GENDER & ENVY

GENDER & ENVY

edited by

NANCY BURKE

Routledge
Taylor & Francis Group
New York   London

Routledge is an imprint of the
Taylor & Francis Group, an informa business

Published in 1998 by

Routledge
29 West 35th Street
New York, NY 10001

Published in Great Britain by
Routledge
11 New Fetter Lane
London EC4P 4EE

Printed in the United States of America on acid-free paper.
Text Design by Debora Hilu

Library of Congress Cataloging-in-Publication Data

Gender and envy / edited by Nancy Burke.
        p.   cm.
    Includes bibliographical references and index.
    ISBN 0-415-91627-5 (hardcover : alk. paper). —
    ISBN 0-415-91628-3 (pbk. : alk. paper)
    1. Psychoanalysis.   2. Sex.   3. Gender identity.   4. Envy.
  I. Burke, Nancy.
  BF175.G44   1998
  155.3—dc21   98-2534
                                         CIP

To the memory of
my mother

CONTENTS

ACKNOWLEDGMENTS

I am deeply indebted to many people for their help during all phases of this project. While I was compiling the manuscript, I was privileged to receive the guidance and insight of John Friedman, Robert May, Frank Summers, Gene Borowitz, Janine Chasseguet-Smirgel, and Sigfried Gold regarding the direction of the work as a whole. Johanna Tabin and Dale Gody also offered much support. I was able to discuss the book as it evolved with the members of the Study Group on Giving and Receiving led by Peter Shabad, the members of the Freud Study Group led by John Friedman, and the members of the Feminism and Psychoanalysis discussion group sponsored by the Chicago Association for Psychoanalytic Psychology. I also want to thank the members of what began as a dissertation support group, including Jeanne Nakamura, Jim O'Brien, and Doug Bell, for their sustenance and insight. I was fortunate to have Maureen MacGrogan and Heidi Freund as my editors at various stages of this project, and to have the editorial assistance of Laska Jimson, Brian Phillips, and Sarita Sahni. Sue Baugh acted as the unofficial adviser to the project, and Beth Kaplan provided the index and much encouragement. I thank my colleagues at the Rehabilitation Program, Northwestern Memorial Hospital, for their flexibility, and my students in Northwestern University Medical School's Division of Psychology, who are consistently surprising and inspiring. Most of all, I want to thank my father, Maurice Burke, who has been a true mentor to me throughout my life, and my husband, Steve Harp, who has made this project, and so many other things, possible.

GENERAL INTRODUCTION

Although Freud was aware, from the time of his self-analysis onward, of the centrality of envy and jealousy as components of human experience, he seemed to focus particular attention on these and related themes in his writings of the early 1920s, during a period coinciding roughly with the birth of his interest in the psychology of women as a subject for specific inquiry. After discussing the topics of jealousy and of women's psychology side by side in his 1919 paper "A Child Is Being Beaten," he went on to interweave them ever more intricately in many subsequent papers, including "The Psychogenesis of a Case of Homosexuality in a Woman" (1920), "The Dissolution of the Oedipus Complex" (1924), and, especially, "Some Psychical Consequences of the Anatomical Distinction Between the Sexes" (1925). Indeed, Freud makes it clear that the co-occurrence of these two preoccupations in the papers of this period is far from coincidental; in fact, envy, in the form of penis envy, is portrayed as the cornerstone and prime mover of woman's development, and jealousy its characteristic outcome. To be sure, Freud never claimed that envy and jealousy were the exclusive province of women, nor penis envy their only source. Nevertheless, at least from the early 1920s onward, Freud was clearly "of the opinion that [jealousy] plays a far larger part in the mental life of women than of men" (*SE* 19: 254), despite the fact that jealousy and envy were quantitatively attributed far more often to men than to women in his writings as a whole.

The suggestion of a fundamental link between gender and envy has not been explored in a sustained way since that time (although it has been the subject of some number of excellent though isolated papers, and of circumscribed bursts of controversy, particularly early on), perhaps for two main reasons. First, because psychoanalysis is, by its very nature, an *inter*discipline that has grown up at the confluence of literature and science, of nature and of culture, the breadth and institutional formlessness of its basic tenets have allowed, on the one hand, for the creation of a complex system of isolated phalanxes, each dominated by a single charismatic authority, and on the other, for a rigid institutional bureaucracy to regulate clinical practice. Thus, the pioneering work of Melanie Klein on envy, for instance, is still not fully integrated into many of the other strains of psychoanalytic theory, even leading the issue of envy itself to be branded as "Kleinian," its importance determined more by a reader's sympathy for its theoretical context than by its clinical relevance. And to some extent, the feeling is mutual; although questions of gender have been central to the vitality of psychoanalytic theory since its inception, and all the more so during the past thirty years, when I approached authors about the prospect of writing for this book, a few prominent self-designated Kleinians declined to contribute, stating that they had little or no understanding of, or even interest in, gender theory. Meanwhile, although the adoption of psychoanalytic ideas into the academic mainstreams of literary and culture theory has continued to invigorate both currents of thought, an unspoken rift has opened up between clinical and academic readers of Freud in this country, so that, for instance, discussions of Lacan's writings on the role of the phallus in psychic life have largely occurred within the context of literary theory, in isolation from the more clinically focused studies offered in professional journals; even though cross-fertilization between clinical and academic readings of psychoanalytic theory has perhaps taken place with greater frequency of late, the reader of *Critical Inquiry* or *October* is still unlikely also to read *Psychoanalytic Dialogues* or *The International Journal*.

The second, no doubt deeper, obstacle to a more sustained discussion of the relationship between gender and envy has also been perhaps its greatest source of inspiration to date; that is, the controversy surrounding the concept of penis envy. Since Freud's time, theorists have consistently targeted the issue of penis envy as a locus of debate, outrage, introspection and generative critique. While some have attempted to reappropriate or reinterpret the concept, others have rejected the notion outright, and with it, some or all of Freud's account of women's development, his theory of sexuality, and his general psychoanalytic theory. I became acutely aware of the role of the theory of penis envy in creating both opportunities and stumbling blocks to further inquiry on the topic of gender and envy in the context of teaching an annual course on feminism and psychoanalysis to graduate students in clinical psychology. Despite the reputation of the school for offering a more psychodynamically-informed training experience than most graduate programs, the students came to this third-year elective often having had no experience of reading Freud, or Klein, Winnicott, or Kohut, for that matter, as primary texts. If, for Freud, penis envy was the crux of female development, on whose resolution the woman's psychic life depended, for these clinicians-in-training, this concept was likewise the crux upon which their allegiance to psychoanalysis as a whole often turned, and thus the direction of their professional development. After expressing surprise at finding Freud on the syllabus, someone would invariably ask, "Does anyone still believe in penis envy?" stating outright that she did not. In this light, Freud's dictum about the goal of therapy was adapted for the classroom—"Where belief was, there thought shall be"—and the aim of the course was more clearly articulated to emphasize the development of an appreciation of the potential fertility of conflict as a necessary tool for conceptual refinement, a goal that has likewise guided the process of compiling the present volume.

The book's structure, made up of five sections, reflects an awareness both of the essentially interdisciplinary nature of psychoanalytic thought and of the opportunities and obstacles presented by its historical obsession with the concept of penis envy. The first section is intended to act as an introduction to the debate, as it presents some of the now-classic texts that have served as starting points for the development and controversy which have unfolded around them. Of Freud's writings, his essay "Female Sexuality" (1931) has as much claim to represent his ideas about penis envy as the essay included here, and in many respects is the richer for its suggestions about the pre-oedipal relationship between mother and daughter in the formation of het-erosexuality, and even for its role as a source for alternative explanations for the girl's turn from the mother. Yet of his extended explorations of penis envy, the essay included here is the one that was most frequently responded to in his day, and in many respects it was also the most influential historical catalyst of the debate that surrounded it. That essay is accompanied here by a paper by Karen Horney, the most vocal and passionate critic of penis envy during Freud's lifetime, as well as the clearest ancestor of a central strain of feminist critique that has evolved to the present. Indeed, the reader will feel the reverberations of Horney's characterizations of penis envy as a neurotic construction evolving within a specific cultural context; of a primary femi-ninity; and of the phallocentric bias of Freud's thought; in several of the essays to follow, even when such ideas are not attributed to her explicitly. The third chapter in this foundational section contains Klein's first reply to this unfolding debate on the topic of gender and envy, although it should ideally be supplemented by a reading of her more extended explorations sup-plemented to be found in her essays on "The Effects of Early Anxiety Situations" in the girl and boy (1932), "The Oedipus Complex in Light of Early Anxieties" (1945), and "Envy and Gratitude" (1957).

The second section is devoted to a series of interpretive responses to the concept of penis envy itself, beginning with John Friedman's careful close reading of Freud. If for Friedman, however, penis envy is the thread of which the psychic lives of both men and women are woven, Luce Irigaray's reading of Freud represents a passionate call to pull the thread, so that the weave of patriarchy might thereby become unraveled at last. The three other authors whose works are included in this section have reappropriated and reinter-preted Freud's concept of penis envy, finding it useful, understandable, or even essential, within the context of the girl's relationship with her mother (in the essays by Maria Torok and Janine Chasseguet-Smirgel), and with her father (in Jessica Benjamin's paper). Reading these essays side by side will, I hope, provide the reader with a glimpse into the subtlety, complexity, and sheer range of psychological forces and experiences that can be argued to account for the phenomenon of penis envy. While Torok creates a compelling argument to suggest that it is born of girls' need to hide qualities and strengths that might be found threatening to their mothers and thereby result in a loss of their love, Chasseguet-Smirgel, who also locates the source of penis envy in the mother-child relationship, suggests instead that it can best be viewed as a manifestation of the child's wish for revenge against a mother who is perceived as terrifying and omnipotent. Meanwhile, Benjamin's explication of one of the "multiple meanings" of penis envy points to the relative neglect of the father-daughter relationship in the psychoanalytic literature, and of the role of penis envy as an internal monument to the corresponding neglect by fathers of their daughters' need to identify with them, and to have this need recognized and accepted. Further, Benjamin's account of the mutual reluctance of fathers and of psychoanalysts to appreciate the significance of cross-gender identification acts in her essay as a lens through which the nature and limits of the concept of gender itself can be radically revisioned.

The authors whose works are included in the third section each argue for the primacy of connections between gender and envy other than penis envy, although most of the essays locate themselves with respect to Freud's account if only to rebut it with an alternative, or at least complementary, one. Of these analyses, Irene Fast's clear and elegant statement has perhaps been the most influential in turning the discussion to a focus on the inextricable link between envy and the development of sexual identity per se for children of both genders. Fast's documentation of the process by which the "undifferentiated and overinclusive earliest matrix for gender identity development" gradually gives way to a recognition of limits and an envy of what one doesn't have after all might be described in Yiddish as the *yenems* (what *you* have) theory of psychosexual development. Although several of the other essays in this section predate Fast's, her writing can be seen not only as describing a matrix from which gender identity emerges, but as supplying the discussion of gender and envy itself with a matrix in the context of which alternative claims can be located.

Thus, the essay that follows Fast's can be read as an account of potential mechanisms for the development of envy in boys as they attempt to move beyond the "original matrix." Eva Feder Kittay builds on Bettelheim's claims regarding the existence of a fundamental "womb envy" in men, highlighting its destructive effects as well as the ways in which social life must evolve to better neutralize these effects. Christiane Olivier, whose work begins with a critique of penis envy, following Irigaray, as a "figment of the imagination" of men, soon moves her focus to stress the centrality of "envy of the maternal breast, forever lost, forever sought" in both girls (who are underdesired) and boys (who are overdesired), as this preoccupation is echoed in the configuration of the family and of social life in general. The reader might be surprised to see an essay by Freud included in this section of alternative accounts of gender and envy, and particularly one that, although it was written not long before his "Psychical Consequences" essay, stresses not only the general tendency of both men and women to feel envious and jealous of the other sex, due to the grief of loss and the narcissistic wounds arising out of the positive and negative oedipal struggles, but also the spectrum of envy-related phenomena in men. It is hoped that this essay will offer a challenge to the assumption that Freud's ideas about envy and jealousy are limited to his theory of penis envy, and thus will open the reader to aspects of his work that are often overshadowed by his more well-known writings. In contrast to these works, Susan Kavaler-Adler paints a vivid picture of the voracious destructiveness of an envy born of parental emptiness and deprivation, as seen in Sylvia Plath in unresolved form and in resolving form in a case study. Though in certain theoretical respects her work resonates with ideas found in the essays by Torok and Benjamin, among others, it creates its argument without reference to penis envy and yet holds fast to an alternative account of the body's role in signifying, experiencing, and giving birth to feelings of envy.

The fourth section of the book arises in the interstice between psychoanalytic and life-span developmental studies. Each of the essays in this section is newly written for this volume, for virtually no psychoanalytically-informed studies of the interactions between gender and envy across the course of life exist to date. Upon the huge blank canvas that is thus unfurled here, these three articles, in addition to their inherent interest, can serve as but beginning sketches for a work that can only evolve over time. Robert May's essay, which focuses on gender and envy in the college years, offers a portrayal of psychic life at a time that is not only developmentally significant but that often represents the first interaction between troubled individuals and the world of psychotherapeutic intervention. Meanwhile, Peter Shabad's work reflects on some ramifications of envious feeling in the parents of children per se, but also focuses on the forms of envy distinctive to, or more prevalent in, mothers and fathers respectively. By highlighting the breadth of the transformation that takes place in the lives of the male artists to whom his essay refers, David Gutmann's study "Male Envy Across the Life-Span" opens up a vast and complex domain of inquiry distinct from, and yet firmly tethered to, the world of infantile psychosexual life.

The book's last section represents perhaps the broadest in the series of concentric circles through which the essays collected here have taken us. Although psychoanalytic thought is often viewed as being restricted to the very early universe of the psychic life of individuals, it has, in fact, been inextricably tied to social and cultural life from its very origins. Despite attempts by some readers to paint Freud as a scientific reductionist, in his work he drew as freely for his insights and inspiration from the poets as he did from the unfolding scientific domain which was the source of so many of his metaphors, and further, often interpreted the scientific theories that guided him through the lens of his thirst for the mythopoetic kernel of psychic life. As Freud constructed his intrapsychic theories, he concerned himself, simultaneously, with a study of social life and culture, as manifested in a series of essays (*Totem and Taboo, Group Psychology*, etc.) which are often read in isolation from his ontogenetic theory, to the reader's detriment. Of the writers included here, Teresa Brennan rereads Freud and Klein with an eye toward locating them within the broader macrocosmic environment of which individual dynamics must be seen as only a microcosm. In highlighting the irreducibly social life of psychoanalytic concepts, she demonstrates the role of gender and envy in the perpetuation of capitalism, in the subjugation of women, and in the attacks against the environment that threaten to undermine the lives not only of the social worlds we have created, but of the individuals those worlds comprise. Although the selection of her work included here, on the "foundational fantasy," cannot incorporate all of these aspects of her thought, it can open the door to a broader discussion of the sway of envy in social life, and thus gesture toward the social context within which many of the essays in this book unfold. Marjorie Garber's reading of fetish envy as a foundation of theater from Shakespeare's time to the present day highlights the extent to which issues of gender and envy permeate cultural production at its very roots. And Clayton Koelb's work echoes this view of sexual envy as essential to cultural and, here, philosophical life, even as he inverts the terms that Garber uses to describe how this envy is played out, stressing Nietzsche's longing not for the phallus but for the empty place left behind in its absence, in which thought and power reside.

Just as each of the essays in this volume stresses simultaneously the effects of what is present and what is absent, I have been increasingly aware, in compiling this book, of my wish that it be useful to the reader both because of what is included within it and because of what it has left out. By placing these many and varied works on gender and envy side by side, I hope that a universe of thought might begin to emerge out of the isolated insights they represent (though each essay is, likewise, a complex universe unto itself). Yet any collection of essays cannot but reveal how much is absent from it, either essential work that has already been published, or work that has not yet been written, or never will be. Thus, I consider this book to be a demonstration of the very interplay of presence, refinding, and lack that each of the essays strives, individually, to describe. It is offered in hopes that the reader will not only absorb the material presented here, but will reintegrate it in her or his own way, and will use it as the basis not only for a search for the more that can be found, but for a deepening and refinement of the sense of what is missing that permeates our lives from birth to death.

Part One

THE EMERGENCE OF A
POINT OF TENSION

INTRODUCTION

There is often a passage in even the most thoroughly interpreted dream which has to be left obscure; this is because we became aware during the work of interpretation that at that point there is a tangle of dream-thoughts which cannot be unravelled and which moreover adds nothing to our knowledge of the content of the dream. This is the dream's navel, the spot where it reaches down into the unknown. The dream-thoughts to which we are led by interpretation cannot, from the nature of things, have any definite endings; they are bound to branch out in each direction into the intricate network of our world of thought. It is at some point where this meshwork is particularly close that the dream-wish grows up, like a mushroom out of its mycelium. (*SE* 5: 525)

Of all the obstacles to the integration of psychoanalytic and gender theories, Freud's concept of penis envy has been, perhaps, the greatest, a mountain in the path of their confluence, around which a city has grown up. Of this city, Freud's 1925 essay, "Some Psychical Consequences of the Anatomical Distinction Between the Sexes," marks its founding, simultaneously the point at which his prior writings on penis envy come retrospectively to have new meaning within the framework of his theory as a whole, and the birth of the controversy, evidenced by the essays of Horney and Klein that followed it, that has defined the landscape of psychoanalytic feminism from that time forward. Whether the reader has anticipated the journey with some dread, or has "booked [her] passage as a matter of course" (*SE* 22: 240), she cannot but sense that she has arrived at a point in the net of theory in which the meshwork is particularly close, a city dense with conflict and context, in which the issue of penis envy stands as "the very omphalos, cynosure and soul around which the town...has organized itself" (Kingsley, 1855).

FREUD'S 1925 PAPER: A BRIEF ARCHAEOLOGY

"Some Psychical Consequences of the Anatomical Distinction Between the Sexes" was not Freud's first exploration of the topic of penis envy; in fact, his attention to the concept was nearly as old as his interest in gender itself, surfacing first in undeveloped form in his 1908 paper "On the Sexual Theories of Children". The growth of Freud's intertwined interests in penis envy and the psychology of women in general can be traced chronologically from that point on in a linear trajectory that stretches from this early reference through to the 1925 paper and beyond. In an effort to provide a context for the "Psychical Consequences" essay, a sketch of that trajectory will be offered here, in the belief that locating it within this linear chronology will provide a useful, perhaps necessary, and ultimately inadequate ground for an appreciation of it. For though the concept of penis envy directly anchors Freud's account of sexual difference, its own conceptual grounding is, as Freud's ideas develop, increasingly nested elsewhere, within the context of his general theory of mind; in that context, penis envy can be seen as one manifestation of a set of broader psychological—that is, philosophical—allegiances, under whose canopy it serves to draw in the issue of sexual difference through the creation of an epistemology of gender. Only by recognizing this broader role, I suggest, can the reader develop an appreciation of the stakes of the battles to follow between Freud's theories and those of his adversarial disciples Horney and Klein. Thus, the short synopsis offered here of the development of Freud's ideas specifically about penis envy will be supplemented by a reworking of this conceptual lineage within the context of concurrent developments in his general psychological theory.

Although "On the Sexual Theories of Children" contained Freud's first mention of penis envy, the ground for his interest in the topic had been laid a decade earlier, in the context of his earliest inquiries into the development of mature sexuality from its infantile roots. By the mid-1890s, in his letters to Fliess, Freud was already grappling with many of the ideas that formed the bedrock of his later theory of sexuality, including sexual monism, bisexuality, infantile sexuality, and the role of repression in shaping libidinal life. When, in 1897, he suggested that although the timing of prior events of sexual history was perhaps different for girls and boys, "the main distinction between the sexes emerges at the time of puberty" (Masson, 1985, p. 280), he already fully realized the importance of illuminating the mechanism through which this divergence occurred. In his earliest account, the search for this mechanism took place within the context of a general view of development as determined by the natural but specifically human tendency to lose interest in some libidinal zones—the nose, mouth, anus, and, in women, he already believed, clitoris—in the process of consolidating sexual organization. Yet if, according to this early theory, the capacity of women to give up an allegiance to the latter zone, and to feel shame in regard to it, could be explained simply on the basis of the repugnance of memory ("memory actually stinks" [Masson, 1985, p. 280]), such an account was soon to be questioned from the vantage point of concepts put forward in the 1908 paper, for reasons that were only hinted at there.

In that paper (which built upon the claims put forward in the *Three Essays on the Theory of Sexuality* (1905), as further clarified in light of his analysis-by-proxy of Little Hans (1909)), Freud emphasized that the child's perception of sexual difference is created within the context of its psychosexual situation, an assertion that in hindsight can be seen as paving the way for his more general insights into the constructed, inherently psychical, nature of sexual identity. For now, however, Freud put forward the two concepts that would later function as the building blocks of his understanding of psychosexuality, penis envy and castration anxiety, side by side, without elaborating on their relationship to each other or on the role of penis envy in the process of gender construction. It is significant for a reading of Freud's ideas about gender and envy to note that the frame for his 1908 meditations was his observation that Little Hans's interest in sexual difference arose only in the context of his sibling rivalry, which appeared to trigger further envy, both of his mother's capacity to have babies, and of his father's (= horse's) large penis. It is against this background of the boy's envy of his parents and sibling, and of his theorizing into where babies come from, that the girl's envy of the penis was inserted in Freud's text, at this point seemingly as an aside. Indeed, only in retrospect is Freud's investment in the idea made clear, when he imports his observations regarding penis envy and castration anxiety wholesale into his 1915 revision of the *Three Essays*, moving the two concepts even closer together there in light of his insight, recorded in a comment in his paper "On Narcissism" of the year before, that these are but two versions, the male and the female, of the same phenomenon: a universal castration complex that determines the relative balance of self- and object-love in both sexes in later life.

When Freud next took up the issue of penis envy, in his paper "On Transformations of Instinct as Exemplified in Anal Eroticism" of 1917, we might suggest that his observation in regard to "anal traits" that at first "my main object was to make known the fact...; I was little concerned about its theoretical significance" (*SE* 17: 127), might apply to his previous discussions of the former concept as well. Indeed, this essay, written while he was in the midst of composing his so-called metapsychological papers, appears to mark the point at which Freud's interest in the theoretical significance of penis envy came to the fore. In it, he reached back to his first curiosity about the mechanism by which earlier libidinal investments in bodily zones receded at the emergence of new ones, in order to trace the reverberations of these earlier investments within the context of genital sexuality. Here, Freud spoke briefly of the boy's reworking of his earlier investment in his feces into a narcissistic investment in his penis under the sway of the castration complex; but he spoke at greater length about the seemingly more complex process through which the girl's anal eroticism converges with her penis envy and her independent early desires for a baby and for a man, allowing her to transform the two former libidinal sources into a further impetus toward aligning her desires with the roles of wife and mother. Through his postulation of an "unconscious equivalence" between penis and baby, Freud set the stage for the appreciation of penis envy not only as an observed phenomenon, but as a factor in the transformation of the girl's relational desires. Meanwhile, Freud traced the more pernicious effects of the girl's penis envy upon her marital relationships in "The Taboo of Virginity" (1917/18), which was written on the heels of the "Transformation of Instincts" paper, and discussed cultural variations in how these effects are accommodated at the social level. He was able to illustrate the role played by latent penis envy in determining later libidinal life and object relationships in his study of "The Psychogenesis of a Case of Homosexuality in a Woman" (1920), in which he came further to appreciate not only the intricacy and ontogenetically ancient origins of a woman's libidinal world, but his own limitations, as a man, in gaining access to the pre-oedipal substrate of her desires. This study was built upon insights Freud had developed in his essay "'A Child is Being Beaten:' A Contribution to the Study of the Origin of Sexual Perversions" (1919), which he later recognized as documenting the effects of penis envy on the fantasies of girls.

If the essay on anal eroticism put the concept of penis envy into play as a phenomenon of theoretical, as well as clinical, significance, its importance was hardly granted a full investigation in that context. It seems, fittingly enough, that Freud needed to develop a clearer appreciation of the lacunae in his earlier accounts of psychosexual development—specifically, a theory of female sexuality—before he was inspired to redress this lack through a reworking of observations of which he had previously had only limited appreciation. He posed his concern about these theoretical deficits quite clearly in his 1924 essay, "The Dissolution of the Oedipus Complex," following his observations on that topic with the comment that "the process which has been described refers, as has been expressly said, to male children only. How does the corresponding development take place in little girls? At this point our material—for some incomprehensible reason—becomes far more obscure and full of gaps" (*SE* 19: 177). Although he follows this statement of his concern with his most elaborate account to date of the role of penis envy as a component of the female castration complex and as a precipitant of the resolution of her Oedipus complex, he maintains that his speculations on the topic are "unsatisfactory, incomplete and vague" (*SE* 19: 179), setting the stage for further consideration of female development as a topic in its own right.

The 1925 essay included in this volume, titled "Some Psychical Consequences of the Anatomical Distinction Between the Sexes," directly followed Freud's 1924 call to arms, and indeed was the first theoretical paper devoted explicitly to the general topic of women's psychosexual development. I will leave it to the reader to follow the thread of Freud's ideas about penis envy, as we have traced them to this point, through the text of the paper, highlighting only that in this essay penis envy has become the crux not only of female psychology but of the sudden opening up of theory to the "dark regions" of the pre-oedipal psychic landscape in both men and women, bestowing upon these regions a significance that was lacking in Freud's earlier considerations of the child's pre-oedipal attachments. In his reworking of these ideas in "Female Sexuality" (1931), Freud locates his inquiry at the outset within this dark (though by this time, not quite as dark) province, emphasizing the uncanny completeness of the girl's relationship with the mother, which not only instigates, but foreshadows isometrically the heterosexual relationship that may (or may not) follow.

Though often viewed as a recapitulation of the 1925 paper, the "Female Sexuality" essay contains subtle but potentially far-reaching variations in the significance granted to penis envy. This phenomenon is now presented as only one among many of the catalysts for the girl's turn from mother to father, and the functional equivalence between penis and baby no longer necessitates that the girl's angry disaffection with the mother be caused specifically by her failure to grant the child that organ. Instead, the fantasy of bearing the mother a child predates a similar wish in regard to the father, and the disappointment of this earlier wish might in itself explain the turn to the father in search of its fulfillment. Although not included in this volume, the reader is strongly encouraged to read the 1931 essay and to decide for herself whether it marks the further establishment of penis envy as the crux of sexual difference in Freud's account of female psychology or, rather, whether penis envy appears there as a residue of an idea that, though decisive in leading Freud to a new land, has been overshadowed by the discoveries he made on his arrival. Suffice it to say here that Freud's own appreciation of the role of penis envy in female psychology only continued to grow over time; in his "New Introductory Lecture" on "Femininity" of 1933, he highlighted the girl's castration complex once again as the single factor distinguishing her relationship with her mother from the boy's, noting that "one cannot very well doubt the importance of envy for the penis" (SE 22:125), a sentiment that is enthusiastically restated yet again in An Outline of Psycho-Analysis (1938), which Freud composed at the end of his life as a synthesis of his most important ideas.

To say that the summary offered above represents a sketch of the linear chronology of Freud's thoughts about penis envy may be superficially correct, inasmuch as his major writings on the topic have been discussed here roughly in the order of their composition. Yet Freud himself was devoted to a form of historiography which called into question the belief that such a chronology constituted a sufficient ground for an appreciation of the evolution of meaning, preferring instead to chart, in the anamneses of his patients (viz., SE 18: 160), the way in which significance unfolds through the back-and-forth motion of Nachträglichkeit, or deferred action, in accordance with which the past is continually refound, and thus recreated, within the context of the present. Just as, in Freud's account, the boy at first finds the girl's anatomy unremarkable, viewing it as significant only from within the context of his own castration fears, so too do each of his discussions of penis envy reinvent past ideas which had previously been of only limited importance from within the developing sphere of his concerns. Did Freud's theory of penis envy exist from the beginning? Perhaps yes, but most definitely no, inasmuch as "the beginning" can only be so designated, and so constructed, from the point of view of our interest in the question itself, as therapists or analysts, as academics, as readers of Freud, as feminists, as individuals of an infinite if circumscribed complexity.

Yet Freud's effort to delineate the peculiar form of temporality characteristic of meaning, and thus to establish its status as constructed—one would hope, rigorously—from within an interpretive context, only highlights the sense that the above attempt to trace his ideas on penis envy through the volumes of the *Standard Edition* is an exercise that is itself strangely disembodied, cut off from the overarching worldview in which, in light of Freud's role as a unified field theorist of the mind, they are inherently embedded. Given the scope of this introduction, I can only gesture, by offering a speculative meditation of my own, toward one path to the reintegration of the theory of penis envy into the body of Freud's work, while referring the reader to others who have undertaken the task more deeply and thoroughly (Freud himself, Friedman in this volume, Lacan, and other contemporary theorists to whom reference will be made in the introductions to the book's other sections). My concern here, rather, is merely to alert the reader to the broader conceptual horizon surrounding this issue and, again, to highlight the philosophical stakes inherent in Freud's viewpoint so that the terms of the debate that arose in response to it can be brought more easily to the fore.

Though Freud maintained an interest in a myriad of specialized topics, the threads of which make up much of the fabric of his work, he also maintained an interest in the creation of a more general psychological theory, an account of mental life per se, through which these various strands of his thought could take on broader theoretical significance. This interest in a general theory of mind can be traced from the 1895 "Project" through to Chapter VII of the *Interpretation of Dreams* (1900), and on to the metapsychological papers (1914-17), *Beyond the Pleasure Principle* (1920), *The Ego and the Id* (1923) (which he viewed as a continuation of the preceding work), and, among other essays, to his short paper on "Negation (1925)." The oscillation of his attention between the general and the specific is reflected in his practice of composition; often, he worked on more than one essay simultaneously, or else composed two or more in immediate chronological proximity; the dream book and the Dora case, the joke book and the *Three Essays*—the writings that unfolded were compartmentalized and cross-referenced to varying degrees, both in the process of their composition and in his later syntheses of his work. His account of the analysis of a homosexual woman appeared between the two drafts of *Beyond the Pleasure Principle*, which itself was written in alternation with the book on group psychology, and July 1925 saw the twin births of the "Negation" essay and of the "Psychical Consequences" essay included here, which, Jones informs us, were presented together in a reading to Ferenczi during the following month (Jones 1957, Vol. 3, p. 118).

Clearly, the task of locating Freud's theory of penis envy within the stream of his general psychological theory is impossible within the scope of this (and no doubt any) introduction; for this reason, I will restrict my focus to the single point of confluence offered by Freud's simultaneous attention to the two 1925 papers, taking them as representative instances, respectively, of his general and specific concerns. How might our reading of Freud's account of penis envy be transformed through the acknowledgment of the temporal proximity of the date of its composition to that of his essay "Negation"? The latter essay might, I suggest, be viewed as a Genesis story, a transformative condensation of Freud's prior thinking about how a specifically psychological realm comes to be formed out of the "complemental series" of temperament and experience that constitutes its ground. In *Beyond the Pleasure Principle*, Freud had told the well-known story of his grandson's Fort-Da game, in which the boy had transformed an experience of passive loss into an *active* game of loss and recovery, first of his toy, as this came to represent his mother, and ultimately, as we read in a footnote to the text (p. 9), of himself. Freud returns to look at the process of loss and recovery in "Negation," where he explicitly links the rhythm of loss and refinding, such as characterized Ernst's game, to the birth of judgment, adding that this faculty is made possible through the evolution of a symbol for the act of expulsion, in the form of the word "not," that can represent this action of the instinct of destruction while allowing the object in question, be it internal or external, to survive for later refinding. According to this perspective, the capacity to develop an independent psychic sphere and, simultaneously, a sense of an outside world that exists beyond this sphere, rests on the success of the effort to create this negation symbol (it is worthwhile to consider Winnicott's essay "The Use of an Object" (1970) as an imaginative re-reading of Freud's essay).

Viewed through the context of Freud's essay on negation, the stories of loss and refinding as experienced by the boy and girl, respectively, in the forms of castration anxiety and penis envy, can be seen as chronicles of the emergence of gender as a psychological phenomenon. Without the perception of potential loss of an exclusively genital kind, the reverberation between the two essays seems to be telling us, there can be no truly psychical sexuality, and indeed no way of giving content to the realm of psychological experience as gendered. The psychic representation of the penis (Lacan and Friedman would call this the phallus) is, in other words, the "not" of gender, the signal of the creation of a psychical world that, although certainly tethered to the anatomical scene of its discovery, nevertheless constitutes an autonomous realm with its own laws and developmental history. This "not" of the phallus is the "not" of *having*, rather than of *being* (such as was stumbled upon by Ernst in his baby-gone games), although presupposing being and conditioned by it, as Freud seems to suggest in what might be thought of as his last creative reworking of the penis envy concept, the posthumously published compilation of paragraphs he brought together under the heading "Findings, Ideas, Problems" (1938). "July 12—...'Having' and 'being' in children," he writes in a fragmentary meditation on penis envy:

> Children like expressing an object-relation by an identification: "I am the object." "Having" is the later of the two; after loss of the object it relapses

into "being." Example: the breast. "The breast is a part of me, I am the breast" Only later: "I have it"—that is, "I am not it." (*SE* 23: 300)

We might draw from this brief note that penis envy and its analog, the castration complex, signify not only the emergence of sexuality as a phenomenon of psychological significance, but the prior loss and refinding of the self, without which existence is itself impossible. Thus, the concept of penis envy accrues, in Freud's work, a significance that transcends its role in the empirical documentation of the course of the girl's development, representing, further, his commitment to establishing the existence of an inherently constructed epistemology of gender within the context of a truly *psychological* theory of mind.

DIALOGUE AND RUPTURE: HORNEY VERSUS FREUD ON THE THEORY OF PENIS ENVY

The Professor's surroundings and interests seem to derive from my mother rather than from my father, and yet to say the "transference" is to Freud as mother does not altogether satisfy me. He had said, "And—I must tell you (you were frank with me and I will be frank with you), I do *not* like to be the mother in transference—it always surprises and shocks me a little. I feel so very masculine!" I asked him if others had what he called this mother-transference on him. He said ironically and I thought a little wistfully, "O, *very many*."   — HD

If, in our tour of the old city, we have begun with Freud's writings on penis envy, we can nevertheless observe in the works of his contemporaries myriad other contributions contained within its walls. Though Freud's ideas about penis envy might best be read within the context of his more general theory of mind, this reading must be nested in turn within the context of the debate that surrounded it. Freud himself consistently stressed the "unsatisfactory, incomplete and vague" (*SE* 19: 179) status of his investigations into women's psychology, calling especially upon his female colleagues to shed light on regions to which, owing to his sex and temperament, he could not hope to go. Indeed, interest in female psychology within psychoanalytic circles coincided with an influx of women into the field, many of whom, Horney and Klein among them, made significant contributions to the debates on femininity early on in their careers, but later moved their attention away from the issue of gender. The written discussion that unfolded prior to and following the publication of Freud's 1925 paper—a debate that was perhaps among the most focused and intense, and most threatening to cohesion, in the history of the psychoanalytic movement—which has come to be known, perhaps somewhat misleadingly, as the Jones-Freud controversy, took penis envy as its focal point. It flourished (or raged) for a decade and then abated, "bound to perish," perhaps, "precisely because it...was so intense," (*SE* 21: 234) (or else, as Mitchell suggests, because of the impasse arising out of a confusion of tongues between the languages of psychology and biology [1971, p. 130]), leaving behind a pattern of foundations upon which more recent attempts to debate "the ultimate question [of] whether a woman is born or made" (Jones, 1935/1948, p. 495) have been built.

Penis envy came first to be a focus of broader debate following the publication of Freud's 1917 paper, "The Taboo of Virginity," which inspired responses both from Johan Van Ophuijsen and from Karl Abraham, whose paper was the second of the two to be composed but the first to be published, and ultimately proved to be the more influential. This essay, delivered in 1920, titled "Manifestations of the Female Castration Complex," melds Freud's ideas in "Taboo" about the origins in penis envy of women's rage toward the men who deflower them with his equation, in the "Transformation of Instinct" paper, between penis and baby, in the service of creating a developmental account of the origins and potential consequences of the girl's castration complex. The paper had an unusually direct influence on Freud's thought during the years following its publication; it inspired Freud's own paper on the "Psychical Consequences" of the girl's castration complex, and indeed, in "Female Sexuality" (1931) Freud described it as "still unsurpassed" (*SE* 21: 241). Meanwhile, however, the paper had an additional, indirect influence upon Freud's discussion of the topic inasmuch as it inspired essays by other theorists whose ideas about penis envy and gender would influence Freud's work and the direction of psychoanalytic thinking as a whole during the course of the Jones-Freud debates.

Among the responses to Abraham's essay, Karen Horney's contribution, the 1922/1923 paper "On the Genesis of the Castration Complex in Women," was perhaps the most influential. Freud himself acknowledged it at the end of the "Psychical Consequences" essay, along with Abraham's paper, as a "valuable and comprehensive" study (*SE* 19: 258), and Jones likewise cited it, along with other papers by Horney, as the inspiration for his own debates with Freud on femininity (Jones, 1927). Horney's paper, the first of her works to be presented publicly, was read to a large audience as part of a panel chaired by Freud in September, 1922 in Berlin; it was presented explicitly as a critical response to the paper by Abraham (who had been her analyst during the years 1910–1912 and perhaps, intermittently, beyond then). The essay took as its starting point Abraham's contention that penis envy was the central determinant of the girl's castration complex, responsible for the variety of residual manifestations he observed in his adult patients. Rather, Horney claimed, women's tendency to regard themselves as anatomically and socially inferior must in fact be the product of "other forces," which she aimed to spell out in her paper.

Horney was not concerned there to dispute the existence of penis envy as a phenomenon in the lives of girls; on the contrary, she elevated their developmental disadvantage, due to inhibitions in urethral eroticism, scopophilia, and masturbation which the boy, as a result of the greater availability of his organ, does not experience, to the status of an "*actual fact*," noting that "unless we are quite clear about the *reality* of this disadvantage we shall not understand that penis envy is an almost inevitable phenomenon in the life of female children, and one that cannot but complicate female development" (1922/23, p. 42). Rather, she argues, this "disadvantage" becomes a determining factor in women's lives only when it is reinforced by a flight into identification with the father as a result of the frustration of her sexual wishes toward him, and of her wishes that he give her a baby. This rejection leaves her with Oedipal guilt, compensatory rape fantasies that lead her to attribute her lack of a penis to violence at the hands of her father, a hatred of men such as that described by Freud in his "Taboo of Virginity" paper, and a revulsion toward her own sexuality, the combined effects of which propel her to regressively recathect her original penis envy and feelings of genital inferiority. Thus, Horney takes issue with Freud's claim that penis envy is the deepest and most central determinant of women's psychology—indeed, in her view, the wish for a penis is more acceptable to a "wounded woman" than a wish for a child, and thus functions as a defense against the latter desire—even while drawing upon Freud's ideas about the importance of identification as the foundation for her argument. Inasmuch as this 1922/1923 paper provides a more thorough account than is offered in Horney's later writings of the mechanisms through which primary penis envy provides the template for the girl's psychic life only as a result of its secondary reinforcement, a familarity with this essay is essential for an appreciation of the early debates regarding gender difference, as well as of Horney's subsequent work.

The paper included in this volume, "The Flight from Womanhood" of 1926, represents Horney's next effort at reworking her ideas about femininity in general and penis envy in particular in light of Freud's 1925 essay. As such, it offers a context for her earlier assertions (e.g., regarding the problematic nature of the girl's oedipal drama), which, although they clearly undergird her thinking in the 1926 paper, are explicitly referred to there only in highly condensed form. In "The Flight from Womanhood," critiques of Freud that were presented less forcefully and globally in her earlier paper are employed more systematically and directly, and the breadth of the implications of her modifications of the Freudian account of the female castration complex for the more general issue of gender and envy are more clearly identified. A brief suggestion in her earlier paper that the prevailing view of penis envy might be attributable to "masculine narcissism" (p. 38) has been expanded, in light of Simmel's observations on "masculine civilization," and is now used as the frame for her inquiry not only into the isomorphism between the boy's account of genital difference and that of psychoanalysis as a whole, but into the envy-based motives, so strikingly underestimated by Helene Deutsch (1925), that might have fueled the development of the latter point of view. Further, while she still maintains the view that penis envy based on genital difference is typical in women, she presents it as even more relatively insignificant, in comparison to the totality of their oedipal experiences, in determining the nature of the female castration complex. In place of the concept of penis envy as a "primal, biological principle" (p. 68), she suggests instead an essential female nature, characterized by a "desire for a child and [a] tender attachment to the father" (or the penis as a part-object representation of him), as signaled by early vaginal sensations.

As might be expected, Horney's paper provoked strong reactions, both positive and negative, in her contemporaries. Though Jones, in his 1927 paper "The Early Development of Female Sexuality," endorsed Horney's views of primary and secondary penis envy on the one hand, and of a primary femininity on the other, Freud himself offered a pointed critique of Horney's paper in his essay "Female Sexuality" of 1931, throwing in comments critical of Jones for good measure. Freud later elaborated on his criticism, as presented there, in a letter to a colleague who expressed a view similar to that of "Horney, Jones, Rado, etc., who do not come to grips with the bisexuality of women and who, in particular, object to the phallic stage," emphasizing:

> I object to all of you to the extent that you do not distinguish more clear-ly and cleanly between what is psychic and what is biological, that you try to establish a neat parallelism between the two and that you, motivated by such intent, unthinkingly construe psychic facts which are unprovable and that you, in the process of so doing, must declare as reactive or regressive much that without doubt is primary. (Freud, 1935/1971)

Indeed, Freud suggests here, the most significant points of conflict between Horney's account and his own do not revolve around specific differences in the details of female development (Horney does not deny the existence of penis envy in girls, for instance), so much as in the fact that they have adopted two incommensurate methods of thought. Whereas Freud is most concerned with creating a psychology of gender, that is, with an account of how gender is constructed out of the perception of difference, Horney is expressing a fundamental essentialism, in which gender is an innate given and thus is not, at least at first, inherently psychological, but is only later elaborated upon through the erection of defenses, the scars of biologically, anatomically, sociologically, or family-determined disappointments. In Horney's view, reality is an objective entity that has the power directly to imprint itself upon the self—girls are at a real anatomical disadvantage, for example, and women try, in analysis, to establish the reality of their father's seductions rather than recognize the "essential unreality of the situation" (p. 44)—while in Freud's thought, external reality is only circuitously related to psychic reality, as mediated by meaning; the rest, he suggests, is trauma (1920). Although Horney abruptly gave up her study of gender in the mid-1930s, the assumptions that ground her suggestion here that "a woman is born and not made" were carried over into her later, more general inquiries into the development of individuals in their cultural context. Meanwhile, feminist authors have drawn attention to the importance of developing a reappreciation of the differences between Horney's and Freud's accounts regarding women's development per se, stressing that to ignore the content of these debates is to leave psychoanalitic feminism in chauvinistic shadow (Fliegel, 1986).

KLEIN ON GENDER AND THE ORIGINS OF ENVY

If the Jones-Freud controversy derived its name in part from Jones's efforts to champion the works of Horney, his defense of Melanie Klein's contribution to the psychoanalytic theory of gender was no less definitive of his role as the spokesperson for what he eventually came to call "Position B" (1933). Indeed, if Horney came to be known first and foremost for her contribution to the debates on gender, Klein's own role in these debates has tended to be overshadowed by her later psychological theory, and by her role as Anna Freud's adversary in the simultaneously unfolding disagreement between the two women over the nature of child therapy, a controversy that was to broaden as further theoretical and political differences emerged (for a thorough and vivid account of the "controversial discussions" that constitute the verbal point of these later debates, see King and Steiner, 1991). Yet the effect of Klein's ideas was and continues to be significant, both upon the evolution of analytic thought about penis envy and gender difference, and about envy in general. Further, although Horney and Klein are often associated in historical accounts of gender and psychoanalysis, and offered each other agreement and support on specific points of theory, their overall missions diverged radically, and gave birth to two very different schools of thought, through which their views on the specific points under consideration here must be read. Indeed, their divergences are all the more significant given the existence of shared roots, both personal (both were analyzed by Abraham, and they analyzed each other's daughters) and theoretical (their thought was shaped within a common intellectual climate in Berlin and was heavily influenced early on by Abraham's ideas).

Klein entered the fray after Horney presented her 1922 and 1926 papers; her first contribution to the controversy is the essay included in this volume, "Early Stages of the Oedipus Complex," which she presented at the Innsbruck Congress in 1927 and published the following year. She earlier had presented a paper on child analysis that had made a strong impression on Jones and shocked the psychoanalytic establishment with its radical suggestion that the Oedipus complex, and the development of the superego, were linked to oral and anal frustrations experienced as early as the first year of life. That paper clearly laid the groundwork for the "Early Stages" essay, in which Klein continued to explore the foundation in oral and anal frustration for the vicissitudes of the "femininity phase" in children of both sexes. There, the outlines of an account of penis envy significantly different from Freud's can be seen. From the very start, in Klein's work, the girl's sense of suffering from the lack of a penis is preceded by a more fundamental sense of deprivation. The wish for a (that is, the mother's) baby comes before the wish for the penis; oral

and anal deprivation instigate both the turn from the mother and the formation of the superego; and the girl is seen as experiencing vaginal sensations
early on that facilitate the turn to the father. Further, as part of Klein's explication of the boy's "femininity complex," she stresses the primacy of his envy
of his mother, which she claims is covered over by his narcissistic overvaluation of the penis.

Clearly, there are points of convergence between Klein's ideas and those
of her colleagues. She appreciates Horney's sensitivity to the girl's anxiety in
regard to her physical well-being, and also her claims that the girl experiences early vaginal sensations, that the girl's wish for a baby precedes that
for a penis, that penis envy is a secondary phenomenon which serves defensive functions, and that the boy experiences significant envy of the mother.
Further, Klein includes in her paper a hearty endorsement of a point made by
Deutsch (who tended to act as a spokesperson, though not always an accurate one, for Freud's position) that "the genital development of the woman
relies on the successful displacement of oral libido on to the genital" (p. 192).
And in the text of her essay, Klein explicitly downplays the radical nature of
her ideas vis-á-vis those of Freud, suggesting that they imply a change in
emphasis regarding a few points (p. 197) but do not contradict his theory in
any significant way.

Just as clearly, however, her claims represent, in many respects, a departure from those of her fellow theorists. Although she agrees with Horney, for
instance, that penis envy is largely a secondary phenomenon which functions at least partly as a defense against prior feelings of disappointment,
that the girl has a dread of internal injury, or that the wish for a baby precedes the wish for the penis, she also contradicts Horney in her claim that
the wish for a child is first and foremost directed toward the mother's babies,
in her assertion that the anxiety about violation comes not from the fear of
the father's overwhelmingly large penis but from the fear of the mother's
vengeful attacks, and in her account of what penis envy is secondary to.
Further, Klein's specific assertions—that the girl turns from her mother primarily due to oral deprivation rather than to deprivation of the penis, that
the girl and boy have, from the outset, a shared foreknowledge of both genitals and of parental intercourse rather than a shared phallic monism, that
both have an extended period of pregenital attachment to the mother—reflect
more overarching theoretical differences deriving from her radical revision-
ing of psychoanalytic theory. While Freud's articulated account of his conflicts with Klein on these specific matters is minimal (viz. his few, clipped
statements in the Freud-Jones correspondence (Paskauskas, 1993), he does
make clear his general objection (certainly substantive, but, some have suggested, intensified by his feelings about Klein's dispute with Anna) to her
more sweeping modifications of his theories.

As noted above, the effort by Klein included in this volume was only the
first of her inquiries into the nature of oedipal envy. It was followed by a
more extensive pair of essays, "The Effects of Early Anxiety-Situations on

the Sexual Development of the Girl" and "The Effects of Early Anxiety-Situations on the Sexual Development of the Boy," which were among a group of papers appended to a series of lectures she first delivered in 1925 that were published as her first book, *The Psycho-Analysis of Children* (1932). In that work, she maintained the claim, apparent in the earlier essay, that the oedipus conflict is initiated at a time when experiences of sadism are at their zenith because of the trauma of weaning, but here she places the story that thus emerges within the context of a conflict between the life and death instincts, citing *Beyond the Pleasure Principle* as a guide to her understanding of sadism in its many forms. Meanwhile, she develops in greater detail her account of the effects of the transitional belief in children of both sexes that the mother contains the father's penis inside her, which is desired as a content of her body. When Klein next revisits the topic of oedipal envy in an extended way, in her 1945 paper "The Oedipus Complex in the Light of Early Anxieties," it is in the light of the discovery of the paranoid and depressive positions which, she notes, "throws new light...on the early stages of the Oedipus complex" (xiv). Whereas previously she saw the Oedipus complex arising out of an influx of sadism and frustration, she now describes the turn toward the father as prompted by feelings of both love and hate, as is the turn from the mother. The child resolves its oedipal dilemma not merely to quell anxiety and the perception of threat, she now suggests, but due to love and to wishes to repair the relationships with both parents so that genital sexuality might itself be redeemed.

If the path Klein had thus far traveled marked a series of reworkings of a set of ideas in light of subsequent, more overarching insights, the culmination of this developmental trajectory was, no doubt, her essay titled "Envy and Gratitude". This essay, like those before it, provoked a storm of controversy; when she read its precursor, "A Study of Envy and Gratitude," at the 1955 Geneva Congress, Winnicott listened with his head in his hands, muttering, "Oh no, she *can't* do this!" (Grosskurth, 1987 p. 414). Here, she details the role of envy of the mother's breast and its resolution as the fundamental building block of later psychological experience for children of both sexes. Penis envy, which was portrayed in her previous works as a semi-independent phenomenon that relied upon reinforcement by envy of the mother for its emergence, is now viewed as originating from the envy of the breast per se, as are the other manifestations of envy in the lives of men and women. In its focused attention to the transformations of and defenses against this earliest oral envy, the importance of gender itself to psychological life has clearly been diminished in comparison with the centrality of the mechanisms by which children of both sexes navigate the rocky road between envy and gratitude.

I will attempt, in the following section of the book, to portray the theories of Horney and Klein on gender and envy not merely as outskirts of Freud's thought, but as centers of growth in their own right, providing foundations upon which ideas of gender and envy can unfold. My view of the primary task presented to the reader of this first section is in line with that of Jones, for whom "the ultimate question is whether a woman is born or made." My hope is that the reader will continue, in reflecting on the papers in this section, to attempt to discern how each of the authors might respond to Jones's inquiry, and to use these observations as the basis for appreciating both the fundamental philosophical differences that are contained there, and the specific points of contrast in their accounts of how and out of what matter, if women (and men, and gender itself) are "made," they have come to be constructed.

REFERENCES

Abraham, K. (1922). Manifestations of the female castration complex. *International journal of psycho-analysis, 3*, 1–29.

Deutsch, H. (1925). The psychology of women in relation to the function of reproduction. *International journal of psycho-analysis, 6*, 405–418.

Fliegel, Z. O. (1986). Women's development in analitical theory: Six decades of controversy. In *Psychoanalysis and women: Contemporary reappraisals*. Alpert, J.L. (ed.) Hillsdale, NJ: The Analytical Press.

Freud, S. (1895). *Project for a scientific psychology*. SE, Vol. 1: (pp. 281–392) (All *SE* citations refer to *The standard edition of the complete psychological works of Sigmund Freud*, 24 Volumes. Edited by James Strachey in collaboration with Anna Freud, assisted by Alix Strachey and Alan Tyson. London: Hogarth Press, 1953–1964. In English translation.)

———— (1900). *The interpretation of dreams. SE*: Vols. 4 and 5.

———— (1905). *Three essays on a theory of sexuality. SE*, Vol. 7 (pp. 123–246).

———— (1908). On the sexual theories of children. *SE*, Vol. 9 (pp. 205–226).

———— (1909). Analysis of a phobia in a five-year-old boy. *SE*, Vol. 10 (pp. 1–147).

———— (1917). On transformations of instinct as exemplified in anal eroticism. *SE*, Vol. 17 (pp. 125–34).

———— (1917/1918). The taboo of virginity. *SE*, Vol. 11 (pp. 191–208).

———— (1919). 'A child is being beaten': A contribution to the study of the origin of sexual perversions. *SE*, Vol. 17 (pp. 175–204).

———— (1920). The psychogenesis of a case of homosexuality in a woman. *SE*, Vol. 18 (pp. 145–172).

———— (1920). *Beyond the pleasure principle. SE*, Vol. 18 (pp. 1–64).

———— (1923). *The ego and the id. SE*, Vol. 19 (pp. 1–65).

———— (1924). The dissolution of the Oedipus complex. *SE*, Vol. 19 (pp. 173–182).

———— (1925). Negation. *SE*, Vol. 19 (pp. 235–240).

———— (1925). Some psychical consequences of the anatomical distinction between the sexes. *SE*, Vol. 19 (pp. 241–260).

———— (1931). Female sexuality. *SE*, Vol. 21 (pp. 221–246).

———— (1932/1933). *New introductory lectures on psycho-analysis. SE*, Vol. 22 (pp. 1–182).

———— (1935/1971). Letter to Carl Mueller-Braunschweig, tr. Stierlin, H. *Psychiatry, 34*, 329.

———— (1936). A disturbance of memory on the Acropolis. *SE*, Vol. 22 (pp. 239–250).

———— (1938). Findings, ideas, problems. *SE*, Vol. 23 (pp. 299–300).

———— (1938/1940). *An outline of psycho-analysis. SE,* Vol. 23 (pp. 139–208).

Freud, S. & Abraham, K. (1965). Letter, Oct. 7, 1923. In *A psychoanalytic dialogue: The letters of Sigmund Freud and Karl Abraham.* New York: Basic Books.

Grosskurth, P. (1987). *Melanie Klein: Her world and her work.* Cambridge, MA: Harvard University Press.

HD (1956). *Tribute to Freud.* New York: McGraw Hill.

Horney, K. (1922/23/1967). On the genesis of the castration complex in women. In H. Kelman (ed.), *Feminine psychology.* New York: W. W. Norton.

———— (1926/1967). The flight from womanhood. In H. Kelman (ed.), *Feminine psychology.* New York: W. W. Norton.

Jones, E. (1927). The early development of female sexuality. *International journal of psychoanalysis, 8,* 459–472.

———— (1933). The phallic phase. *International journal of psycho-analysis, 14,* 1–13.

———— (1935/1948). Early female sexuality. In *Papers on psycho-analysis.* London: Maresfield.

King, P. and Steiner, R. (1991). *The Freud-Klein controversies, 1941–45.* New York: Routledge.

Kingsley, W. (1855). *Oxford English Dictionary* listing under "omphalos."

Klein, M. (1928/1975). Early stages of the Oedipus complex. In *Love, guilt and reparation and other works, 1921–1945.* New York: Delacorte.

———— (1932/1975). The effects of early anxiety-situations on the sexual development of the girl. In *The psycho-analysis of children* (p. 194–239). New York: Dell.

———— (1932/1975). The effects of early anxiety-situations on the sexual development of the boy. In *The psycho-analysis of children* (p. 240–278). New York: Dell.

———— (1945/1975). The Oedipus complex in the light of early anxieties." In *Love, guilt and reparation and other works, 1921–1945.* New York: Delacorte.

———— (1957/1975). Envy and Gratitude. In *Envy and gratitude & other works, 1946–1963.* New York: Delacorte.

Lacan, J. (1985). The meaning of the phallus. In *Feminine sexuality* (p. 74–85). New York: W. W. Norton.

Masson, J. M. (1985). *The complete letters of Sigmund Freud to Wilhelm Fliess, 1887–1904.* Cambridge. MA: Harvard University Press.

Mitchell, J. (1971). *Psychoanalysis and feminism.* New York: Random House.

Paskauskas, R. A. (1993) *The complete correspondence of Sigmund Freud and Ernest Jones, 1908–1939.* Cambridge, MA: Harvard University Press.

Winnicott, D. W. (1970). The use of an object and relating through identifications. In *Playing and reality* (pp. 86–94). New York: Routledge.

SOME PSYCHICAL CONSEQUENCES OF THE ANATOMICAL DISTINCTION BETWEEN THE SEXES[1]

Sigmund Freud

In my own writings and in those of my followers more and more stress is laid on the necessity that the analyses of neurotics shall deal thoroughly with the remotest period of their childhood, the time of the early efflorescence of sexual life. It is only by examining the first manifestations of the patient's innate instinctual constitution and the effects of his earliest experiences that we can accurately gauge the motive forces that have led to his neurosis and can be secure against the errors into which we might be tempted by the degree to which things have become remodeled and overlaid in adult life. This requirement is not only of theoretical but also of practical importance, for it distinguishes our efforts from the work of those physicians whose interests are focused exclusively on therapeutic results and who employ analytic methods, but only up to a certain point. An analysis of early childhood such as we are considering is tedious and laborious and makes demands both upon the physician and upon the patient which cannot always be met. Moreover, it leads us into dark regions where there are as yet no sign-posts. Indeed, analysts may feel reassured, I think, that there is no risk of their work becoming mechanical, and so of losing its interest, during the next few decades.

In the following pages I bring forward some findings of analytic research which would be of great importance if they could be proved to apply universally. Why do I not postpone publication of them until further experience has given me the necessary proof, if such proof is obtainable? Because the conditions under which I work have undergone a change, with implications which I cannot disguise. Formerly, I was not one of those who are unable to hold back what seems to be a new discovery until it has been either confirmed or corrected. My *Interpretation of Dreams* (1900) and my 'Fragment of an Analysis of a Case of Hysteria' (1905) (the case of Dora) were suppressed by me—if not for the nine years enjoined by Horace—at all events for four or five years before I allowed them to be published. But in those days I had unlimited time before me—'oceans of time'[2] as an amiable author

---

1. [Ed: SE 19:241-260. Originally published in 1925 in *Int. z. psychoanal.* 11, 401ff.]
2. [In English in the original. It is not clear what author Freud had in mind. The reference to Horace is to his *Ars Poetica*, 388.]

puts it—and material poured in upon me in such quantities that fresh experiences were hardly to be escaped. Moreover, I was the only worker in a new field, so that my reticence involved no danger to myself and no loss to others.

But now everything has changed. The time before me is limited. The whole of it is no longer spent in working, so that my opportunities for making fresh observations are not so numerous. If I think I see something new, I am uncertain whether I can wait for it to be confirmed. And further, everything that is to be seen upon the surface has already been exhausted; what remains has to be slowly and laboriously dragged up from the depths. Finally, I am no longer alone. An eager crowd of fellow-workers is ready to make use of what is unfinished or doubtful, and I can leave to them that part of the work which I should otherwise have done myself. On this occasion, therefore, I feel justified in publishing something which stands in urgent need of confirmation before its value or lack of value can be decided.

In examining the earliest mental shapes assumed by the sexual life of children we have been in the habit of taking as the subject of our investigations the male child, the little boy. With little girls, so we have supposed, things must be similar, though in some way or other they must nevertheless be different. The point in development at which this difference lay could not be clearly determined.

In boys the situation of the Oedipus complex is the first stage that can be recognized with certainty. It is easy to understand, because at that stage a child retains the same object which he previously cathected with his libido— not as yet a genital one—during the preceding period while he was being suckled and nursed. The fact, too, that in this situation he regards his father as a disturbing rival and would like to get rid of him and take his place is a straightforward consequence of the actual state of affairs. I have shown elsewhere[1] how the oedipus attitude in little boys belongs to the phallic phase, and how its destruction is brought about by the fear of castration—that is, by narcissistic interest in their genitals. The matter is made more difficult to grasp by the complicating circumstance that even in boys the Oedipus complex has a double orientation, active and passive, in accordance with their bisexual constitution; a boy also wants to take his *mother's* place as the love-object of his *father*—a fact which we describe as the feminine attitude.[2]

As regards the prehistory of the Oedipus complex in boys we are far from complete clarity. We know that that period includes an identification of an affectionate sort with the boy's father, an identification which is still free from any sense of rivalry in regard to his mother. Another element of that stage is invariably, I believe, a masturbatory activity in connection with the genitals, the masturbation of early childhood, the more or less violent suppression of which by those in charge of the child sets the castration complex in action. It is to be assumed that this masturbation is attached to the Oedipus complex and

1. 'The Dissolution of the Oedipus Complex' (1924) (Ed: *SE* 19:173) [Much of what follows is an elaboration of that paper.]
2. [Cf. ibid., p. 176.]

serves as a discharge for the sexual excitation belonging to it. It is, however, uncertain whether the masturbation has this character from the first, or whether on the contrary it makes its first appearance spontaneously as an activity of a bodily organ and is only brought into relation with the Oedipus complex at some later date; this second possibility is by far the more probable. Another doubtful question is the part played by bed-wetting and by the breaking of that habit through the intervention of training measures. We are inclined to make the simple connection that continued bed-wetting is a result of masturbation and that its suppression is regarded by boys as an inhibition of their genital activity—that is, as having the meaning of a threat of castration;[1] but whether we are always right in supposing this remains to be seen. Finally, analysis shows us in a shadowy way how the fact of a child at a very early age listening to his parents copulating may set up his first sexual excitation, and how that event may, owing to its after-effects, act as a starting-point for the child's whole sexual development. Masturbation, as well as the two attitudes in the Oedipus complex, later on become attached to this early experience, the child having subsequently interpreted its meaning. It is impossible, however, to suppose that these observations of coitus are of universal occurrence, so that at this point we are faced with the problem of 'primal phantasies'.[2] Thus the prehistory of the Oedipus complex, even in boys, raises all of these questions for sifting and explanation; and there is the further problem of whether we are to suppose that the process invariably follows the same course, or whether a great variety of different preliminary stages may not converge upon the same terminal situation.

In little girls the Oedipus complex raises one problem more than in boys. In both cases the mother is the original object; and there is no cause for surprise that boys retain that object in the Oedipus complex. But how does it happen that girls abandon it and instead take their father as an object? In pursuing this question I have been able to reach some conclusions which may throw light precisely on the prehistory of the oedipus relation in girls.

Every analyst has come across certain women who cling with especial intensity and tenacity to the bond with their father and to the wish in which it culminates of having a child by him. We have good reason to suppose that the same wishful phantasy was also the motive force of their infantile masturbation, and it is easy to form an impression that at this point we have been brought up against an elementary and unanalysable fact of infantile sexual life. But a thorough analysis of these very cases brings something different to light—namely, that here the Oedipus complex has a long prehistory and is in some respects a secondary formation.

The old paediatrician Lindner [1879] once remarked that a child discovers the genital zones (the penis or the clitoris) as a source of pleasure while indulging in sensual sucking (thumb-sucking).[3] I shall leave it an open question whether it is really true that the child takes the newly found source of pleasure in exchange for the recent loss of the mother's nipple—a possibility to

1. [Cf. ibid., p. 175.]
2. [Cf. the discussions in the 'Wolf Man' analysis (1918), SE, 17, especially 48–60 and 95–7, and Lecture XXIII of the Introductory lectures (1916–17).]
3. Cf. Three essays on the theory of sexuality (1905) [SE, 7:179].

which later phantasies (fellatio) seem to point. Be that as it may, the genital zone is discovered at some time or other, and there seems no justification for attributing any psychical content to the first activities in connection with it. But the first step in the phallic phase which begins in this way is not the linking-up of the masturbation with the object-cathexes of the Oedipus complex, but a momentous discovery which little girls are destined to make. They notice the penis of a brother or playmate, strikingly visible and of large proportions, at once recognize it as the superior counterpart of their own small and inconspicuous organ, and from that time forward fall a victim to envy for the penis.

There is an interesting contrast between the behavior of the two sexes. In the analogous situation, when a little boy first catches sight of a girl's genital region, he begins by showing irresolution and lack of interest; he sees nothing or disavows[1] what he has seen, he softens it down or looks about for expedients for bringing it into line with his expectations. It is not until later, when some threat of castration has obtained a hold upon him, that the observation becomes important to him: if he then recollects or repeats it, it arouses a terrible storm of emotion in him and forces him to believe in the reality of the threat which he has hitherto laughed at. This combination of circumstances leads to two reactions, which may become fixed and will in that case, whether separately or together or in conjunction with other factors, permanently determine the boy's relations to women: horror of the mutilated creature or triumphant contempt for her. These developments, however, belong to the future, though not to a very remote one.

A little girl behaves differently. She makes her judgement and her decision in a flash. She has seen it and knows that she is without it and wants to have it.[2]

Here what has been named the masculinity complex of women branches off.[3] It may put great difficulties in the way of their regular development towards femininity, if it cannot be got over soon enough. The hope of some day obtaining a penis in spite of everything and so of becoming like a man may persist to an incredibly late age and may become a motive for strange and otherwise unaccountable actions. Or again, a process may set in which I should like to call a 'disavowal',[4] a process which in the mental life of children seems neither uncommon nor very dangerous but which in an adult would mean the beginning of a psychosis. Thus a girl may refuse to accept the fact of being castrated, may harden herself in the conviction that she *does* possess a penis, and may subsequently be compelled to behave as though she were a man.

1. [See Strachey's footnote to 'The Infantile Genital Organization', *SE* 19:143.]
2. This is an opportunity for correcting a statement which I made many years ago. I believed that the sexual interest of children, unlike that of pubescents, was aroused, not by the difference between the sexes, but by the problem of where babies come from. We now see that, at all events with girls, this is certainly not the case. With boys it may no doubt happen sometimes one way and sometimes the other; or with both sexes chance experiences may determine the event. [The statement mentioned at the beginning of this footnote appears in more than one place: e.g. in the paper on 'The Sexual Theories of Children' (1908), *SE* 9:212, in the case history of 'Little Hans' (1909), *SE* 10:133, and in a passage added in 1915 to the *Three essays* (1905d), *SE* 7:195. In a passage earlier than any of these, however, in a paper on 'The Sexual Enlightenment of Children' (1907), *SE* 9:135, Freud in fact takes the opposite view—the one advocated here.]
3. [This term seems to have been introduced by Van Ophuijsen (1917). Freud adopted it in '"A Child is Being Beaten"' (1919), *SE* 17:191. Cf. also 19:178].
4. [For the parallel process in boys, see 'The Infantile Genital Organization' (1923) *SE* 19:43-4.]

The psychical consequences of envy for the penis, in so far as it does not become absorbed in the reaction-formation of the masculinity complex, are various and far-reaching. After a woman has become aware of the wound to her narcissism, she develops, like a scar, a sense of inferiority.[1] When she has passed beyond her first attempt at explaining her lack of a penis as being a punishment personal to herself and has realized that that sexual character is a universal one, she begins to share the contempt felt by men for a sex which is the lesser in so important a respect, and, at least in holding that opinion, insists on being like a man.[2]

Even after penis-envy has abandoned its true object, it continues to exist: by an easy displacement it persists in the character-trait of *jealousy*. Of course, jealousy is not limited to one sex and has a wider foundation than this, but I am of opinion that it plays a far larger part in the mental life of women than of men and that that is because it is enormously reinforced from the direction of displaced penis-envy. While I was still unaware of this source of jealousy and was considering the phantasy 'a child is being beaten', which occurs so commonly in girls, I constructed a first phase for it in which its meaning was that another child, a rival of whom the subject was jealous, was to be beaten.[3] This phantasy seems to be a relic of the phallic period in girls. The peculiar rigidity which struck me so much in the monotonous formula 'a child is being beaten' can probably be interpreted in a special way. The child which is being beaten (or caressed) may ultimately be nothing more nor less than the clitoris itself, so that at its very lowest level the statement will contain a confession of masturbation, which has remained attached to the content of the formula from its beginning in the phallic phase till later life.

A third consequence of penis-envy seems to be a loosening of the girl's relation with her mother as a love-object. The situation as a whole is not very clear, but it can be seen that in the end the girl's mother, who sent her into the world so insufficiently equipped, is almost always held responsible for her lack of a penis. The way in which this comes about historically is often that soon after the girl has discovered that her genitals are unsatisfactory she begins to show jealousy of another child on the ground that her mother is fonder of it than of her, which serves as a reason for her giving up her affectionate relation to her mother. It will fit in with this if the child which has been preferred by her mother is made into the first object of the beating-phantasy which ends in masturbation.

1. [Cf. *Beyond the pleasure principle* (1920), SE 18:20–1.]
2. In my first critical account of the 'History of the Psycho-Analytic Movement' (1914) [*SE* 14:54–5], I recognized that this fact represents the core of truth contained in Adler's theory. That theory has no hesitation in explaining the whole world by this single point ('organ-inferiority', the 'masculine protest', 'breaking away from the feminine line') and prides itself upon having in this way robbed sexuality of its importance and put the desire for power in its place! Thus the only organ which could claim to be called 'inferior' without any ambiguity would be the clitoris. On the other hand, one hears of analysts who boast that, though they have worked for dozens of years, they have never found a sign of the existence of a castration complex. We must bow our heads in recognition of the greatness of this achievement, even though it is only a negative one, a piece of virtuosity in the art of overlooking and mistaking. The two theories form an interesting pair of opposites: in the latter not a trace of a castration complex, in the former nothing else than its consequences.
3. "A Child is Being Beaten" (1919e) [*SE* 17:184–5].

There is yet another surprising effect of penis-envy, or of the discovery of the inferiority of the clitoris, which is undoubtedly the most important of all. In the past I had often formed an impression that in general women tolerate masturbation worse than men, that they more frequently fight against it and that they are unable to make use of it in circumstances in which a man would seize upon it as a way of escape without any hesitation. Experience would no doubt elicit innumerable exceptions to this statement, if we attempted to turn it into a rule. The reactions of human individuals of both sexes are of course made up of masculine and feminine traits. But it appeared to me nevertheless as though masturbation were further removed from the nature of women than of men, and the solution of the problem could be assisted by the reflection that masturbation, at all events of the clitoris, is a masculine activity and that the elimination of clitoridal sexuality is a necessary precondition for the development of femininity.[1] Analyses of the remote phallic period have now taught me that in girls, soon after the first signs of penis-envy, an intense current of feeling against masturbation makes its appearance, which cannot be attributed exclusively to the educational influence of those in charge of the child. This impulse is clearly a forerunner of the wave of repression which at puberty will do away with a large amount of the girl's masculine sexuality in order to make room for the development of her femininity. It may happen that this first opposition to auto-erotic activity fails to attain its end. And this was in fact the case in the instances which I analysed. The conflict continued, and both then and later the girl did everything she could to free herself from the compulsion to masturbate. Many of the later manifestations of sexual life in women remain unintelligible unless this powerful motive is recognized.

I cannot explain the opposition which is raised in this way by little girls to phallic masturbation except by supposing that there is some concurrent factor which turns her violently against that pleasurable activity. Such a factor lies close at hand. It cannot be anything else than her narcissistic sense of humiliation which is bound up with penis-envy, the reminder that after all this is a point on which she cannot compete with boys and that it would therefore be best for her to give up the idea of doing so. Thus the little girl's recognition of the anatomical distinction between the sexes forces her away from masculinity and masculine masturbation on to new lines which lead to the development of femininity.

So far there has been no question of the Oedipus complex, nor has it up to this point played any part. But now the girl's libido slips into a new position along the line—there is no other way of putting it—of the equation 'penis-child'. She gives up her wish for a penis and puts in place of it a wish for a child: and *with that purpose in view* she takes her father as a love-object.[2] Her mother becomes the object of her jealousy. The girl has turned into a little woman. If I am to credit a single analytic instance, this new sit-

1. [A reference to clitoridal masturbation in girls appeared in the first edition of the *Three essays* (1905), *SE* 7:220. In the course of his 'Contributions to a Discussion on Masturbation' (1912), Freud expressed regret at the lack of knowledge about female masturbation (*SE* 12:247).]
2. [cf. 'The Dissolution of the Oedipus Complex", *SE* 19:179.]

uation can give rise to physical sensations which would have to be regarded as a premature awakening of the female genital apparatus. When the
girl's attachment to her father comes to grief later on and has to be abandoned, it may give place to an identification with him and the girl may thus
return to her masculinity complex and perhaps remain fixated in it.

I have now said the essence of what I had to say: I will stop, therefore,
and cast an eye over our findings. We have gained some insight into the
prehistory of the Oedipus complex in girls. The corresponding period in boys
is more or less unknown. In girls the Oedipus complex is a secondary formation. The operations of the castration complex precede it and prepare for
it. As regards the relation between the Oedipus and castration complexes
there is a fundamental contrast between the two sexes. *Whereas in boys the
Oedipus complex is destroyed by the castration complex,*[1] *in girls it is made
possible and led up to by the castration complex.* This contradiction is
cleared up if we reflect that the castration complex always operates in the
sense implied in its subject-matter: it inhibits and limits masculinity and
encourages femininity. The difference between the sexual development of
males and females at the stage we have been considering is an intelligible
consequence of the anatomical distinction between their genitals and of the
psychical situation involved in it; it corresponds to the difference between
a castration that has been carried out and one that has merely been threatened. In their essentials, therefore, our findings are self-evident and it
should have been possible to foresee them.

The Oedipus complex, however, is such an important thing that the manner in which one enters and leaves it cannot be without its effects. In boys (as
I have shown at length in the paper to which I have just referred [1924] and
to which all of my present remarks are closely related) the complex is not simply repressed, it is literally smashed to pieces by the shock of threatened castration. Its libidinal cathexes are abandoned, desexualized and in part sublimated; its objects are incorporated into the ego, where they form the nucleus
of the super-ego and give that new structure its characteristic qualities. In
normal, or, it is better to say, in ideal cases, the Oedipus complex exists no
longer, even in the unconscious; the super-ego has become its heir. Since the
penis (to follow Ferenczi [1924]) owes its extraordinarily high narcissistic
cathexis to its organic significance for the propagation of the species, the catastrophe to the Oedipus complex (the abandonment of incest and the institution of conscience and morality) may be regarded as a victory of the race over
the individual. This is an interesting point of view when one considers that
neurosis is based upon a struggle of the ego against the demands of the sexual function. But to leave the standpoint of individual psychology is not of
any immediate help in clarifying this complicated situation.

In girls the motive for the demolition of the Oedipus complex is lacking.
Castration has already had its effect, which was to force the child into the
situation of the Oedipus complex. Thus the Oedipus complex escapes the

1. [Ibid., p. 177.]

fate which it meets with in boys: it may be slowly abandoned or dealt with by repression, or its effects may persist far into women's normal mental life. I cannot evade the notion (though I hesitate to give it expression) that for women the level of what is ethically normal is different from what it is in men. Their super-ego is never so inexorable, so impersonal, so independent of its emotional origins as we require it to be in men. Character-traits which critics of every epoch have brought up against women—that they show less sense of justice than men, that they are less ready to submit to the great exigencies of life, that they are more often influenced in their judgements by feelings of affection or hostility—all these would be amply accounted for by the modification in the formation of their super-ego which we have inferred above. We must not allow ourselves to be deflected from such conclusions by the denials of the feminists, who are anxious to force us to regard the two sexes as completely equal in position and worth; but we shall, of course, willingly agree that the majority of men are also far behind the masculine ideal and that all human individuals, as a result of their bisexual disposition and of cross-inheritance, combine in themselves both masculine and feminine characteristics, so that pure masculinity and femininity remain theoretical constructions of uncertain content.

I am inclined to set some value on the considerations I have brought forward upon the psychical consequences of the anatomical distinction between the sexes. I am aware, however, that this opinion can only be maintained if my findings, which are based on a handful of cases, turn out to have general validity and to be typical. If not, they would remain no more than a contribution to our knowledge of the different paths along which sexual life develops.

In the valuable and comprehensive studies on the masculinity and castration complexes in women by Abraham (1921), Horney (1923) and Helene Deutsch (1925) there is much that touches closely on what I have written but nothing that coincides with it completely, so that here again I feel justified in publishing this paper.

2

THE FLIGHT FROM WOMANHOOD[1]

The Masculinity-Complex in Women as Viewed by Men and by Women

Karen Horney

In some of his latest works Freud has drawn attention with increasing urgency to a certain one-sidedness in our analytical researches. I refer to the fact that till quite recently the minds of boys and men only were taken as objects of investigation.

The reason for this is obvious. Psychoanalysis is the creation of a male genius, and almost all those who have developed his ideas have been men. It is only right and reasonable that they should evolve more easily a masculine psychology and understand more of the development of men than of women.

A momentous step toward the understanding of the specifically feminine was made by Freud himself in discovering the existence of penis envy, and soon after, the work of van Ophuijsen and Abraham showed how large a part this factor plays in the development of women and in the formation of their neuroses. The significance of penis envy has been extended quite recently by the hypothesis of the phallic phase. By this we mean that in the infantile genital organization in both sexes only one genital organ, namely the male, plays any part, and that it is just this that distinguishes the infantile organization from the final genital organization of the adult.[2] According to this theory, the clitoris is conceived of as a phallus, and we assume that little girls as well as boys attach to the clitoris in the first instance exactly the same value as to the penis.[3]

The effect of this phase is partly to inhibit and partly to promote the subsequent development. Helene Deutsch has demonstrated principally the inhibiting effects. She is of the opinion that at the beginning of every new sexual function (e.g., at the beginning of puberty, of sexual intercourse, of

1. "Flucht aus der Weiblichkeit," *Intern. zeitschr. f. psychoanal.*, XII (1926), pp. 360–74; *Int. j. psycho-anal.*, VII (1926), pp. 324–39.
2. Freud, "The Infantile Genital Organization of the Libido." *Collected Papers, Vol. II*, No. XX. [Horney's references to Freud are usually to editions prior to the Standard one (*The complete psychological works of Sigmund Freud* and the *collected papers*, published by the Hogarth Press, London).]
3. H. Deutsch, *Psychoanalyse der weiblichen sexualfunktionen* (1925). (Ed: *The psychology of women's sexual functions*. Vienna: Verlag. Reviewed by Horney in *The international journal of psycho-analysis*, 7:92–100)

pregnancy and childbirth), this phase is reactivated and has to be overcome every time before a feminine attitude can be attained. Freud has elaborated her exposition on the positive side, for he believes that it is only penis envy and the overcoming of it which give rise to the desire for a child and thus form the love bond to the father.[1]

The question now arises as to whether these hypotheses have helped to make our insight into feminine development (insight that Freud himself has stated to be unsatisfactory and incomplete) more satisfactory and clear.

Science has often found it fruitful to look at long-familiar facts from a fresh point of view. Otherwise there is a danger that we shall involuntarily continue to classify all new observations among the same clearly defined groups of ideas.

The new point of view of which I wish to speak came to me by way of philosophy, in some essays by Georg Simmel.[2] The point that Simmel makes there and that has been in many ways elaborated since, especially from the feminine side,[3] is this: Our whole civilization is a masculine civilization. The State, the laws, morality, religion, and the sciences are the creation of men. Simmel by no means deduces from these facts, as is commonly done by other writers, an inferiority in women, but he first of all gives considerable breadth and depth to this conception of a masculine civilization: "The requirements of art, patriotism, morality in general and social ideas in particular, correctness in practical judgment and objectivity in theoretical knowledge, the energy and the profundity of life—all these are categories which belong as it were in their form and their claims to humanity in general, but in their actual historical configuration they are masculine throughout. Supposing that we describe these things, viewed as absolute ideas, by the single word 'objective,' we then find that in the history of our race the equation objective = masculine is a valid one."

Now Simmel thinks that the reason why it is so difficult to recognize these historical facts is that the very standards by which mankind has estimated the values of male and female nature are "not neutral, arising out of the differences of the sexes, but in themselves essentially masculine....We do not believe in a purely 'human' civilization, into which the question of sex does not enter, for the very reason that prevents any such civilization from in fact existing, namely, the (so to speak) naïve identification of the concept 'human being'[4] and the concept 'man,'[5] which in many languages even causes the same word to be used for the two concepts. For the moment I will leave it undetermined whether this masculine character of the fundamentals of our civilization has its origin in the essential nature of the sexes or only in a certain preponderance of force in men, which is not really bound up with the question of civilization. In any case this is the reason why, in the most varying fields, inadequate achievements are contemptuously called 'feminine,' while distinguished achievements on the part of

1. Freud, "Uber einige psychische Folgen der anatomischen Geschlechtsunterschiede," *Intern. zeitschr. f. psychoanal.*, XI (1925). (Ed: "Some psychical consequences of the anatomical distinction between the sexes" *SE* 19:241-60)
2. Georg Simmel, *Philosophische kultur.*
3. Cf. in particular Vaerting, *Männliche Eigenart im Frauenstaat und Weibliche Eigenart im Männerstaat.*
4. German *Mensch.*
5. German *Mann.*

women are called 'masculine' as an expression of praise."

Like all sciences and all valuations, the psychology of women has hitherto been considered only from the point of view of men. It is inevitable that the man's position of advantage should cause objective validity to be attributed to his subjective, affective relations to the woman, and according to Delius[1] the psychology of women hitherto actually represents a deposit of the desires and disappointments of men.

An additional and very important factor in the situation is that women have adapted themselves to the wishes of men and felt as if their adaptation were their true nature. That is, they see or saw themselves in the way that their men's wishes demanded of them; unconsciously they yielded to the suggestion of masculine thought.

If we are clear about the extent to which all our being, thinking, and doing conform to these masculine standards, we can see how difficult it is for the individual man and also for the individual woman really to shake off this mode of thought.

The question then is how far analytical psychology also, when its researches have women for their object, is under the spell of this way of thinking, insofar as it has not yet wholly left behind the stage in which frankly and as a matter of course masculine development only was considered. In other words, how far has the evolution of women, as depicted to us today by analysis, been measured by masculine standards and how far therefore does this picture fail to present quite accurately the real nature of women.

If we look at the matter from this point of view our first impression is a surprising one. The present analytical picture of feminine development (whether that picture be correct or not) differs in no case by a hair's breadth from the typical ideas that the boy has of the girl.

THE BOY'S IDEAS	OUR IDEAS OF FEMENINE DEVELOMENT
Naïve assumption that girls as well as boys possess a penis.	*For both sexes it is only the male genital which plays any part.*
Realization of the absence of the penis.	*Sad discovery of the absence of the penis.*
Idea that the girl is a castrated, mutilated boy.	*Belief of the girl that she once possessed a penis and lost it by castration.*
Belief that the girl has suffered punishment that also threatens him.	*Castration is conceived of as the infliction of punishment.*
The girl is regarded as inferior.	*The girl regards herself as inferior. Penis envy.*

1. Delius, *Vom Erwachen der Frau.*

The boy is unable to imagine how the girl can ever get over this loss or envy.	*The girl never gets over the sense of deficiency and inferiority and has constantly to master afresh her desire to be a man.*
The boy dreads her envy.	*The girl desires throughout life to avenge herself on the man for possessing something which she lacks.*

We are familiar with the ideas that the boy entertains. I will therefore only sketch them in a few succinct phrases, and for the sake of comparison will place in a parallel column our ideas of the development of women.

The existence of this over-exact agreement is certainly no criterion of its objective correctness. It is quite possible that the infantile genital organization of the little girl might bear as striking a resemblance to that of the boy as has up till now been assumed.

But it is surely calculated to make us think and take other possibilities into consideration. For instance, we might follow Georg Simmel's train of thought and reflect whether it is likely that female adaptation to the male structure should take place at so early a period and in so high a degree that the specific nature of a little girl is overwhelmed by it. Later I will return for a moment to the point at which it does actually seem to me probable that this infection with a masculine point of view occurs in childhood. But it does not seem to me clear offhand how everything bestowed by nature could be thus absorbed into it and leave no trace. And so we must return to the question I have already raised—whether the remarkable parallelism I have indicated may not perhaps be the expression of a one-sidedness in our observations, due to their being made from the man's point of view.

Such a suggestion immediately encounters an inner protest, for we remind ourselves of the sure ground of experience upon which analytical research has always been founded. But at the same time our theoretical scientific knowledge tells us that this ground is not altogether trustworthy, but that all experience by its very nature contains a subjective factor. Thus, even our analytical experience is derived from direct observation of the material that our patients bring to analysis in free associations, dreams, and symptoms, and from the interpretations we make or the conclusions we draw from this material. Therefore, even when the technique is correctly applied, there is in theory the possibility of variations in this experience.

Now, if we try to free our minds from this masculine mode of thought, nearly all the problems of feminine psychology take on a different appearance.

The first thing that strikes us is that it is always, or principally, the genital difference between the sexes which has been made the cardinal point in the analytical conception and that we have left out of consideration the other great biological difference, namely, the different parts played by men and by women in the function of reproduction.

The influence of the man's point of view in the conception of motherhood is most clearly revealed in Ferenczi's extremely brilliant genital theory.[1] His view is that the real incitement to coitus, its true, ultimate meaning for both sexes, is to be sought in the desire to return to the mother's womb. During a period of contest man acquired the privilege of really penetrating once more, by means of his genital organ, into a uterus. The woman, who was formerly in the subordinate position, was obliged to adapt her organization to this organic situation and was provided with certain compensations. She had to "content herself" with substitutes in the nature of fantasy and above all with harboring the child, whose bliss she shares. At the most, it is only in the act of birth that she perhaps has potentialities of pleasure denied to the man.[2]

According to this view the psychic situation of a woman would certainly not be a very pleasurable one. She lacks any real primal impulse to coitus, or at least she is debarred from all direct—even if only partial—fulfillment. If this is so, the impulse toward coitus and pleasure in it must undoubtedly be less for her than for the man. For it is only indirectly, by circuitous ways, that she attains to a certain fulfillment of the primal longing—i.e., partly by the roundabout way of masochistic conversion and partly by identification with the child she may conceive. These, however, are merely "compensatory devices." The only thing in which she ultimately has the advantage over the man is the surely very questionable pleasure in the act of birth.

At this point I, as a woman, ask in amazement, and what about motherhood? And the blissful consciousness of bearing a new life within oneself? And the ineffable happiness of the increasing expectation of the appearance of this new thing? And the joy when it finally makes its appearance and one holds it for the first time in one's arms? And the deep, pleasurable feeling of satisfaction in suckling it and the happiness of the whole period when the infant needs her care?

Ferenczi has expressed the opinion in conversation that in the primal period of conflict which ended so grievously for the female, the male as victor imposed upon her the burden of motherhood and all it involves.

Certainly, regarded from the standpoint of the social struggle, motherhood *may* be a handicap. It is certainly so at the present time, but it is much less certain that it was so in times when human beings were closer to nature.

Moreover, we explain penis envy itself by its biological relations and not by social factors; on the contrary, we are accustomed without more ado to construe the woman's sense of being at a disadvantage socially as the rationalization of her penis envy.

But from the biological point of view woman has in motherhood, or in the capacity for motherhood, a quite indisputable and by no means negligible physiological superiority. This is most clearly reflected in the unconscious of the male psyche in the boy's intense envy of motherhood. We are familiar with this envy as such, but it has hardly received due consideration as a dynamic factor. When one begins, as I did, to analyze men only after a fairly long experience of analyzing women, one receives a most surprising

---

1. Ferenczi, *Versuch einer Genitaltheorie* (1924).
2. Cf. also Helene Deutsch, *Psychoanalyse der Weiblichen Sexualfunktionen*; and Groddeck, *Das Buch vom Es*. (Ed: *The book of the it*. New York: Random House, 1923/1949).

impression of the intensity of this envy of pregnancy, childbirth, and motherhood, as well as of the breasts and of the act of suckling.

In the light of this impression derived from analysis, one must naturally inquire whether an unconscious masculine tendency to depreciation is not expressing itself intellectually in the above-mentioned view of motherhood. This depreciation would run as follows: In reality women do simply desire the penis; when all is said and done motherhood is only a burden that makes the struggle for existence harder, and men may be glad that they have not to bear it.

When Helene Deutsch writes that the masculinity complex in women plays a much greater part than the femininity complex in man, she would seem to overlook the fact that the masculine envy is clearly capable of more successful sublimation than the penis envy of the girl, and that it certainly serves as one, if not as the essential, driving force in the setting up of cultural values.

Language itself points to this origin of cultural productivity. In the historic times that are known to us, this productivity has undoubtedly been incomparably greater in men than in women. Is not the tremendous strength in men of the impulse to creative work in every field precisely due to their feeling of playing a relatively small part in the creation of living beings, which constantly impels them to an overcompensation in achievement?

If we are right in making this connection, we are confronted with the problem of why no corresponding impulse to compensate herself for her penis envy is found in woman. There are two possibilities: Either the envy of the woman is absolutely less than that of the man; or it is less successfully worked off in some other way. We could bring forward facts in support of either supposition.

In favor of the greater intensity of the man's envy we might point out that an actual anatomical disadvantage on the side of the woman exists only from the point of view of the pregenital levels of organization.[1] From that of the genital organization of adult women there is no disadvantage, for obviously the capacity of women for coitus is not less but simply other than that of men. On the other hand, the part of the man in reproduction is ultimately less than that of the woman.

Further, we observe that men are evidently under a greater necessity to depreciate women than conversely. The realization that the dogma of the inferiority of women had its origin in an unconscious male tendency could only dawn upon us after a doubt had arisen whether in fact this view were justified in reality. But if there actually are in men tendencies to depreciate women behind this conviction of feminine inferiority, we must infer that this unconscious impulse to depreciation is a very powerful one.

Further, there is much to be said in favor of the view that women work off their penis envy less successfully than men, from a cultural point of view. We know that in the most favorable case this envy is transmuted into the desire for a husband and child, and probably by this very transmutation it forfeits the greater part of its power as an incentive to sublimation. In unfavorable cases, however, as I shall presently show in greater detail, it is burdened with

1. K. Horney, "On the Genesis of the Castration Complex in Women," *Int. j. psycho-anal.*, Vol. V (1924). (Ed: (1923/1967). In *Feminine psychology*. New York: W. W. Norton, pp 37–53).

a sense of guilt instead of being able to be employed fruitfully, while the man's incapacity for motherhood is probably felt simply as an inferiority and can develop its full driving power without inhibition.

In this discussion I have already touched on a problem that Freud has recently brought into the foreground of interest:[1] namely, the question of the origin and operation of the desire for a child. In the course of the last decade our attitude toward this problem has changed. I may therefore be permitted to describe briefly the beginning and the end of this historical evolution.

The original hypothesis[2] was that penis envy gave a libidinal reinforcement both to the wish for a child and the wish for the man, but that the latter wish arose independently of the former. Subsequently the accent became more and more displaced on to the penis envy, till in his most recent work on this problem, Freud expressed the conjecture that the wish for the child arose only through penis envy and the disappointment over the lack of the penis in general, and that the tender attachment to the father came into existence only by this circuitous route—by way of the desire for the penis and the desire for the child.

This latter hypothesis obviously originated in the need to explain psychologically the biological principle of heterosexual attraction. This corresponds to the problem formulated by Groddeck, who says that it is natural that the boy should retain the mother as a love object, "but how is it that the little girl becomes attached to the opposite sex?"[3]

In order to approach this problem we must first of all realize that our empirical material with regard to the masculinity complex in women is derived from two sources of very different importance. The first is the direct observation of children, in which the subjective factor plays a relatively insignificant part. Every little girl who has not been intimidated displays penis envy frankly and without embarrassment. We see that the presence of this envy is typical and understand quite well why this is so; we understand how the narcissistic mortification of possessing less than the boy is reinforced by a series of disadvantages arising out of the different pregenital cathexes: the manifest privileges of the boy in connection with urethral erotism, the scoptophilic instinct, and onanism.[4]

I should like to suggest that we should apply the term *primary* to the little girl's penis envy, which is obviously based simply on the anatomical difference.

The second source upon which our experience draws is to be found in the analytical material produced by adult women. Naturally it is more difficult to form a judgment on this, and there is therefore more scope for the subjective element. We see here in the first instance that penis envy operates as a factor of enormous dynamic power. We see patients rejecting their female functions, their unconscious motive in so doing being the desire to be male. We meet with

1. Freud, *Uber einige psychische Folgen der anatomischen Geschlechts-unterschiede.*
2. Freud, "On the Transformation of Instincts with Special Reference to Anal Erotism," *Collected Papers*, Vol. II, No. XVI. (Ed: *SE* 17:125–134).
3. Groddeck, *Das Buch vom Es.*
4. I have dealt with this subject in greater detail in my paper "On the Genesis of the Castration Complex in Women."

fantasies of which the content is: "I once had a penis; I am a man who has been castrated and mutilated," from which proceed feelings of inferiority that have for after-effect all manner of obstinate hypochondriacal ideas. We see a marked attitude of hostility toward men, sometimes taking the form of depreciation and sometimes of a desire to castrate or maim them, and we see how the whole destinies of certain women are determined by this factor.

It was natural to conclude—and especially natural because of the male orientation of our thinking—that we could link these impressions onto the primary penis envy and to reason *a posteriori* that this envy must possess an enormous intensity, an enormous dynamic power, seeing that it evidently gave rise to such effects. Here we overlooked the fact, more in our general estimation of the situation than in details, that this desire to be a man, so familiar to us from the analyses of adult women, had only very little to do with that early, infantile, primary penis envy, but that it is a secondary formation embodying all that has miscarried in the development toward womanhood.

From beginning to end, my experience has proved to me with unchanging clearness that the Oedipus complex in women leads (not only in extreme cases where the subject has come to grief, but *regularly*) to a regression to penis envy, naturally in every possible degree and shade. The difference between the outcome of the male and the female Oedipus complexes seems to me in average cases to be as follows. In boys the mother as a sexual object is renounced owing to the fear of castration, but the male role itself is not only affirmed in further development but is actually overemphasized in the reaction to the fear of castration. We see this clearly in the latency and prepubertal period in boys and generally in later life as well. Girls, on the other hand, not only renounce the father as a sexual object but simultaneously recoil from the feminine role altogether.

In order to understand this flight from womanhood we must consider the facts relating to early infantile onanism, which is the physical expression of the excitations due to the Oedipus complex.

Here again the situation is much clearer in boys, or perhaps we simply know more about it. Are these facts so mysterious to us in girls only because we have always looked at them through the eyes of men? It seems rather like it when we do not even concede to little girls a specific form of onanism but without more ado describe their autoerotic activities as male; and when we conceive of the difference, which surely must exist, as being that of a negative to a positive, i.e., in the case of anxiety about onanism, that the difference is that between a castration threatened and castration that has actually taken place! My analytical experience makes it most decidedly possible that little girls have a specific feminine form of onanism (which incidentally differs in technique from that of boys), even if we assume that the little girl practices exclusively clitoral masturbation, an assumption that seems to me by no means certain. And I do not see why, in spite of its past evolution, it should not be conceded that the clitoris legitimately belongs to and forms an integral part of the female genital apparatus.

Whether in the early phase of the girl's genital development she has organic vaginal sensations is a matter remarkably difficult to determine from the analytical material produced by adult women. In a whole series of cases I have been inclined to conclude that this is so, and later I shall quote the material upon which I base this conclusion. That such sensations should occur seems to me theoretically very probable for the following reasons. Undoubtedly the familiar fantasies that an excessively large penis is effecting forcible penetration, producing pain and hemorrhage, and threatening to destroy something, go to show that the little girl bases her oedipus fantasies most realistically (in accordance with the plastic, concrete thinking of childhood) on the disproportion in size between father and child. I think too that both the oedipus fantasies and also the logically ensuing dread of an internal—i.e., vaginal—injury go to show that the vagina as well as the clitoris must be assumed to play a part in the early infantile genital organization of women.[1] One might even infer from the later phenomena of frigidity that the vaginal zone has actually a stronger cathexis (arising out of anxiety and attempts at defense) than the clitoris, and this because the incestuous wishes are referred to the vagina with the unerring accuracy of the unconscious. From this point of view frigidity must be regarded as an attempt to ward off the fantasies so full of danger to the ego. And this would also throw a new light on the unconscious pleasurable feelings that, as various authors have maintained, occur at parturition, or alternatively, on the dread of childbirth. For (just because of the disproportion between the vagina and the baby and because of the pain to which this gives rise) parturition would be calculated to a far greater extent than subsequent sexual intercourse to stand to the unconscious for a realization of those early incest fantasies, a realization to which no guilt is attached. The female genital anxiety, like the castration dread of boys, invariably bears the impress of feelings of guilt, and it is to them that it owes its lasting influence.

A further factor in the situation, and one that works in the same direction, is a certain consequence of the anatomical difference between the sexes. I mean that the boy can inspect his genitals to see whether the dreaded consequences of onanism are taking place; the girl, on the other hand, is literally in the dark on this point and remains in complete uncertainty. Naturally this possibility of a reality test does not weigh with boys in cases where the castration anxiety is acute, but in the slighter cases of fear, which are practically more important because they are more frequent, I think that this difference is very important. At any rate, the analytical material that has come to light in women whom I have analyzed has led me to conclude that this factor plays a considerable part in feminine mental life and that it contributes to the peculiar inner uncertainty so often met with in women.

Under the pressure of this anxiety the girl now takes refuge in a fictitious male role.

What is the economic gain of this flight? Here I would refer to an experience that all analysts have probably had: They find that the desire to be a

---

1. Since the possibility of such a connection occurred to me, I have learned to construe in this sense—i.e., as representing the dread of vaginal injury—many phenomena that I was previously content to interpret as castration fantasies in the male sense.

man is generally admitted comparatively willingly and that when once it is accepted, it is clung to tenaciously, the reason being the desire to avoid the realization of libidinal wishes and fantasies in connection with the father. Thus the wish to be a man subserves the repression of these feminine wishes or the resistance against their being brought to light. This constantly recurring, typical experience compels us, if we are true to analytical principles, to conclude that the fantasies of being a man were at an earlier period devised for the very purpose of securing the subject against libidinal wishes in connection with the father. The fiction of maleness enabled the girl to escape from the female role now burdened with guilt and anxiety. It is true that this attempt to deviate from her own line to that of the male inevitably brings about a sense of inferiority, for the girl begins to measure herself by pretensions and values that are foreign to her specific biological nature and confronted with which she cannot but feel herself inadequate.

Although this sense of inferiority is very tormenting, analytical experience emphatically shows us that the ego can tolerate it more easily than the sense of guilt associated with the feminine attitude, and hence it is undoubtedly a gain for the ego when the girl flees from the Scylla of the sense of guilt to the Charybdis of the sense of inferiority.

For the sake of completeness I will add a reference to the other gain that, as we know, accrues to women from the process of identification with the father, which takes place at the same time. I know of nothing with reference to the importance of this process itself to add to what I have already said in my earlier work.

We know that this very process of identification with the father is one answer to the question of why the flight from feminine wishes in regard to the father always leads to the adoption of a masculine attitude. Some reflections connected with what has already been said reveal another point of view that throws some light on this question.

We know that whenever the libido encounters a barrier in its development an earlier phase of organization is regressively activated. Now, according to Freud's latest work, penis envy forms the preliminary stage to the true object love for the father. And so this train of thought suggested by Freud helps us to some comprehension of the inner necessity by which the libido flows back precisely to this preliminary stage whenever and insofar as it is driven back by the incest barrier.

I agree in principle with Freud's notion that the girl develops toward object love by way of penis envy, but I think that the nature of this evolution might also be pictured differently.

For when we see how large a part of the strength of primary penis envy is accrued only by retrogression from the Oedipus complex, we must resist the temptation to interpret in the light of penis envy the manifestations of so elementary a principle of nature as that of the mutual attraction of the sexes.

Whereupon, being confronted with the question of how we should conceive psychologically of this primal, biological principle, we would again have to confess ignorance. Indeed, in this respect the conjecture forces itself more and more strongly upon me that perhaps the causal connection may be the exact converse and that it is just the attraction to the opposite sex, operating from a very early period, which draws the libidinal interest of the little girl to the penis. This interest, in accordance with the level of development reached, acts at first in an autoerotic and narcissistic manner, as I have described before. If we view these relations thus, fresh problems would logically present themselves with regard to the origin of the male Oedipus complex, but I wish to postpone these for a later paper. But, if penis envy were the first expression of that mysterious attraction of the sexes, there would be nothing to wonder at when analysis discloses its existence in a yet deeper layer than that in which the desire for a child and the tender attachment to the father occur. The way to this tender attitude toward the father would be prepared not simply by disappointment in regard to the penis but in another way as well. We should then instead have to conceive of the libidinal interest in the penis as a kind of "partial love," to use Abraham's term.[1] Such love, he says, always forms a preliminary stage to true object love. We might explain the process too by an analogy from later life: I refer to the fact that admiring envy is specially calculated to lead to an attitude of love.

With regard to the extraordinary case with which this regression takes place, I must mention the analytical discovery[2] that in the associations of female patients the narcissistic desire to possess the penis and the object libidinal longing for it are often so interwoven that one hesitates as to the sense in which the words "desire for it"[3] are meant.

One word more about the castration fantasies proper, which have given their name to the whole complex because they are the most striking part of it. According to my theory of feminine development, I am obliged to regard these fantasies also as a secondary formation. I picture their origin as follows: When the woman takes refuge in the fictitious male role, her feminine genital anxiety is to some extent translated into male terms—the fear of vaginal injury becomes a fantasy of castration. The girl gains by this conversion, for she exchanges the uncertainty of her expectation of punishment (an uncertainty conditioned by her anatomical formation) for a concrete idea. Moreover, the castration fantasy, too, is under the shadow of the old sense of guilt—and the penis is desired as a proof of guiltlessness.

Now these typical motives for flight into the male role—motives whose origin is the Oedipus complex—are reinforced and supported by the actual disadvantage under which women labor in social life. Of course we must recognize that the desire to be a man, when it springs from this last source, is a peculiarly suitable form of rationalization of those unconscious motives. But we must not forget that this disadvantage is actually a piece of reality and that it is immensely greater than most women are aware of.

Georg Simmel says in this connection that "the greater importance attach-

---

1. Abraham, *Versuch einer Entwicklungsgeschichte der Libido* (1924). (Ed: A short study of the development of the libido. (1979) In *Selected papers of Karl Abraham, M.D.* New York: Brunner/Mazel).
2. Freud referred to this in "The Taboo of Virginity". (Ed: *SE* 11:191–208).
3. German, *Haben-Wollen.*

ing to the male sociologically is probably due to his position of superior strength," and that historically the relation of the sexes may be crudely described as that of master and slave. Here, as always, it is "one of the privileges of the master that he has not constantly to think that he is master, while the position of the slave is such that he can never forget it."

Here we probably have the explanation also of the underestimation of this factor in analytical literature. In actual fact a girl is exposed from birth onward to the suggestion—inevitable, whether conveyed brutally or delicately—of her inferiority, an experience that constantly stimulates her masculinity complex.

There is one further consideration. Owing to the hitherto purely masculine character of our civilization, it has been much harder for women to achieve any sublimation that would really satisfy their nature, for all the ordinary professions have been filled by men. This again must have exercised an influence upon women's feelings of inferiority, for naturally they could not accomplish the same as men in these masculine professions and so it appeared that there was a basis in fact for their inferiority. It seems to me impossible to judge to how great a degree the unconscious motives for the flight from womanhood are reinforced by the actual social subordination of women. One might conceive of the connection as an interaction of psychic and social factors. But I can only indicate these problems here, for they are so grave and so important that they require a separate investigation.

The same factors must have quite a different effect on the man's development. On the one hand they lead to a much stronger repression of his feminine wishes, in that these bear the stigma of inferiority; on the other hand it is far easier for him successfully to sublimate them.

In the foregoing discussion I have put a construction upon certain problems of feminine psychology, which in many points differs from current views. It is possible and even probable that the picture I have drawn is one-sided from the opposite point of view. But my primary intention in this paper was to indicate a possible source of error arising out of the sex of the observer, and by so doing to make a step forward toward the goal that we are all striving to reach: to get beyond the subjectivity of the masculine or the feminine standpoint and to obtain a picture of the mental development of woman that will be more true to the facts of her nature—with its specific qualities and its differences from that of man—than any we have hitherto achieved.

3

EARLY STAGES OF THE OEDIPUS COMPLEX[1]

Melanie Klein

In my analyses of children, especially of children between the ages of three and six, I have come to a number of conclusions of which I shall here present a summary.

I have repeatedly alluded to the conclusion that the Oedipus complex comes into operation earlier than is usually supposed. In my paper, 'The Psychological Principles of Infant Analysis', I discussed this subject in greater detail. The conclusion which I reached there was that the oedipus tendencies are released in consequence of the frustration which the child experiences at weaning, and that they make their appearance at the end of the first and the beginning of the second year of life; they receive reinforcement through the anal frustrations undergone during training in cleanliness. The next determining influence upon the mental processes is that of the anatomical difference between the sexes.

The boy, when he finds himself impelled to abandon the oral and anal positions for the genital, passes on to the aim of *penetration* associated with possession of the penis. Thus he changes not only his libido-position, but its *aim*, and this enables him to retain his original love-object. In the girl, on the other hand, the *receptive* aim is carried over from the oral to the genital position: she changes her libido-position, but retains its aim, which has already led to disappointment in relation to her mother. In this way receptivity for the penis is produced in the girl, who then turns to the father as her love-object.

The very onset of the oedipus wishes, however, already becomes associated with incipient dread of castration and feelings of guilt.

The analysis of adults, as well as of children, has familiarized us with the fact that the pregenital instinctual impulses carry with them a sense of guilt, and it was thought at first that the feelings of guilt were of subsequent growth, displaced back on to these tendencies, though not originally associated with them. Ferenczi assumes that, connected with the urethral and anal impulses, there is a 'kind of physiological forerunner of the super-ego', which he terms 'sphincter-morality'. According to Abraham, anxiety makes its

1. (Ed: Originally published in 1928 in *Int. j. psycho-anal.*, 9.)

appearance on the cannibalistic level, while the sense of guilt arises in the succeeding early anal-sadistic phase.

My findings lead rather further. They show that the sense of guilt associated with pregenital fixation is already the direct effect of the oedipus conflict. And this seems to account satisfactorily for the genesis of such feelings, for we know the sense of guilt to be in fact a result of the introjection (already accomplished or, as I would add, in process of being accomplished) of the oedipus love-objects: that is, a sense of guilt is a product of the formation of the super-ego.

The analysis of little children reveals the structure of the super-ego as built up of identifications dating from very different periods and strata in the mental life. These identifications are surprisingly contradictory in nature, excessive goodness and excessive severity existing side by side. We find in them, too, an explanation of the severity of the super-ego, which comes out specially plainly in these infant analyses. It does not seem clear why a child of, say, four years old should set up in his mind an unreal, fantastic image of parents who devour, cut and bite. But it is clear why in a child of about *one year* old the anxiety caused by the beginning of the oedipus conflict takes the form of a dread of being devoured and destroyed. The child himself desires to destroy the libidinal object by biting, devouring and cutting it, which leads to anxiety, since awakening of the oedipus tendencies is followed by introjection of the object, which then becomes one from which punishment is to be expected. The child then dreads a punishment corresponding to the offence: The super-ego becomes something which bites, devours and cuts.

The connection between the formation of the super-ego and the pregenital phases of development is very important from two points of view. On the one hand, the sense of guilt attaches itself to the oral- and anal-sadistic phases, which as yet predominate; and, on the other, the super-ego comes into being while these phases are in the ascendant, which accounts for its sadistic severity.

These conclusions open up a new perspective. Only by strong repression can the still very feeble ego defend itself against a super-ego so menacing. Since the oedipus tendencies are at first chiefly expressed in the form of oral and anal impulses, the question of which fixations will predominate in the oedipus development will be mainly determined by the degree of the repression which takes place at this early stage.

Another reason why the direct connection between the pregenital phase of development and the sense of guilt is so important is that the oral and anal frustrations, which are the prototypes of all later frustrations in life, at the same time signify *punishment* and give rise to anxiety. This circumstance makes the frustration more acutely felt, and this bitterness contributes largely to the hardship of all subsequent frustrations.

We find that important consequences ensue from the fact that the ego is still so little developed when it is assailed by the onset of the oedipus tendencies and the incipient sexual curiosity associated with them. The infant, still undeveloped intellectually, is exposed to an onrush of problems and questions. One of the most bitter grievances which we come upon in the unconscious is that these many overwhelming questions, which are apparently only partly conscious and even when conscious cannot yet be expressed in words, remain unanswered. Another reproach follows hard upon this, namely, that the child could not understand words and speech. Thus his first questions go back beyond the beginnings of his understanding of speech.

In analysis both these grievances give rise to an extraordinary amount of hate. Singly or in conjunction they are the cause of numerous inhibitions of the epistemophilic impulse: for instance, the incapacity to learn foreign languages, and, further, hatred of those who speak a different tongue. They are also responsible for direct disturbances in speech, etc. The curiosity which shows itself plainly later on, mostly in the fourth or fifth year of life, is not the beginning, but the climax and termination, of this phase of development, which I have also found to be true of the oedipus conflict in general.

The early feeling of *not knowing* has manifold connections. It unites with the feeling of being incapable, impotent, which soon results from the oedipus situation. The child also feels this frustration the more acutely because he *knows nothing* definite about sexual processes. In both sexes the castration complex is accentuated by this feeling of ignorance.

The early connection between the epistemophilic impulse and sadism is very important for the whole mental development. This instinct, activated by the rise of the oedipus tendencies, at first mainly concerns itself with the mother's body, which is assumed to be the scene of all sexual processes and developments. The child is still dominated by the anal-sadistic libido-position which impels him to wish to *appropriate* the contents of the body. He thus begins to be curious about what it contains, what it is like, etc. So the epistemophilic instinct and the desire to take possession come quite early to be most intimately connected with one another and at the same time with the sense of guilt aroused by the incipient oedipus conflict. This significant connection ushers in a phase of development in both sexes which is of vital importance, hitherto not sufficiently recognized. It consists of a very early identification with the mother.

The course run by this 'femininity' phase must be examined separately in boys and in girls, but, before I proceed to this, I shall show its connection with the previous phase, which is common to both sexes.

In the early anal-sadistic stage the child sustains his second severe trauma, which strengthens his tendency to turn away from the mother. She has frustrated his oral desires, and now she also interferes with his anal pleasures. It seems as though at this point the anal deprivations cause the anal tendencies to amalgamate with the sadistic tendencies. The child desires to get possession of the mother's faeces, by penetrating into her body, cutting it to pieces, devouring and destroying it. Under the influence of his genital impulses, the boy is beginning to turn to his mother as a love-object. But his sadistic impulses are fully at work, and the hate originating in earlier frustrations is powerfully opposed to his object-love on the genital level. A still greater obstacle to his love is his dread of castration by the father, which arises with the oedipus impulses. The degree to which he attains the genital position will partly depend on his capacity for tolerating this anxiety. Here the intensity of the oral-sadistic and anal-sadistic fixations is an important factor. It affects the degree of hatred which the boy feels towards the mother; and this, in its turn, hinders him to a greater or lesser extent in attaining a positive relation to her. The sadistic fixations exercise also a decisive influence upon the formation of the super-ego, which is coming into being whilst these phases are in the ascendant. The more cruel the super-ego the more terrifying will be the father as castrator, and the more tenaciously, in the child's flight from his genital impulses, will he cling to the sadistic levels, from which levels his Oedipus tendencies, too, in the first instance, take their colour.

In these early stages all the positions in the oedipus development are cathected in rapid succession. This, however, is not noticeable, because the picture is dominated by the pregenital impulses. Moreover, no rigid line can be drawn between the active heterosexual attitude which finds expression on the anal level and the further stage of identification with the mother.

We have now reached that phase of development of which I spoke before under the name of the 'femininity-phase'. It has its basis on the anal-sadistic level and imparts to that level a new content, for faeces are now equated with the child that is longed for, and the desire to rob the mother now applies to the child as well as to faeces. Here we can discern two aims which merge with one another. The one is directed by the desire for children, the intention being to appropriate them, while the other aim is motivated by jealousy of the future brothers and sisters whose appearance is expected, and by the wish to destroy them in the mother. (A third object of the boy's oral-sadistic tendencies inside the mother is the father's penis.)

As in the castration complex of girls, so in the femininity complex of the male, there is at bottom the frustrated desire for a special organ. The tendencies to steal and destroy are concerned with the organs of conception, pregnancy and parturition, which the boy assumes to exist in the mother, and further with the vagina and the breasts, the fountain of milk, which are coveted as organs of receptivity and bounty from the time when the libidinal position is purely oral.

The boy fears punishment for his destruction of his mother's body, but, besides this, his fear is of a more general nature, and here we have an analogy to the anxiety associated with the castration-wishes of the girl. He fears that his body will be mutilated and dismembered, and this dread also means castration. Here we have a direct contribution to the castration complex. In this early period of development the mother who takes away the child's faeces signifies also a mother who dismembers and castrates him. Not only by means of the anal frustrations which she inflicts does she pave the way for the castration complex: in terms of psychic reality she is also already the *castrator*.

This dread of the mother is so overwhelming because there is combined with it an intense dread of castration by the father. The destructive tendencies whose object is the womb are also directed with their full oral- and anal-sadistic intensity against the father's penis, which is supposed to be located there. It is upon this penis that the dread of castration by the father is focused in this phase. Thus the femininity-phase is characterized by anxiety relating to the womb and the father's penis, and this anxiety subjects the boy to the tyranny of a super-ego which devours, dismembers and castrates and is formed from the image of father and mother alike.

The incipient genital positions are thus from the beginning criss-crossed by and intermingled with the manifold pregenital tendencies. The greater the preponderance of sadistic fixations, the more does the boy's identification with his mother correspond to an attitude of rivalry towards the woman, with its blending of envy and hatred; for, on account of his wish for a child, he feels himself at a disadvantage and inferior to the mother.

Let us now consider why the femininity complex of men seems so much more obscure than the castration complex in women, with which it is equally important.

The amalgamation of the desire for a child with the epistemophilic impulse enables a boy to effect a displacement on to the intellectual plane; his sense of being at a disadvantage is then concealed and over-compensated by the superiority he deduces from his possession of a penis, which is also acknowledged by girls. This exaggeration of the masculine position results in excessive protestations of masculinity. In her paper ('Die Wurzel des Wissbegierde'),[1] Mary Chadwick, too, has traced the man's narcissistic over-estimation of the penis, and his attitude of intellectual rivalry towards women, to the frustration of his wish for a child and to the displacement of this desire on to the intellectual plane.

A tendency in boys to express excessive aggression, which very frequently occurs, has its source in the femininity complex. It goes with an attitude of contempt and 'knowing better,' and is highly asocial and sadistic; it is partly determined by an attempt to mask the anxiety and ignorance which lie behind it. In part it coincides with the boy's protest (originating in his fear of castration) against the feminine *rôle*, but it is rooted also in his dread of his mother, whom he intended to rob of the father's penis, her children and her female sexual organs. This excessive aggression unites with the pleasure in attack which proceeds from the direct, genital oedipus situation, but it represents that part of the situation which is by far the more asocial factor in character-formation. This is why a man's rivalry with women will be far more asocial than his rivalry with his fellow-men, which is largely prompted through the genital position. Of course the quantity of sadistic fixations will also determine the relationship of a man to other men when they are rivals. If, on the contrary, the identification with the mother is based on a more securely established genital position, on the one hand his relation to women will be positive in character, and on the other the desire for a child and the feminine component, which play so essential a part in men's work, will find more favourable opportunities for sublimation.

1. *I.Z.P.A.*, vol. xi, 1925.

In both sexes one of the principal roots of inhibitions in work is the anxiety and sense of guilt associated with the femininity-phase. Experience has taught me, however, that a thorough analysis of this phase is, for other reasons as well, important from a therapeutic point of view, and should be of help in some obsessional cases which seem to have reached a point where nothing more could be resolved.

In the boy's development the femininity-phase is succeeded by a prolonged struggle between the pregenital and the genital positions of the libido. When at its height, in the third to the fifth year of life, this struggle is plainly recognizable as the oedipus conflict. The anxiety associated with the femininity-phase drives the boy back to identification with the father; but this stimulus in itself does not provide a firm foundation for the genital position, since it leads mainly to repression and over-compensation of the anal-sadistic instincts, and not to overcoming them. The dread of castration by the father strengthens the fixation to the anal-sadistic levels. The degree of constitutional genitality also plays an important part as regards a favourable issue, i.e. the attainment of the genital level. Often the outcome of the struggle remains undecided, and this gives rise to neurotic troubles and disturbances of potency.[1] Thus the attainment of complete potency and reaching the genital position will in part depend upon the favourable issue of the femininity-phase.

I will now turn to the development of girls. As a result of the process of weaning, the girl-child has turned from the mother, being impelled more strongly to do so by the anal deprivations she has undergone. Genital trends now begin to influence her mental development.

I entirely agree with Helene Deutsch,[2] who holds that the genital development of the woman finds its completion in the successful displacement of oral libido on to the genital. Only, my results lead me to believe that this displacement begins with the first stirrings of the genital impulses and that the oral, receptive aim of the genitals exercises a determining influence in the *girl's turning to the father.* Also I am led to conclude that not only an unconscious awareness of the vagina, but also sensations in that organ and the rest of the genital apparatus, are aroused as soon as the oedipus impulses make their appearance. In girls, however, onanism does not afford anything like so adequate an outlet for these quantities of excitation as it does in boys. Hence the accumulated lack of gratification provides yet another reason for more complications and disturbances of female sexual development. The difficulty of obtaining full gratification by masturbation may be another cause, besides those indicated by Freud, for the girl's repudiation of onanism, and this may partly explain why, during her struggle to give it up, manual masturbation is generally replaced by pressing the legs together.

Besides the receptive quality of the genital organ, which is brought into play by the intense desire for a new source of gratification, envy and hatred of the mother who possesses the father's penis seem, at the period when these

1. Cf. here W. Reich: 'Die Funktion des Orgasmus', reprinted in *The discovery of the orgone* (New York, 1942).
2. H. Deutsch: *Psychoanalyse der weiblichen sexualfunktion.* (Ed: (1925) The psychology of women's sexual functions. Vienna:Verlag).

first oedipus impulses are stirring, to be a further motive for the little girl's turning to the father. His caresses have now the effect of a seduction and are felt as 'the attraction of the opposite sex'.[1]

In the girl identification with the mother results directly from the Oedipus impulses: the whole struggle caused in the boy by his castration anxiety is absent in her. In girls as well as boys this identification coincides with the anal-sadistic tendencies to rob and destroy the mother. If identification with the mother takes place predominantly at a stage when oral- and anal-sadistic tendencies are very strong, dread of a primitive maternal superego will lead to the repression and fixation of this phase and interfere with further genital development. Dread of the mother, too, impels the little girl to give up identification with her, and identification with the father begins.

The little girl's epistemophilic impulse is first roused by the Oedipus complex; the result is that she discovers her lack of a penis. She feels this lack to be a fresh cause of hatred of the mother, but at the same time her sense of guilt makes her regard it as a punishment. This embitters her frustration in this direction, and, in its turn, exercises a profound influence on the whole castration complex.

This early grievance about the lack of a penis is greatly magnified later on, when the phallic phase and the castration complex are fully active. Freud has stated that the discovery of the lack of a penis causes the turning from the mother to the father. My findings show, however, that this discovery operates only as a reinforcement in this direction: it is made at a very early stage in the oedipus conflict, and penis-envy succeeds the wish for a child, which again replaces penis-envy in later development. I regard the deprivation of the breast as the most fundamental cause of the turning to the father.

Identification with the father is less charged with anxiety than that with the mother; moreover, the sense of guilt towards her impels to over-compensation through a fresh love-relation with her. Against this new love-relation with her there operates the castration complex which makes a masculine attitude difficult, and also the hatred of her which sprang from the earlier positions. Hate and rivalry of the mother, however, again lead to abandoning the identification with the father and turning to him as the object to love and be loved by.

The girl's relation to her mother causes her relation to her father to take both a positive and a negative direction. The frustration undergone at his hands has as its very deepest basis the disappointment already suffered in relation to the mother; a powerful motive in the desire to possess him springs from the hatred and envy against the mother. If the sadistic fixations remain predominant, this hatred and its over-compensation will also materially affect the woman's relation to men. On the other hand, if there is a more positive relation to the mother, built up on the genital position, not only will the woman be freer from a sense of guilt in her relation to her children, but her love for her husband will be strongly reinforced, since for the woman he always stands at one and the same time for the mother who gives what is

1. We regularly come across the unconscious reproach that the mother has seduced the child whilst tending it. This reproach goes back to the period when genital desires come to the fore and the Oedipus tendencies are awaking.

desired and for the beloved child. On this very significant foundation is built up that part of the relation which is connected exclusively with the father. At first it is focused on the act of the penis in coitus. This act, which also promises gratification of the desires that are now displaced on to the genital, seems to the little girl a most consummate performance.

Her admiration is, indeed, shaken by the oedipus frustration, but unless it is converted into hate, it constitutes one of the fundamental features of the woman's relation to the man. Later, when full satisfaction of the love-impulses is obtained, there is joined with this admiration the great gratitude ensuing from the long-pent-up deprivation. This gratitude finds expression in the greater feminine capacity for complete and lasting surrender to one love-object, especially to the 'first love'.

One way in which the little girl's development is greatly handicapped is the following. Whilst the boy does in reality *possess* the penis, in respect of which he enters into rivalry with the father, the little girl has only the *unsatisfied* desire for motherhood, and of this, too, she has but a dim and uncertain, though a very intense, awareness.

It is not merely this uncertainty which disturbs her hope of future motherhood. It is weakened far more by anxiety and sense of guilt, and these may seriously and permanently damage the maternal capacity of a woman. Because of the destructive tendencies once directed by her against the mother's body (or certain organs in it) and against the children in the womb, the girl anticipates retribution in the form of destruction of her own capacity for motherhood or of the organs connected with this function and of her own children. Here we have also one root of the constant concern of women (often so excessive) for their personal beauty, for they dread that this too will be destroyed by the mother. At the bottom of the impulse to deck and beautify themselves there is always the motive of *restoring* damaged comeliness, and this has its origin in anxiety and sense of guilt.[1]

It is probable that this deep dread of the destruction of internal organs may be the psychic cause of the greater susceptibility of women, as compared with men, to conversion-hysteria and organic diseases.

It is this anxiety and sense of guilt which is the chief cause of the repression of feelings of pride and joy in the feminine *rôle*, which are originally very strong. This repression results in depreciation of the capacity for motherhood, at the outset so highly prized. Thus the girl lacks the powerful support which the boy derives from his possession of the penis, and which she herself might find in the anticipation of motherhood.

The girl's very intense anxiety about her womanhood can be shown to be analogous to the boy's dread of castration, for it certainly contributes to the checking of her oedipus impulses. The course run by the boy's castration anxiety concerning the penis which *visibly* exists is, however, different; it might be termed more *acute* than the more chronic anxiety of the girl concerning her internal organs, with which she is necessarily less familiar. Moreover, it is bound to make a difference that the boy's anxiety is deter-

1. Cf. Hárnik's paper at the Innsbruck Psycho-Analytical Congress: 'Die ökonomischen Beziehungen zwischen dem Schuldgefühl und dem weiblichen Narzissmus.'

mined by the paternal and the girl's by the maternal super-ego.

Freud has said that the girl's super-ego develops on different lines from that of the boy. We constantly find confirmation of the fact that jealousy plays a greater part in women's lives than in men's, because it is reinforced by deflected envy of the male on account of the penis. On the other hand, however, women especially possess a great capacity, which is not based merely on an over-compensation, for disregarding their own wishes and devoting themselves with self-sacrifice to ethical and social tasks. We cannot account for this capacity by the blending of masculine and feminine traits which, because of the human being's bisexual disposition, does in individual cases influence the formation of character, for this capacity is so plainly maternal in nature. I think that in order to explain how women can run so wide a gamut from the most petty jealousy to the most self-forgetful loving-kindness, we have to take into consideration the peculiar conditions of the formation of the feminine super-ego. From the early identification with the mother in which the anal-sadistic level so largely preponderates, the little girl derives jealousy and hatred and forms a cruel super-ego after the maternal imago. The super-ego which develops at this stage from a father-identification can also be menacing and cause anxiety, but it seems never to reach the same proportions as that derived from the mother-identification. But the more the identification with the mother becomes stabilized on the genital basis, the more will it be characterized by the devoted kindness of a bountiful mother-ideal. Thus this positive affective attitude depends on the extent to which the maternal mother-ideal bears the characteristics of the pregenital or of the genital stage. But when it comes to the active conversion of the emotional attitude into social or other activities, it would seem that it is the paternal ego-ideal which is at work. The deep admiration felt by the little girl for the father's genital activity leads to the formation of a paternal super-ego which sets before her active aims to which she can never fully attain. If, owing to certain factors in her development, the incentive to accomplish these aims is strong enough, their very impossibility of attainment may lend an impetus to her efforts which, combined with the capacity for self-sacrifice which she derives from the maternal super-ego, gives a woman, in individual instances, the capacity for very exceptional achievements on the intuitive plane and in specific fields.

The boy, too, derives from the feminine phase a maternal super-ego which causes him, like the girl, to make both cruelly primitive and kindly identifications. But he passes through this phase to resume (it is true, in varying degrees) identification with the father. However much the maternal side makes itself felt in the formation of the super-ego, it is yet the *paternal* super-ego which from the beginning is the decisive influence for the man. He too sets before himself a figure of an exalted character upon which to model himself, but, because the boy is 'made in the image of' his ideal, it is not unattainable. This circumstance contributes to the more sustained and objective creative work of the male.

The dread of injury to her womanhood exercises a profound influence on the castration complex of the little girl, for it causes her to over-estimate the penis which she herself lacks; this exaggeration is then much more obvious than is the underlying anxiety about her own womanhood. I would remind you here of the work of Karen Horney, who was the first to examine the sources of the castration complex in women in so far as those sources lie in the oedipus situation.

In this connection I must speak of the importance for sexual development of certain early experiences in childhood. In the paper which I read at the Salzburg Congress in 1924, I mentioned that when observations of coitus take place at a later stage of development they assume the character of traumata, but that if such experiences occur at an early age they become fixated and form part of the sexual development. I must now add that a fixation of this sort may hold in its grip not only that particular stage of development, but also the super-ego which is then in process of formation, and may thus injure its further development. For the more completely the super-ego reaches its zenith in the genital stage, the less prominent will be the sadistic identifications in its structure and the more likely will be the securing of mental health and the development of a personality on an ethically high level.

There is another kind of experience in early childhood which strikes me as typical and exceedingly important. These experiences often follow closely in time upon the observations of coitus and are induced or fostered by the excitations set up thereby. I refer to the sexual relations of little children with one another, between brothers and sisters or playmates, which consist in the most varied acts: looking, touching, performing excretion in common, fellatio, cunnilingus and often direct attempts at coitus. They are deeply repressed and have a cathexis of profound feelings of guilt. These feelings are mainly due to the fact that this love-object, chosen under the pressure of the excitation due to the oedipus conflict, is felt by the child to be a substitute for the father or mother or both. Thus these relations, which seem so insignificant and which apparently no child under the stimulus of the oedipus development escapes, take on the character of an oedipus relation actually realized, and exercise a determining influence upon the formation of the Oedipus complex, the subject's detachment from that complex and upon his later sexual relations. Moreover, an experience of this sort forms an important fixation-point in the development of the super-ego. In consequence of the need for punishment and the repetition-compulsion, these experiences often cause the child to subject himself to sexual traumata. In this connection I would refer you to Abraham,[1] who showed that experiencing sexual traumata is one part of the sexual development of children. The analytic investigation of these experiences, during the analysis of adults as well as of children, to a great extent clears up the oedipus situation in its connection with early fixations, and is therefore important from the therapeutic point of view.

To sum up my conclusions: I wish first of all to point out that they do not, in my opinion, contradict the statements of Professor Freud. I think that the

1. Karl Abraham, *Selected papers*, International Psycho-Analytical Library, No. 13. (Ed: (1979) *Selected papers of Karl Abraham, M.D.*. New York: Brunner/Mazel).

essential point in the additional considerations which I have advanced is that I date these processes earlier and that the different phases (especially in the initial stages) merge more freely in one another than was hitherto supposed.

The early stages of the oedipus conflict are so largely dominated by pregenital phases of development that the genital phase, when it begins to be active, is at first heavily shrouded and only later, between the third and fifth years of life, becomes clearly recognizable. At this age the Oedipus complex and the formation of the super-ego reach their climax. But the fact that the oedipus tendencies begin so much earlier than we supposed, the pressure of the sense of guilt which therefore falls upon the pregenital levels, the determining influence thus exercised so early upon the oedipus development on the one hand and that of the super-ego on the other, and accordingly upon character-formation, sexuality and all the rest of the subject's development— all these things seem to me of great and hitherto unrecognized importance. I found out the therapeutic value of this knowledge in the analyses of children, but it is not confined to these. I have been able to test the resulting conclusions in the analysis of adults and have found not only that their theoretical correctness was confirmed but that their therapeutic importance was established.

Part Two

PENIS ENVY: FOUNDATION OR DELUSION?

INTRODUCTION

The vitality of any doctrine depends on the possibility of rethinking certain aspects without disrupting the whole structure.

—Chasseguet-Smirgel

By the end of the 1930s, the centrifugal interest in women's psycho-sexuality in general and penis envy in particular within the psychoanalytic community seemed to wind down, but its quiescence, in retrospect, constituted a period of latency rather than a true loss of momentum. From the early '70s onward, lines of thought arising from a variety of perspectives have emerged and intertwined, creating a spreading metropolis around the old city comprised by the works of Freud, Horney, Klein, Jones, and their contemporaries. To be sure, many theorists suspected, during the interim, that what had been a thriving center was now a dying town, closing in on itself as its infrastructure was dismantled piece by piece. Yet fears that this landscape of controversy had yielded only "deadlock" (Chasseguet-Smirgel, 1964/1970, p. 2) and even calls to raze what was left of it in light of a growing sense that it had been built upon the flawed foundation of Freud's "gross male-supremacist bias" (Millett, 1969, p. 258) seem to have served only to promulgate its growth; Chasseguet-Smirgel used her concern as the impetus to reexamine the debate by producing an edited volume (1964/1970), from which two of the essays included in this section are drawn, which did much to revitalize European interest in the concept of women's sexuality, and Millett's challenge and others like it paved the way for an equally influential book by Mitchell (1974), which argued that the psychoanalytic theory of gender must be read within its proper context, so that Freud's analysis of patriarchy could clearly be seen. Further, *Psychoanalyse et Politique*, a women's group in France, through its complex legacy and effects, highlighted the work of Lacan as providing the grounds for a revitalization, in the eyes of some, of psychoanalytic feminism itself and, in the eyes of others, of a tradition of psychoanalytic "phallocentrism" (Jones's word). The reader is left, in this context, to grapple not only with these more recent comments on Freud's ideas about penis envy, but his with his injunction that "the use of analysis as a weapon of controversy (a 'knife that cuts both ways') can clearly lead to no decision" (*SE* 11: 230 and n.).

Some of the contemporary currents of European psychoanalytic gender studies have been incorporated, slowly, into an equally burgeoning American tradition of inquiry. In general, the theorists writing during the period following the 1950s argue, simultaneously following and modifying the ideas of Horney, Mahler, and American Ego Psychology, for the existence of a pre-oedipally derived female gender identity that provides the background into which later discoveries of sexual difference are, or are not, integrated. If this pre-oedipal gender identity is viewed as constructed at all rather than as given, it is seen as made up of an amalgam of social and constitutional forces, as a bricollage of influences rather than a residue of conflicts. Hence Stoller (1976) proposes the existence of a "core gender identity," a "primary femininity" that grounds all later development, and he and other theorists have devoted themselves to elucidating precisely what this ground consists of. Building on the attention paid to the girl's early history by Greenacre (1958) and Jacobson (1936, 1964), Kestenberg (1956, 1982, 1990) has postulated the existence of an "early maternal" or "inner genital" phase that precedes the phallic phase in girls, while Tyson (1982, 1990) has worked to discriminate the strands that comprise core gender identity.

While many of these efforts in Europe and America have offered visions of gender different from Freud's, each one has nevertheless drawn, to a greater or lesser extent, from his conceptual framework, and thus it is not surprising that virtually all of them have included specific attention, whether to reject, defend, or reconfigure it, to the notion of penis envy. Indeed, despite the plurality of viewpoints on the theory of women's development, discussions of penis envy still constitute the most prevalent inquiries into the topic of gender and envy as a whole, and in their content the outlines of their original foundations in the controversies that preceded them can still be seen. While Lacan and his followers generally maintain phallic monism and castration as central to an understanding of the sexual psychologies of both men and women—emphasizing, in their readings of Freud, that penis envy refers not to a lack of the penis itself, but of its symbolic representation (the phallus)—other primarily European thinkers follow Klein in viewing penis envy as a construction that emerges out of the earlier mother-child relationship and functions defensively in the service of expressing and resolving conflicts from that era. Meanwhile, theorists who share with Horney, Jones, and in some respects Klein an interest in elucidating a pre-oedipal, essential femininity have themselves created a broad spectrum of accounts of this essence; Irigaray's search occurs within the context of an appreciation of its repression not just in Freud's work, but in the whole dominant strain of Western philosophy, whereas American theorists tend to see this essence either as the foundation upon which later attempts to grapple with anatomical difference are erected, or as the sole necessary basis for a sense of one's gender, which can but need not be augmented by penis envy as symptom, defensive tool, or transitional phenomenon.

The five essays included in this section represent merely a small sample of the points of view that have been expressed in the resurgence of interest in the concept of penis envy. This section begins with the essay "Gender and Envy in Freud's Discourse," in which John A. Friedman develops an argument for the appreciation of Freud's account of penis envy from a careful reading of Freud's texts on psychosexuality as they are located within the context of his more general psychological theory. He contrasts this reading with accounts of the alternative theories of Klein and Winnicott in an effort to clarify what is at stake in the decision to adopt (or not) a view of sexuality as constructed and achieved, rather than as simply assumed. Friedman's analysis, grounded as it is within his previously developed account "The Idea of Narcissism in Freud's Psychoanalysis" (1988), which argued for the role of phallic primacy in establishing a relationship between an individual's psychology and the world, proceeds from the idea that the capacity to develop a psychologically mediated relationship to that which is anatomically given defines us as truly human. Against claims that Freud's concept of *penisneid* leads inevitably to a denigration of women, Friedman highlights its capacity, rather, to liberate women from prejudicial assumptions about their nature that throughout history have provided the tools for their oppression.

The writing of Luce Irigaray stands in direct opposition to Friedman's claims about the constructed, symbolically mediated nature of sexuality; in fact, she argues, it is this very emphasis upon gender as constructed that has served to obscure and indeed to enslave women within the discourse of the Western philosophical tradition, and thus in social life. Her deconstructive critique of psychoanalysis as one moment in that tradition (on the basis of which she was expelled from Lacan's school) highlights its blindness to the real otherness of woman, due to its privileging of a libidinal economy of masculine domination that subserves woman's otherness to its own projective needs. The concepts of penis envy and phallic primacy, she continues, are the tools, par excellence, of his project of domination. When the phallus, representing the law, comes between the originary mother-daughter bond, the girl is sent into exile, barred from access to her own beginnings and story, and to her own source of pleasure, in deference to the man's. Horney, Klein, and Jones, she suggests, were aware that penis envy marked the end of the girl's story rather than the beginning, but Irigaray takes this claim further, allowing her ideas to come forward in a style that is deliberately "hysterical," that speaks from outside the rules of grammar, logic, and representation, as she attempts to give voice to a bodily sense that the phallus, as it is wielded by Freud, otherwise throws into shadow.

Torok and Chasseguet-Smirgel also take, as their starting point, the assumption of a primal relationship with the mother, but they place a very different valance on the girl's earliest connection, and on her (and the boy's) relationship to the phallus in that context. Penis envy, the instrument that their compatriot Irigaray sees as the tool of the repression of woman's nature, is seen by these authors as serving important defensive purposes, albeit also exacting a high price in self-esteem and later relational comfort. As noted, these essays were originally published in a book referred to above, *Female Sexuality*, or *Recherchés psychoanalytiques nouvelles sur la sexualite feminine*, edited by Chasseguet-Smirgel, that did much to revive interest in the topic of gender within psychoanalytic circles; in its introduction, their commentator, Frederick Wyatt, presents the writers as guided by, or making use of, "the Klein-Jones frame of reference" (p. vii); although while both Torok and Chasseguet-Smirgel have clearly absorbed Klein's ideas, both also depart from them in significant ways. Further, while the two authors begin with common assumptions—regarding the girl's need to extricate herself from the original position with the mother, the defensive uses of penis envy in doing so, and an assumed primal femininity characterized by distinctively feminine desires—they differ significantly in their views of the primal mother and of the challenges inherent in separating from her, and correspondingly of the specific defensive uses to which penis envy is put. While for Torok, penis envy is the cover for desires which the girl feels would harm or destroy her relationship with a controlling, and yet castrated and empty, primal mother, Chasseguet-Smirgel focuses on the mother's omnipotent aspects and the wish for the penis as a tool to allow the girl to escape from such a feared and powerful figure.

Although Benjamin takes, as one of her many starting points, Chasseguet-Smirgel's observations on the girl's need to escape the omnipotent mother through the use of an identification with the father, she makes this latter form of identification itself the primary focus of her paper, thus shifting the emphasis from the girl's relationship with her mother to look more closely at the father-daughter bond. In doing so, she is inspired by the writings of Horney, who, she argues, has been underappreciated in the psychoanalytic literature; like Horney, she views penis envy as a marker of the girl's disappointment in the relationship with her father, due to his unavailability. While both theorists' analyses draw heavily upon, and give new prominence to, the importance of identification in the creation of the self, however, Benjamin offers a new and transformative perspective on the centrality of identification with the father not as an indicator of pathology or as a project doomed to failure, but as a core developmental need. In tracing the effects of a failure of the father's recognition of his daughter as like him—in some ways as his son—Benjamin builds upon her previous suggestion in *The Bonds of Love* (1988) that such a failure in recognition can result in the development of masochism, particularly in women. In the essay "Father and Daughter" included in this volume, she attempts to take her original argument further by highlighting more explicitly the centrality of identificatory love as both "an important precursor and ongoing constituent" of the Oedipal configuration. Thus, in Benjamin's view, an understanding of penis envy marks the entrance into a broader and deeper psychoanalytic account of love per se.

Benjamin's emphasis on the importance of a love between father and daughter based on identification demonstrates the potential function of the concept of penis envy to testify not simply to the distinction between the sexes, but to the limits of that distinction as well. In her appreciation of the importance of both identificatory and object love in the girl's relationships with both her mother and her father, Benjamin revitalizes the tension, so clearly highlighted by Freud, between the terms *feminine/masculine* on the one hand and *female/male* on the other. Whereas for Deutsch (1925), penis envy is the fulcrum for a true psychological distinction between the sexes, Benjamin suggests the ways in which it rather problematizes this distinction, inasmuch as it marks the failure of the environment to accommodate the girl's femininity as bisexually grounded. Further, while Chasseguet-Smirgel suggests that madness stems from the inability to maintain a clear distinction between the sexes, that is, between the psychologies and gender roles of women and men (Baruch & Serrano, 1988, p. 113), Benjamin's reading of penis envy suggests that the rigid reification of gender identity through the failure of potential avenues of identification is a likely source of future psychic pain, and accordingly advocates for the more fluid sharing of gender-associated tasks (Baruch & Serrano, 1988, p. 330). Thus, Benjamin's discussion of penis envy opens onto other current efforts to question the rigid perception of gender as a binary opposition, which theories about men or women are always in danger of reinforcing (Benjamin, 1996; Butler, 1990; Goldner, 1991).

Other than Friedman, each of the authors included in this section in some way takes issue with, or recasts, Freud's original account of penis envy, and all, including Friedman, thus commit themselves, implicitly or explicitly, to a position regarding the assertion by Chasseguet-Smirgel that serves as the epigraph to this section. Friedman and Irigaray are perhaps strange partners in their shared objection to Chasseguet-Smirgel's claim, for both appear to recognize that the concept of penis envy, or at least Freud's account of it, cannot be cleanly excised from the body of his other writing, leaving the rest perhaps revisioned, but intact. In fact, each might suggest that the very vitality of Freud's theory is reflected in its richly integrated consistency, such that his theory of penis envy is but one microcosm and essential component, simultaneously, of the whole. No doubt the two authors would strongly disagree, however, on the implication of that view, Friedman highlighting Freud's achievement in creating an integrated theory of psychosexuality, and Irigaray stressing that the common assumptions that underlie the general and specific theories suggest that the entire Freudian corpus must be removed from women's sight in order for their own sensibilities to emerge. Meanwhile, the reader can assess whether, or to what extent, the modifications offered by the work of the three remaining authors do indeed "disrupt the whole," and if so, how the landscape is transformed in light of this disruption.

REFERENCES

Baruch, E. H. & Serrano, L. J. (1988). *Women analyze women.* New York: New York University Press.

Benjamin, J. (1988). *The bonds of love.* New York: Pantheon.

———— (1996). In defense of gender ambiguity. *Gender & psychoanalysis, 1*(1), 27–43.

Butler, J. (1990). *Gender trouble.* New York: Routledge.

Chasseguet-Smirgel, J. (1964/1970). *Female sexuality.* Ann Arbor: University of Michigan Press.

Deutsch, H. (1925). The psychology of women in relation to the function of reproduction. *International journal of psycho-analysis, 6,* 405–418.

Freud, S. (1931). Female sexuality. *SE* 21, (pp. 221–246).

Friedman, J. (1988). The idea of narcissism in Freud's psychoanalysis. *International review of psychoanalysis 15,* 499–514.

Goldner, V. (1991). Toward a critical relational theory of gender. *Psychoanalytic dialogues 1,* 249–272.

Greenacre, P. (1952). Pregenital patterning. *International journal of psychoanalysis 33,* 410–415.

———— (1953/1971). Penis awe and its relation to penis envy. In *Emotional growth, Vol. 1,* (p. 31–49) New York: International Universities Press.

———— (1958). Early physical determinants in the development of the sense of identity, In *Emotional growth* (p. 113–27). New York: International University Press.

Jacobson, E. (1936/1968). On the development of a girl's wish for a child. *Psychoanalytic quarterly 37,* 523–538.

———— (1964). *The self and the object world.* New York: International Universities Press.

Kestenberg, J. (1956). Vicissitudes of female sexuality. *Journal of the American psychoanalytic association 4,* 453–476.

———— (1982). The inner-genital phase: Prephallic and preoedipal. In D. Mendell (Ed.), *Early female development* (p. 71–126). New York: S.P. Medical and Scientific Books.

———— (1990). Two-and-a-half to four years: From disequilibrium to integration. In S. Greenspan and G. Pollock (Eds.), *The Course of life, Vol. 3* (p. 25–51). New York: International Universities Press.

Millett, K. (1969). *Sexual politics.* New York: Ballantine.

Mitchell, J. (1974). *Psychoanalysis and feminism.* New York: Random House.

Stoller, R. (1976). Primary femininity. *Journal of the American psychoanalytic association 24 (Suppl.),* 59–78.

Tyson, P. (1982). A developmental line of gender identity, gender role, and choice of love object. *Journal of the American psychoanalytic association 30,* 61–86.

Tyson, P. & Tyson, R. (1990). Gender development: Girls. In *Psychoanalytic theories of development: An integration* (p. 258–276). New Haven, CT: Yale University Press.

4

GENDER AND ENVY IN FREUD'S DISCOURSE

John A. Friedman

Coming to terms with notions of gender and envy as they appear in Freud's writings is highly problematic at best, and this for a number of reasons. First, our entry into Freud's thought is obstructed by the layers of understanding and misunderstanding that have encased it. Attempts to extricate ourselves from these "readings" are quite complicated and difficult (see Friedman, 1988, 1992a, 1992b, 1998; Friedman & Alexander, 1983).

Yet there is nothing accidental or inessential about such renderings. Freud's discourse is originary; it is foundational thinking and constitutes, in a sense, a world of discourse. Therefore, it demands and commands a response. It places a burden on us as it renders our actions and motives in its terms; it produces its own resistance in its character as such.

Can we think of another discourse in the field of psychoanalysis that exacts such a toll on us *as psychoanalysts, as practicing psychoanalysis*? Does Jung's genius produce such an effect? Do the extraordinary insights and brilliant formulations of Klein make these demands upon us? And this is not even to mention the impressive array of more modern contributors to the field. Are we compelled to respond to their most recent essays? Is the significance of our conduct forced to show itself, even against our interests and will, in these modern works?

Toward the end of his brilliant career as a psychoanalyst, Winnicott too defined himself in and through his correlation with Freud. In keeping with this connection, Winnicott made the following remarks about his own thinking and practice:

> At the beginning I do know that—like everybody, I suppose, in this room—as soon as I found Freud and the method that he gave us for investigating and for treatment, I was in line with it. This was just like when I was at school and was reading Darwin and suddenly I knew that Darwin was my cup of tea. I felt this tremendously, and I suppose that if there's anything I do that *isn't* Freudian, this is what I want to know. I don't mind if it isn't, but I just feel that Freud gave us this method which we can use, and it doesn't matter what it leads us to. The point is, it *does* lead us to things; it's an objective way of looking at things and it's for people who can go to something without preconceived notions, which, in a sense, is science. (1967/1989, p. 574)

Even after Winnicott has made his own significant contributions to psychoanalysis, he still feels entirely in the grip of Freud. I present this as merely one example of a response to Freud.

Let me add that I am here referring only to the situation produced by the foundational and originary character of Freud's work, its constitutive nature. I do not wish to take for granted either the advances of Freud's associates and our contemporaries, or the manner in which they often retreat from psychological positions that Freud, with so much effort, achieved. So, in addition to the various sociocultural/historical pressures involved in any discussion of gender, we are forced to reckon with these considerations when we respond to Freud's work.

Given these various and pervasive difficulties, it is of the greatest importance that we gain an initial foothold or orientation as we confront/respond to Freud's discourse on gender and envy. In this effort, I will begin with a few general and provisional comments about how Freud understood gender in the context of infantile sexuality.

When discussing the great sexologist of his day, Havelock Ellis, Freud is reported to have said: "He knows about sex, but nothing about sexuality." Any effort to understand human sexuality must, for Freud, take into account its origins as "infantile sexuality." Infantile sexuality is unique to humans and operates within the register of "drive" (*Trieb*) as opposed to "instinct" (*Instinkt*). It is this rootedness in drive that lies at the heart of the constitution of the psyche with its mysterious folds and contours.

Freud never loses sight of the fact that the psychically based and historically grounded world of humans is merely one more development out of a more fundamental and archaic environment from which all life springs, so that he takes the *bios* and *logos* of biology quite seriously. At the same time, Freud does not confuse sex/sexual reproduction with sexuality/desire (sexual libido). For humans, sexuality begins as infantile, as unorganized (*Partialtrieb*; see Freud, 1905). It *becomes* organized in a distinctly human "biphasic" manner, that is to say, sexual life develops or comes into an organization in childhood and then again is (re)organized in adolescence.

For Freud, sex and sexuality in humans are *not* givens and are not to be taken for granted. The development of what Freud (1905) calls "genital organization" is an *achievement*. For human beings, creation and procreation are always problematic and present themselves as a response to some psychically constituted difficulty. As Freud (1914) quotes Heine as saying: "We create in order to not fall ill." And even in the realm of reproduction and procreation, conception, birth, and child rearing have never been simple or straightforward for humans, at least not in the past of which we have historical record. (Even the 25,000-year-old cave paintings have representations of the fertile woman and the sexually excited man; no Adam and Eve innocents are to be found here.)

In Freud's thought, the psychical basis for any and all of these achievements is in infantile sexuality. Freud's claim has always been that the roots of the highest achievements are found in the "lowest," the most primitive–

that is, the instinctual. Like all other animals, human beings have always and already been given over to their basic instinctual (the *bios* of "biology") condition. With humankind, we add two features not found in any other species of animal. First is the fact that we are "born too soon" or prematurely. If delivery is delayed in normal fetal development, the infant's head would become too large to pass through the narrow birth canal. So the human infant is born profoundly unorganized and in need of extended and involved care by those who raise it. Winnicott (1963/1965) has called this dependency "radical" or "double" in that the infant is wholly dependent on the parent figure and entirely unaware of this dependent relationship as such.

This "radical dependency" has an extraordinary consequence not found in other animals. For the human infant, the world is, from the start, in the other—in the eyes, gaze, facial expressions, skin-to-skin contact, ministrations, vocalizations of this other. For most other mammals, the infant is born more organized, not as dependent on the parent, capable almost immediately of some form of imitative behavior. So for these newborns, their world will be essentially the same as that of their parents. They will track their parents' direction into the world, try to manipulate what their parents manipulate, and so on. By contrast, the world of the human infant is an other with a definite and consuming interest in the child (for better or for worse). So the infant's world is actually and originally constituted, at least in part, by the psyche and desire of the other.

Being born so helpless and unorganized (Freud's idea of a "polymorphous" libidinal situation), the human infant nonetheless is driven in its pursuits of its gratifications (pleasures) and elimination of suffering (unpleasure). Here we find the various zonal gratifications of infant life (from oral through phallic). Yet in order for these instinctual (*trieblich*) pursuits to find their object, there is a psychical factor preliminary to this. Freud (1921, 1923a) calls this the infant's "primary identification" (*primare Identifizierung*). That this psychic phenomenon has been overlooked or misrepresented has led to some extraordinary misunderstandings.

Freud's essential comments on primary identification appear in his 1923 work *The Ego and the Id*, and are presented in the context of his discussion of the relations between "ego and superego/ego ideal." I would like to quote this passage at length.

> The effects of the first identifications made in earliest childhood will be general and lasting. This leads us back to the origin of the ego ideal; for behind it *there lies hidden an individual's first and most important identification, his identification with the father in his own personal prehistory. This is apparently not in the first instance the consequence or outcome of an object-cathexis; it is a direct and immediate identification and takes place earlier than any object-cathexis.* (p. 31, emphasis added)

Regarding this "father-identification," Freud adds the following footnote:

> Perhaps it would be safer to say [identifies] "with the parents"; for before a
> child has arrived at definite knowledge of the *difference* between the sexes,
> *the lack of a penis,* it does not distinguish in value between its father and
> its mother. (p. 31, emphasis added)

This is Freud's statement that underlies his claims about the primacy of the phallus and penis envy. Critics of Freud and Freud's psychoanalysis would do well to start here. These ideas of Freud's are seemingly indefensible. "Identification with the father"? Or, even worse, that this primary identification has something to do with the "phallus" or "lack of a penis"? It would seem that we have finally caught Freud in his most extreme ideological/patriarchal posture. We can now cite this fundamental misunderstanding of his, ridding ourselves of these (we hope) "outdated" prejudices and moving on in our psychoanalytic thinking and work.

If the reader and psychoanalyst want to reach these conclusions, this is certainly their prerogative. My only interest would be that they have a more adequate grasp of what it is that they are rejecting and the kind of ideas that tend to follow a rejection of this aspect of Freud's thought.

I have elsewhere given a more complete account of what will follow concerning "primary identification" (see Friedman, 1998). To understand what Freud means by this "immediate and direct identification, taking place before any object-cathexis" we must go back again to the original, infantile arrangement. Following Winnicott, I will say that "there is no baby without a mother." Even more, the infant's dependency on mother is, as we have said, double or absolute in that the baby is not aware of this dependency (see Winnicott, 1963).

What is the nature of the baby's dependency? I would like to emphasize two essential elements or aspects of this infantile condition. On the one hand, the baby requires caretaking that tends to his needs and wants. Here we find both his biophysiological needs (hunger and the like) and his psychical push for pleasure (sucking, handling, and being handled or held, and so on). For most psychoanalytic theorists, including Klein and Winnicott, "the breast" or "mother's breast" or even "the technique of mothering" is used to represent both the meeting of the need and the gratification of the urge. On the other hand, another factor is necessary to maintain the infant's developing organization precisely so it can have its needs met and experience gratification. In other words, the human infant, born unorganized and radically dependent, requires some additional factor around which it can organize and pursue its driven/instinctual interests. Though the child is born a human subject, it is not born a "self." This is why we hear Freud saying, *Wo es war, soll Ich werden*: Where "It" was, there I shall (it is my obligation/duty to) become (someone).

There is more. For the human infant, the failure or breakdown of its developing organization is experienced traumatically. Freud (1920) names this quite aptly as *Schreck*, which has been adequately rendered by Strachey as "fright," but is better named as "terror." Beyond the limit of the human individual's ability to maintain his/her organization is terror. This is true for all human beings, infants to adults. In Conrad's *Heart of Darkness* we hear Kurtz saying "the horror, the horror" in reference to this limit. Christian ideas of hell are made up of this terror experience (as are all the horror and suspense stories and films that we all enjoy so much). What separates the infant from the adult is the former's vulnerability to *Schreck,* how its life conditions and early dependent, unorganized setup are so conducive to *Schreck* (this is at the root Rank's idea of the "birth trauma"). Humans are, in a sense, creatures of *Schreck,* unlike any other animal. (Here we find the psychical location for religious beliefs, beyond their historical, cultural, and political moorings.) It is not just a matter of "unmet needs" or "frustration of a driven interest." These are certainly significant, but the human condition derives its poignancy and pathos from its inner, ownmost possibility of terror, trauma.

This is where the organizing "x" factor comes into play to avert the infant's own terror. It is here that Freud's idea of primary identification takes on its proper significance, even in its phallic aspect. But before elaborating on Freud's notion, let us look briefly at two original and profound psychoanalytic thinkers who could not make use or sense of Freud's idea, and so came up with their own idea of the infant's original organization. I am referring to Melanie Klein and Donald Winnicott. Though much can be made of their differences, they have a certain basic feature in common, one that has now superseded Freud's view on this matter.

For both Klein and Winnicott, "the breast"—sometimes identified as *mother's* breast—forms the core of the ego and is the basis of identity and a sense of self. They both recognize that the infant, born unorganized and helpless, requires some "x" factor outside of its own interests and responses in order to grow and develop physically and psychically. They claim that all healthy, developing human infants first identify with this body part (part-object).

Klein says: " I have repeatedly put forward the hypothesis that the primal good object, the mother's breast, forms the core of the ego." (1957, p. 5). Additionally, the breast is the prototype for "goodness, patience, generosity and creativeness"; it is the "foundation for hope, trust and belief in goodness" (pp. 5–6). For Klein, this breast is also the original embodiment of evil.

Klein uses "breast" and "mother's breast" interchangeably, though we know that there is a world of difference in the two characterizations. The healthy human infant has a "good feed"—has its need met and is satisfied— as it organizes itself around *eye contact with its caretaker.* Furthermore, seemingly from the very start, human infants respond differentially to the "familiar" (same root as "family") *voice.* Just as "the breast" is not at all the same as "mother's" breast, "a voice" is not the same as "Mother's/Father's" or "God's" or "conscience's" voice ("calling" to us). Klein is unable to differentiate between the (part-)object of the infant's instinctual interest, which is breast, from that which organizes this interest, which is *mother's* (meaning face and voice) breast. Before showing how these considerations take us to

Freud's idea of "primary identification," let us turn our attention to Winnicott's modification of Klein's position.

Winnicott does sense that there is a serious problem in characterizing the necessary external factor, required by the human infant, as the breast or even mother's breast. Here is an example of one of Winnicott's attempts to make a correction on Klein's breast idea:

> When it is said that the first object is the breast, the word "breast" is used, I believe, to stand for the technique of mothering as well as for the actual flesh. It is not impossible for a mother to be a good-enough mother (in my way of putting it) with a bottle for the actual feeding (1951/1958, p. 239)

Winnicott is trying to get past the breast that Klein proclaimed as the basis for the ego and the foundation of the ego ideal. His "technique of mothering" idea is one possible solution to this difficulty. Yet, Winnicott is also unable to get beyond the infant's act of feeding and grasp the psychical preconditions for this feed (visual/auditory contact with the familiar/family). Only with these preconditions can the breast become mother's (good or bad) breast.

In a discussion of Klein's ideas of the "depressive position" and the child's movement from "part" to "whole-objects," Winnicott (1955/1958) makes the following remarks:

> To reach the depressive position a baby must become established as a whole person. Here *I am counting the breast as whole person, because, as the baby becomes a whole person, then the breast, the mother's body, whatever there is of her, any part, becomes perceived by the baby as a whole thing.* (p. 264, emphasis added)

Without a clear sense of the preconditions for part-object gratifications, Winnicott is left with "parts," even "any parts." He cannot adequately account for how these "parts" belong to mother, or anyone else for that matter. Winnicott, one would think, is trying to base the identificatory aspect on "the feed." Yet, incredibly, this is not the case. Winnicott wants to take the original identification beyond instinct and instinctual relating.

For Winnicott, in a psyche wherein the subject has taken shape through the breast and "any part" of mother, both "doing" and "drive" are (potentially) alien and alienating. So Winnicott divides psychic life into male and female elements, placing *both active and passive doing* under the male heading. Here then is the female:

> The pure female element relates to the breast (or to the mother), in the sense that the object is the subject. I see no instinct drive in this. (1971, p. 79)

The "pure female" is equated with the breast idea. Our "female principle" finds its nature outside of all sexuality and all doing, as it often does when psyche and libido are taken out of our understanding of the human infant (so now all of our prejudices and naïve assumptions about "the female" power-fully flow back into our account, backed by a sense of certainty that only disavowed drive elements can bring).

Now that Winnicott has done away with the instinctual breast, we find the Breast, beyond Klein's breast idea or even mother's breast. Winnicott states this as follows: "The breast here is a symbol not of doing but being" (p. 81). Of course, even with this statement he runs into a similar confusion that he and Klein had before. They give "the breast" priority on the one hand (the mother image derived from the breast), but also make it somehow "mother's" breast on the other. So while the "pure female"/breast element and "experience of being" would not allow for mediation (which is a doing and a symbolization/repre-sentational act), Winnicott nonetheless makes the claim that the breast is a symbol of being (not doing). Winnicott's thinking on these matters is as mud-dled as he is certain of his findings. And it gets even more muddled.

Breasts themselves can be more or less breastlike (that is, partake of the female element):

> Clinically one needs to deal with the case of the baby who has to make do with an *identity with a breast that is active, which is a male element breast, but which is not satisfactory for the initial identity which needs a breast that is, not a breast that does. Instead of "being like" this baby has to "do like," or be done to, which from our point of view here is the same thing* (p. 82, emphasis added).

In trying to establish a basis for the ego outside of psychical reactions and instinct, Winnicott is forced to speak in these peculiar terms. Breasts can now be alienated from themselves, their pure being interrupted and replaced by a "doing/done-to." Like the story of Adam and Eve, "doing" is a sin; our story is now reduced to the Transgression of the Breast (as opposed to Adam/Man and Eve/Woman).

For Winnicott, "when the girl element in the boy or girl baby or patient finds the breast *it is the self that has been found*" (p. 82, emphasis added). Here the human infant takes on qualities of the breast; the "Breast" itself is the basis for humanity.

In their efforts to replace Freud's vision of the psychical/libidinal origins of the ego, Winnicott and Klein fall prey to some serious misunderstandings regarding the psychic life of the human infant. In place of Freud's active, striving, human infant, we find the Pure Being of the Breast, with which the human infant is to identify. Even more, the striving of the infant is alien and alienating to this Pure Being, at least for Winnicott. In Klein, the infant's dri-ven interests do not fare much better as they are seen as organized around a breast-thing. Klein endows the breast with all manner of human qualities and characteristics, begging the question, of course, as to the origin of these qual-ities (unless the breast is granted some supernatural powers—which, in fact, it is). Opposing these confusions, and prior to them, stands *Freud's idea of primary identification.*

It is true that the human infant requires some factor or presence beyond itself and its own resources at birth, and if this resource is absent or somehow fails, the child experiences the terror (*Schreck*) of trauma. The breast, which can be called mother's breast if neither the child or mother is psychotic, is the child's first (part-)object and has object cathexes directed toward it. Freud was quite aware of this and so purposely stated that the primary identification is "immediate and direct and takes place before any object cathexis." What then is this an identification with, if not some omnipotent breast?

If I tell you that the *hyle* or material of this primary identification is, in health, the human/mother's *face* and (the familiar/family) *voice*, we are least oriented correctly. We are now in a human environment, where human subjects can take shape; no longer in the breast-world where things somehow take on human qualities, which then form the basis for the infant's ego and self. The identity of the subject is prefigured in this primary (immediate and direct) identification with the (human/mother) face/voice. The healthy infant organizes its "omnipotent," libidinally driven activities around and through these psychic images; this especially includes sucking and feeding on mother's breast (which is really the infant's possession as so organized around voice/face) This face/voice (also) *belongs to the infant.* Just as Klein and Winnicott mistakenly claim about the breast, these images of face/voice *"are" the infant as subject and constitute the basis for the self.*

All of this is prelude. While the claim here is that the raw material (*hyle*–stuff) of the child's primary identification usually belongs to the mother, we still must account for its form (*morphe*). Freud's claim is that the father (or parents) as phallic gives this identification its shape or form; it is, says Freud, the father who serves as the model (*Vorbild*; "*Vor*" means "before," and "*Bild*" means image, so "*Vorbild*" is a primary image, a "before image," a model).

As paradoxical as this may seem, the identificatory images the healthy infant carries have a total or complete quality about them, in spite of the fact that we understand that they are derived from/supported by interactions with part-objects. Therefore, the voice/face that "is" the baby has an all-powerful (omnipotent) aspect (within its absolute dependency on the caretaker). This complete, powerful, commanding, aggressive quality is that of the (primal) father, or, as in Freud's footnote, the "phallic parent(s)." This is how the infant becomes organized "as his own ideal" (see Freud, 1914). In healthy development, this will serve as the basis for the ego ideal and conscience. In religious experience, this image is rendered as God's voice within us (which can also be experienced delusionally). This all-powerful god is most often modeled as Father (*Vorbild*).

This account is also a rendering of the child's state of primary narcissism, to be differentiated from autoerotism (which originally has to do with oral gratifications and the presence or absence of the/mother's breast). Furthermore, this primary identification constitutes the child's hidden indebtedness to the other (primal Father as form/*morphe* and environmental Mother as material/*hyle*) that lies at the heart of the "mysterious masochistic trends in the ego" (Freud, 1920) and the ego's "primary masochism" (Freud, 1924). This is how the infant can be aggressive/sadistic as it operates within the primal identification, yet already be masochistically and passively given over to this Great Other (not "The Breast").

So Freud envisions this primary identification as the "x" factor around which the human infant becomes organized, out of which it develops a gendered sense of self and pursues its libidinal interests. I would hope we can see how superior this approach is to those approaches that merely posit "male and female elements" as givens, then introduce these into the psychic life of men and women. Freud reminds us that the givens for human life are activity and passivity, which become associated with phallic–castrated, then male and female. *Freud understood that gender and sexuality are, for humans, constructions and achievements*, though with a somewhat limited range of possible configurations.

In an effort to avoid some new set of confusions surrounding this notion of primary identification, a few more clarifications might be helpful. For the human subject, even the most stable and healthy primary identification requires subtle and ongoing environmental support. For example, when the anthropologist Malinowski takes up residence in a culture entirely foreign to him, he becomes besieged with terrible mood swings and the intrusion of primitive sexual and aggressive ideas. A similar experience awaits the religious hermit when he first goes into the desert (though he calls this the work of the devil). The horrors of war can and do break down this primary identification as well. Any destruction of this organizing structure is terrible and traumatic, leading to delusional or near-delusional states (as psychic attempts to get reorganized). Cults, religious and mystical orders, even the military rely on the instability of the primary identification and so, through training or indoctrination, impose a new identity on the individual. Physical and psychological torture can be used in a similar fashion. While much of this has been presented before in the context of discussions about the "ego ideal" and its function (see Freud, 1921), it is important that we understand how fundamental this underlying and primary identificatory structure is.

Though both adult and infant require environmental support to sustain their identificatory organization, the infant's situation is worth treating separately for a few important reasons. First, there is no preexisting identification, so one needs to be established. Second, the requirements needed to maintain this identification are more intensive than those of an adult. Third, and not least important, the ease with which this organizing aspect can fall apart and fail the child makes the child particularly susceptible to being thrown it into a state of terror (*Schreck*) and trauma. Even its own reactions (rage/frustration) to discomfort and deprivation can produce this terrible result. For all the talk and focus on the love of the parent towards the child (a worthy achievement that is not as common as one would think or hope), the critical function of the parent (and therapist in working with disturbed patients) is to assist in holding the child together (Winnicott's "holding environment"). This has to do with the neutralization and management of persecutory fears and anxieties. Parental love for children certainly allows for more patience, energy and vigilance in performing this all-important task, though merely loving, in and of itself, might not be enough (this is certainly and especially true for therapists and their patients [see Friedman, 1995]).

In the realm of the primary identification, that original organizing structure of the infant's instinctual pursuits and interests, there is the "Father model" (*Vorbild*). The raw materials for this are most often brought to the baby by the mother. In healthy infants, instinctual gratifications lead to cathectic investments in objects, the first (part-)object being mother's breast (the good feed). In childhood psychosis, different primary identifications and object-cathexes occur, as with autistic children (and their "inanimate" identificatory objects) and childhood schizophrenics ("breast-selves" can be found here). *It is on the basis of this original Father model that gender and sexuality find their shape in the human realm.* As always, given the enormous amount of distortion and misunderstanding that surrounds this idea of Freud's, it is important that we look carefully at what this involves.

To recall certain aspects of this primary identificatory image, it is whole and complete, active and omnipotent, all of these psychically maintained through visually based perception (this is the importance of eye contact with the caretaker) and auditory contact (baby talk). This is the original form of the "Ideal Ego" which is a "Body Ego" (see Freud, 1905, 1914, 1923a). While the healthy infant's instinctual aims are both passive and active, the Ideal Ego is constituted as active. This is the basis for the following statement of Freud's, seemingly incredible to today's ears: "So far as the autoerotic and masturbatory manifestations of sexuality are concerned, we might lay it down that the sexuality of little girls is of a wholly masculine character" (1905, p. 219). Freud is not espousing some metaphysics of Male/Female (as Winnicott, Jung, Ferenczi tend to do). Rather, Freud is reconstructing the masculine and feminine from their psychical roots in the dimension of activity/passivity (see Freud, 1905, p. 219). Freud maintains this view from the beginning of his reflective career until the end. For example, in 1930 he writes: "For psychology the contrast between the sexes fades away into one between activity and passivity" (p. 106).

So Freud clearly stakes out the claim for a certain primary masculinity (activity) in and for all infants and children. Yet Freud also argues (1905) for an original and ongoing bisexual aspect in every individual. How can these two views be reconciled? In fact, there is no inconsistency in these two ideas; rather, together they constitute a complete account of the psychical basis for gender and sexuality in each human subject.

First, we find the infant organized around this primary identification, which is also the ideal (body) ego. Though this is a psychical construction within the infant's own sphere of omnipotence, it nonetheless uses the parent as *Vorbild* or model. So the model is active and identified with as such, but the infant is "taken over" by this model and is, in a sense, passively wedded to the ideal (this is the basis for "primary masochism," [see Freud, 1924]). Though it is too soon in this account of things to speak of gender, we can see that there already is a primary passive aspect to the infant's original active organization.

When we turn to early object-cathexes and aims, we find the same double-sided arrangement. We have both active and passive instinctual aims (feeding/being fed, grasping/being held, and, later, looking/being looked at, and all variations of the sadistic/masochistic styles). Strictly speaking, we still have not arrived at the point of gender distinction, though we can see the ground being laid for the psycho-sociohistorical construction(s) of gender. We are, however, in the domain of the sexual, with its active/passive bipolarity.

We should not underestimate the uniquely human aspects of this active-passive instinctual (*trieblich*, not *Instinkt*) arrangement. Just as no other animal is born into such an extended period of helplessness as to require the psychical maintenance of a primary identification (never to be permanently secured, always in need of some support from the *Lebenswelt*—life world), so is no other animal given over so thoroughly to both active and passive gratifications. Furthermore, human sexuality or desire serves primarily as a basis for living, rather than being only or essentially a hormonally-based drive to reproduce. And so, as Freud has so brilliantly demonstrated, the significations or signs of this sexuality can and are easily spread over any and all aspects of our lives. Thus even the act of writing can represent coitus and so become inhibited or prohibited (see Freud, 1926). It is precisely this two-sided and doubled point of origin, in primary identification and passive/active instinctuality, that first produces this phenomenon of desire (libido).

From whence gender? Now that we are versed in a more adequate account of Freud's understanding of primary identification and the drives (*Triebe*, not *Instinkt*), we can turn our attention to another controversial passage in Freud. Following his claim that the Father-like parent is the model (*Vorbild*), Freud says:

> The main characteristic of this "infantile genital organization" is its *difference* from the final genital organization of the adult. This consists in the fact that, for both sexes, only one genital, namely the male one, comes into account. What is present, therefore, is not a primacy of the genitals, but a primary of the phallus (Freud, 1923b, p. 142)

Freud does not say "primacy of the penis"; there are distinct reasons for this. The phallus is a *representation*, an *image* of the penis. As I have said elsewhere:

> This differentiation between signifier and signified has a long history. Greek vase painting attests to the symbolic power of the male organ when translated into phallic representation. There the celebrants carry before them huge penises, larger than their bodies. The organ itself remains inconsequential when compared with its representation. (Friedman, 1988)

Not a breast nor a womb, this phallus (as a signifier) *constitutes a relation to the world*, just as Little Hans goes about looking for animals that have a visible *Wiwimacher* and those that do not (see Freud, 1909). To understand how Freud can think in such a fashion, we need to add another element to our presentation: castration and the castration complex. This will be the linchpin in the constructions of gender and sexuality.

Once again, I would like to cite comments from a previous study:

> For Freud, it is much less important that boys have penises than that girls do not. It is this absence that endows the phallus with "presence," that gives it its primacy. The phallus is the fulcrum of sexual difference. Boys and girls are different in that girls do not have a penis. Therefore, the boy is always at risk. In a definite sense, the girl defines and guides the boy's identity more than the girl's "penis envy" serves as the basis for her femininity. (Friedman, 1988)

The phallus is the representation of the missing penis; it is founded on the "fact" of castration. So Freud says that "the significance of the castration complex can *only be rightly appreciated if its origin in the phase of phallic primacy is also taken into account*" (Freud, 1923b, p. 144, emphasis added). The phenomena of human gender and desire become organized around absence, not presence. *Only as absent can an object serve in this organizing signifying fashion.* As evidence of this, think of the role the dead play in our lives through the work of mourning, of how society builds monuments to the past, of how religions are always founded on some "original, past loss." As Kierkegaard claimed about Jesus, it would always be a disadvantage to be his contemporary. The meaning of his life appears only once he is gone.

Phallic primacy becomes constitutive of gender and psyche itself. It works within the original primary identification, with its double-edged and bisexual instinctual arrangement. This is why Freud can claim:

> The antithesis here is between having a *male genital* and being *castrated*. It is not until development has reached its completion at puberty that the sexual polarity coincides with *male* and *female*. (Freud, 1923b, p. 145)

Freud was never a simple nor naïve realist. The human world (*Lebenswelt*) is one of refindings and re-presentations. (Even Winnicott [1969/1971] will argue that the basis for the sense of reality and the externality of objects is *fantasy*). So it is the fact of sexual difference (as castration), signified through the absent penis—now phallus—that allows for a sense of (gender) identity and the externality of the world.

> The phallus is the representation of the essential lost object, the penis. The penis is represented in psychoanalysis as the phallus, as being "alienable" in that possession is never guaranteed. In the traditionally rendered sense, the threat of castration, of being dispossessed, turns the boy away from his mother and forces his desire elsewhere. For the girl too this alienable part will produce a transformation of desire. Upon discovering her own and her mother's lack, her

love will turn to the father. In other words, the character of the phallus, its nature as "absent," organizes desire, gives shape to the oedipal passions and forces the question concerning the latter's renunciation. (Friedman, 1988)

For Freud, there are no female breasts or male breasts. There is, however, phallic primacy, castration, and the creation of gender and sexuality out of an original active/passive instinctuality. Freud's is precisely not a metaphysics of sexuality and gender, where all historical prejudice is merely placed at the beginning (so the female is maternal and peaceful, while the male is aggressive and warlike [see Ferenczi, 1988; Friedman, 1995]). Though biology and history provide the limits of the human gender and sexual configurations, it is their signification that puts these limits and the possibilities that accompany them into play. Freud's psychoanalytic understanding reflects on and traces these developments. It does so, I would like to add, with *minimal historical prejudice*, especially when compared with the ideological renderings of some of his most important, and presently admired, followers (Ferenczi, Winnicott, and Klein, to name just a few).

I would like to conclude with a few general remarks about the now-famous "penis envy" (*Penisneid*) idea. Since we now have a more adequate understanding of the role of the "absent penis" (represented as the phallus) in the signifying of objects, we must now provide a clearer statement about envy and its roots.

Only humans experience envy; that is to say, only the human subject can covet the pleasure or circumstances or experience of another. Envy requires a certain kind of imagining of what the other person's experience is. Of course, what we come to imagine can range from the empathically accurate to the projection-filled delusion, with a lot of ground in between. But the point remains nonetheless. Envy comes from our preoccupations with the Other. And though no other animal operates in these terms, nothing could be more natural for the human individual. Born so radically dependent, operating in an organized, omnipotent manner, with his most essential environment being the *Mit-welt* (world of others), the child's envy is merely a sign that a world beyond his projection exists.

Envy reactions in children and adults are not, in and of themselves, pathological. That the Ten Commandments condemn covetousness merely indicates the universality of envy. As in anything human, there are pathological variations of envy. The chronic and spoiling envy that we find in borderline children and adults, and adults with severe character pathology, is just such an example (see Boris, 1994; Klein, 1957). In the case of healthier individuals, envy that has been worked through contributes to the formation of a more personal and cultivated ego ideal structure and, along with this, a capacity for admiration (as opposed to mere idealizations and "worship"). So while we might be condemned to envy, envy does not necessarily condemn us.

Now to Freud's notion of penis envy. This concept is, no doubt, a lightning rod for both misguided criticisms of Freud's psychoanalysis and superficial adherence to psychoanalytic "doctrine." If the phallus is a representation of the absent or missing penis and the boy's castration complex is predicated on this absence, then *penis envy* is the name of the girl's castration complex (see Freud, 1914, 1917, 1925, 1931, 1933). The girl's sexuality, originally phallic within the primary identification, now turns on her lack of the penis (which is also her mother's lack—the earliest mother is, no doubt, the "phallic mother" found in fairy tales as a powerful witch or fairy).

In order to understand what is at stake here, we must be clear on the centrality of this factor of *absence*. *Nothing along the lines of human sexuality* (which is not identical to "sex") *would exist without this signifying/representational aspect put into play by absence* (not presence). If the boy's organ represents the "absence of absence," then the girl's is the "presence of absence." Though this may sound confusing, it is important that we think in these terms. If we do not, we will find ourselves quickly caught up in an infantile "penis ideology" or in the compulsion to renounce this ideology (often leading to naïve—ideology-based—ideas about male and female elements as givens). Human desire is itself built around, constituted by, the dominion of absence (and lost objects); all creativity and culture find their *raison d'être* here. Both boy and girl have a primary identification; both boy and girl are conditioned, in their sexuality and desire, by absence. This conditioning by absence is named by the phallus and phallic primacy and concerns the absent penis (as itself the signifier of sexual difference).

Penis envy is the name Freud gives to what is here called the "presence of absence." Again, I ask the reader to bear with me in speaking this way so that the most common misunderstandings and distortions can be avoided and a more adequate rendering of sexuality and desire can be given. So the boy experiences an absence of absence. This is precisely the castration complex, built upon absence. Since the boy's experience is also founded on absence, his possession of the phallus is *never* fully secured (forever forcing a renunciation of "primary narcissism"; see Friedman, 1988). With the threat of castration becoming an aspect of his relationship to his father, the boy's desire is forced away from his mother and the (re)finding of a "mate" can proceed on that basis. Let me add that this mating aspect is, as we all know, not so simple for creatures with desire based on absence. Then what about the girl and her penis envy?

Just as the boy is compelled to preserve the absence of absence, so the girl is driven to transform the presence of absence into the presence of presence. Again, I need the reader to allow human sexuality or desire its representational, signifying aspect, which it so obviously has. This manner of speaking forces us to take this seriously. So how does the girl make this transformation of absence into presence? Remember, she begins just as the boy in a primary identification/narcissism that is phallic (though carried by both parents). So her transformation is named by Freud as her castration complex. In this psychic dilemma, the girl finds her mother to be of no value in this attempt to transform absence into presence; the mother herself is lacking.[1]

---

1. I am here leaving aside discussion of certain and mostly pathological variations on this theme which include the girl's relation to a "phallic" mother (the story of Rapunzel) and her wish to have a baby with her mother ("mother babies" as opposed to "father babies"; see Freud, 1933).

This will set the stage for the girl's turning away from mother and toward father with the "wish" (*Wunsch*) that this absence of hers be transformed into presence. As Freud (1933) states:

> The wish with which the girl turns to her father is no doubt originally the wish for the penis which her mother has refused her and which she now expects from her father. *The feminine situation is only established, however, if the wish for a penis is replaced by one for a baby, if, that is, a baby takes the place of a penis in accordance with an ancient symbolic equivalence.* (p. 128, emphasis added)

Let me repeat this crucial point one more time: There is nothing in human experience that is not a matter of absence/loss, which always opens up a field of signifiers and significations. This includes the woman's wish for a baby, a wish that Freud does not take for granted. There is no *female element* nor *maternal element* already and fully made, of which a good mother has a lot and a bad mother very little. This kind of thinking, I believe, only leads us back to shallow maternalisms and other prejudices. The woman's wish for a baby is a psychic construction. So it is equally true that while getting pregnant might just be a matter of having sex (again a psychical event for humans) with conception occurring, having (and raising) a child is a psychical construction. Humans do all manner of things to their infants, from affectionate child rearing to torture and death and everything in between. In order to attempt an adequate response to these variations, an acceptance of the constructed nature of the mother-child relationship is the crucial first step. And this is precisely what Freud's understanding offers us.

The baby turns absence into presence. With the baby (especially with a male child, says Freud), the woman's castration complex (the presence of absence) is, to some extent, neutralized and resolved. Human desires/libidinal interests are all built up through this phallic linchpin (as absent/missing penis representing sexual difference). Maternal love and affection, "good enough mothering" and "maternal preoccupation" *all presuppose these psychical developments; they themselves are not and cannot be the starting point of any discussion about mother-child relationships.*

So penis envy and the two castration complexes bring a relation to a world inhabited by desire and desired (lost/refound) objects. So embodiments of, substitutes for, and symbols for the phallus are forever sought (this all occurring in the patriarchal order within which, of course, there must appear the "story" of an overturned matriarchy [see Lerner, 1986; Rosaldo & Lamphere, 1974]). It is in such a world that love and reproduction can occur together in a choice of mate. In addition, work and production can also make their claims on us in such a symbol-rich environment (*Lebenswelt*). With castration and penis envy, we find the roots of love and sublimation.

REFERENCES

Boris, H. (1994). *Envy.* Northvale, NJ: Jason Aronson.

Ferenczi, S. (1988). *The clinical diary of Sandor Ferenczi.* Cambridge, MA: Harvard University Press.

Freud, S. (1905). *Three essays on the theory of sexuality. SE,* Vol. 7.

―――― (1909). Analysis of a phobia in a five-year-old boy. *SE,* Vol. 10.

―――― (1914). On narcissism: An introduction. *SE,* Vol. 14.

―――― (1917). On transformations of instinct as exemplified in anal erotism. *SE,* Vol. 17.

―――― (1920). *Beyond the pleasure principle. SE,* Vol. 18.

―――― (1922). *Group psychology and the analysis of the ego. SE,* Vol. 18.

―――― (1923a). *The ego and the id. SE,* Vol. 19.

―――― (1923b). The infantile genital organization. *SE,* Vol. 19.

―――― (1924). The economic problem of masochism. *SE,* Vol. 19.

―――― (1925). Some psychical consequences of the anatomical distinction between the sexes. *SE,* Vol. 19.

―――― (1926). *Inhibitions, symptoms and anxiety. SE,* Vol. 20.

―――― (1930). *Civilization and its discontents. SE,* Vol. 21.

―――― (1931). Female sexuality. *SE,* Vol. 21.

―――― (1933). *New introductory lectures on psycho-analysis. SE,* Vol. 22.

Friedman, J. (1988). The idea of narcissism in Freud's psychoanalysis. *Int. rev. psychoanal.,* 15: 499–514.

―――― (1992a). Freud's Todestrieb: An introduction. Part 1. *Int. rev. psychoanal.,* 19, 189–196.

―――― (1992b). Freud's Todestrieb: Part 2. *Int. rev. psychoanal.,* 19: 309–322.

―――― (1995). Ferenczi's Clinical diary: On loving and hating. *Int. j. psychoanal,* 76, 957–975.

―――― (1998). *Living and dying in Freud's psychoanalysis.* New York: Jason Aronson, in press.

Friedman, J., & Alexander, J. (1983). Psychoanalysis and natural science: Freud's 1895 Project revisited. *Int. rev. psychoanal.,* 10, 303–318.

Klein, M. (1957). *Envy and gratitude.* London: Tavistock Publications.

Lerner, G. (1986). *The creation of patriarchy.* New York: Oxford University Press.

Rosaldo, M., & Lamphere, L. (1974). *Woman, culture and society.* Stanford, CA: Stanford University Press.

Winnicott, D. (1958). The depressive position in normal emotional development. In *Through pediatrics to psycho-analysis.* New York: Basic Books. (Original work published 1955)

―――― (1958). Transitional objects and transitional phenomenon. In *Through pediatrics to psycho-analysis.* New York: Basic Books. (Original work published 1951)

―――― (1965). From dependence towards independence in the development of the individual. In *Maturational processes and the facilitating environment.* Madison, CT: International Universities Press. (Original work published 1963)

―――― (1971). Creativity and its origins. In *Playing and reality.* New York: Routledge.

―――― (1971). The use of the object and relating through identifications. In *Playing and reality.* New York: Routledge. (Original work published 1969)

―――― (1989). Postscript: D.W.W. on D.W.W. In *Psychoanalytic explorations.* Cambridge, MA: Harvard University Press. (Original work published 1967)

5

THE BLIND SPOT OF AN OLD DREAM OF SYMMETRY (EXCERPT FROM *SPECULUM OF THE OTHER WOMAN*)

Luce Irigaray

ANOTHER "CAUSE"—CASTRATION

As Might Be Expected

The little girl's hostility toward her mother finds other justifications. Such as: the impossibility of satisfying the child's sexual desires; the mother inciting the child to masturbate and then forbidding it to do so; the fact that the bond to the mother is supposedly destined to disappear as a result of its primitive character, since early object cathexes are always highly ambivalent; "it is the special nature of the mother-child relation that leads, with equal inevitability, to the destruction of the child's love; for even the mildest upbringing cannot avoid using compulsion and introducing restrictions, and any such intervention in the child's liberty must provoke as a reaction an inclination to rebelliousness and aggressiveness." But "all these factors...are, after all, also in operation in the relation of the *boy* [Freud's italics] to his mother and are yet unable to alienate him from the maternal object." So some specific factor must intervene in the mother-daughter relation and in the development of that relation which would explain "the termination of the attachment of girls to their mother" (p. 124).[1]

> I *believe* we have found this specific factor, and indeed *where we expected to find it*, even though in a surprising form. *Where we expected to find it*, I say, for it lies in the castration complex. After all, the *anatomical* distinction [between the sexes] *must* express itself in *psychical* consequences. *It was, however, a surprise to learn from analyses that girls hold their mother responsible* for their lack of a penis and do not forgive her for their being thus put at a disadvantage (p. 124).

One might cite or even recite Freud at length, the Freud of "female sexuality" at least, on the basis of these "I believes," these "where we expected to find its,"

---

1. (Ed: All quotations are from Freud's essay "Femininity," lecture XXXIII, *New introductory lectures on psychoanalysis* (SE 22: 112–135) unless otherwise noted).

these "castration complexes"; and also relate them to his failure to be "surprised" at the "psychical consequences" of an "anatomical distinction," or to his rather univocal appeal to anatomy to explain a psychical economy—which would supposedly know no other mimesis than that of "nature" according to this interpretation?—and to all those expressions of surprise which, perhaps, mask the upsurge of an *unheimlich* that is much more uncanny, blinding....

The Gaze, Always at Stake

So the little girl does not forgive her mother for not giving her a penis. At the "*sight* of the genitals of the other sex," girls "*notice the* [sexual?] *difference* and, it must be admitted, its significance too. They feel seriously *wronged*, often declare that they want to '*have something like it too*'...and fall victim to *envy for the penis*, which will leave ineradicable traces on their development and the formation of their character" (p. 125).

The dramatization is quite good, and one can imagine, or dream up, recognition scenes along these lines in the consulting room of psychoanalyst Freud. By rights, though, the question should still be raised of the respective relationships between the gaze and sexual difference, since, he tells us, you have to see it to believe it. And therefore, one must lose sight of something to see it anew? Admittedly. But all the same....Unless all the potency, and the difference (?) were displaced into the gaze(s)? So Freud will see, without being seen? Without being seen seeing? Without even being questioned about the potency of his gaze? Which leads to envy of the omnipotence of gazing, knowing? About sex/about the penis. To envy and jealousy of the eye-penis, of the phallic gaze? He will be able to see that I don't have one, will realize it in the twinkling of an eye. I shall not see if he has one. More than me? But he will inform me of it. Displaced castration? *The gaze is at stake from the outset.* Don't forget, in fact, what "castration," or the knowledge of castration, owes to the gaze, at least for Freud, The gaze has always been involved.

Now the little girl, the woman, supposedly has *nothing* you can see. She exposes, exhibits the possibility of *a nothing to see.* Or at any rate she shows nothing that is penis-shaped or could substitute for a penis. This is the odd, the uncanny thing, as far as the eye can see, this nothing around which lingers in horror, now and forever, an overcathexis of the eye, of appropriation by the gaze, and of the *phallomorphic* sexual metaphors, its reassuring accomplices.[1]

This nothing, which actually cannot well be mastered in the twinkling of

---

1. Cf. the relationship Freud establishes between castration anxiety, the fear of losing one's sight, and the fear of one's father's death (in "The Uncanny," *SE*, 17:219–52). Or again this: "It often happens that neurotic men declare that they feel there is something uncanny about the female genital organs. This *unheimlich* place, however, is the entrance to the former *Heim* (home) of all human beings. to the place where each one of us lived once upon a time and in the beginning. . . . In this case, too, then, the *unheimlich* is what was once *heimlich*, familiar; the prefix "un" is the token of repression" ("The Uncanny," *SE* 17:245). For the moment let us concentrate on the strange disquiet felt about the female genitals. The woman-mother would be *unheimlich* not only by reason of a repression of the primitive relationship to the maternal but also because her sex/organs are strange, yet close; while *heimisch* as a mother, woman would remain "un" as a woman. Since woman's sexuality is no doubt the most basic form of the *unheimlich*.

an eye, might equally well have acted as an inducement to perform castration upon an age-old oculocentrism. It might have been interpreted as the intervention of a difference, of a deferent, as a challenge to an imaginary whose functions are often improperly regulated in terms of sight. Or yet again as the "symptom," the "signifier," of the possibility of an *other* libidinal economy, of a heterogeneity unknown in the practice of and discourse about the (designated) libido. Now the "castration complex" in becoming a woman will merely close off, repress? or censure? such possible interpretations. Woman's castration is defined as her having nothing you can see, as her *having* nothing. In her having nothing penile, in seeing that she has No Thing. Nothing *like* man. That is to say, *no sex/organ* that can be seen in a *form* capable of founding its reality, reproducing its truth. *Nothing to be seen is equivalent as having no thing. No being* and *no truth.*[1] The contract, the collusion, between *one* sex/organ and the victory won by visual dominance therefore leaves woman with her sexual void, with an "actual castration" carried out in actual fact. She has the option of a "neutral" libido or of sustaining herself by "penis-envy."

Anatomy is "Destiny"

This "neuter" is hard for Freud to account for in his theory of the difference of the sexes, as we can see from his repeated admissions that the subject of woman's sexuality is still very "obscure." As for what he will have to say about it, what has become "apparent" to him about it, female sexuality can be graphed along the axes of visibility of (so-called) masculine sexuality. For such a demonstration to hold up, the little girl must immediately become a little boy. In the beginning...the little girl was (only) a little boy. In other words THERE NEVER IS (OR WILL BE) A LITTLE GIRL. All that remains is to assign her sexual function to this "little boy" with no penis, or at least no penis of any recognized value. Inevitably, the trial of "castration" must be undergone. This "little boy," who was, in all innocence and ignorance of sexual difference, *phallic,* notices how ridiculous "his" sex organ looks. "He" *sees* the disadvantage for which "he" is *anatomically destined:* "he" has only a tiny little sex organ, no sex organ at all, really, an almost invisible sex organ. The almost imperceptible clitoris. The humiliation of being so badly equipped, of cutting such a poor figure, in *comparison* with the penis, with *the* sex organ, can only lead to a desire to "have something like it too," and Freud claims that this desire will form the basis for "normal womanhood." In the course of the girl's discovery of her castration, her dominant feelings are of envy, jealousy, and hatred toward the mother—or in fact any woman—who has no penis and could not give one. She desires to be a man or at any rate "like" a

---

1. This echoes Leibniz's questions in *Principles of Nature and of Grace Founded on Reason:* "Why is there something rather than nothing?" Or again: That which is truly not *one* entity, is not truly one *entity* either": Leibniz, letter to Arnauld, April 30, 1687. (Leibniz, *Philosophical Writings*, ed. G. H. R. Parkinson, trans. Mary Morris and G. H. R. Parkinson. [London: Dent, 1934 and 1973], pp. 199 and 67.)

man since she cannot actually become one.[1] The little girl does not submit to the "facts" easily, she keeps waiting for "it to grow," and "believes in that possibility for improbably long years." Which means that no attempt will be made by the little girl—nor by the mother? nor by the woman?—to find symbols for the state of "this nothing to be seen," to defend its goals, or to lay claim to its rewards. *Here again no economy would be possible where-by sexual reality can be represented by/for woman.* She remains forsaken and abandoned in her lack, default, absence, envy, etc. and is led to submit, to follow the dictates issued univocally by the sexual desire, discourse, and law of man. Of the father, in the first instance.

What the Father's Discourse Covers Up

So, borrowing Freud's own terms, let us question him for example, about his relationship to the parental function. That is, to the exercise of the law—notably the psychoanalytic law—of castration. Why this fear, horror, phobia...felt when there is nothing to be seen, why does having nothing that can be seen threaten *his* libidinal economy? And remember in this regard that in the castration scenario Freud has just outlined, it is the boy who looks and is horrified first, and that is the little girl merely doubles and confirms by reduplication what he supposed to have seen. Or not seen. "In [boys] the castration complex arises after they have learnt *from the sight of the female genitals* that the organ which they value so highly need not necessarily accompany the body. At this the boy calls to mind the threats he brought on himself by his doings with that organ, he begins to give credence to them and falls under the influence of *fear of castration,* [Freud's italics] which will be the most powerful motive force in his subsequent development" (p. 125). After which, Freud goes on: "The castration complex of girls is *also* started by the *sight* of the genitals of the other sex. Etc."

Here again the little girl will have to act *like* the little boy, feel the same urge to see, look in the same way, and her resentment at not having a penis must follow and corroborate the horrified astonishment the little boy feels when faced with the strangeness of the nonidentical, the nonidentifiable. The "reality" of the girl's castration could be summed up as follows: you men can see nothing, can know nothing of this; can neither discover nor recognize yourselves in this. All that remains, therefore, is for me, for her (or them), to accept this fact. As a biological fact! The girl thus "enters" into the castration complex in the same way as the boy, like a boy. She "comes out" of it feminized by a decision, which she is duty bound to ratify, that there cannot be a nothing to be seen. The idea that a "nothing to be seen," a something not subject to the rule of visibility or of specula(riza)tion, might yet have some reality, would indeed be intolerable to man. It would serve to threaten the theory and practice of the representation by which he aims to sublimate, or avoid the ban on, masturbation. Auto-erotism

---

1. In other words, the "fact of castration" will leave woman with only one option—the semblance, the mummery of femininity, which will always already have been to "act like" the value recognized by/for the male. The fact that certain men want to "act like" women thus raises the question whether they thereby take back for themselves that "femininity" which was assigned to woman as an inferior copy of their relation to the origin.

has been permitted, authorized, encouraged insofar as it is deferred, exhibitited in sublated ways. All this is endangered (caught in the act, one might say) by a *nothing*—that is, a nothing the same, identical, identifiable. By a fault, a flaw, a lack, an absence, outside the system of representations and autorepresentations. Which are man's. By a *hole* in men's signifying economy. A nothing that might cause the ultimate destruction, the splintering, the break in their systems of "presence," of "re-presentation" and "representation." A nothing threatening the process of production, reproduction, mastery, and profitability, of meaning, dominated by the phallus—that *master signifier* whose law of functioning erases, rejects, denies the surging up, the resurgence, the recall of a *heterogeneity* capable of reworking the principle of its authority. That authority is minted in concepts, representations and formalizations of language which prescribe, even today, the prevailing theory and practice of "castration." And what weak instruments these are, products of the very system they pretend to challenge. Such collusion with phallocentrism serves only to confirm its power.

The Negative in Phallocentric Dialectic

Thus the matter before us leads us to ask ourselves, and to ask them:

(1) Does the little girl, the woman, really have "penis-envy" in the sense Freud gives to that expression; that is, of wanting "to have something like it too"? This assumption, in fact, governs everything said now and later about female sexuality. For this "envy" programs all of woman's instinctual economy, even, though she does not realize it, *before* the discovery of her castration, at the point when, supposedly, she only was, and wanted to be, a boy.

(2) What is the relationship of that "envy" to man's "desire"? In other words, is it possible that the phobia aroused in man, and notably in Freud, by the uncanny strangeness of the "nothing to be seen" cannot tolerate *her* not having this "envy"? *Her* having other desires, of a different nature from *his* representation of the sexual and from *his* representations of sexual desire. From his projected, reflected *auto representations* shall we say? If woman had desires other than "penis-envy," this would call into question the unity, the uniqueness, the simplicity of the mirror charged with sending man's image back to him— albeit inverted. Call into question its flatness. The specularization, and speculation, of the purpose of (*his*) desire could no longer be two-dimensional. Or again: the "penis-envy" attributed to woman soothes the anguish man feels, Freud feels, about the coherence of his narcissistic construction and reassures him against what he calls castration anxiety. For if his desire can be signified only as "penis-envy," it is a good thing that he has it (one). And that what he has should represent the only goods acceptable for sexual trading.

(3) Why does the term "envy" occur to Freud? Why does Freud choose it? Envy, jealousy, greed are all correlated to lack, default, absence. All these terms describe female sexuality as merely the *other side* or even the *wrong side* of a

male sexualism. It could be admitted that the little girl accords a special status to the penis as the instrument of her sexual pleasure and that she displays a centrifugal-centripetal tropism for it. But "penis-envy," in the Freudian and indeed psychoanalytic sense, means nothing less than that the little girl, the woman, must despise *her own* pleasure in order to procure a—doubtless ambiguous—remedy for man's castration anxiety. The possibility of losing his penis, of having it cut off, would find a real basis in the *biological* fact of woman's castration. The fear of not having it, of losing it, would be re-presented in the anatomical amputation of woman, in her resentment at lacking a sex organ and in her correlative "envious" urge to gain possession of it. The castration anxiety of not having it,or losing it, would thus be supported by the representation of the female sex, whereas *the desire to have it* would confirm man in the assurance that he has it, still, while reminding him at the same time—in one of the essential rules of the game—that he risks having her take it away from him. The fact remains that "penis-envy" must above all be interpreted as a symptomatic index—laid down as a law of the economy of woman's sexuality—of the pregnancy of the desire for the same, whose guarantee, and transcendental signifier or signified, will be the phallus. The Phallus. If it were not so, why not *also* analyze the "envy" for the vagina? Or the uterus? Or the vulva? Etc. The "desire" felt by each pole of sexual difference "to have something like it too"? The resentment at being faulty, lacking, with respect to a heterogene, to an other? The "disadvantage" mother nature puts you to by providing only *one* sex organ? All of this would require, entail, demand an other sex, a different sex—a sex that shared in the same while remaining different[1]— for sexual pleasure to be possible. But finally, in Freud, sexual pleasure boils down to being plus or minus one sex organ: the penis. And sexual "otherness" comes down to "not having it." Thus, woman's lack of penis and her envy of the penis *ensure the function of the negative*, serve as representatives of the negative, in what could be called a *phallocentric*—or phallotropic—dialectic.[2] And if "sexual function" demands that the little boy should turn away from his—real—mother whom convention forbids he should get with child, if what is indicated by the "castration complex" forces him to "sublimate" his instincts toward his mother, let us say that, as far as he is concerned, man will *lose nothing* thereby, and that the loss will amount only to a risk, a fear, a "fantasy" of loss. And that the *nothing* of sex, the *not* of sex, will be borne by woman.

But, ipso facto, "castration" cannot be what makes the relation between the sexes practicable or assures the possibility for both repetition and "displacement" of the relation *between two sexes*. It must serve as a reminder of the negative which is attributed to woman, to the female sex—in *reality* too, for more verisimilitude—an attribution that would guarantee its "sublation"[3] in the sublimation of the penis. With sex and sexualness being sublated into representations, ideas, laws, dominated by the Phallus. The relationship to the negative, for man, will always have been imaginary—imagined, imaginable,—

1. Of course this will initially imply bisexuality, but here it would evoke instead the "brilliance" of the mirror which explodes into sexual pleasure, like and unlike according to each sex.
2. This might be understood as a tautology, unless the word "a" is re-marked. In other words, if dialectic has *the* one, *the* same as the horizon of its process, then it is necessarily phallocentric.
3. Translation of *Aufhebung*.

hence the impetus it gives to fictive, mythic, or ideal productions that are only afterward defined as laws assuring the permanence and circularity of this system. The legislation re-establishes, then, the castration complex, notably of woman, which will serve, along with other edicts, to transform into a historical program the fables relating to men's sexual practices.

(4) As for woman, one may wonder why she submits so readily to this make-believe, why she "mimics" so perfectly as to forget she is acting out man's contraphobic projects, projections, and productions of her desire. Specifically, why does she accept that her desire only amounts to "penis-envy"? What fault, deficiency, theft, rape, rejection, repression, censorship, of representations of her sexuality bring about such a subjection to man's desire-discourse-law about her sex? Such an atrophy of her libido? Which will never be admissible, envisionable, except insofar as it props up male desire. For the "penis-envy" alleged against woman is—let us repeat—a remedy for man's fear of losing one. If *she* envies it, then *he* must have it. If *she* envies what *he* has, then it must be valuable. The only thing valuable enough to be envied? The very standard of all value. Woman's fetishization of the male organ must indeed be an indispensable support of its price on the sexual market.

Is Working Out the Death Drives Limited to Men Only?

So let us speculate that things happen this way because, in psychoanalytic parlance, *the death drives can be worked out only by man,*[1] never, under any circumstances, by woman. She merely "services" the work of the death instincts. Of man.

Thus, by suppressing her drives, by pacifying and making them passive, she will function as pledge and reward for the "total reduction of tension." By the "free flow of energy" in coitus, she will function as a promise of the libido's evanescence, just as in her role as "wife" she will be assigned to maintain coital homeostasis, "constancy." To guarantee that the drives are "bound" in/by marriage. She will also be the place referred to as "maternal" where the automatism of repetition, the reestablishment of an earlier economy, the infinite regression of pleasure, can occur. Back to the sleep of Lethe, to lethargy. Except that she is charged at the same time with preserving, regenerating, and rejuvenating the organism, notably through sexual reproduction. She is wholly devoted to giving life, then, source and re-source of life. To being still the restoring, nourishing mother who prolongs the work of death by sustaining it; death makes a detour through the revitalizing female-maternal.

You will have realized that the "sexual function" also requires aggressiveness from the male, and that this authorizes an economy of death drives

1. For the following section, the reader should refer to *Beyond the pleasure principle*, "Instincts and their Vicissitudes," *SE*, 16, and "The Economic Problem of Masochism," *SE*, 19.

whereby the "subject" disengages and protects himself by diverting his energies to the "object." And, by maintaining the subject-object polarity in sexual activity, woman will provide man with an outlet for that "primary masochism" which is dangerous and even life-threatening for the "psychic" as well as the "organic" self. Now, Freud states that this "primary" or "erogenous" masochism will be reserved to woman and that both her "constitution" and "social rules" will forbid her any sadistic way to work out these masochistic death drives. She can only "turn them around" or "turn them inward." The sadism of the anal-sadistic stage is also transformed, at a secondary level, into masochism: activity is turned into passivity, sadism is "turned back" from the "object" onto the "subject." Secondary masochism added to primary masochism—this is apparently the "destiny" of the death drives in woman, and they survive only because of their unalterably sexuate nature, through the erotization of this "masochism."

But further, in order to transform his death drives and the whole instinctual dualism, in order to use his life to ward off death for as long as it takes to choose a death, man will have to work on building up his ego. On raising his own tomb, if you like. This new detour along the road to death, through/for the construction of narcissistic monuments, involves pulling the libido back from the object onto the self and desexualizing it so it can carry out more sublimated activities. Now, if this ego is to be valuable, some "mirror"[1] is needed to reassure it and re-insure it of its value. Woman will be the foundation for this specular duplication, giving man back "his" image and repeating it as the "same." If an *other* image, an *other* mirror were to intervene, this inevitably would entail the risk of mortal crisis. Woman will therefore be this sameness—or at least its mirror image—and, in her role of mother, she will facilitate the repetition of the same, in contempt for her difference. Her own sexual difference. Moreover, through her "penis-envy," she will supply anything that might be lacking in this specula(riza)tion. Calling back, now and forever, that *remainder* that melts into the depths of the mirror, that sexual energy necessary to carry out the work. The work of death.

So "woman" can function as place—evanescent beyond, point of discharge—as well as time—eternal return, temporal detour—for the sublimation and, if possible, mastery of the work of death. She will also be the representative-representation (*Vorstellung-Repräsentanz*), in other words, of the death drives that cannot (or theoretically could not) be perceived without horror, that the eye (of) consciousness refuses to recognize. In a protective misprision that cannot be put aside without the failure of a certain gaze; which is the whole point of castration. Up to this point, *the main concepts of psychoanalysis, its theory, will have taken no account of woman's desire*, not even of "her" castration. For their ways are too narrowly derived from the history and the historicization of (so-called) male sexuality. From that process by which consciousness comes into being and woman remains the place for the inscription of repressions. All of which demands that, without knowing it, she should provide a basis for such

---

1. A certain flat mirror would thus serve to desexualize drives and thereby work out funeral monuments for the "subject's" ego.

fantasies as the amputation of her sex organ, and that the "anatomy" of her body should put up the security for reality. She provides irrefutable, because natural, proof that this is not a matter of the silent action of the death drives. She will therefore be despoiled, without recourse, of all valid, valuable images of her sex/organs, her body. She is condemned to "psychosis," or at best "hysteria," for lack—censorship? foreclusion? repression?—of a valid signifier for her "first" desire and for her sex/organs.

This doesn't mean that the question of castration isn't raised for woman but rather that it refers back in reality to the father's castration, including the father of psychoanalysis—to his fear, his refusal, his rejection, of an *other* sex. For if to castrate woman is to inscribe her in the law of the *same* desire, of *the desire for the same*, what exactly is "castration"? And what is the relationship of the agent of castration to the concept and its practice?

"Penis-envy"

Waiting in Vain

The little girl, therefore, having seen the genital organs of the other sex, scorns all the pleasure that her own had afforded her and now has only one wish—to have a penis herself one day. And she does not "submit easily to the fact of being without a penis." On the contrary, "she believes...for improbably long years" in the possibility of possessing the male organ. "And analysis can show that, at a period when knowledge of reality has long since rejected the fulfillment of the wish as unattainable, it persists in the unconscious and retains a considerable cathexis of energy." In fact "the wish to get the longed-for penis eventually may contribute to the motives that drive a mature woman to analysis."

Of course, let us not neglect the fact that the woman, the hysteric, is particularly liable to submission, to suggestion, to fabrication even, where the discourse-desire of the other is concerned. And that what she comes to say while in analysis will not be very different from what she is expected to say there. And if she didn't say it there, why should she bother to come? To this scene that is organized, also, by/for her "penis-envy." And what could an analyst make of a desire of hers that would not correspond to *his* wish? For the penis. He would be, Freud confides in us, quite helpless. Therefore, she will express and express again her greed for the male organ and perhaps she will get, from the analytic treatment of this "envy," "a capacity to carry on an intellectual profession," "a sublimated modification of this repressed wish."

An Indirect Sublimation

You must understand that the analytic scene will not solve "penis-envy" for woman, it will not free her from her condition as sexual proletarian, it will not help in interpreting the credit surplus given to this "sex/organ" of the man (father), but it will allow her—perhaps—to enter into the system of a discourse whose "sense," whose "meaning" is based exclusively on a phallic standard. "Penis-envy" would represent, would be the only effective representative of woman's desire to enter into symbolic exchange as a "subject" and raise woman from her status as a mere "commodity."[1] So, she will have to undergo treatment for this "envy" in order to achieve sublimation. Which means, here, paying the price of repression of the appetite for sexual potency so as to gain access to a discourse that denies woman any right on the exchange market. Woman can realize the "capacity to carry on an intellectual profession," once again, only by indirect means. The casting couch, or the analyst's couch!

For there is no way out of this "envy." For her in particular. "One cannot very well deny the importance of envy for the penis. You may take it as an instance of male injustice if I assert that envy and jealousy play an even greater part in the mental life of women than of men...but I am inclined to attribute their greater amount in women to this latter influence [i.e. of penis-envy]" (p. 125). Which in no way lays to rest the question of "injustice" that was raised. Social injustice, obviously. For, once again, woman as such has no means of participating in so-called "spiritual" life (?), since she takes no part in working it out, in its "symbolization," its exchanges. This accounts for her grievance at being excluded as "subject" from a phallocentric scene upon which she can appear only if she accepts derision, guilt, and the loss of what they call, or he calls, her "femininity." In any case, only if she disavows, represses? or, rather perpetuates, the repression of what she herself might put forward as exchange values. Intellectuality only at the price of her female condition.

"Envy" or "Desire" for the Penis?

"Some analysts, however, have shown an inclination to depreciate the importance of this first installment of penis-envy in the phallic phase. They are of the opinion that what we find of this attitude in women is in the main a secondary structure which has come about on the occasion of later conflicts by regression to this early infantile impulse. This, however, is a general question of *depth* psychology. In many *pathological*—or even *unusual*—instinctual attitudes (for instance, in all the *sexual perversions*) the question arises of how much of their strength is to be attributed to early infantile fixations and how much to the influence of later experiences and developments" (pp. 125–26). "In all cases," with regard to the matter in hand—which we find to be equated with a "pathological" attitude, or at least to something "unusual" like a "sexual perversion," even though this "envy" is stated to be indispensable in the making of a "normal woman"—"the infantile factor sets the pattern, but does not always determine the issue, though it often does. Precisely in the case of penis-envy I should argue decidedly in favour of the preponderance of the infantile factor" (p. 126).

How has Freud read, or understood, these psychoanalysts (male or female) who depreciate the importance of penis-envy? For it seems that they don't all

---

1. And as the analytic scene has not raised the question of woman's social and economic condition, the language of the hysteric will become a "commodity" that serves the (theoretical) exchanges between psychoanalysts.

consider it as coming "first."[1] Yet it is as a function of this archaism, of something that comes before another, that Freud answers them. What is at stake in this need to establish priority? Particularly since the "envy" that Freud now, for the purposes of argument, is claiming to be primary was earlier defined as coming after the girl's castration complex. The little girl could not have felt this "envy" earlier on because, according to Freud himself, the difference between the sexes did not exist then, since the little girl was simply a little boy. She had a clitoris-penis. Therefore she could not have an "envy" for one in the sense Freud gives to the term until after the intervention of the castration complex.

Therefore let us turn the question around again. Is the primitive, or most primitive, character of "penis-envy" not an essential factor in establishing the *primacy of the male organ*? In making the phallus necessarily the archetype for sex? The primal sex? And making the penis the best representational equivalent of the Idea of sex? There can only be one desire: the desire to ensure dominion by greed, by appetite for appropriation. If anything were to contradict this desire—the little girl's pleasures, for example—the whole economy of sexual affects, and affectations, would have to be reinterpreted. And it is difficult to predict where a shift in the attribution of sexual powers might lead. But the misprisions needed to maintain the established order lead one to suspect that such an operation might take us far.

Arguments that premise the early onset of penis-envy to justify a belief in it are still heard within the field of analytic prolematics. Thus, woman's avidity for his sex organ supposedly means for man, among other things, a projection of his "primitive" oral instincts, of his wish to devour the mother's breast. And in this reminder of primary appetites, one might detect also the fear of having destroyed woman's sex, of having castrated her out of insatiable hunger, biting in an attempt to seize, incorporate, or eliminate something that is becoming elusive. Whence the guilt, the horror at the sight of the reality of these fantasies, which thereby become all-powerful, perhaps. And hence the terrible anxiety that *she*, the maternal-substitute, in retaliation or also moved by hunger, might do the same thing to his penis-breast.

Repression, or Inexorable Censorship

Be this as it may, when she sees the penis, when she compares—as if this were possible—her sex organ to the little boy's, the little girl is supposed to give up all her previous libidinal workings; her oral, sadistic-anal, and phallic instincts, her desire to bear the mother's child or give her a child, and her infantile masturbation. That whole economy would in some way be blotted out, forgotten, repressed—but by whom or what? how? from what motives of pleasure or displeasure?—or "converted" so that "penis-envy" might thus be validated as the basis of female sexuality from now on.

---

1. In actual fact, these men and women analysts discuss the little girl's "desire" for the penis, which would suggest that she "discovers" her genitals long before Freud thinks. Cf. the articles of Horney, Klein and Jones on female sexuality.

"We know how children react to their first impressions of the absence of a penis. They disavow the fact and believe that they *do* [Freud's italics] see a penis all the same. They gloss over the contradiction between observation and pre-conception by telling themselves that the penis *is still small and will grow bigger presently*; and they then slowly come to the emotionally significant conclusion that after all the penis *had at least been there before and been taken away afterwards.* The lack of a penis is regarded as a result of castration, and so now the child is faced with the task of coming to terms with castration in relation *to himself.*"[1] Why are these feelings, these representations, these defenses, attributed *also* to the little girl? She is supposed to experience her lack of penis as an "accomplished fact" that is presumably a punishment for her earlier (phallic-viril-clitoral) masturbations.[2] She believes that "it had at least been there before." She would refuse the facts, telling herself that "the penis is still small and will grow bigger presently," hoping against hope that her(?) wish will some day come true. Etc. All of which is a postulate of the phallic imperialism that will also lead the little girl to "turn away from her mother" and despise herself and all women since all lack a penis. "We know, too, to what a degree *depreciation* of women, *horror* of women, and a *disposition to homosexuality* are derived from the final conviction that women have no penis."[3] Or again: "two reactions...permanently determine the boy's relation to women: horror of the mutilated creature or triumphant contempt for her."[4] Or: "One thing that is left over in men from the influence of the Oedipus complex is a certain amount of disparagement in their attitude toward women, whom they regard as being castrated."[5]

Mimesis Imposed

Why make the little girl, the woman, fear, envy, hope, hate, reject, etc. in more or less the *same terms* as the little boy, the man? And why does she comply so readily? Because she is suggestible? Hysterical? But now we begin to be aware of the vicious circle. How could she be otherwise, even in those perversities which she stoops to in order to "please" and to live up to the "femininity" expected of her? How could she be anything but suggestible and hysterical when her sexual instincts have been castrated, her sexual feelings, representatives, and representations forbidden? When the father forces her to accept that, while he alone can satisfy her and give her access to pleasure, he prefers the added sexual enjoyment to be derived from laying down the law, and therefore penalizes her for her (or his own?) "seduction fantasies"?

And anyway why would she not be "hysterical"? Since hysteria holds in reserve, in suspension/suffering, something in common with the mime that is a sine qua non of sexual pleasure. The problem is that the ludic mimicry, the fiction, the "make believe," the "let's pretend"—which, as we know, made the hysteric subject to all kinds of disbelief, oppression, and ridicule—are stopped

1. "The Infantile Genital Organisation," *SE*, 19:143 44.
2. "The Dissolution of the Oedipus Complex," *SE*, 19:177–79.
3. "The Infantile Genital Organisation," *SE* 19:144.
4. "Some Psychical Consequences of the Anatomical Distinction between the Sexes," *SE*, 19:252.
5. "Female Sexuality," *SE*, 21:229.

short, impeded, *controlled by a master-signifier*, the Phallus, and by its repre-
sentative(s). Emblem(s) not so much of interplay between the sexes as of power
that masters and appropriates the relationship to the origin (of desire, "for
example"). After that, the hysteria scenario, that privileged dramatization of
feminine sexuality, is condemned as so many "bad" copies or gross caricatures
of a "good," and valuable and valid, relationship to origin. Hysteria is stigma-
tized as a place where fantasies, ghosts, and shadows fester and must be
unmasked, interpreted, brought back to the reality of a repetition, a reproduction, a representation that is congruent to, consistent with, the original. And,
of course, someone will at this point cite the "initial trauma," the supposed origin of the "illness," but the game is all over by this time. And the question
would rather be–to risk repetition–that woman's symbolization of her beginning, of the specificity of her relationship to the origin, has always already
been erased, or is it repressed? by the economy that man seeks to put in place
in order to resolve the problem of his primary cause. A problem to be solved
by putting the Phallus at the beginning, and at the end. As the signifier of sexual potency and precedence, in the face of which there can only be "lack,"
"atrophy," "envy," "acting as if one had it," "pretending to be it or to have it,"
etc. But as the Phallus is never stated as *terminus, origin,* and *cause of desire,*
there will be no possibility of interplay between two different modes of relationship to the origin, the primary, the desire for origin. With each modality
comprising measure and folly. On the one hand the "serious role"–truth?–
played out in a genealogy, a genetics, and on the other hand, copies, fantasies,
reflections, semblances, specular anamorphoses, that will transform the part,
the parts, even before they are produced, or reproduced. Now, under these conditions, one might have a relationship between the sexes, an enactment of sexual difference–which obviously precludes the predominance of one sex.
But....Between the "obsessive' on this side, who wants and demands and
repeats, and turns around and around in his original desire, which he claims to
master in order, finally, to establish his omnipotence, and the "hysteric" on the
other side, who drifts aimlessly, wanting nothing, no longer knowing her own
mind or desire, acting "as if " or "as you like it," her body the only reminder
of what has been...the game seems to have got off to a bad start. At best a
mournful pleasure seems in store. Sadly repetitive, painstaking, or infinitely
fragmenting things, rambling on with pauses only for explosions. Pleasure (?)
full of histories but no possible historiography.

6

THE SIGNIFICANCE OF PENIS
ENVY IN WOMEN

Maria Torok

1

In every woman's analysis, there is inevitably a period in which appears a feeling of envy and covetousness for both the male sex organ and its symbolic equivalents. This penis envy may be simply episodic with some patients, but with others it can be central. The exacerbated desire to possess what women believe themselves deprived of by fate, or the mother, is an expression of a fundamental dissatisfaction which some people believe to be woman's lot. Indeed, the conviction that what they feel themselves deprived of is exactly what other people have is common to patients of both sexes and is found in all analyses. Jealousy and demand, spite and despair, inhibition and anxiety, admiration and idealization, inner void and depression: all these are among the varied symptoms of this state of deficiency. Yet it is interesting that only women relate this feeling of deficiency to the very nature of their sex: "It is because I am a woman." One must understand such a statement to mean: I do not have a penis; that accounts for my weakness, my inertia, my lack of intelligence, my dependent state or even my illnesses.

"All things considered, my predicament is common to all women, therefore I can only hold them in contempt, as I do myself." "It is they, the men, who command everything of value, all the attributes which render them worthy of being loved and admired."

Is such an extreme devaluation of one's own sex conceivable? Do its roots lie in a real biological inferiority? Freud felt finally compelled to accept the idea after he had vainly tried to remove this obstacle to treatment—the coveting of an object which is, by nature, unattainable. One would do better to go "preaching to the winds"—to quote Freud's own expression—than to wear oneself out on such a vain enterprise: making patients renounce once and for all their infantile desire to acquire a penis. Faced with so many failures, should one not, after all, resign oneself to allowing some legitimacy to penis envy and to ascribe it to the proper nature of things: "the biological inferiority of the feminine sex"? In considering another point of view, namely, the child's affective development, Freud arrived at the same conclusion. When he discovered an intermediate (the phallic) stage between the anal and the genital stages, he imagined it similar for both sexes, that is, entirely devoted to the penis. If it is true that only one sex, the male sex, is known to the child, one can understand the little girl's jealous spite at being deprived of it. All her theories concerning her castrated state and the overestimation of the other sex would find their origins here—due to a psychobiological "phallo-centrism" inherent in the phallic stage itself; that is why woman's penis envy, as well as the efforts to make her renounce it, can (in Freud's analytic perspective) only end in deadlock. But, if the theory of unisexuality at the phallic stage is constantly confirmed in the fantasies relating to this stage, it seems that this state of affairs could be given an accurate psychoanalytical explanation. Therefore, we must not concede our helplessness and rely on a biological explanation.

One can understand Freud's exasperation on being told: "What is the good of continuing the analysis if you cannot give me *that*." But one also can understand the patient's despair, when asked to *renounce* a desire which seems so dear to her. Freud would have been the first to agree that it is not part of an analyst's function to recommend giving up any desires whatever.

It is none the less true that in analysis, the woman's desire to have a penis (that is to say, to be a man) reveals itself as a subterfuge, because of its envious character. A desire can be satisfied, envy never can. Envy can bring about only more envy and destruction. Pseudo-desire, promulgated by envy, achieves a semblance of satisfaction, as shown in the phallic attitudes of some women, who are immersed in imitation of the other sex, or at least of the image they have of it. The fragile structure which they build shelters only feelings of inner void, anxiety, and frustration. The problem of analysis is precisely to bring back into the open the authentic but repressed desire which, disguised as envy, has remained hidden. Here, as with other fantasies, if one took the patient's protestations literally one would preclude analysis. A sure way of doing this would be to legitimatize woman's penis envy through accepting an alleged castration as her lot, for which phylogenesis would bear the responsibility. Another way just as certain of making analysis fail would be to attribute the desire to extra-analytical causes, such as the inferior sociocultural status of women.

For the analyst who dares face up to this impasse in treatment—namely penis envy—the first step is to clarify the nature of the conflict which produced such a desperate solution. He should not underestimate the advantages which it unfailingly provides, and he should utilize in treatment the painful contradictions in which it inevitably locks the patient.

Among post-Freudian authors, Jones and M. Klein distinguish themselves by no longer holding penis envy to be an irreducible problem. Indeed, both believe that the nature of the first relationship with the maternal breast is the determining factor. As soon as the analyst has improved this first relationship (by allaying the conflict caused by introjection of the part-object) envy in general and penis envy in particular lose their reason for existence.

In the light of what these authors say it is worthwhile emphasizing this: for the analyst the part-objects could simply be *indications* of conscious or unconscious fears or desires, in other words, reminders of those early circumstances which led the individual to establish them. For Freud the object as such and the human object as a whole are in the individual's economy *mediators* on the way to the goal of his instinctual drive: satisfaction. *Part-objects*, of course, have their real names and can be said to exist objectively in space. The fact that everyone can recognize them makes them ideal signposts for communicating and also for concealing desires. It is the analyst's job to probe beyond the objective appearance and unearth the desire it denies as it appears to fulfill it. Therefore, analysis of envied *things* like the penis or the breast (even if they be the analyst's) will exacerbate the contradictions which affect the part and whole objects instead of removing them. This results in the appearance (and at the same time concealment) of internal conflicts which are implied by the *satisfaction* of a vital desire. Fulfillment of the desire is independent of objective anatomical circumstance. It depends on the patient's capacity for satisfaction and on his conviction of the right to satisfaction; that is, on the freedom he has to establish relations to others through his body. The objective circumstances (generally not subject to modification) brought forth as objects of deficiency or as reasons for covetousness are in fact snares set up for treatment, in order to hide (and thereby maintain) the inhibitions accompanying these relationships, snares which often keep the desire covered up for life.

That is why the penis itself—considered as a thing, an objective, biological, or even sociocultural reality—must be left aside in this essay on penis envy. For the penis itself is not involved in penis envy, even if this at first seems paradoxical. This part-object turns out to be an *ad hoc* invention to camouflage a desire, like an obstacle blocking the path to a reunified self as it would emerge if the prohibition of inhibited acts were lifted. What is the purpose of this subterfuge and what does it protect the patient from? One must *understand* it before denouncing it.

However disguised, however hidden, the desire underlying penis envy cannot fail to show through. For this reason, this symptom, like all others, deserves our respect and attention. If our analytic work has reached the origins of penis envy and rendered it superfluous, it has done so only by exchanging a desire for a renunciation. Penis envy will disappear by itself the day the patient no longer has that painful feeling of deficiency which caused it.

II

If one agrees to abandon an object-oriented view of the envied penis—and to defer all questions concerning the sociocultural legitimacy of the envy—then one can undertake a truly psychoanalytical approach. Penis envy is the symptom, not of an illness, but of a certain state of unfulfilled desire—unfulfilled because of conflicting needs. Only an inquiry which disregards the object nature of the penis reveals the general significance of penis envy, the conflict which the symptom is trying to solve and the way it attempts to do this.

Freud believes that the little girl's visual discovery of the boy's sex organ was sufficient reason for her to envy it and, concomitantly, sufficient for her to hate her mother who (in the little girl's hypothesis) is responsible for her castrated state. Penis envy comes from experience, even when it is a pretext. But one problem still remains. At what ripe moment must this experience have taken place for the envy to last an entire lifetime? People only find what they are willing to find. "The polar bear and the whale...each one confined to his own surroundings...cannot meet," says Freud. If the moment was decisive it was not because of the difference between the boy and the girl but because of the similarity: in other words, because they both have a sex. One may suppose that the little girl's discovery of the boy's sex is part of the process of discovering her own little girl's sex. The discovery of the penis must have occurred at an important moment for it to have been more than a mere incident of early childhood. When the little girl thinks: "My mother didn't give me *that*, so I hate her," she is using a convenient pretext for expressing a hatred without explaining it.

The association of penis envy with conscious or unconscious hatred toward the mother is frequently observed. But there is another clinical fact, just as noticeable, which, if examined, will enable one to detect the deeper motives of this hatred. This fact, so constant in clinical experience and also so significant, could be called *penis idealization*. Many women have the fanciful idea that the male sex organ possesses supreme qualities: infinite power for good or evil, a guarantee of its possessor's security, absolute freedom, immunity against anxiety or guilt, and a promise of pleasure, love, and the fulfillment of all his wishes. *Penis envy is always envy of an idealized penis.*

> "When one has *it* (the penis)," says Ida, "one has everything, one feels protected, nothing can touch you...one is what one is, and the others can only follow you and admire you...it is absolute power. They (men) can never find themselves feeling need, or lacking love. Woman? She is incomplete, perpetually dependent, her role is of a Vestal Virgin guarding the torch. No matter how much they told me about the Virgin Mary...God the Father, he is a real man, 'Purity' makes me think of 'puke'...I have always had a certain contempt for women."

> "I don't know why I have this feeling," says Agnes, "as it corresponds to nothing in reality but it has always been like this for me. As though, only man was fit to fulfill himself, to have opinions, to mature, to go always further. And everything to him is so naturally easy...nothing, nothing can stop him...he is a force that can stop anything if he wants to. Me, I am getting nowhere, hesitating, there's a kind of wall in front of me....I always had the feeling I wasn't finished. Like a statue waiting for the sculptor to decide at last to model its *arms*...."

> A little girl, Yvonne, always thought that boys "could at once succeed in doing anything...they instantly speak all languages...they could go into a church and take all the candles and nobody would stop them. If ever they find something in the way, they would naturally jump over it."

These are eloquent descriptions of an *idealized* penis. It is obvious that this always means: "*the thing* whatever it is that one doesn't have oneself." Yet such a vital defect could not be a natural one, but could only be the effect of a deprivation or a renunciation. And then the question arises: Why is she deprived of such a precious part of herself, for the benefit of an external object, supposedly inaccessible, and, on the patient's own admission, definitely nonexistent? For the moment let us merely examine the fact. It has a name: repression. For all idealization there is a corresponding repression as a counterpart. But whom does the repression benefit? The Mother, of course, as is shown by the hatred addressed to her. Indeed, though the idealized penis has no actual existence, its counterparts, depression, self-devaluation, rage, have a very real existence. No one would believe that these affective states of such intensity could be due to an *idea* one has about an object one has once encountered. When the little girl says to the Mother within her: "I hate you because of this thing you haven't given me," she is also saying, "this is a legitimate hatred as is evident from my lack of this thing. But don't worry, I consider the real living hatred within me illegitimate because of the repression you imposed upon my desire."

What is this repression? It is not by chance that the penis, absent from the girl's anatomy, was chosen for the investment of those qualities which the patient must have deprived herself of: the sex organ one does not have represents perfectly that which is inaccessible, in that the sex organ can naturally not represent needs experienced in one's own body. In short, the choice of an inaccessible object for her envy shows that the patient's desire is blocked by an impassable barrier. The overinvestment of the envied thing testifies to the primordial value belonging to the abandoned desire. Women want to ignore the occasion responsible for repression: for them it is a persecutor with an anonymous face; and in order to identify it one would have to confront those obscure areas where hate and aggression are smoldering against the object one could not but love.

A complex, unconscious speech is concentrated in "penis envy," and this speech is addressed to the maternal imago. One could expound it by the following propositions:

1) "You see, it is in a *thing* and not in *myself* that I am looking for what I am deprived of."
2) "I am searching in *vain*, because this thing can never be mine. The obvious vanity of my search must be a guarantee of the definitive renunciation of those desires you disapproved in me."
3) "I shall insist on the value of this inaccessible *thing* so that you may realize the greatness of my sacrifice in letting myself be deprived of my desire."

4) "I should accuse you and, in turn, deprive you, but that is precisely what I want to avoid, deny, and ignore, because I need your love."

"In short, idealizing the penis, in order to envy it more, is reassuring you by showing you that this will never come between us, and that consequently I shall never be reunified, I shall never fulfill myself. I tell you, it would be just as impossible as changing bodies."

"Penis envy" marks this oath of fidelity.

When the little girl, in the speech to her imago, refers to the forbidden part of herself, which is the counterpart of the "penis," this can only be her own sex, condemned to repression.

An amazing statement! It seems to mean that the little girl's sex—as she experiences it—can be symbolized by the boy's penis-*thing*; in other words, by the penis regarded as an anal object. There is, in fact, some genetic link missing in the explanation of the symbolization and that is the anal relation to the Mother. The notion of "thing"—whether it be accessible or inaccessible, permitted or forbidden—clearly refers to this. It is to the Mother that the little girl is addressing her request: "That *thing*, I want it." Furthermore, the vanity of this request, in its formulation and in its meaning, implies a reassurance for the Mother; her privileges will be maintained. It is interesting that the authority, the mother's high-handedness, does not concern the "things" which belong to her as much as the very acts of mastering the sphincter; acts which she claims to command according to her whims. Because of this the child (and later, of course, the adult) has difficulty in assuming the responsibility for these acts without recourse to the imago. Such is the context for penis envy. One can now see that it is not the "thing" itself that the patient is coveting, but the acts which allow one to master "things" in general. Coveting a *thing* is precisely the same as demonstrating to the imago the renunciation of an *act*. During the anal relationship with his mother, the child surrendered his capacity for sphincter control to please his mother. This results in overwhelming aggression directed toward her. Let us assume that the following process takes place: the Mother's control of the sphincter can only be interpreted by the child as a manifestation of her interest in possessing the feces, even while they are still in the body. Consequently, *at the same time, the body's interior also comes under maternal control.* How can one free oneself from such sovereignty, other than by reversing the relation? This is when murderous fantasies—about disemboweling, evacuation of the Mother's insides, destruction of the seat and means of her control—take place.

This is why the Mother must be reassured. We now clearly understand that the covetousness attached to the inaccessible penis-thing plays this role to perfection.

But one must answer the ultimate question: What motivated this specific choice? Why was it precisely the "penis" that was chosen?

To press the question further we shall use a complementary way of examining the symptom; as well as trying to reconstruct its *retrospective* genesis, as we have done up till now, we shall consider another equally important dimension—its *prospective* one. This new explanation might in turn enlighten us further about the origins of the symptom.

By *prospective dimension* of a symptom or of the conflict which underlies it we mean the negative aspect of the symptom. This is not a solution to a problem, since it is determined by something still nonexistent or unachieved, that is, the step forward is prevented. Yet it is this prospective moment that gives repression its dynamic character. The obstructed stages of affective maturation are claiming their fulfillment. They are certainly present despite the repression that blocked them, but the prospective aspect of the symptom is not explicit in the speech to the imago. Indeed, the little girl could not, even unconsciously, address the following sentences to her imago: "I can tell you that I am coveting the penis-thing to appropriate it myself and become a boy, but I cannot even feel my aborted desire to *have pleasure with* the penis as women do, and which was *intended* in my sexual destiny." But it is precisely the fact of genital failure that gives us the clue to identifying the prohibitions responsible for the repression. The very experience which should have *prepared the way for the genital stage and its accompanying identifications* is only too clearly involved, and this experience is evidently connected with that "precious part" of oneself which has been repressed.

We have already shown that this "precious part" was the complex range of acts which had become the anal Mother's privilege. Yet the little girl possessed a means by which she could have indirectly recovered what she had been deprived of, namely *identification* with the Mother, sovereign of her powers. But one notices that penis envy testifies to a total lack of identification. To conclude, we are led to consider that not only the repression of anal-pregenital conflicts underlies penis envy, but also a specific, total or partial, inhibition of masturbation of orgasm, and of their concomitant fantasy activities. Penis envy appears now to be a disguised claim—not for the organ and the attributes of the other sex—but for one's *own desires for maturation and development by means of the encounter with oneself in conjunction with orgastic experience and sexual identification.* These seem to be the first conclusions one can draw about the general significance of "penis envy" considered as a *symptom* in the Freudian sense of this term.

III

M. Klein, E. Jones, K. Horney, and J. Müller long ago pointed out the early discovery of vaginal sensations and their repression. I myself have noticed that the encounter with the other sex was always a reminder, or occasioned the awakening, of one's own sex. Clinically, penis envy and discovery of the boy's sex are often associated with the repressed memory of orgastic experiences.

> During several sessions Martha has violent bursts of crying or laughing. Slowly, her emotions regain a meaning; when a little girl, she met some boys in the swimming pool. Since then she often repeats the same phrase: "I can-

not live like *this*."

It was this phrase which came up, during her analysis, in moments of deep depression. Consciously, "this" means "being deprived of a penis." But we must also understand that, on that occasion, she "squeezed her thighs together," "rolled up a little bit of swimsuit inside" and felt a kind of "sensitive shiver." The laughter mixed with tears (mingled joy and guilt) reflected her idea: if I am made "this" way (feeling this shiver) then, "at home, will they want me?" At puberty, this same patient had such a feeling of guilt toward her mother that she kept her periods—the sign of her genital maturity—a secret from her mother for a whole year.

Her own sexuality, far from being ignored, was a constant, but latent, preoccupation; in those days, the need to please her mother was greater than orgastic pleasure. During the sessions she expressed the desire for an orgasm, through the fits of laughter, but repressed it through penis envy itself. First of all there had been "an indescribable joy," "an immense hope." Then, she does not know why, she was convinced that "something infinitely desirable exists, not in me but over there, not in my body but in an *object*, an absolutely inaccessible object." One can see the contradiction: the "sensitive shiver of infinite goodness" makes the little girl lose her feeling of *being good* for the sake of her family. The penis is then felt, as we shall see, to be the "good" sex which gives the possessor pleasure without guilt; this pleasure is not tied up with masturbatory or internalized guilt. It has all the conditions of a perfect harmony: pleasure for oneself and harmony with others. Feeling the "shiver" is aggressive, wicked to others. So all that is "good" is abandoned and an external object substituted— the idealized penis. The void thus created in the patient is filled by sadness, bitterness, jealousy. But this smoldering aggression can never be a substitute for what she has missed, the growing and voluptuous awakenings of maturity. Only analysis can arouse those feelings by loosening up machinery, as it were.

This joy of awakening maturity goes beyond immediate satisfaction. To the patient it means a sudden opening up of the future. That is when the time of great discoveries comes, the "Ah! I understand!" "So this is how I become myself, adult; I find my worth through the joy I experience in becoming *myself*." (J. Müller points out that freedom of infantile sexuality guarantees self-esteem.) Indeed, the orgastic joys of infancy are the true means by which genital sexuality, and through it the unfolding personality, are prepared and molded. What does the patient discover while developing the ability to have an orgasm? The possibility of identifying with the parents in fantasy and of imagining herself in all the different positions of the *primal scene* according to the moment at which it is considered. *The orgasm, once achieved, has the value of confirmation: the fantasy is valid because it has brought about sensual pleasure.* One realizes that any inhibition regarding such an encounter with herself leaves the patient with a blank in place of an identification, however vital it is for her. The result is an unfulfilled body-self (some would say body–image) and, correspondingly, a world of fragmented reality.[1]

1. Indeed, masturbation could appear later on with different fantasy content, but what has been repressed earlier leaves its negative mark on all future personality development.

Certain dreams remind us of the importance of those openings up of the future which give orgastic experiences their meaning:

> Agnes remembers her early orgastic experiences together with emotions accompanying them. First there is a dream of "inexpressible joy," turning into depression. Beside the sea. She is waiting. An excited crowd gathers around her (this refers to the waiting for an orgasm). Behind her there is a toilet (a reminder of a masturbation scene). She is seated. Suddenly a marvelous animal, soft and silky to stroke, settles on her taut skirt. She inhales deeply, stretches out her arms and strokes it. In admiration, the whole crowd vibrates with her. Everything was "so full," "so wonderful." This moment, she says, *was a concentration of everything, all I have been, everything I shall be.* Like saying to oneself: I want to be in a lovely country, I have an immense desire for it, and I've no sooner said it than I'm there.

So, the repressed fantasy, as the dream shows, involves the incorporation of the penis in its function as the agent of instinctual drive and as the *generator of orgasm.* This same patient thought her body was unfinished and wished a sculptor would come and "make her *arms.*" She could only make very limited use of her hands, tied up in masturbation's fundamental fantasy function of being a *penis for the vagina.*

Ferenczi has shown that masturbation goes with a duality in the individual: he identifies simultaneously with both partners and achieves copulation in an autistic manner. One must add that this duality, the "touching oneself," the experience of "I-myself," authenticated by the orgasm, also suggests: "As I can do it to myself, alone, I am emancipated from those who have hitherto permitted or forbidden me this pleasure according to their whim." Masturbation, literally touching oneself, and reflective fantasy free the child from maternal dependence and at the same time establish an autonomous maternal imago, that is to say, one which can find its pleasure somewhere other than with the child, a possibility missing when the mother forbids masturbation. Such an imago is rooted in excessive or premature anal training and would influence all similar activities. A mother who is too exacting will cause a jealous, empty, unsatisfied maternal imago. How could she manage by herself if only mastery of the child can give her satisfaction? How could she not be jealous or suspicious if the child frees herself from her while growing to maturity? The ban on masturbation has the effect of tying the child to his mother's body and interfering with his essential growth. Patients often express this situation by saying, "some part of my body (hand, penis, feces) is still in my mother, but how can I get it back? She needs it so much! It is her only pleasure."

The hand "belonging to the Mother" can only symbolize for the patient what the mother herself forbids; this hand will never represent the penis.[1] The path leading to the father is thus blocked, and the dependent relation with the Mother perpetuates itself. The little girl will experience this insoluble dilemma: identifying with a dangerously aggressive mother who needs to be

---

1. It is worth noting that the hand as a means for the introjection of the primal scene always represents the genital organ of the opposite sex.

completed by having or being the useless appendage of an incomplete body (namely, that of the child). The patient might repeat the two possibilities in relation to her husband. But analysis is there precisely to help her break the magic circle of "being" and "having." It will certainly not provide an appendage-penis; the "arms" Agnes has just recovered are equivalent to a complementary penis, which represents something beyond being and having, *the right to act and to become.* When the envy of an appendage-penis is not any longer hiding the desire for a complementary one, then the father's approach need no longer be blocked by the feeling that she has a body which is dangerous for the penis. This also means that masturbation, and identifications, are no longer felt as destructive to the Mother.

The removal of orgastic inhibition during analysis is always accompanied by a feeling of power. A woman's analysis could not possibly bring her to general maturity without solving penis envy, which conceals the masturbatory and the anal conflicts underlying it. For example, it is impossible that penis envy could be resolved as a desire to have a child by the father. Indeed, if the child has to play the part of a converted penis-object and supply the completion lacking up till then, how can her maturity be accepted, the fulfillment of her ambitions wished for and encouraged by a mother who, without her, would lapse into bitterness and envy! Such a mother has in the girl's fantasy only one wish: to keep the child-penis (an illusory guarantee of her own completeness) eternally in the role of an appendage.

Inasmuch as penis envy represses *pregenital* anxieties, it completely blocks genital fulfillment. The path from penis envy to genital fulfillment necessarily passes through an intermediary stage: the fantasy of *having pleasure with the father's penis.* Once this fantasy is allowed, the "desire to have a child" by the father will no longer mean what one actually *has* or receives, but will mean what is a natural part of growing up.

IV

Arrested in the process of her genital fulfillment, the woman who suffers from penis envy lives with a feeling of frustration, the nature of which she cannot guess. She has only a vague idea of what genital orgastic completion is. At any rate she cannot achieve it while the repression continues.

We have seen that the symptom consists of idealizing the penis, investing it with all she has lost hope of her herself: her aim in life, genital maturity. This is what the child has to achieve because she does not have it yet. Indeed, the desire is eternal; it never goes away, but it is either without content or fixed on stereotyped images. The greatest desire of a woman who suffers from penis envy is to meet the male in full orgastic union, and to realize herself in an authentic act, but this is what she has to avoid most. Clinicians often see women trying to obtain the complementary penis, the instrument of their fulfillment, at the cost of having to struggle with a threatening jealous imago. Then envy for the idealized penis and hatred toward its possessor arise. From then on deception will prevail over love, frustration over ample gratification.

During analysis the shift to what is usually called the genital stage is always like this: I am no longer "castrated" because "I can." This means, first of all, the disinhibition of masturbatory gestures and fantasies, otherwise the analysis will not progress. If repression means that something is missing in the ego which limits one's capacities, then freeing the repression will bring a sense of power, self-esteem and, especially, *faith* in one's own possibilities and future development.

> "I don't know how I can tell you," says Olga, "what impression your words had on me. I can't get over it. ...It is as though you had *transferred a power* to me. Yet, I was very depressed the other day. But after going out of here, I repeated to myself everything you said. And all that anxiety melted away! I have rarely cried as much as I have this week....It is like a sudden light....And last night I...no, I've never mentioned those things to anybody. Briefly, it was like *waking up*. I had some pleasure....Now I want to try myself out and I keep smiling at all the men, and you know, they answer me very kindly. And, I can't get over it, people have paid me compliments!"

During the last session, we had realized how, by means of idealization, she was forbidding herself a gratification within her reach and how, in fact, this prohibition referred to the maternal interdiction against having anything to do with her father's virility. The dismissal of the prohibiting imago revealed the knot of the problem—masturbation. At a later session Olga arrives with "*one* very cold hand," as if it did not belong to her. She mentions all the objects her mother forbade her to touch, particularly her own genitals. This "very cold" hand was nothing but a manifestation of her obedience to the forbidding maternal imago.

Recognizing that the idealization of the penis comes from the repression of masturbation is equal to liberating energy and, as we can see, easily confers new possibilities to one's own sex. These are the ones of which the child was deprived and which are now recovered, the possibility of identifying with the protagonists of the primal scene, at each of its stages, and of verifying the validity of such identifications by the orgasmic pleasure obtained through them.[1,2]

1. This is so true that the identification with the castrator, the one who forbids "autoeroticism," is necessarily part of a masturbatory fantasy. Without this identification, however paradoxical or neurotic it might seem, the interdiction is experienced as a true castration and is manifested by inability to do anything and by extreme tension. The psychotic autocastration has no meaning other than that of trying, in desperation, a paralyzing identification in order to remove an inhibition which is just as deadly.
2. There are two ways of compromising the child's maturing identifications. First, to forbid the orgasm which would confirm the validity of his efforts to fulfill himself. 2d, to suppress the fantasy by substituting an objective reality for it (seduction). In this case the fantasy identification is stopped by an effective but premature achievement, and the mutilating effects of inhibition which result from this trauma are similar to those of the other stringency. That is why people who are inhibited about masturbation have fantasies to the extent of mythomania about scenes of rape, and these "precociously ravished" women behave in exactly the same way as those who are inhibited about orgasms.

To give the reader a more concrete idea of these theories it will be helpful to read a brief sequence from analytical treatment (about twenty sessions). Ida, a young woman of Hungarian origin, had sought analytical help because of numerous professional difficulties and emotional problems:

> It gave me a shock to see Jacques doing the dishes. I was ashamed as though somebody had exposed a hidden part of my body. I am incapable of doing needlework, repairing, sewing....I'm ashamed to have a woman's body. I am ashamed to see Jacques becoming...how can I put it?...a woman. Of course, this doesn't mean that he is...but why was it so worrying? *Maybe because, for you, "woman" doesn't have the usual meaning. To be a "woman," for you, means to be "without a sex."* I don't know. I am very muddled. Why did I think that with a torch (name given to the penis) one had everything, that everything was lovely? Why have I given this great power to men? Are they really like that? No, of course, they aren't like that! *At least, if they are as you described them to be for you, I can understand your envy of the torch.* Jacques isn't like that, neither is my father, grandfather, or anybody. It was my own idea. For my mother, women were enemies. Oliver wasn't. Oliver, my brother, could be a friend. He could say to men: this is my mother, she is wonderful. She herself, she was abandoned by her own mother. She thought children were born through the navel. It is exactly as we said last year: the child didn't give her a "lower body." For me a child is all the life of "down there," it is all one has down there, all that can grow from down there. Then she had jaundice, my mother. Deep down, I must have been like her. (This is a reminder of a dream in which she gives birth to a yellowy-orange child.) In fact, I must have been like an enemy for her. But I was also a friend....Why did she say to me, "You will never be as beautiful, nor as delicate, nor as sensitive as Susan?" She never protected me, she has never been a support for me. I have never had anything for myself. I have never kept anything. I have always given all my things away.

It is obvious that for Ida "woman" means "castrated." Trying to castrate men is justified by the desire to acquire the unique sex, the male sex, with all its advantages. In such an interpretation one tries to acknowledge two things: (1) the idealized character of the desired penis; (2) the subjective character of this idealization.

Having recognized that she herself was the source of the meaning "woman" and "penis" had for her, and having realized that these were not absolute, unshakable meanings, Ida can now go beyond them toward their origin—"my mother." "It is because my mother lives like that in me that 'woman' must mean for me 'castrated,' without a lower body, 'monstrous,' and I must envy and idealize the penis." Uncompleted, empty, frustrated, the Mother has devalued her and castrated her in the sense of depriving her of her future fulfillment. That is why, she realizes, she can keep nothing for herself:

> Poor mummy, she feels very let down. She believes that now I shall only look after my baby. I dreamed of a snake. He came out of my breasts and could have bitten other people. The midwife told me the baby was ready to come

out. Poor mummy. She telephoned today, but it was to speak to Jacques. She must be very lonely. In the children's home there were only girls. Then this kind doctor, that nice old man. I liked him a lot. He gave me injections. At school there were always boys, too. My mother never sent me to school on time. I always had to wait around before leaving and stay longer with her. She always wanted to prolong the holidays too. She didn't like school. Yet school is strength, authority, regularity, security. I like school. (Ida has serious inhibitions about continuing her university studies.)

Ida continues to understand further the significance of her relation to her mother. She can now see that if she has her baby, mummy will become "impoverished." Daughter and mother are indissolubly tied together; one complements the other's emptiness.

The equivalence between the snake-baby which bites and that nice old doctor who injects is that they are pleasure-objects for Ida, which means that they are dangerous for the Mother. Thanks to these pleasure-objects she will be able, as she knows, to free herself. This is why she thinks her mother stops her from coming into contact with that "strength," "that authority," which school represents. Ida arrives late at her sessions for the same reason. The "empty" Mother, "with no lower body," needs to keep Ida near her in order to fill up her emptiness, with Ida as a pleasure-object *for herself.* In short, whether to be autonomous and have pleasure *with* the penis or to be the appendage of the Mother—that is the dilemma. If I have pleasure, my mother becomes empty; that is unbearable for me.

I dreamed that we were asking my mother for a little dog. Not me, my husband. When I was little, I liked to keep back my pee. The old ironing lady would send me off to the bathroom when she saw me hopping from one leg to the other. That's odd, after having made love I also go straight to the bathroom....People always made me believe that woman had nothing. Nothing but a hole out of which things come. They must retain nothing. That little bear makes me laugh. I bought it for the baby, but for the time being I am keeping it for myself. I am as tight as a virgin, I can't put the dutch cap on right. It bleeds, it falls into the john. I'll pay you today.

There is something to claim from the Mother: the liberty to retain the "pee" in one's body, to play and have pleasure with it. Talking about all this is a start for the dissolution of that depressing tie with the Mother. Ida must reassure her mother—she is not trying to empty her; on the contrary, she is paying her; anyway it is so tight in there that she could not retain anything even if she wanted to. "There is no question of my satisfying myself alone, there is no danger for you, you can keep me as an appendage." In this case, to be able to retain means that one can have pleasure by oneself and, thereby, become independent. We also notice that Ida's own "lower body" begins to come up in her talks.

Now, in giving birth, I had great difficulty in getting the child out. Then sud-

denly I thought of all the things we have said here, I called you very loudly, very loudly, and then it was over, the anxiety had dissipated. I came late
because of my cooking. And you know, I've left my work. I said to myself,
suddenly, "I'm a real woman." *A real woman? What is that, for you?* Oh a
few dresses, a hairdo, five minutes rest from time to time, a well-made
boeuf bourguignon. But you are right, there is something odd. I saw Jacques
at his desk, he was writing. I wanted to do the same. I was kind of...jealous.
My studies...they are still part of my anxiety. I still have mountains to climb.
(This is a reminder of a dream in which she was climbing a mountain with
her mother. Down below there is an abyss, "it's terrible," it is a box filled by
a crab, a huge red crab.) My mother in that kitchen...terrible. That day I had
two mothers, that was my impression—one like the everyday one, smiling,
talking, doing hundreds of things; the other, that unknown woman, that
intangible woman who's absurd. (This refers to a scene in the kitchen. Her
mother had one day wounded her father during an argument in the
kitchen.) I remember, I dreamed there was a shop, a haberdasher's, and they
sold buttons there. I wanted a sewing box.

Ida is reassuring me that I am good for her; thanks to me she was able to
get her child out. No danger of her asserting herself in independence. But will
I allow her another pleasure, the real one, the one precisely which the Mother
forbids—study? There can be no question of it. She asserts that now she feels
a "real woman"—in other words, a real, castrated person. But that is safer
than freeing herself from Mother. Hurt, incomplete, the Mother would
become dangerous, as in that scene in the kitchen. Besides, to renounce one's
own completeness (as when Ida pretends to be a "real woman") carries the
same danger: the aggression of dissatisfaction. The only way out is total
inhibition. To study, to retain, like "keeping in pee" or having pleasure in
intercourse, are all forbidden. The empty Mother holds on to Ida, she stops
her from going away, from going toward that "strength."

It is impossible to arrive on time. I'm always arriving late. *Like at school.* I
felt you were angry the other day. Now I can handle the baby well. When
my mother didn't send me to school, I wasn't pleased, I wanted to get angry,
but then in the end I acquiesced. I'm worried by the idea of starting my
studies again. You mentioned that mountain dream. I was with my mother.
I was behind her, very frightened. It was horrible down below. *Like everything that happens "down below."* Then I was also very frightened of falling.
Oh, last night, I had a dream. I am in the sand, or something clayey. It's
growing hollow, I'm sinking into it more and more. I had this impression that
in order to save myself I was supposed to make certain gestures, certain
movements. I was supposed to let myself go and not resist...do some, I don't
know what...particular gestures. On the edge of a hole—an indeterminate
man, I couldn't see his face, I didn't know who he was. An indifferent person, neutral (the analyst). I had the impression he would try to save me, also
that he was incapable, and that he could do nothing for me. And I sank in
more and more, still trying to recall those gestures—I absolutely *had* to

remember them! But, really, in the end, it wasn't as bad as all that. I believed it would save me, in spite of everything. I don't know any more, I don't know any more. It was like when I gave birth.

The memory of the "mountain dream" (she is on the summit with her mother; there is an abyss and a crab down below) reminds her now of another, more recent, dream. This time she is "down below" with a man, in the abyss itself: she now dares explore it. She goes into it (like a baby in her body). She is able now to identify herself with the penis that penetrates her. She is reassured—it was not in danger—and even experienced orgastic pleasure. To penetrate oneself, to allow oneself to be attracted "inside," as in a masturbatory duality, means already to envisage intercourse with a man, and thereby to emancipate oneself from the "summit of the mountain," from the relationship to the Mother which made the "down below" like an "abyss of crabs." The orgastic aspect of the dream will be more explicit in a following session. "It was like giving birth," when the child separates itself from the Mother. This separation occurs by means of an orgasm by intromission. At this stage Ida can give up being the doll she was for her mother and can deal with a new problem, the genital relationship:

> I have a terrific panic when Jacques holds me! I thought about your interior corridor. I have been to see the gynecologist. This time I wasn't afraid at all. I was quite at ease. When Jacques holds me I can't free myself, I stamp my feet. I can't bear it that someone wants to tie me down. Yet, when he caresses me, I like it, but I have a terrific panic. Then, I think of something else (his home town, where his mother is still living). I was ugly in my childhood. It was because I wanted to be so. I would say to myself: I shall start by will, through really hard work. I became fat with eating so much bread all the time. That pleasure was allowed. *Instead of another one, forbidden?* (Ida laughs.) Yes, I understand what you mean. In fact, you mean that I am just as afraid of you as I am of Jacques. Perhaps that is why I always arrive late.

The mother is now endowed with an "interior corridor"—her body is no longer empty. In turn, Ida can now speak of her own inside. The woman "with no lower body" no longer threatens to tie her to herself. Ida is now attempting to formulate in the transference her panic in the face of sexual intercourse:

> For my mother I was like a doll she could dress. I am ashamed at the idea of having wandered naked in my father's country. Jacques, like you, tells me that I am running away from him. Though he is very kind, I do go into fits with him....I left him and went to sleep on the carpet. He rejoined me and we both slept on the carpet in the end. I am looking at the things that are here. When I was little I couldn't stay still in my bed. I thought it was boring. I would look at the things in the room for a long, long time....For my mother, yes it is very odd....I was her doll. Sometimes she wanted me to be her mother. When I am with her I disappear, I cannot exist as me. She insists that I look after her, only her. She phoned me, I said that I was ill, tired, that I had metritis. When I come

to think of it, my baby is a very curious thing. He could nearly fit into a basket. Babies are funny things. Now I can handle the dutch cap very well, but I am a bit frightened. I told Jacques that it was bleeding...*and that it was no good inside.* I had a dream last night. Oh...I am not going to tell you this dream. I am going to keep you in suspense, I am going to make you wait for nothing. It was at the Galeries Lafayette. We were there with Jacques to buy some curtains. We were on the fifth floor. Then suddenly, something was burning, there was fire, smoke. Jacques climbed up to the sixth floor. It was safer to go up than down. One day he really played the role of a fireman in a house on fire. A friend said to me: I am embarrassed when I make love. I made several hypotheses about why he had gone up. I had stayed on the floor below. And I fainted. It was exactly the same impression as when I was sinking into the sand in that other dream. Why did I have this dream? Sometimes Jacques puts his tongue out at me and it is horrible. (We analyze a problem related to fellatio.) It feels good to have talked about that. You are not afraid of fire.

"It was the same impression." But no longer the same symbol. If in the dream about the "abyss" Ida enters into her own inside, in the dream about the "fire," she sees the possibility of putting the man's tongue (as a penis) inside her, and she is not afraid of fire (torch: name given to the penis in her childhood), just as the analyst, representing here the paternal imago, is not afraid of Ida's "internal fire."

I am not going to stay with you, I am going to leave! By the way I have found out how to get a reduction in my rail fare. *A reduction of me. So that nothing can go from me into you. People have always told you to take nothing from daddy!* I had a dream. There was Brigitte Bardot and me; I got angry like a child, I stamped my feet on the ground: I want it, I want it! It was about a dress. I am thinking of my father on the beach. There was something in his pants, and it was because of that I wasn't allowed to play with him. *Not allowed to have a BB[1] in your pants either?* Oh, something happened to me....I bought a bird and I brought it home. Soon after it was dead. It was terrible. Yes, at the beach I thought: in order to play with him he would have not to have that in his pants. I was told, when there was a question of my parents divorcing, that he might take me away and therefore I had to be hidden at my grandparent's home: they would protect me. That bird, that poor little bird, and I wanted to make a nice warm nest for it. *You wanted so much to nest the "bird" warmly in you. But you feel that in you it would not be comfortable. So it is better to go away rather than to come near it. Haven't you been told to keep away from Daddy? Perhaps meeting him represented some danger for you and for him?*

But the maternal interdiction manifests itself when the desire becomes explicit: "There is no question of your having a BB." So Ida "reduces" the father's penis in order to render it ineffectual. Thus, she shelters herself from the desire to take hold of it and put it into herself. The idea of danger and

---

1. BB means at the same time Brigitte Bardot and "baby" in French. (Tr. note.).

the idea of the forbidding Mother appear simultaneously. The interpretation turns on this development.

> I went home to my mother's. I was ill. I vomited. My mother has never want-ed to teach me the secrets of cooking. She hardly allowed me to chop up the onion and the parsley. Chop and cut, nothing else. Never real cooking, I mean cooking as an art. *Just as she didn't teach you the art of approach-ing your father.* I had a dream last night. It was like a film. And also like going to the office. Tiring yet at the same time agreeable. There was some-thing like an arena....The lion was supposed to be inside, but, in fact, he was outside. He was running all around the arena....I was with a friend and I asked him to protect me. I was beside him and we were running too. The lion was running in the same direction as us. He was like a man. How odd. I turned round and saw that he was doing leaps like a dancer, he was doing the splits in the air....I went and presented myself for my nomination. It is annoying to speak in front of fifty people. I did it. How much do I owe you for this month? I was in a funk when I was there, I didn't dare speak. I would like to tell you something...you know I have always thought that it was all dead in me, quite dead. And then, now, I felt something...that my vagina was sensitive. It's staggering. I felt that I could have some pleasure! Before, I was very frightened. Now "it" is coming. I can no longer be afraid. Yes. I can feel that it is going to come. That it's already there. I don't know. I never speak about it with Jacques. I have the feeling he's frightened. If we can't resolve this, he will have to go into analysis. That's odd, I am speaking to you as though you weren't there. It's a bit as though I had nothing to say. *Perhaps you think that your pleasure frightens me?* I don't know why, but I suddenly thought of daddy and mummy, and the Germans. Mummy wasn't pleased when he came to see me. She was jealous. And it was as though something could happen when daddy held me by the hand. People were hostile. Yet he was handsome. But everyone knew they were divorcing. I also thought that I could have been born from a mother and a father who were apart....Then I was afraid that something would happen to mummy. That she would be unhappy. I feel happy....I was terribly worried she would have some sort of attitude towards me. I imagine her angry, screaming, saying unbearable things, like she did with daddy. I would have done anything to avoid that. She had never been as happy as when I was at boarding school. But nowa-days I don't know, I don't bear her a grudge anymore. Sometimes, lately, I have been full of hatred. It's diminishing now. I think I am not responsible for them. I am thinking of something silly: I have a lovely baby and you, you haven't got one. Maybe it's not true, after all I don't know. But that's how I feel and...I feel sorry for you. It's silly. I want to know how much I owe you? *For the baby?* (Ida laughs.) No, I didn't mean it that way. That's odd, it is as though I had pleasure in depriving you. These things are silly...

Having named the obstacle, the desire for *incorporation* can now be for-mulated. The complex symbol of the "lion" (man-eating man) condenses the image of the penis (pleasure-object) and the gestures of man and woman in intercourse (the "leaps" and the "splits"). The desire to have an orgasm by introducing the penis shows that she is seeking integration (the lion is running after her), but that she cannot yet accept it entirely: the lion stayed "outside." The desire to have pleasure *with* the penis becomes more precise, but Ida is frightened at the idea of feeling the orgastic sensations mentioned in the previous session. They imply a break of the tie to the mother. Frustrated, hurt, would the Mother in turn hurt the daughter, as she hurt the Father? Nevertheless, the mere fact of foreseeing the possibility of orgastic pleasure allows Ida to envisage resuming her previously inhibited professional activity.

> I am becoming insomniac. I haven't slept all night. As though I had something better to do than sleep. Yet I dreamed. Beside a swimming pool there was something like a brothel. A woman was there, a prostitute, quite sympathetic, not mean at all. It was very hot. I wanted very much to have a swim. She didn't want to. Finally, she agreed. Then there were four men, it was horrible, they wanted me to be...like a call girl. I was terrified, we left. Then I was in the train. I said: you must help me, there are some people who want to do terrible things to me. In such circumstances I am very efficient: I spoke to a soldier, to tell him that it was his civic duty to help me. He gave me a telephone number. I seem to remember that I failed in the end. Oh! I am so tired, I can hardly distinguish things around me. How much do I owe you? My husband told me that I was intelligent. It was nice, because it was as though someone had reassured me from outside. I don't know why I think women are worth nothing. And it is always men who are in command of everything, who do everything. Oh! My finger is cut. It bled all day yesterday. I can't imagine how I came to cut it! With a knife? It bled so much! Why? How did I do this to myself? Oh, I'm tired! And also I didn't feel at all like getting ready, like dressing myself. But how much do I owe you for this month, I never know, oh what a bore! *For the moment, you think you owe me a finger for the pleasure you took in your inside.* On the beach, in my country, I was always alone. The other children had their parents, I was alone, always. *Are you sure?* Ah, not that time, you are right....Oh, but in the dream, it was the same beach as the one where I saw daddy.

Because of her guilt, Ida is trying to cancel the previous progress. "You see," she says to me, "I have put nothing inside, I have done nothing, anyway women have nothing, they have no 'lower body,' you have nothing to worry about, I will still be your doll." The equivalence is between the finger and the penis. Her finger, how did she cut it? She is sure the Mother is responsible for this. Isn't it she who stopped Ida from putting her finger-penis into herself and thus stopped her from becoming independent? But as this "finger" (her pleasure-object) is kept by the Mother, inasmuch as she cuts it off, Ida already expresses, even though in a self-punishing way, her desire to break the tie of belonging to her mother.

> Last night I dreamed that daddy was dead. We were at C...Really I haven't

had any letters from my parents for some time. Daddy's death would explain their silence. He was in a car. Mummy was with him. As they drew up in front of the memorial to the dead, he wasn't feeling well. He had difficulty in driving. Mummy had to ask for a light from another man. That was a sign that things weren't going well. I thought to myself: he should be careful. Then he was dead. It was his heart. There was nothing sad. An emotion just similar to the one I had when my grandmother died. A strong but irrelevant emotion. In any case with no link to anything I could understand. It was more like a feeling of shame. Then, in the dream, I had to leave town. I was with my mother. I wanted to leave but she wouldn't let me. Always the same blackmailing, the same fits of hysteria...I thought of mummy and I said to myself: he must have suffered a lot but now no more problems. No more worries about the person who is dead. I am less and less afraid of death. I've started work again, and reading and thinking...that is important. Then I went to this meeting. I felt like talking at it but I didn't do it. I am still waiting for my nomination. That would give me time for my studies. My father, poor thing, he was always threatened by my mother, always in danger of being abandoned. I also dreamed that there were fires everywhere: left, right, below, above, in front, behind. Very strange.

She is making the father "die" and in doing so separating the "Mother's fire" from the Mother. But this father is also Ida who herself suffered, like him, from pressures and threats of abandonment. Ida's desire is becoming more precise: to withdraw from the Mother, but gaining autonomous erotic pleasure of the Oedipal relationship. Yet guilt regains its importance, and in the second half of the dream Ida has become once again complementary to the Mother. Nevertheless, her fear of breaking away is diminishing. She can envisage taking up her activities again and invests all the space around, that is to say, all her body, with "fire" ("fire is life").

I am late again. Yesterday we had our wedding anniversary. I gave Jacques a pipe. Last year I hardly told you about my wedding, I had to hide it from you, to steal it from you in some sense. I am very pleased. It is no longer as before, but there is still a lot to do. And I was always waiting for you to make my decisions for me. Now I decide by myself. I had a funny dream last night. At home there was a sort of political meeting. Something suspect. My husband was in the house opposite. I wanted to comb my hair and I looked for a mirror. I arrived in the bathroom and horror! I noticed...I saw my skull! On it there were still a few hairs...like a brush...a few bristles. The hairs on the neck had been saved, they were falling, as if burned. It was horrible, hideous....I called for help: Do something fast! "Yes, they told me, it's a serious illness, you must treat it." Then I went to see my husband....I told him there was great danger, a terrible catastrophe, but he wouldn't understand....When I was ten I used to imagine what would happen if they were to die and I were to become an orphan. I still want to have parents....I saw an old friend in my dream, and I kissed her very warmly. There are a lot of hidden things in my relations with women. I'm glad to think that fire doesn't frighten you, that means I will be able to live. I have made this discovery—people don't really live. They are extinct. My husband is a smoldering fire. I have great confidence in him. I would like to say that I am happy but I immediately become afraid of a catastrophe.

"To comb oneself," "to touch oneself," that is to say to masturbate, means to be in danger. The meaning of the dream becomes clearer later on: Ida is trying to remember a scene. Masturbation implies the desire of freeing herself through the death of her parents. The "reunion" means that by touching herself she can achieve a reunion of the self with the self, like the parents who unite in the sexual act.

I have a friend who said to me one day: You know, you're slow to start, but once you've started, you charge. I dreamed of a locomotive and a child threatened by kidnappers. The train was between the beach and the swimmers. One had to cross the rails. I'm thinking of a lion who bit the arm of the person who was stroking him....I'm afraid of Jacques. I have always been very clumsy with my hands. When I sew, I prick myself; I cut my fingers. By the way how much do I owe you? *By the way of what?* I don't know, I can never calculate a debt. I would prefer you to tell me. I don't like handling money. It was my mother's privilege. She was in charge of the cash. Money, to open the drawer, touch it...for me would be like touching fire! *The torch?* (Ida laughs). That's odd. It pleases me to think that last time, when I didn't come, you waited for me. Perhaps you waited for me from one minute to the next; since the whole hour is mine it's my session. Nobody can come in my place. And that you...that you thought of me. But when I will be cured...I mean when everything will be going well, when I have started my work and my studies again, what will become of you? *My cash-box will be empty? My room will be empty?* By the way, my husband gave your address to someone. Because he thinks you are good and that's rare. I don't know what I think about it. *That it will fill the gap? Comfort me?* I don't know. It's the first time in my life that I have something which is really my own.

If autonomy, the definition and elaboration of oneself, occurs in the self-experience of masturbation then this contact may fall within that store of deep guilt associated with anal characteristics. It is the Mother's privilege to handle the "cash-box," to fill it up, empty it. Ida is trying to restore to the Mother the power she once usurped with her own fingers. By this act she gives herself up to the Mother, and becomes once again the manipulated object.

Monstrous. What do you think of someone who kisses her baby on the mouth? I thought, I must tell you immediately. It's like when one is condemned, I mean in my dream. There was a dried-up water course with big worms in it. You were supposed to eat them or was it that when you ate them you died? It was at my grandparents. Impression of horror. Big, big worms. It reminded me of that mashed meat I left in a plastic pot; then it rotted and there were worms in it. I was in the classical position of a woman who doesn't want to show her fear. My husband, just as disgusted as I was, was pretending to be courageous. At last I regained composure. I put the little box in a big one and went and put it in the rubbish bin. I nearly fainted. I was determined to show that I was courageous. And then, it's silly, just think, I interpreted this dream. I don't know anything about psychoanalysis and I didn't think, it came spontaneously. Well, I interpreted. I thought that I must be frightened that during sexual intercourse people could die. You know it does happen, the newspapers..., well, I don't know who, a president or someone died that way. It's silly to want to interpret one's own dreams. *Why should it be silly?* Because I don't know anything about psychoanalysis and it's your job....Deep down it's like with mummy. She always said to me: you're stupid, there's sawdust in your head. She was always wanting me to depend on her, to need her absolutely. That's odd, that dream with my grandparents. I feel that the kitchen is something very important. I remember my grandfather in the kitchen, when I was living with them....I had been just at the height of his...in such a way that my face...these things are terrible...*that you could do with his penis what you had done with your baby?* Oh, it reminds me, I also dreamed I had a tiny little baby, hardly any bigger than my pen. He was in a transparent case and I was putting him into everything! In the pocket, in the drawer, up, down, by the front, by the back. It was very amusing.

Ida's guilt no longer expresses itself in the form of a simple inhibition. She is now trying to give a demonstration for the mother imago. In spite of the apparently depressing side of the dream, she can now allow herself to handle herself—and to speak about it—"to comb herself," "to give interpretations," "to put the baby into her," "to eat the worm." At the same time this is an introjection of the analyst's function, indicating an important modification of the maternal imago.

(This is about a young girl's "kidnapping" in the street.) It gives me a strange uneasiness. It makes me think of something in the kitchen. This kitchen is haunting me. I had a dream: people were dancing, I agree to dance, then the room becomes an amphitheatre, and I'm sitting down. Then the amphitheatre becomes a kitchen. A woman offers me a crab, something gelatinous, slightly disgusting for me to eat. I hesitate, then I accept. I cut a little bit off and give her back the rest. After all I prostituted myself when I lived with the nuns. I had a fit of anger last night. I said that people should have the right to be stupid after all, if they wanted to. Why did I say it? Everybody belittled my father, I was the only one to love him. In fact my mother must have been under her parents' influence....That woman....What did she leave unsaid about my husband!...I dreamed that I had twins and then that my baby had a little detachable penis, one could take it off, put it back on, and handle it. Things have never been as good as they are now with my husband; and even so, I'm jealous, I'm afraid that some woman will take him away from me. *Perhaps, precisely because you are happy?* And I'm also frightened of fire in the house. I'm frightened of hurting my husband. Yes, I am frightened of hurting him. *Of being like mummy who hurt daddy in the kitchen?* You should take my husband into analysis.

A new difficulty appears here. Although she can achieve an emancipation from the Mother in fantasy by introjecting her anal power into masturbatory acts, she has difficulty in assuming this power which is then felt to be dangerous for the partner. There is a contradiction in the imago. That is why Ida undertakes only a partial introjection by sharing the crab. Yet it requires total introjection of the "crab" to remove inhibitions concerning "the dance" and "the studies" (shared orgasm and intellectual activities). The contradiction lies precisely in the fact that at the same time she also must be the violent but frustrated Mother, who although she "cuts," does not "eat" (may not give herself any pleasure). Does not the violence manifested toward the Mother show the castration of her own genital?

> I have the impression that there are hidden vibrations between people. I am looking for other people's secret. How are they? What are they doing? Oh, they will see that my shoes are badly polished, my skirt not well put on. When I was a young girl I wanted everybody to look at me, to fall in love with me. To be seen, to be looked at. That is how one becomes an actress. I read something about the Russian revolution while coming here on the bus. Yesterday, Jacques left home; he has gone on a voyage and I cut my finger with the scissors. Mummy didn't like having to treat me. You shouldn't be sick, she would say. I am thinking that I would like a cup of tea. When they went to bed at night, mummy and daddy, I often had tummy pains. I was delighted with daddy on Sundays. Jacques's mummy is ill. Perhaps she has something very serious in her uterus.

Jacques's departure on a voyage is compared with the scene in the kitchen. This time she used the scissors to "cut" Jacques from his mother, causing guilt, self-mutilation and fear of illness. Nevertheless, the Oedipal structure becomes clearer.

> I cannot swallow anything. I'm on a diet. Maybe I've got an ulcer, or something in my stomach. I must have some X rays taken I never used to complain when I was little. Never! *Not even when you were in your little bed?* Yes, after all it is true, I often cried. I had a dream last night. A mountain, in it things of great value, ancient precious stones, it was a very hard mountain, very hard. Jacques went inside it.

Ida does not want to "swallow" the nocturnal intimacy of her parents. The dream mountain (the Mother) has things of great value inside it. There is no question of Ida—this is implied but not expressed—entering it and taking them. On the contrary she seems to give Jacques back to the "mountain." We might surmise that she has secretly made her husband into an ally who will be able to take the "riches" and give them to her.

I've been to see the doctor about my stomach. That's why I didn't come here. I have a little bit of money this month. The analysis is boring me. *It bores you to have to think once and for all that you have to take away from here some "riches" for yourself. That's why you think you must be ill, weak, impoverished. And in the long run, if you are poor, I am impoverished, I am not paid.* That's true, after all I don't know what is happening to me. I'm excited and aggressive and I don't know why. Yet you know, my husband—I love him very much and all the same I am very angry with him. I don't know what I would do to him if I could. *When you are angry with yourself this is what you do: you prick your-self, you cut and hurt yourself, and you deprive yourself of intellectual nour-ishment and love. Maybe this is what you want to do to someone else when you are angry.* At the nuns...there were no mirrors at all. I was never able to see myself in a mirror. *But you did in a dream.* Ah yes, when my hair was all burnt. *Yes and you had the impression that there was something "suspect" there.* Yes, I remember well. At the nuns, I wasn't able to wash myself entirely. I mean you had to do it bit by bit. It was ridiculous. I never looked at the bottom half of myself. That's odd. When my arm hangs from the bed between the wall and the mattress and it touches the carpet, even though it's silky and soft down there, I have the impression that somebody might cut it off or bite it. Often I even take my arm back quickly. It's such a strange feeling. *What is down below is dan-gerous?* I remember at the nuns, that soldier, he came one day....I remember him well, that German. I was doing...anyway I was sleeping....I suppose I might have been...and he said to me: If you are not good, baby...*and if you put your hand down there*....No, only, if you are not good, I will cut your arm off. Then it was Christmas and I could ask for something. I asked for a little brother. I was three years old. I was sure one could ask for that. In fact I got a teddy bear but that wasn't good enough....I wasn't pleased at all. A little brother is alive, one can play with him. And especially, a little brother, this could have been a proof! *Of what?* That...that my parents exist somewhere, that they made him, so therefore they exist. *If that was the proof you wanted a little sister would have done, but you, you wanted a little brother.* A little brother is like an extension. Yes, it has a penis and after all, I didn't know my father very well, there were hardly any men in the convent, apart from the priest, the good old doctor...really that teddy bear...a little brother would have been like an extension toward my father. After all (that's odd, why am I thinking of that?), it's shameless that I shouldn't know it, it...the hymen, whereabouts is it? It can't be immediately at the entrance; it's more likely to be a little higher. A little girl can put her finger to it. Oh, I always swept the staircase going from the top of the bottom. At first, I didn't think of sweeping, only of holding the broomstick in my hand. One could handle it; I think of the way children climb stairs: they put one leg on the step first of all, then the other leg rejoins the first one. I liked to handle the broom when going up the stairs. One could put it between one's legs...*it extends the finger, the arm, it went toward your father.* You see? I could have played with a little brother, and a little boy is something kind, well behaved, good! *It is not like "an enemy for mummy" as you explained to me one day.*

Ida draws away from the aggression contained in the desire to "empty" the Mother of her "riches." She is running away from me in order to protect me. She refuses to see what is pushing her to "deprive" me, to "cut " me, to "prick" me, to "take back" her autonomy that I am "keeping" for myself. This session shows us *in statu nascendi*, the progression which led to penis envy. We see the exacerbation of the conflict with the anal Mother. This kind of conflict usually resolves itself due to masturbatory acts and fantasies. And, indeed, in thinking of this Ida finally mentioned the memories about masturbation which led to remembering the traumatic moment that made her give it up. It was at that moment of desperation that she invented (in the utopian solution of getting a little brother) her penis envy. To have a penis like the boy meant in the little girl's mind a great number of advantages, but they all come down to one: the ability to keep a harmonious relation with the Mother. What is the magical power of the penis due to? The answer to this question has to be looked for on three different levels, which cannot always be distinguished easily. On an anal level it seems as though the penis, seen as a fecal stick, undetachable from the body, is a sign that its owner has not been dispossessed of his sphincter autonomy. He therefore has no reason either to be aggressive with the Mother (boys are "well-behaved, kind, good") or to be guilty. On the level of personality formation, the presence of the penis is important in that it frees one from masturbatory conflict (no need to put one's finger to it, as it is a per-manent "finger") and, consequently, from conflict with the family: the little boy can have his pleasure, without becoming wicked. The path to the future is open. Lastly, on a prospective level (genital future) the penis is an extension toward the father and, as Ida puts it, permits her to come nearer the little girl's genital object. These are the infantile reasons underlying Ida's penis envy, an envy which has very little to do with the male genital organ itself. It expresses the repressed identificatory autoerotic fantasies directed toward the anal Mother.

> I had a strange dream last night, but I've forgotten it. Yet I remember a lit-tle....That job, I wouldn't find it disagreeable at all. And after all, it would be a good discipline...it would force me to be neat. To do my hair, to make myself pretty....I don't know....I sing and then I want to grumble, like daddy. I do contradictory things. I am going to work. I'm thinking that Jacques's mother is well. On that side things are going better....That is odd, I think that I'm ashamed to work, to study. As though I wasn't allowed to. When I was little I couldn't work in peace. It was like a scandalous privilege. My mother often said to me, "Leave it, you'll be able to think of yourself later." And then the more I worked the more pleasure I had and the more mummy became sad, very sad. It's like a nail still stuck in me. She needed me so much, and then suddenly one day, she was happy on her own! She didn't need me!...Before, I was completely enslaved and she absolutely needed me, and then I thought to myself, "You will not be alone." When I was little, she left me....This dependence also had a nice side to it. It was like depending on God. I could avoid having to live all alone. Sometimes we were as good friends as two schoolgirls. But it was only on the surface....Then daddy, poor

thing, he was totally excluded from this strange paradise. It was more like hell. Yet he was a bit frightened of us. When two women get together they become wicked. She wanted to make an ally out of me. Sometimes he was tender to us, and it makes me feel so sad. After all, I am ashamed of him, ashamed of daddy. *Ashamed of daddy, ashamed of studies*...daddy thinks that from now on I shall write to him and not to mummy. It upsets me. I wonder why?

Remembering the scene with the soldier allows Ida to foresee the possibility of an identification with the father. And we notice a new difficulty. The identification must fail because of the father's weakness, like the daughter he is dominated by the Mother.

I'm worn out. I went yesterday for that job...I'm delighted. So, because of that I bought some hairpins, lipstick, etc. It amuses me. I'm going to be late in paying you...at the beginning, when I couldn't pay you, it was unbearable. Now I say to myself—"After all, you can wait a bit." See? You just shouldn't have chosen that profession. You earn your money at other people's expense. It's scandalous to have a career like that! *The other day you told me that working, studying, were like a privilege, a "scandalous" pleasure. One could say that you are now doing to me what your mother did to you—you are reproaching me for my pleasures, my work, my career, the fact that I earn money....*(Ida laughs.) Yes, it's as though I bear you a grudge like with....Then that dream...that nightmare....I was at home with Jacques. I had to hide him. There was something illegal. We were pursued by the authorities, a dramatic story. Some soldiers were supposed to come and fetch him. At first he was in the room next door. The chief commissioner came personally. He explained to me that I had to hide him under the blanket in the bed; that way no one would find him. That's funny, the superior authority of those same soldiers was explaining to me how to escape his own authority. But Jacques was taking the whole thing too lightly. He kept moving, going out. I thought: they are going to knock, they are going to come in, but he wouldn't stay still, he was moving all the time. As though there had been a baby there....I was on the lookout. They could come back a second time. Somebody knocks on the door. I tell Jacques to stay still, but it's no use, he gets up and goes to open the door. Then it is an old lady who comes in. "Oh! You're there!" she says, "Hello!" And then she left and I saw her speak with some soldiers. I thought, we have been betrayed....I was afraid they would take him from me and kill him. Last night...we made love...me, as usual,...But this time I wanted to go on. I was feeling very sensual. (But an external event interrupted.) I felt kind of amputated. It's odd, with daddy, as though mysterious, curious things could happen....I was not supposed to be with him. After all, everyday life is full of mysteries. That German soldier...loaded with rifles and tommy-guns. He said to me, "Hello baby!" and I said, "Hello Andrew!" *Hello! Like the old lady in the dream, the soldier's associate?* Yes, exactly. And then, in the dream I thought, "My God, she saw what she wasn't meant to see. It is treacherous....Those Germans, perhaps they were looking for the Maquis, or something else that would have been hidden well within me. I mean in the bed.

There were my arms and perhaps hands at the end. (Ida laughs.) It is funny to say that. After all, hands are always at the end. *Perhaps when they feel threatened they feel somehow detached from the end.* In the boarding school you know that's exactly the style of the nuns. One doesn't sleep with one's hands under the sheets. It's odd, sometimes I don't dare look at people in the street, observe them or see exactly how they are. Before, even when I spoke to them, I didn't dare look at them....I was thinking about the mother superior. She was a witch. Everybody knew that she stole fruit. And then, I wonder why she slept in a big bed? We had our little beds, our little blankets....

Ida continues, using the same words as her mother, to negate her ambitions and achievements. Yet the dream shows the modification of the imago's demands; this time it is a superior authority who shows her how to escape its hold, allowing her to relive the "scene with the soldier" and to keep the pleasure-object under her blanket (hand, penis, husband). The external event which interrupted coitus is interpreted by Ida according to her guilt: "I felt kind of amputated." One might add that this castration does not concern the orgasm but the acts and the pleasure involved in it. The pleasure-objects under her blanket appear "stolen" or at least related to an aggressive act (she is persecuted). As the persecution lessens ("the hands are still at the end"), Ida acquires the right to dispose of the pleasure-object. Concomitantly, penis envy, having lost its purpose, will disappear.

Ida's analysis continues but from now on several problems are on the way to solution. She has a growing feeling of confidence in herself and is beginning to feel equal to a professional field.

V

To conclude our study, we might formulate a question avoided until now in this essay: Why is the feeling of castration and its corollary, penis envy, the universal lot of womanhood? Why do women so often renounce creative activity, their means of making the world? Why do they agree to shut themselves up in "women's quarters," to "be quiet in church," in short, to prefer a dependent state? The question is far from simple and would require research into various sectors and a documentation I do not yet have. Yet, we can study the problem from a psychoanalytical point of view, and try to formulate hypotheses from the material we have.

From a psychoanalytical viewpoint an institution is not established and does not survive unless it resolves some particular interpersonal problem. In principle, an institutional solution must have advantages for both men and women over the situation that preceded it. We should make explicit what advantages each has in the institutional inequality of the sexes, at least in the domain accessible to psychoanalysis—that is to say in affective life.

We are right when we suppose that this age-old inequality requires woman's complicity, in spite of her apparent protest shown by penis envy.

Men and women must be exposed to specific, complementary affective conflicts to have established a *modus vivendi* which could last through many
civilizations.

As for the woman, consider the following: at the end of the anal stage the
little girl should be able to achieve in masturbatory fantasy simultaneously
both parents envisaged in terms of their genital functioning. But there are two
obstacles: first, the one originating in the anal period; namely, that autonomy in masturbatory satisfaction necessarily means a sadistic dispossession of
the Mother and her prerogatives; second, the Oedipal obstacle, according to
which the fantasy-achievement of the primal scene, by identification with
both parents, also implies supplanting the Mother. As long as these obstacles
are not overcome—and usually they are not—something will be missing in the
identification with: (1) the father, who can give pleasure with his penis; (2)
with the Mother, who can receive pleasure from the father. This fundamental
deficiency is in conjunction with a particular maternal imago: that of an
exacting, jealous, and castrated Mother, and an envied, depreciated, and at the
same time overvalued Father. The only way out of this impasse to identification is the establishment of an inaccessible phallic ideal (mythical image of an
idealized Father), which is a reassurance to the Mother that she can keep her
prerogatives, and also the nostalgic wish to make up for the deficiency fatal
to genital fulfillment: the identification with the Father. When women holding such imagoes have to deal with married life, they suddenly find themselves confronted with their latent genital desires, even though their affective
life is immature for want of heterosexual identification, as they are still dominated by problems of the anal stage. Thus, the fleeting Oedipal hopes will
soon give way to a repetition, this time with the husbands, of the anal relationship to the Mother, a relation which is then confirmed by penis envy. The
advantage of this situation consists in avoiding a frontal attack on the maternal imago and also in avoiding the feeling of deep anxiety at the idea of
detaching oneself from her domination and superiority.

The little girl's drama, particularly in relationship to the Mother, is made concrete in the following situation: when, in order to disengage herself from the
anal Mother, she tried to use the Father as a prop, she found herself confronted
with the heterosexual object which belongs to the Mother and, consequently, in
opposition to her over matters of interest. Simultaneously attacked from both
sides, the Mother continuously appears as very dangerous: threatened with total
destruction, she might, in turn, threaten to destroy totally. The superimposition
in the same object of both mastery and rivalry blocks the way out of the anal
stage and forces the girl to renounce her desires. She will then make herself
into an anal appendage (the "cork," the "doll") of the Mother, and later into
the "phallus" of her husband. It certainly seems that this is a universal difficulty in woman's development, a difficulty which more or less explains why
such a condition of dependence toward man, the heir of the anal Mother
imago, is accepted. That is the price for some of the disguised genital
achievements which, in some instances, women allow themselves.

At first one sees easily the advantages which man acquires for himself from this disposition to dependence created by feminine guilt. Yet, on examining the question more closely, it is not obvious a priori that men should naturally want such a relationship of mastery. The falsity, the ambivalence, and the refusal of identifications it conceals should appear to him as so many snags on which his own full and authentic achievement comes to grief. And yet...who could doubt that in order to achieve his own interests in superiority man is almost universally the accomplice of woman's state of dependence and that he thrives in elevating all this into religious, metaphysical, or anthropological principles. What interest has he in giving in to his need to dominate the being through whom he could understand himself and who could understand him? To discover oneself through the other sex would be a genuine fulfillment of one's humanity, yet this is exactly what escapes most of us.

Having seen the woman's problems, let us now try to see which specific problems are in the way of man's fulfillment. When the little boy is about to free himself from the anal Mother, he can identify with the Father, possessor of the "phallus." In this way he frees himself from maternal domination; the phallic Father is his ally and the Mother is not yet his genital object. Thus, he will have to cope with two periods of anxiety in his development: (1) the liquidation of his anal relationship to the Mother by a particularly dangerous identificatory incorporation (dangerous because of the rejection of her domination as well as the inverse Oedipal exclusion of the Mother) and (2) the Oedipal moment itself, which implies an identification with the genital rival as well as his elimination. This double failure in the boy's identification is, as we see, quite symmetrical to the failure we noticed in the little girl. In the case of the boy, too, an impossible desire is crystallized into an envy, paralleling that of the girl, of the same illusory object, the "penis." It is obvious that these envies are beyond any real genital differentiation and refer to the nonintegrated anal relationship. If at this stage a difference appears between the two sexes it is about the possession or nonpossession (one is just as illusory as the other) of the penis-thing and its varied symbolic significance. From then on, phallic deception leads the way for the institutionalized relation between the sexes. The whole problem of the failure in identification will by fetishistic means be concealed behind active or passive fascination. The possession of the "fetish" is intended to arouse envy, and envy in turn is intended to confirm the value of the fetish for the man. We can now understand the meaning of the fact that men encourage "penis envy" in the other sex and try to make it part of their social institutions. Once it is conceded that the exclusive possessor of the fetish is man, is not this so-called privilege, sustained by covetousness alone, nothing but a variant of envy, projected on to woman? The penis-emblem allows the man to be enviable and thus, logically, avoid living a life of envy. Man cannot be other than envious as long as he needs to objectify as well as hide in a fetish what is missing in his genital fulfillment. Thanks to this subterfuge he will continue to ignore his dangerous desire to take the Mother's part in the anally conceived Primal Scene. The woman, envious and guilty, is the ideal support for the projection of this desire. She can thus become man's unacknowledged "feminine part," which he must then master and control. That is why man will be driven to prefer a mutilated, dependent, and envious woman to a partner, successful in her creative fullness.

The biblical myth of the first couple gives us an eloquent articulation of these problems. Eve, split off from Adam's self, represents what he refuses to allow himself. To her is also attributed the original sin for which he thus completely avoids responsibility. Eve shall transgress the divine interdiction, she shall "castrate" the heavenly Father. Thus, she must bow beneath the weight of this double guilt: her own and that which man has projected on her. She is doomed to double servitude: toward God (the castrated Father) and toward her husband (the Mother who must not be castrated). She will live in enmity with the Serpent. Such is the divine decree which lays the basis for "penis envy." Part of Adam's body, Eve is at the same time his chattel (his servant) and his attribute. Object of his projections, controlled and enslaved, she is compelled to live in submissiveness—not with a real partner of the opposite sex—but with a tyrannical representative of the anal Mother image.

This, briefly, is our psychoanalytical hypothesis concerning the affective aspects of the institution which postulates female dependence and passivity and imposes on woman the envy of an emblem which serves to conceal her desires. This hypothesis has at least one advantage over various cultural and philosophical concepts: it is drawn from clinical experience and is of therapeutic value. Indeed, we believe that on an individual level, the solution to penis envy is the job of the analyst—on condition that he himself be free from this phallocentric prejudice, old as humanity itself.

7

THE FEMALE CASTRATION COMPLEX AND PENIS ENVY (*EXCERPT*)

Janine Chasseguet-Smirgel

"I've got one, and you've got none!" (Gay little song sung by a three-and-a-half-year-old boy to his six-year-old sister.)

On the subject of penis envy Freud's views are opposed to those of Josine Müller, Karen Horney, Melanie Klein, and Ernest Jones. Freud holds that, until puberty, there is a *phallic sexual monism*, and therefore a total sexual identity between boys and girls up till the development of the castration complex. According to Hélène Deutsch, who agrees with Freud on these points, the little girl has no complete sexual organ from the age of four (age of the castration complex) to puberty—she has only her clitoris, which is seen as a *castrated penis*. She has no vagina as she has not yet discovered it and does not even know of it *unconsciously*.[1] We can understand easily why Freud and those who followed him in his theory on female sexuality believed *penis envy to be a primary phenomenon* and fundamental to women's psychosexuality, since the little girl wants to compensate for the instinctual and narcissistic defects which mark most of her childhood.

Authors who do not agree with Freud's theory of female sexuality refuse to consider woman as *"un homme manqué"* (Jones). According to these authors the vagina is the first sexual organ to be libidinally cathected. The little girl is a woman from the start. The cathexis of the clitoris is secondary and serves a defensive function with regard to conflicts concerning genital impulses linked to the vagina: "The undiscovered vagina is a vagina denied" (Karen Horney).

These authors agree that repression of vaginal impulses is due to narcissistic anxieties concerned with attacks against the inside of the body. Therefore, the erotic cathexis is transferred to the clitoris, a safer, external sexual organ.[2] This throws a new light on the theory of penis envy.

Josine Müller believes that self-esteem is linked to the satisfaction of the impulses peculiar to one's own sex. Penis envy, therefore, is due to the nar-

---

1. This assertion was maintained by Freud even in his "Short Account of Psychoanalysis" (1924), after many people had opposed him in theory and by clinical observation. Yet in the article Ruth Mack Brunswick wrote with him ("The Pre-Oedipal Phase," 1940), he seems to have more or less accepted that early sensations do exist in the vagina.
2. I think this transfer of cathexis is due to the guilt associated with the anal-sadistic incorporative drives.

cissistic wound resulting from unsatisfied genital (vaginal) desires, which have been repressed.

For Karen Horney penis envy results from certain characteristics of the penis (its visibility, the fact that its micturition is in the form of a jet, and so on),[1] but also from a fear of the vagina which exists in both sexes. In the girl such fears are related to her Oedipal desire to be penetrated by the father's penis, which becomes fearful because she attributes to it a power of destruction.

According to Melanie Klein, *the libidinal desire for the penis* is a primary one. It is first of all an oral desire, the prototype of vaginal desire. The fulfillment of this desire is linked to the fantasy of sadistically taking the paternal penis from the mother, who has incorporated it. This results in fear of retaliation from the mother, who might try to wound or destroy the inside of the girl's body. Therefore, penis envy can be related to the following ideas in the girl's unconscious: By using the external organ she demonstrates her fears are unfounded, testing them against reality. She regards the penis as a weapon to satisfy her sadistic desires toward her mother (cleaving to her so as to tear away the penis which is hidden inside her, to drown her in a jet of corrosive urine, etc.). The guilt resulting from these fantasies may make her wish to return the penis which she has stolen from the mother, and thus restitute her by regressing to an active homosexual position for which the possession of a penis is necessary.

Ernest Jones follows Melanie Klein's theory of penis envy in his article "The Phallic Phase" (1932), centering his ideas on the primary characteristic of the "receptive" cathexes of all the orifices of a woman's body (her mouth, anus, vagina).

All these authors attribute a large part in female psychosexuality to the father and to penis envy, whereas Freud believed the Oedipus complex to be mainly masculine. Ruth Mack Brunswick thought female neuroses lack an "Oedipus complex" and J. Lampl de Groot claims that the paternal image really exists for the little girl only when once she is six, and maintains, that until that age, the relation with the father is the same as the child's relation with any other member of the household: sometimes friendly, sometimes hostile, according to her mood.

In his article on "Female Sexuality" (1931) Freud argues against the *secondary* nature of penis envy, because the woman's envy is so violent that it can only have drawn its energy from *primary* instincts.

I believe that the fact that there may be primary receptive instincts in women, be they oral, anal, or vaginal,[2] does not prevent penis envy from being primary, too. However, even if one holds that a female sexual impulse exists right from the start, that the little girl has an adequate organ of which she has some certain knowledge, in other words, that she has all the instinctual equipment, yet we learn from clinical experience that from a narcissistic point of view the girl feels painfully incomplete. I believe the cause of this

---

1. The narcissistic cathexis of these characteristics is linked, according to Grunberger, with the anal-sadistic phase, and thus the only objects of value are those which can be measured, compared, and precisely graded.

2 Freud not only ignores the vagina but, until the castration complex, that is, the Oedipus complex,

feeling of incompleteness is to be found in the primary relation with the mother and will therefore be found in children of both sexes.

THE OMNIPOTENT MOTHER

In the article she wrote with Freud, "The Pre-Oedipal Phase of the Libido Development" (1940), Ruth Mack Brunswick insists on the powerful character of the primitive maternal imago ("She is not only active, phallic, but *omnipotent*"). She shows that *the first activity to which the child is submitted is the mother's*. The transition passage from passivity to activity is achieved by an *identification with the mother's activity*. Because of his dependence on the omnipotent mother "who is capable of everything and possesses every valuable attribute" the child obviously sustains "early narcissistic injuries from the mother" which "enormously increases the child's hostility."

I believe that a child, whether male or female, even with the best and kindest of mothers, will maintain a terrifying maternal image in his unconscious, the result of projected hostility deriving from his own impotence.[1] This powerful image, symbolic of all that is bad, does not exclude an omnipotent, protective imago (witch *and* fairy), varying according to the mother's real characteristics.

However, the child's primary powerlessness, the intrinsic characteristics of his psychophysiological condition, and the inevitable frustrations of training are such that the imago of the good, omnipotent mother never covers over that of the terrifying, omnipotent, bad mother.

It seems to me that when the little boy becomes conscious[2] that this omnipotent mother has no penis and that he, subdued so far by her omnipotence, has an organ which she has not, this forms an important factor in his narcissistic development.

Analysts have mainly stressed the horror (the *Abscheu*) the little boy feels when he realizes that his mother has no penis, since it means to him that she has been castrated, thus confirming his idea that such a terrifying possibility

he believes the girl's sexuality to be identical with that of the boy. She merely hopes for receptive satisfactions from her mother, but she does not expect them to be phallic and denies the penis as well as the vagina. When she turns to the father wanting a child by him, it is not yet a desire for incorporation of the paternal penis. For Freud, the girl's Oedipus complex occurs without interfering with incorporation desires (or desires of being penetrated in any manner); in a similar way the boy has no desire to penetrate the mother. He is ignorant of her possessing an organ complementary to his own. It is only at puberty that erection of the penis indicates a new aim—the penetration of a cavity. Apart from numerous indications that there are early desires of penetration (which many people have noted), erections are frequent before puberty, and one finds babies having erections, particularly while being suckled. E. Jones, Melanie Klein, Josine Müller, Karen Horney, and, more recently, Phyllis Greenacre, in discussing the girl's discovery of the vagina, stress the fact that we are used to talking about external and visible organs without taking deep coenesthetic sensations into consideration. Girl's ignorance of their vaginas does not prove the nonexistence of a genital desire to incorporate the penis, just as a congenital malformation obstructing the mouth would not deny the existence of hunger. Indeed, the impossibility of satisfying the instinct increases guilt, in face of the "condemned" vagina.

1. Once frustration has brought the primary narcissistic phase to an end.
2. Unconsciously, he has probably always known she had no penis just as, unconsciously, he always knew she had a vagina. But this does not exclude representations of a phallic or castrated mother, since the primary processes readily admit contradiction.

exists. This in turn may lead to fetishistic perversion and certain kinds of homo-sexuality. Few people take note of Freud's other statements stressing the nar-cissistic satisfaction felt by the little boy at the thought that he has an organ which women do not have. Thus, Freud says (in a note on exhibitionism added to the *Three Essays* in 1920): "It is a means of constantly insisting upon the integrity of the subject's own (male) genitals and it reiterates his infantile satis-faction at the absence of a penis in those of women." Elsewhere, Freud men-tions the little boy's triumphant disdain for the other sex. He believes that this feeling of triumph (a note in *Group Psychology and the Analysis of the Ego*)[1] always arises from a convergence of the ego and the ego ideal. So it is indeed a narcissistic satisfaction, a triumph at last, over the omnipotent mother.

In his 1927 article on "Fetishism" Freud pointed out the ambivalent role of the fetish. It is supposed to conceal the horrifying castration while it is at the same time the means of its possible reparation. Freud says of the fetishist that "to point out that he reverses his fetish is not the whole story; in many cases he treats it in a way which is obviously equivalent to a representation of castration," and at this point Freud refers to the people who cut off braids. When considering the Chinese custom of mutilating women's feet and then venerating them, which he believes to be analogous to fetishism, Freud states: "It seems as though the Chinese male wants to thank the woman for having submitted to being castrated."

Countless clinical details relating to both sexes testify to the frequency and wealth of wishes to castrate the mother of her breast and of her phallus. If it were not for this deep satisfaction and its associated horror, the fantasy of the castrated mother would probably be less forceful.

Is it not at this point that myths begin to prevail over scientific thought? Are we not all tempted to talk as Freud did of "the castrated condition of women," or of "the necessity for women to accept their castration," or as Ruth Mack Brunswick put it, "The real quality of the representation of the castrated mother and the fantasy quality of the phallic mother," instead of putting these two representations back under the sway of the pleasure principle?

Images of woman as deficient, as containing a hole or wound, seem to me to be a denial of the imagoes of the primitive mother; this is true for both sexes, but in women identification with such an imago leads to deep guilt.

The protective imago of the good omnipotent mother and the terrifying imago of the bad omnipotent mother are both in opposition to this repre-sentation of the castrated mother.

Generous breast, fruitful womb, softness, warmth, wholeness, abundance, harvest the earth, all symbolize the mother.

Frustration, invasion, intrusion, evil, illness, death, all symbolize the mother.

In comparison with the ideal qualities attributed to the early mother-image, the fall of the "castrated" mother appears to result from a deep desire to free oneself from her domination and evil qualities.

The little boy's triumph over the omnipotent mother has many effects on his

---

1. International Psychoanalytic Press, 1922. [Reprinted in *SE*, Vol. 18]

future relations with women. Bergler points out that man attempts to reverse the infantile situation experienced with the mother and live out actively what he has endured passively, thus turning her into the dependent child he had been. This idea seems to be supported by certain aspects of woman's role, often noted by other authors. One also observes in patients the narcissistic effect of a man's realization that his mother does not possess a penis.

If the little boy has not been traumatized by the omnipotent mother, if her attitude has been neither too restraining, nor too invasive, he will be sufficiently reassured by the possession of his penis to dispense with constant reiteration of the triumphant feeling he once experienced. The need to reverse the situation might be restricted to a protective attitude toward women (this is not necessarily a reaction formation; it might be a way of linking his need for mastery to his love). But if the child was a fecal part-object serving to satisfy the mother's desire for power and authority, then the child's future object-relations with women will be deeply affected.[1]

In analysis we rarely encounter male patients who show defused anal-sadistic impulses in a pure state, nor do we find mothers in *analyses* who satisfy perverse desires through their children. But many male patients present contained sexual and relational problems, linked to a need for a specific form of narcissistic gratification which we regard as being the result of regression to the phallic-narcissistic phase.

It seems that Jones's description of the deutero-phallic phase in boys (with narcissistic overestimation of the penis, withdrawal of object-libido and lack of desire to penetrate sexually and certain aspects of ejaculatio praecox noted by Abraham) are to be found in these narcissistic-phallic men who have been disturbed in their early relation with the mother. They lack confidence in the narcissistic value of the penis and constantly have to put it to the proof; theirs is the "little penis" complex, they regard a sexual relation as narcissistic reassurance rather than an object relationship of mutual value.[2]

Such men constantly doubt their triumph over women, as they doubt the fact that she has no penis, and are always fearful of finding one concealed in the vagina. This leads to ejaculation *ante portas*, in order to avoid such a dangerous encounter. The fantasy represents not only the paternal phallus but also (as Jones pointed out) the destructive anal penis of the omnipotent mother.[3]

But, in general, possessing the penis proves to be the satisfactory narcissistic answer to the little boy's primary relation with his mother.

Like the boy, the little girl, too, has been narcissistically wounded by the

1. Of course other causes also dictate a man's future attitude to women, one of which is an identification with the real father in his relation to the mother.
2. See Karen Horney, "The Dread of Women." The little boy feels an aggressive desire for his mother. In her role as educator she is obliged to dominate him and frustrate him. He desires to penetrate her, but feels humiliated at being small and incapable of achieving this, which leads to his feeling narcissistically wounded and immensely inferior, but he also feels a violently aggressive desire for revenge, which is projected, along with those desires caused by the first frustrations, onto the mother and her vagina.
3. One patient suffering from ejaculatio praecox was content in his first sexual relations at the

mother's omnipotence—maybe even more than he, for the mother does not cathect her daughter in the same way that she cathects her son. But the girl cannot free herself from this omnipotence as she has nothing with which to oppose the mother, no narcissistic virtue the mother does not also possess. She will not be able to "show her" her independence (I think this expression relates to phallic exhibitionism). So she will envy the boy his penis and say that he can "do everything." I see penis envy *not as "a virility claim" to something one wants for its own sake, but as a revolt against the person who caused the narcissistic wound: the omnipotent mother.*

Clinical experience often shows that penis envy is stronger and more difficult to resolve when the daughter has been traumatized by a domineering mother. The narcissistic wound aroused by the child's helplessness and by penis envy are closely related.

Realization that possession of the penis presents the possibility of healing

age of twenty-two with merely external contact "because he did not know" that the vagina existed. Such "ignorance" is due to frightening sexual fantasies. For him the female organ was a threat, full of fecal content (crumbling caves full of garbage, cow's cloaca blocked with dung "as hard as granite," corpses found in rooms, crashed cars spread across an icy road, etc.). Therefore, penetration is dangerous: In order to avoid it one must "fill the vagina with powdered glass, use it as a chamber pot and fill it to the brim," think of it as a john where one puts the lid down before urinating or else tries to get rid of the contents first. Thus, at puberty, this patient spent a lot of time disemboweling flies; one of his favorite fantasies was the following: He was master of a harem and ruled women of all ages with a whip. He had established very strict rules in which the women had to defecate by orders and under close scrutiny. This illustrates the child's inversion of sphincter education and his victory over the anal penis of the intrusive mother. (This patient also had fantasies about excision of the clitoris.)

Men fear the mother's power, and her anal penis in particular. Later they try to stop women from using their anal impulses. As woman is guilty about her own anal wishes toward the father, she becomes an accomplice to the man's defenses. This conjunction results in the visible inhibition of women's anality in society: A woman must never swear, spit, eat strong food or wine, and until recently was not allowed to discuss money or business. Charm and grace are on the whole either reaction formations or sublimations of anal impulses (the opposite of vulgarity). At the same time, women are represented as illogical, vague, incapable of the rigors of science, engineering, etc.—all signs of successful integration of the anal components.

(Owing to the enforced repression it undergoes, the anal instinct may become somewhat "corrosive." The weaker muscular structure of women also favors this corrosive aspect of feminine aggression, as it does not allow for adequate motor discharge. Women are said to scratch, bite, or poison, whereas men punch or knock down.) In fact this desire for victory over the omnipotent mother is often displaced by men onto all women. An exception is the *daughter*, perhaps because she is in a dependent situation. The father projects onto her an *idealized image* which is opposed to the *"normal lasting contempt"* (Freud, Ruth Mack Brunswick, Hélène Deutsch) he feels for other women. His daughter often represents the best part of himself and of the good, primitive object. She is tenderness, purity, innocence, and grace and represents for him a privileged relationship which escapes his ambivalence.

Of course, this relation is not always there, as some men extend their maternal conflicts onto their daughters, too. An obsessional patient suffering from ejaculatio praecox was discussing his six-year-old daughter who was working hard at school in order to attract his attention, a fact he was well aware of: "I push her away from me but, being truly feminine, she still tries to attract my attention"; but the relation I have described exists frequently enough for it to be noticeable. Three patients told me at the outset of their treatment that one of their reasons for coming to analysis was a desire to help their daughters.

the narcissistic wound imposed by the omnipotent mother[1] helps to explain some of the unconscious significance of the penis, whether it is that of a treasure of strength, integrity, magic power, or autonomy. In the idea connected with this organ we find condensed all the primitive ideas of power. This power becomes then the prerogative of the man, who by attracting the mother destroyed her power. Since women lack this power they come to envy the one who possesses the penis. Thus, woman's envy has its source in her conflict with her mother and must seek satisfaction through aggression (that is, what she considers to be aggression) toward her love object, the father. Any achievement which provides her with narcissistic pleasure will be felt as an encroachment on the father's power, thereby leading to many inhibitions, as already mentioned. In fact there is often an unfortunate connection between violent penis envy and the inhibition or fear of satisfying this envy. The connection arises because penis envy derives from conflict with the mother, giving rise to idealization of the father, which must be maintained thereafter.

I think that women's fear of castration can be explained by this equation of the narcissistic wound and the lack of a penis. Freud could see no reason for the little girl to fear castration as she had already undergone it. This led him to alter his proposition that all anxieties were castration fears to that in *Inhibitions, Symptoms, Anxiety* (1936), in which he claimed that woman's fear of losing love is the equivalent of castration anxiety.

Jones pointed out that fears of castration do exist in women since they have as many fears about the future as men have; he also stressed the importance of fears about the integrity of their internal organs. In fact, the fears of both sexes are similar (fear of going blind, being paralyzed, becoming mad, having cancer, having an accident, failing, and so on). In the unconscious, all narcissistic fears at any level are equivalent to castration, because of the narcissistic value given to the phallus by both sexes. Thus, women as well as men constantly fear castration; even if they already have lost the *penis*, there are still many other things with a phallic meaning which one might lose. And men as well as women experience penis envy because each attempt to compensate a deficiency implies a phallic acquisition. The fear of loss or of castration centers in the mother as it is from her the daughter wishes to escape, *at the same time that she gives herself a penis and turns to the father.*

During the change of object even though retaining the unconscious image of the phallic mother the daughter fully realizes that *the father is the only true possessor of the penis.* The change of object and the development of the Oedipal situation come about only when the imago of the phallic mother has become that of a mother who has dispossessed the father of his penis. In order to acquire the penis the girl now turns to her father *just as her mother did*; she does this with all the guilt we have discussed earlier, grappling

---

1. In her article on "The Pre-Oedipal Phase" (written with Freud), Ruth Mack Brunswick reconsiders the idea that the desire for a child is a substitute for penis envy: The desire for a child expresses mainly the desire to have what the mother possessed: a child.

    I believe that if the child's desire is linked both with penis envy and with the omnipotent mother, it is because of a certain connection between penis envy and the omnipotent maternal imago.

with both her parents at the same time, and also attacking the loved object.

As Freud said, she turns to the father to acquire the penis, but her fears, owing to the temporary split between her libidinal and aggressive cathexes *at the time of the change of object*, are tied to the mother, the guilt to the father.

I believe that it is at this stage that the imago of the phallic mother *who holds in herself the paternal penis* (Melanie Klein) becomes much more important than the imago of the phallic mother who on her own possesses a phallus. Even if this latter imago persists in the unconscious it is not the prevailing one. But the father's penis, the mother's property, loses its genital and positive characteristics and acquires the same intrusive, destructive, anal properties of the phallic mother's own penis, thereby being cathected in the same way as its owner.

If the imago of the phallic mother as possessor of a penis remains the more important one, then the homosexual situation threatens to establish itself permanently, but if the imago of the mother as holder of the paternal penis dominates, the triangular situation begins in outline.

In Freud's view, then, *the girl turns away from her mother in order to acquire a penis*; and by turning to the father enters the positive Oedipus phase.

If, however, *penis envy is caused by the desire to liberate oneself from the mother*, as I propose, the sequence of events is somewhat different: the girl will *simultaneously* be envious of the penis *and* turn to her father, powerfully aided by a basic feminine wish to free herself from the mother. Thus, penis envy and the erotic desire for a penis are not opposed to each other but complementary, and if symbolic satisfaction of the former is achieved this becomes a step forward toward integration of the latter.

In his article on "Manifestations of the Female Castration Complex" (1921), Karl Abraham states that women who have professional ambitions thereby manifest their penis envy.[1] This can be demonstrated clinically,[2] but I think the desire to fulfill oneself in any field, professional or otherwise, as well as penis envy, springs from the same narcissistic wound, and is therefore an attempt at reparation. Freud in his essay on narcissism states that once the primary stage of narcissism is passed, personal achievement provides narcissistic rewards. It is important to take this into account in analytic treatment. If one interprets desire for achievement as the manifestation of "masculine demands" (as Abraham did with regard to professional activities), if women's professional desires are invariably interpreted as penis envy, there is a risk of awakening profound guilt feelings. I believe that if one accepts that penis envy is caused by a deep narcissistic wound, then one is able to bind this wound as well as open the way to a normal Oedipus conflict. Sexuality itself is often seen as men's prerogative and, in fact, from a symbolic point of view *normal female sexuality* (a vagina which functions normally) can be regarded as the possession of a phallus, due to the fact that the penis represents wholeness even in regard to orgasm. Certain analysts, basing their views on this fantasy, go so far as to say that normal women

1. For Freud (in "Femininity," 1932), if a woman comes to analysis in order to be more successful in her profession, she is by the same token displaying her penis envy.
2. The same is true of men: For a man to achieve his professional ambitions is symbolically to have a penis *like the father*.

never have an orgasm. This is tantamount to acquiescing to the patients' guilt, leading indeed to castration not only of the penis but also of the vagina and of the whole of femininity. Basically, penis envy is the symbolic expression of another desire. Women do not wish to become men, but want to detach themselves from the mother and become complete, autonomous *women.*

PENIS ENVY AS A DEFENSE AND FEARS FOR THE INTEGRITY OF THE EGO

I do not wish to ignore *the role of penis envy* as a feminine defense. I have insisted upon *guilt* because this aspect of female psychosexuality seems to have been more neglected than that of *the narcissistic fears for the ego's integrity.*

Many women want a penis *to avoid being penetrated,* since penetration is felt as a threat to their integrity;[1] they want to castrate this dangerous penis in order to prevent it from approaching them. But then one wonders, *which* penis?

In "The Change of Object," Luquet-Parat suggests that, if penetration is desired and imagined as a danger for body as well as ego integrity, that is, if the penis continues to represent exaggerated phallic power (the immense penis the little girl desires, too big in comparison with her, is the heir to the invading, destructive, annihilating phallic power of the *primitive maternal* phallus), then sexual penetration is experienced as an intolerable desire which the ego cannot accept, since it is in contradiction to self-preservation.

I agree with Dr. Luquet-Parat that this destructive penis is the equivalent of the maternal phallus of the anal phase; this, in turn, is linked for the girl with persecution and passive homosexual attitudes and provides the basis for paranoia in women. In these cases I wonder if one can truly speak of a "change of object" (since emotions concerning the paternal penis are the same as they had been for the mother's phallus). It may be more correct to say that this was already part of the positive Oedipal situation.

The "transfer" to the father of what was invested in the mother and the fact that these cathexes are equal (as the projections have simply been displaced) seem to point to the creation of a mechanism of defense aimed at escaping the dangerous relation with the phallic mother by establishing a relation with the father. But this mechanism of defense fails because the projections remain the same while the two objects are insufficiently differentiated.

It seems as if in these cases the father did not adequately support the projection of the good aspects of the object, because the primitive object itself was particularly bad. The process of idealization could not be established and thus could not allow for the true triangular situation. Castration as a defense and penis envy which prevents penetration seem to me to be linked mainly to the phallic maternal imago even though they appear to take the father as their aim. The latter does not yet have *the attributes of the paternal role* and

1. Protecting oneself from penetration is also a way of safeguarding the object. A whole series of aggressive acts toward the father can be understood as an attempt to protect him from *contact.*

only plays the role of a substitute for the mother, who possesses the destructive anal phallus.[1]

Fears for ego integrity are best analyzed from the angle of passive homosexuality and identifications and provide a deeper understanding of the meaning of this narcissistic defense against penetration by the penis (unconsciously, the mother's phallus), which causes so many conjugal difficulties. Women who attack and castrate their husbands have unconsciously married the bad mother, and this is often equally true for the husband. Freud noticed that many women marry mother substitutes and act ambivalently toward them.

I believe this results both from Oedipal guilt (one must not take the father from the mother; not incorporate the father's penis) and the repetition compulsion. The issue here is to master the traumatic childhood situation, to live out actively what has been passively experienced, rather than integrated, in relation to the mother. In this case the relationship is homosexual.

It does happen—and this is a proof that the husband does not represent the father in this case—that the idealized paternal imago remains untouched and identical with the ideal portrait created by the little girl.

For example, Adrienne, a young and pretty mother who has made an important advance in the social and financial scale, has retained a genuine simplicity. She tells me that she married her husband on the spur of the moment. At the time she was "going out" with a young man whom she loved, but for some reason which she cannot explain she yielded to her present husband's proposal. He is a rather sadistic man who beats her and makes perverse demands upon her. At the same time he is very attentive to her, which gives him an eminently ambiguous position in her eyes. She is full of bitterness toward him and grievances: he deprives her of her freedom; he does not let her gad about, or hum to herself, or whistle; he demands that she wear a girdle, etc. On top of this he is unfaithful to her. It soon became obvious that this husband was an equivalent of Adrienne's mother, who used to take her things away, keep her under her control, force her to work, and never stop pestering her.

When the mother was angry at mealtimes she would throw forks at the children's heads.

From the very beginning this aspect of the mother was projected onto me, and at the outset the analysis was very difficult, especially as she had not come of her own accord but only because her husband insisted on it. Yet she found sufficient satisfaction in the treatment to keep up the analysis despite her pointedly hysterophobic character.

Thus, when she leaves at the end of her session, she feels that she has become very small, her handbag has become a satchel, she senses that I follow her everywhere: into the subway, the streets, and even her bedroom. The smell of my flat follows her everywhere, too. I am always behind her, etc. (In spite of the content of her feelings, their relation and structure are not at all paranoiac, there is a true possibility of insight.)

She liked her father but it was always the mother "who wore the trousers,"

---

1. Of course, this may also be due to regression.

who took the father's pay, controlling even the smallest expenditure, shutting him out if he came home late, etc.

Adrienne made an attempt at suicide the day her grandfather had his leg amputated. Later, she visited him in the hospital, went to much trouble for him, pampered him, even wished to become a nurse. To this day, every month she goes and gives her blood at the hospital (the links between the suicide attempt, the grandfather's amputation, and the efforts to put it right only became clear late in the analysis; they came up as separate facts, because they were unconscious). This grandfather is the mother's father whom the mother treats with indifference, hardly bothering or worrying about him, unlike Adrienne. When he died, after a second amputation, Adrienne described her mother's attitude at the grandfather's deathbed (the mother had stolen his cigarettes and his money) in the following words:

"How can she think of profiting from him?...I can see an animal in the forest, something like a huge wild boar surrounded by hunters. They are trying to strip him of everything he has."

Her husband had then gone hunting. He had sent her some game which she could not bring herself to eat. Adrienne's attitude to her husband is quite different from her attitude to her father or grandfather. She openly attacks him, forces him to give her money, a personal car, etc., without any inhibition whatsoever. She ridicules him, thinks he looks like a clown, and says so in front of him.

One day, the imago she had projected onto her husband became clear:

"In his dressing gown he looks amazingly like my mother-in-law."

Not long before this, she had a dream in which her mother was dressed up as a priest in a robe.

She sometimes projects onto me the good image of the idealized father, the victim of the mother's castration, at other times the image of the phallic mother, with whom she wishes and fears an anal relation, experiencing once again the intrusive sphincter-training period.

"I can still feel you behind me, I am frightened....I don't want to speak. I can feel you're going to interrogate me, and I'm frightened. It's stupid; in fact, you never do ask questions...or, at least, not in that way....I shall say nothing."

"The image of my husband is haunting me. I keep thinking of him, and yet he infuriates me. I don't want to make love to him....I dreamed of a rat whose claws were pinching my daughter's bottom...."

It seems to me obvious that the relationships to the husband and to me in the transference express a defense against a passive homosexual relation with the phallic mother, whom she attacks, whom she defies, whom she castrates in order to prevent her approach and in order to prove that there is no collusion between them; whereas her relation with her father is based on a counter-identification with the phallic mother and so on an idealization of the paternal image she is trying to restore.

The relation with the phallic husband-mother is connected with *narcissis-*

tic fears for the body ego, whereas the relation to the father-grandfather is connected with guilt.

* * *

8

FATHER AND DAUGHTER: IDENTIFICATION WITH DIFFERENCE—A CONTRIBUTION TO GENDER HETERODOXY

Jessica Benjamin

Since the 1970s most of Freud's views on feminine development have been subjected to critical revision. Whereas Freud (1933) saw the girl beginning life as "a little man," most analysts now regard girls' early attachment to their mothers as a bond of identification that fosters their femininity. Numerous papers have disputed Freud's (1925, 1931, 1933) main contentions that girls are not aware of their own genitals, that they do not develop a firm superego, and that they are guided by envy of the opposite sex more than boys are. More generally, a new theory of gender identity (Stoller, 1968, 1973; Chodorow, 1978; Person and Ovesey, 1983; Fast, 1984) has been evolving that views gender development as a relational process of integrating identifications and separation issues. This new paradigm of gender not only corrects the flagrant depreciation of women but offers an explanation of developmental difficulties that boys as well as girls must negotiate. It offers a notion of gender that is not motivated by, although it does encompass, genital difference.

The new paradigm of gender is, however, somewhat at odds with current feminist theorizing, produced largely outside the auspices of psychoanalysis in academic disciplines, notably literature and philosophy. That theoretical approach questions the notion of unitary gender identity and challenges our acceptance of gender as a binary system (see Dimen 1991, and Goldner 1991). Once this system is questioned, femininity and masculinity no longer appear to be such seamless categories. Indeed, they are barely adequate to contain their volatile, sometimes explosive, subject matter. The confrontation between gender identification theory and this radical critique of gender categories may help to push our thinking into further unexplored territory.

I suggest that the paradigm of gender identification can expand to include flexible and metaphoric reinterpretations of the emblems of sexual difference. For example, once we question the goal of a normative "femininity" that excludes all elements of "masculinity," once we are aware of the opposing gendered aspects every self must negotiate, penis envy may become interesting again in a new way. The contemporary psychoanalytic mainstream seems to have accepted the clinical reinterpretation of penis envy as a "developmental metaphor" (Grossman and Stewart, 1977), but the possibilities of this metaphor have only begun to be explored. Actually, penis envy could become a kind of metaphor for the development of theory; its expanded capacity to represent multiple meanings and to allow multiple interpretations over time exemplifies the decentering of our method. Its wider epistemological implication would be to challenge notions of correct interpretation and definitive meaning—notions that have given way before the postmodern tide of uncertainty in all the related disciplines, especially in regard to gender. In this paper, I offer a new developmental analysis of penis envy, and I try to show how this perspective on development opens the way to accepting the multiplicity of meanings and interpretations of gender that appear in clinical work.

For Freud, of course, envy of the penis required no further explanation; it was the explanation. It provided a central question—How does the girl turn to her father and enter her Oedipus complex?—with a simple, elegant answer. In the genital phase, girls, primed by their focus on the clitoris as an active organ, instantaneously recognize the superiority of the penis and, resentful of their mothers, turn to the father, from whom they may finally hope to gain the penis or its substitute, the baby. This turn to a passive relation to the father and his phallus is the point at which the music stops and the girl is without a chair.

Those who dissented from Freud's original opinion—Horney (1924, 1933), Jones (1927, 1933), and Klein (1928)—did see penis envy as a phenomenon to be explained. They never disputed the existence of this phenomenon, observable in little girls. But why should a girl's envy of the penis exceed the narcissistic wish to possess everything, a wish parallel to a boy's wish for breasts or babies? These analysts did not agree that the superiority of the penis was so self-evident as to require no further thought. Both Klein and Horney argued that girls had much to cherish in their anticipation of motherhood and fertility. At the same time, Freud's question about why the little girl gives up her mother and turns to love the father did appear to have a self-evident answer. Assuming heterosexuality, they thought that little girls know about their vagina and its complementarity to the penis; consequently they desire to have that place in relation to father that mother now has.

Perhaps, Horney (1924, 1926) theorized, penis envy becomes salient only when the little girl backs off from father love, fears competing with her mother, and chooses, instead, to identify with father. Thus penis envy would not be the trigger of the Oedipus complex, as Freud thought, but, indeed, the result of a misfired oedipal situation, a "flight from womanhood." The perception of her own organs as damaged or inadequate might occur, Horney and Klein agreed, because the little girl fears injury as retribution for her envious wish to supplant mother by stealing her father's penis or injure her by stealing her babies. Klein's sense of the multiple meanings of penis envy

remains clinically interesting and fresh, I find, and Horney's work, in particular, deserves to be rescued from the disparagement it received at the hands
of the psychoanalytic establishment. It has been noted that Horney and Klein
answered Freud's original question about the switch to the father in a rather
Freudian way, by their own appeal to anatomical destiny (see Mitchell, 1974).
But, in fact, the idea of identification played a great part in their analysis as
well. Horney (1924), with considerable prescience, actually closed her
remarks on the castration complex by suggesting that Freud's latest writings
on identification show how important that process is in the evolution of
these difficulties.

Indeed, it was not until psychoanalysis produced a more developed theory
of identification and relocated the development of sexual difference in a much
earlier period that the questions of both Freud and his critics could be
reframed. At that point it became possible to explicate the importance of identifications, unconscious as well as conscious, in the formation of gender
(Chodorow, 1978; Fast, 1984; Stoller, 1968).

The idea of gender identity development did not, however, raise gender or
genitality into a conscious, conflict-free zone, as some defenders of Freud's
position feared. Rather, it moved the struggle with gender difference back
into the pre-oedipal period of separation-individuation; this move offered the
possibility of reinterpreting genital and other bodily preoccupations in light
of conflicts in self-development and object relations. This theoretical vantage
point can now reframe some of the dissenters' ideas as well. Take, for example, the flight from womanhood that Horney used to explain the persistence
of penis envy (or the masculinity complex), the girl's insistence on being like
the father rather than having him heterosexually. While Horney thought the
girl was retreating from an oedipal threat, we might see this insistence on
being like father as a pre-oedipal move to resolve difficulties in separation
by repudiating identification with the mother and identifying with the father.

Current reinterpretations of penis envy have emphasized the girl's need to
identify with the father as a figure of separation from the pre-oedipal mother. Emphasizing the power of the pre-oedipal mother and early object relations, the French analysts like McDougall (1980), Torok (1970), and
Chasseguet-Smirgel (1970) and the American feminists Chodorow (1978) and
Dinnerstein (1976) concur that the father and the phallus represent a power
independent of the mother. The French analysts see this "beating back the
mother" (Chasseguet-Smirgel, 1970) as a response to early maternal omnipotence, in particular the anally controlling, sexually repressive mother (Torok,
1970). In standing for difference and separation, the phallus becomes the
desired object for children of both sexes. The meaning of the penis as a symbol of revolt and separation derives from the nature of the child's struggle to
separate from the original maternal power.

The father, not the phallus, then becomes the point of departure for our
interpretation—the father as he is represented internally, refracted through
the conflicts that are currently dominant in the child's psyche. I have sug-

gested that in the period of maximal separation conflict—in rapprochement a representation of the father emerges that is significant for both boys and girls (Benjamin, 1986, 1988). The psychological imperatives of early narcissism and separation-individuation lead the child to invest the father and phallus with idealized attributes. These idealized attributes are crucial not only to self but also to sexual development.

Although psychoanalytic theory has given far less weight to the father than to the mother in the pre-oedipal period, it has generally recognized the importance of the father as a figure of identification for the boy. Father is crucial because the boy has been primarily parented by a woman; the boy needs, in Greenson's (1968) terms, to disidentify with mother in order to separate and assume his masculinity (Stoller, 1973). In conjunction with this view, some writers on male development (Blos, 1984; Tyson, 1986) have stressed the importance for the boy of the loved, not rivalrous, pre-oedipal or dyadic father. In "Group Psychology and the Analysis of the Ego" Freud (1921) noted the importance of the dyadic father in "the early history" of the Oedipus complex: "A boy will exhibit a special interest in his father; he would like to grow like him and be like him, and take his place everywhere....He takes his father as his ideal" (p. 105). This father of identification is beginning to be recognized as crucial to early separation and self-development; a boy's difficulties in separation are often traced to the father's unavailability for identification in this phase. No comparable value, however, is given to the father as an object in the girl's life and inner world, especially at this period. Only a few women analysts have given thought to the implications of paternal identification for girls (Bernstein, 1983; Chasseguet-Smirgel, 1970; Clower, 1977; Levenson, 1984; Rees, 1987; Spieler, 1984).

Abelin (1980), developing Mahler's position, has shown how the father's differences from the mother first assume salience for the child in the rapprochement phase, when gender difference and genital difference begin to be recognized. At that point the struggle to differentiate becomes fatefully intertwined with the consolidation of gender identity (see Mahler, Pine, and Bergman, 1975). I emphasize that this period not only involves separation anxiety, loss, or loss of omnipotence, but also the struggle for recognition, particularly, the difficult matter of being recognized as independent by the one on whom the child was dependent. The child is becoming conscious of intention, will, and agency in a new way; mother's leaving, for example, is not only about tolerating separation but also about recognizing that mother will not do as one wishes. At this point the child not only needs but also wants; that is, the child self-consciously wills to have or do something, for example, the child needs to eat but wants, even insists, on eating from the bowl with the clown picture. In each concrete expression of want lies a general wish to be recognized as a subject of desire rather than merely subject to a need. Rapprochement inaugurates the first of many such struggles to effect one's intent and be recognized in one's desire, and many later struggles will carry the imprint of this first paradigmatic struggle.

Now at this point, also, gender and genital difference begin to be registered, and the difference between mother and father begins to take hold symbolically in the psyche. As the conflict between the fear of separation and the desire to be independent comes to a head, the contradiction between security and autonomous will often feels unmanageable. The two irreconcilable needs then begin to be formulated as a gender split; mother represents attachment, and father represents the recognition of independence.

This split assumes, of course, traditional gender divisions in parenting, in which mother is the primary nurturing figure, associated with dependency, inside, security. But even in the increasing number of families that do not reproduce this stereotype we can often observe the creation of a fantasy father-hero who is able to represent the link to the exciting outside and assume the role of standing for freedom, separation, and desire. This observation does not mean, however, that psychic changes will not follow from changes in parenting and gender organization. Psychic structure evolves through the interaction of internal and external worlds. Thus, when the mother is the "coming and going," outside parent, this situation may reverse the structure (Pruett, 1987); it may, for example, lead a little boy to a much greater insistence on likeness with his mother, even on having the same anatomy or appearance as she does. This reversed gender structure, however, would probably not mesh with the culturally dominant representations of "outside" encountered a bit later, for example, male media heroes, and thus would not yield such an *apparent* coherence of gender identity as the traditional model does. For that matter, I do not believe that gender identity really is coherent at this point or that most boys need to or do disidentify with mother. The latter assumption derives from the questionable proposition (Stoller,1973) that the early identification with mother is gendered (see also Person and Ovesey, 1983). I suspect boys at this point do become more separate and simultaneously begin to differentiate paternal from maternal, adding and organizing aspects of the father in a more integrated and distinct way.

As Abelin explains, the child now needs to be able to represent himself or herself as a subject who desires, and the child meets this need by forming a symbolic representation of another subject with whom to identify. The father offers the boy toddler his first model of desire, and the boy now imagines himself to be the father, the subject of desire, in relation to the mother. While Abelin attributes central importance to the wish "I want Mommy," I believe that this formulation telescopes oedipal and pre-oedipal reactions; and is based largely on a case in which a new sibling took the mother away. Actually, I think Mahler's (1966, cited in Abelin, 1980) interpretation is more fundamental, that the father is a "knight in shining armor" because he comes from "outer space" and brings the excitement of outsideness, because he is not "contaminated" by conflicts around dependency.

In any event, the father now represents a different kind of object—a subject—who is not so much the source of goodness as the mirror of desire. He represents a subject who can want and act appropriately to fill those wants. The child gains from him not merely direct recognition through approval or confirmation but recognition through symbolic identification with this powerful subject who is his or her ideal. In a sense, the father's entry is a deus ex machina that solves the rapprochement dilemma of having to get the confirmation of independence from the one the child still longs to depend on. Identification with the father is a vehicle for avoiding conflict as well as for separation, for denying helplessness and the loss of practicing grandiosity. In the boy's mind, the magical father with whom he identifies is still as omnipotent as the boy would like to be (and as mother might be). Recognition through identification and its elaboration in fantasy are now substituted for the more conflictual need to be recognized by the primary parent with whom he feels his dependency. Of course, the child identifies with, and looks for recognition from, both parents at this time and attributes omnipotence to both. But while the mother's power appears to lie in control over the child and may be "contaminated" by the child's enmeshment with her, the power of the exciting father lies more in his relation to the world outside, beyond maternal power.

The affirmed identification with father, then, has a double aspect: on the one hand, a denial of rapprochement helplessness and on the other hand, a confirmation of the core experience of being the subject of desire. On the one hand, the identificatory impulse functions defensively to avoid the ambivalent mother; on the other hand, the wish to be like father expresses an intrinsic need to make desire one's own, to experience it as legitimate and self-originated, not as the property of the object, but as one's own, inner desire. Thus, many facets of the child's development may now impel him or her toward the father as a symbolic figure of recognition—the need to separate, the need to avoid ambivalence, and the need to find a subject who represents desire and excitement.

More generally, one upshot of this interpretation of the father is to acknowledge that identification plays a key role in love and desire. Identification, being like, is the chief mode in which a child of this age can acknowledge the subjectivity of another person. Identification is not merely an internal process but also a kind of relationship; Freud (1921) actually described identification as the first emotional tie to the object before he finalized its place as the precipitate of abandoned object cathexes (Freud, 1923). Peculiar to this phase of development, then, is a kind of identificatory love. This relationship of identification is with someone outside and different from the first object, someone who is a subject, not a source of goodness. Identificatory love is the relational context in which, for males, separation and gender identification occur. The strong, mutual attraction between father and son allows for recognition through identification, a special erotic relationship. The practicing toddler's "love affair with the world" turns into a homoerotic love affair with the father, who represents the world. The boy is in love with his ideal. This homoerotic, identificatory love serves as the boy's vehicle of establishing masculine identify and confirms his sense of himself as subject of desire.

Of course, this process of identification can be successful only when it is reciprocal, when the father identifies with his son and makes himself available to him. Fathers, it seems, do respond to their sons' need for identification more positively than to their daughters'. Fathers prefer their boy infants and form a more intense bond based on identification, which is followed by greater mutual attachment and mutual identification in toddlerhood (Lamb, 1977; Gunsberg, 1982). For its part, psychoanalytic theory has uncritically reflected this reality. It has made the girl's relationship to the father, in contrast to the boy's, hinge on the phallus rather than on identification with him. Her desire surfaces in a defensive, part-object context rather than a whole-object context. In fact, identification with the father has been given no structured place in the girl's pre-oedipal development comparable to that of the mother for the boy. The observation that little girls in rapprochement become more depressed and lose more of their practicing enthusiasm than do boys was linked by Mahler et al. (1975) to the recognition of the anatomical difference. Roiphe and Galenson (1981) wrote a book on the early genital phase to advance that proposition. Abelin (1980), too, argued that the father plays a small part for the girl—perhaps, he said, because of her penis envy. In this view, the father's unavailability is secondary, contingent on the girl's castration reaction, that is, her recognition of anatomical difference.

My argument is just the opposite. I suggest that the rapprochement girl's wish for a penis is not a self-evident response to anatomical difference. She desires it even as the boy cherishes it (or will come to cherish it) because she is struggling to individuate. Girls seek what toddler boys recognize in their fathers and wish, through identification, to affirm in themselves—recognition of their own desire. Girls' ambivalence around separation may be more intense than that of boys because of the bond of likeness between mother and daughter—all the more reason for them, too, to seek a different object in whom to recognize their independence. This other object is very often the father, and his otherness is guaranteed and symbolized by his other genital. Precisely when this father is unavailable, envy of the penis expresses the girl's longing for him.

Even Galenson and Roiphe (1982), in their effort to prove that the girl's rapprochement depression derives from a castration reaction, inadvertently provide only examples of girls who miss their absent fathers. They sum up one little girl's longing for a departed father and say that "the missing excitement and erotic nature of their relationship, which had earlier been attached to the father in toto was now identified as emanating from his phallus in particular" (p. 162). Mahler et al. (1975) report a similar case, Cathy, whose father is away and who begins to express envy of a little boy's penis during that time. No doubt, the transformation from excitement and desire in general to the (unattainable) phallus does begin here, especially enhanced when the father himself is "missing." But this clamoring for the symbol expresses the loss behind the rapprochement depression—it does not cause it.

Still, we might ask, Can the girl, through a more positive identification with the father, resolve this difficulty and come to feel that desire and agency are properly hers? Ideally, we look forward to the evolution of a cultural context and familial constellations that allow girls (and boys) to identify with a mother who is outside as well as inside, who can represent subjectivity just as well as the father. But in the familial culture that is characterized by a traditional gender division, daughters have tried (and will probably continue to try) to use paternal identification in this way. However misinterpreted, the fact of penis envy does testify to this effort. For psychoanalytic theory the question remains, Could a more positive father-daughter relationship, in fact, allow a different integration of identification?

This question points to the broader theoretical issue: the need to decenter the notion of gender identification, so that it refers to the plurality of developmental positions rather than to a unilinear line of development, which is ultimately referable to the anatomical difference. I propose that children do use cross-sex identifications to formulate important parts of their self-representations as well as to elaborate fantasies about sexual relations (e.g., to fill out the character of the other in their sexual dramas). One support for this proposition would be Fast's theory of gender differentiation, which suggests that initially children do not recognize that certain possibilities are excluded because of an anatomical difference. Children in the pre-oedipal phase are "overinclusive"; Fast says that they believe they can have or be everything; for both girls and boys identifications with both parents continue until the oedipal recognition of sexual complementarity precipitates a crisis of loss and renunciation. The sense of self and secondary characteristics that are integrated through these identifications may continue even when specific, opposite-sex capacities are renounced.

In fact, I think a careful study of gender differentiation suggests that there are more phases and more tension between inclusion and exclusion than psychoanalytic theory has yet recognized. Once core gender identity is established in the first 12 to 18 months of life, the child proceeds to elaborate gender role identity in conjunction with separation-individuation issues, hence in a conflictual and variable context (Person and Ovesey, 1983). Children continue throughout the second and third years to identify with both parents, even though their roles are somewhat differentiated and the father may assume special importance. Toward the end of the overinclusive pre-oedipal phase, Fast (1984) theorizes, the child shows simultaneous awareness of the limits of gender (complementarity) and a determined protest against them; this is the period of penis envy and pregnancy envy par excellence. Here, castration fear means being robbed of what the other sex has. As the oedipal phase begins, as the child realizes he or she can be only one thing, an overly rigid notion of complementarity and a repudiation of the opposite sex set in. This early oedipal stance is marked by the defense against loss and envy: sour grapes but also romance—the heteroerotic desire for the idealized other. At this time castration anxiety begins to mean, for girls as well as boys, loss of one's own genitals (Mayer, 1985). Later on in the oedipal phase (or in the adolescent replay), both castration fear and repudiation of the opposite sex can be toned down. Ideally this allows reintegration of cross-sex identifications and access to a transitional sense of overinclusiveness (Bassin, 1990)—a happy outcome that, for reasons I have discussed elsewhere, most notably the disparagement and sub-jugation of women (Benjamin, 1988), can by no means be taken for granted.

In any event, it is important to differentiate those longings and anxieties related to the rapprochement father identification from heterosexual feelings that appear in the oedipal phase. The assumption has too often been made that the girl's pre-oedipal interest in her father, because erotic, is heterosex-ual. But the interest in the penis at this phase is not heterosexual, and it is not about reuniting with father or mother; it is about homoerotic incorpora-tion, about having something that competes with the powerful breast. It is a homoerotic desire, a desire for likeness, which often resurfaces in the laten-cy wish to be a buddy. Optimally, the father's affirmation of this bond does not preclude the development of oedipal complementarity later on, does not reflect the father's denial of the daughter's femininity. The complex nature of the father-daughter relationship has often been obscured by analytic accep-tance of the fallacy that all opposite-sex love is heterosexual. As Harris (1991) pointed out in her discussion of Freud's "Case of Homosexuality in a Woman," whether a loved object is perceived as different or like, whether it is a heteroerotic or homoerotic choice, is not determined merely by the object's sex. To assume that it is so determined would be, to borrow a phrase, to do psychoanalysis in the missionary position.

Each love object embodies multiple possibilities of sameness and difference, masculinity and femininity, and one love relationship may serve a multitude of functions. In each relationship the axis of similarity and complementarity is aligned somewhat differently with the axis of gender. Paradoxically, the other who appears to be different may be loved in order to be or become more like him or her; through incorporation and assimilation in our fantasy, as well as through loving recognition by the person we take as our ideal, we hope even-tually to become that ideal. "The female tendency to love the embodiment of her own sacrificed ego ideal in the man" (Jacobson, 1937, p. 536; see also A. Reich, 1940) was recognized by early women analysts but was explained psy-cho-sexually as founded in the wish to incorporate the penis orally. My argu-ment is the reverse—that the incorporation of the genital is a means of becom-ing the ideal object rather than being an end in itself.

The father, then, can be an object of homoerotic love for the girl. This homoerotic love, impelled by the developmental force of separation, may, indeed, lead the way into a later heterosexuality. At the beginning of the oedi-pal phase, when she confronts the exclusivity of genital difference and realizes she cannot be or have everything, the girl may switch from homoerotic to het-eroerotic love; she may choose to love in men the masculinity that she once wished to have herself. Still, this love will be less tainted with submission and guilt to the degree that her identificatory love has been recognized: she will not have to steal or envy his masculinity. It is also true that a girl's oedipal conflicts and striving to be the stereotyped heterosexual object may mask or negate her earlier striving for identificatory love, especially if it was unsuccessful. But the rapprochement phase, even with its incipient recognition of the genital difference, is not yet the Oedipus complex.

Here I would like to address some of the main consequences of disappointment in identificatory love of the father. I have argued previously (Benjamin, 1986, 1988) that the idealization of the phallus and the wish for a missed identificatory love with father inspires adult women's fantasies about loving men who represent their ideal. The early deflation of omnipotence in daughters who miss their father's recognition may, as some analysts appear to think, have its rewards in ego development and identification with mother; but too often such daughters wind up admiring the men who get away with their grandiosity intact. As mothers, they may become especially indulgent and proud of their sons' grandiosity. Or this admiration (concealing unconscious envy or resentment) may be expressed in a special kind of relationship to their ideal, a relationship often tinged with service or submission, sometimes with sexual masochism. The adult woman's ideal love scenarios often show identificatory, homoerotic themes, in which a woman is finally recognized by the one who represents the subject she would like to be. There is a genre of male-female adventure films that express this fantasy, in which sexual romance can be achieved only after the success of the cooperative venture in which the woman displays or assimilates much of the man's abilities and daring.

A confirmed recognition from the father—"Yes, you can be like me"—helps the child consolidate the identification and so enhances the sense of being a subject of desire. But the lack of recognition and the denial of the identificatory bond damage the sense of being a sexual subject and lead the woman to look for her desire through a man—and frequently to masochistic fantasies of surrendering to the ideal man's power. The search for identificatory love is thematic in many relationships of submission. (This observation is true not only of women with men, but also, of course, of male submission to more powerful, older males; the search for a father of identification culminating in a deferential or submissive relationship is very typical for men in adolescence or young adulthood. As fathers, these same men may remain distant from their sons in order to defend against what they feel to be the sadistic quality of the homoerotic bond, a quality that reflects their own anger and masochism toward their fathers.)

In line with this perspective on women's submission, I also suggested that the daughter's homoerotic love of the father might shed light on Freud's (1919) discussion of the masturbation fantasy, "A Child Is Being Beaten." One thing that puzzled Freud at first was that the girl's fantasy always depicted a boy being beaten by the father, and it was the boy with whom she masochistically identified. Freud concluded that girls used a boy in the fantasy because they were turning away from the incestuous love of the father that "spurs their masculinity complex" (a phrase he used here for the first time). I am proposing that the beaten child had to be a boy because the fantasy of being the father's son was, in fact, the central frustrated wish. The humiliation associated with the disappointment of this wish was expressed in the sexually exciting punishment— a humiliation that was likely to be iatrogenically intensified by the misunderstanding of penis envy and the condemnation of the masculinity complex in the "dark ages" of psychoanalysis.

A striking illustration of how the wish to be the father's son might underlie the woman's masochistic fantasy can be found in an analysis of the origins of Freud's essay. Young-Bruehl (1988), in her biography of Anna Freud, contends that Anna was actually the patient on whom Freud probably based much of this material. Since Anna was in analysis with her father during this period and wrote a paper on beating fantasies three years later in order to be admitted to the Vienna Psychoanalytic Society, at a time when she was not yet seeing patients, Young-Bruehl concludes that her paper and Freud's thesis were based on her own analysis. And Anna also fitted the description of the patient in her own paper who obsessively created what she called "nice stories" about younger men being punished by older men to cover the earlier beating fantasies; she, too, finally successfully sublimated these into stories of male heroes. The story of Anna's rebelliousness against her mother's control, her struggle against masturbation and the obsessional "stories," her place at her father's side, even her use of this paper to gain admission to her father's world, and, indeed, Freud's own confession that he would "feel like Junius Brutus the elder when he had to judge his own son" (cited in Young-Bruehl, 1988, p. 108)—all suggest how the wish to be son to her father, a forbidden homoerotic love, might underlie that sexual fantasy. In any event, the happy ending was that Anna's paper was accepted, and when one of the membership said that Anna's patient was "totally abnormal," her father came to her rescue and "defended her little girl" (p. 108). Is it possible that this solution, Freud's acceptance of Anna as his "son," helped her to resolve her struggle with the masochistic, sexual form of this fantasy?

It is also worth noting that Freud's paper essentially proposed the same argument that Horney (1926) later elaborated in "The Flight from Womanhood," that the girl regresses from her genital, incestuous love into a masculine identification. This interpretation raises again the question of which motive, identification or object love, comes first and how to disentangle the two. This question has always been tricky, even for Freud; on the one hand, identification was the earliest emotional tie to the object, and on the other, it was the precipitate of object relations. The problem could be solved by decentering our explanation and saying, "All of the above." It seems generally likely that, by the time she has reached adulthood, the daughter's identification as her father's son would incorporate more than one motive, none of the motives mutually exclusive. That identification could express a defense against heterosexual involvement with father, or a defensive repudiation of the mother, or an unsatisfied wish for identificatory love complicated by rejection, humiliation, and punishment. The formal problem in our theory has been the insistence on *one* motive, usually oedipal; the substantive problem has been conflating the fantasy of pain with the desire for pain and thus missing the real wish—the wish for a close, identificatory bond with the father and the humiliation associated with rejection of it.

Psychoanalysts have generally assumed that the positive father transference of their women patients is oedipal and heterosexual in content. The longing to identify with the idealized father of separation in order to be empowered, to separate from mother, and to feel excited, a longing that appeared in the guise of penis envy, was interpreted as resistance to oedipal feelings, or it was simply conflated with oedipal wishes ("You want to have my baby"). Psychoanalysis also interpreted the idealized father transference of male patients, or the urge to submit to father in order to incorporate the phallus, as a negative oedipal stance (an identification with a passive mother) rather than an expression of the longing to recognize themselves in, and be recognized by, the early dyadic father.

This reinterpretation of oedipal material and penis envy fits well with some of the case material in recent literature. For example, Kohut (1977) recounts a reanalysis of a case in which penis envy played a significant role (although Kohut's alignment of mirroring with the mother and cohesion with the father does not capture the role of the father as mirror of desire). The patient, Miss V, dreamed that she was standing urinating over a toilet and that someone was watching her from behind. (Interestingly, Horney [1924] cites a woman who had a similar formulation—"I am urinating like my father, standing up"—as her chief masturbation fantasy.) Kohut tells us that Miss V's previous analyst had made repeated attempts to get her to recognize that her hopelessness stemmed from her insoluble wish to get the penis. He interpreted that this dream and her wish to see the father's penis stemmed from a need to "extricate herself from her relation with her bizarre and emotionally shallow mother and turn toward her emotionally more responsive and down-to-earth father" (p. 221). What I would add here is that this turn to the father not only is a defense against mother, and a result of mother's inadequacy, but also reflects a developmentally appropriate wish to be seen by the father (the analyst) as like him. Furthermore, the defensive direction (away from mother) should not eclipse the erotic direction (toward father), which reflects the original eroticism of identificatory love.

I would speculate that the more confirmation and the less humiliation a girl meets with when she tries to fulfill the wish for identificatory love, the more the wish emerges free of self-abnegating or masochistic elements. For example, the wish was articulated in the dream of a married woman who was involved in an intense, ideal love of an admired mentor. He treated her as a favorite student, indeed, as a daughter, invited her to spend time with him and his wife, and greatly encouraged her work, which progressed accordingly. In this simple dream she was masturbating and, while doing so, speaking to someone who, she reflected on waking, must certainly have been the mentor. The words she uttered were, "I want to be your little boy."

In a case reported by Bernstein (1983), the wish to be the father's son emerges in the transference to a woman analyst. The patient dreams she appears at the analyst's office dressed as a boy, "feeling sort of sheepish but seems to be asking you if it is okay." The associations are about "fathers who wanted their sons to follow in their footsteps, sons who wanted to be like

ter for herself, that is, at a pre-oedipal level. In one session the patient reports reading about the Oedipus complex:

> The father is supposed to interrupt the mother-child relationship, but that was not allowed in my family. In the formula I read the child wants to stay with mother, but I was longing to have father step in. But then he didn't so I had to find some one else....What I want is not sex; it's union with the father without mother, and sex gets in the way. They say the phallus mediates the union of child and father. I say the penis gets in the way. What I want is to be little kids, those two whole little kids, and play....I'm thinking of the time I made this little boat, and he insisted on floating it on the stream at the end of the field, despite my mother's vociferous protests and mine. And then it got lost, and was he in the doghouse....That was the recurring thing, Daddy wants to do something irresponsible and she is protecting me...but maybe he was trying to show me we could have fun with something. [I say, maybe he was trying to show you that the boat could go off by itself, and you saw your mother was right that it couldn't, but you partly wished he had been right.]

The phrase "whole little kid" is from her memory of getting out of the bath, standing in front of the mirror, and feeling great about herself, memory coupled with the fantasy of having alongside her another kid, boy who is a twin, also whole. Each is complete and has everything (pre-oedipal—being, not having, the phallus). The relationship is one of mirroring, and she would like this without the oedipal-sexual penis getting in the way; she and father would be alike, whole and independent—preserving the grandiosity that the rapprochement depression and all subsequent experiences of maternal dependency and control have deflated.

Then again, she edges up to the erotic edge of identification with father. She is talking about how she and her dad are skinny and her husband is fat like her mother. "We are both skinny, unencumbered, sexy, fleet of foot, more active than thinking." I ask, "What do you want from Dad?" She says emphatically, "Me!" Immediately, she thinks how angry she is at a supervisor at work who has been preventing her from getting to her sessions with me by asking her to do things when it is time to leave. She has felt too guilty to stand up for herself because therapy is too self-indulgent and what she wants from me is forbidden. Her associations make me the forbidden "sexy man" who is outside mother's sphere. But when I frame this sequence in terms of her fear of being unfaithful to mother, she tells me she is preoccupied with a recent incident in which she felt spurned and ridiculed by a woman colleague with whom she is enchanted. The woman actually seemed to make fun of her solicitude and discerned that my patient was infatuated with her. This experience was like the searing childhood memory of giving her brother a present from the fair and his spurning it because his friends were with him—"I was just a little girl." Not only the mother's prohibition but the humiliation of being spurned by father, brother, or me bars the way.

Again, we can note the changing positions of men and women: the woman who plays the role of brother, the analyst who is able to be both father and mother, sometimes brother. (The woman analyst represents the father directly and not just the mother who embodies in a "transitional" way the love of the father [Ogden, 1987].) As the associations make clear, the fear associated profoundly with disappointed identificatory love is not only fear of separation or mother's prohibition but humiliation by the beloved. I believe that this humiliation, the narcissistic injury of refusal by the idealized beloved, is one key to the humiliation and punishment associated with envy of the man.

The idealized phallus of the pre-oedipal father can devolve on male or female. The analyst can more easily hold that position, regardless of her or his sex, because the father of identificatory love stems from a phase in which gender is not perceived as fixed; he is a volatile figure. In this case, the figure assumes many guises, including the brother, the idealized older woman, and the sexy man. Each of these holds in common the possibility of mirroring the woman's self and allowing her to experience herself as separate, unencumbered, desiring, and having something of her own. Like the figure who possesses it, the phallus that represents desire also shifts in its relation to her own sexuality—sometimes it is a penis, sometimes her whole body, sometimes her own feminine sexuality.

More generally, this material shows how the symbolic identifications like "mother" and "father" establish fixed points on the internal map on which the parents, the analyst, and the self can be imagined as movable spheres. Real objects chart their trajectory across these points and along the axes of "masculinity" and "femininity," not in straight lines but in complex patterns. Thus we are justified, I believe, in hoping that even the persistence of a gender order can allow for great change, including the possibility that mothers, as well as fathers, may occupy the position of representing desire.

It also follows that the phallus, the father, indeed, any love object, has more than one part to play. In our earliest experience of desire, that of identificatory love, forces that later clash seem magically reconcilable: eros and separation are uniquely blended as are idealization of the other and autonomy. Perhaps this tension, though hidden, plays an important part in adult love, too, in which object love and identification, as well as sameness and difference, both contribute. In any event, the father of separation is also an erotic father, and the child's longing to be recognized in and by his father is not only defensive or hostile to the mother. Whether it be only father or, as we hope, both mother and father who represent the first subject of desire, whoever holds this position also represents the child's love of the world. It is up to us as analysts to recognize this love in all its guises.

REFERENCES

Abelin, E. L. (1980). Triangulation, the role of the father and the origins of core gender identity during the rapprochement subphase. In: *Rapprochement,* ed. R.F. Lax, S. Bach & J.A. Burland. New York: Aronson, pp. 151–170.

Bassin, D. (1990). The reconciliation of gender polarities at the genital stage. Presented at meeting of Division 39, American Psychological Association, New York City.

Benjamin, J. (1986). The alienation of desire: Woman's masochism and ideal love. In: *Woman and psychoanalysis,* ed. J. Alpert. Hillsdale, NJ: The Analytic Press, pp. 113–138.

———— (1988). *The bonds of love.* New York: Pantheon Books.

Bernstein, D. (1983). The female superego: A different perspective. *Internat. j. psychoanal.,* 64:187–202.

Blos, P. (1984). Son and father. *J. Amer. psychoanal. assn.,* 32:301–324.

Chasseguet-Smirgel, J. (1970). Feminine guilt and the Oedipus complex. In: *Female sexuality,* ed. J. Chasseguet-Smirgel. Ann Arbor: Michigan University Press, pp. 94–134.

————(1976). Freud and female sexuality. *Internat. j. psycho-anal.,* 57: 275–286.

Chodorow, N. (1978). *The reproduction of mothering.* Berkeley: University of California Press.

————(1979). Difference, relation and gender in psychoanalytic perspective. *Socialist rev.,* 9, no. 4:51–70.

Clower, V.L. (1977). Theoretical implications in current views of masturbation in latency girls. In: *Female psychology,* ed. H. Blum. New York: International Universities Press, pp. 109–126.

Dimen, M (1991) Deconstructing difference: Gender, splitting, and transitional space. *Psychoanalytic dialogues,* 1(3): 335–352.

Dinnerstein, D. (1976). *The mermaid and the minotaur.* New York: Harper & Row.

Fast, I. (1984). *Gender identity.* Hillsdale, NJ: The Analytic Press.

Freud, S. (1919). A child is being beaten. *SE,* 17:179–204. London: Hogarth Press, 1955.

————(1921). *Group psychology and the analysis of the ego. SE,* 18:67–144. London: Hogarth Press, 1955.

————(1923). *The ego and the id. SE,* 19:1–66. London: Hogarth Press, 1961.

————(1924a). The dissolution of the Oedipus complex. *SE,* 19:173–182. London: Hogarth Press, 1961.

————(1924b). The economic problem of masochism. *SE,* 19:159–172. London: Hogarth Press, 1961.

————(1925). Some psychical consequences of the anatomical distinction between the sexes. *SE,* 19:248–260. London: Hogarth Press, 1961.

————(1931). Female sexuality. *SE* 21: 225–246. London: Hogarth Press, 1961.

————(1933). *New introductory lectures on psychoanalysis*: Femininity. *SE,* 22:112–135. London: Hogarth Press, 1961.

Galenson, E. & Roiphe, H. (1982). The preoedipal relationship of a father, mother, and daughter. In: *Father and child,* ed. S.H. Cath, A.R. Gurwitt & J.M. Ross. Boston: Little, Brown, pp. 151–162.

Gilligan, C. (1982). *In a different voice.* Cambridge, MA: Harvard University Press.

Goldner, V. (1991) Toward a critical relational theory of gender. *Psychoanalytic dialogues.* 1(3): 249–272.

Greenson, R. (1968). Dis-identifying from mother: Its special importance for the boy. *Internat. j. psycho-anal.*, 49:370–374.

Grossman, W.I. & Stewart, W.A. (1977). Penis envy: From childhood wish to developmental metaphor. In: *Female psychology*, ed. H. Blum. New York: International Universities Press, pp. 193–212.

Gunsberg, L. (1982). Selected critical review of psychological investigations of the early father-infant relationship. In: *Father and child*, ed. S.H. Cath, A.R. Gurwitt & J.M. Ross. Boston: Little, Brown, pp. 65–82.

Harris, A. (1991). Gender as contradiction. *Psychoanal. dial.*, 1:197–224.

Horney, K. (1924). On the genesis of the castration complex in women. In: *Feminine psychology*. New York: Norton, 1967, pp. 37–54.

———(1926). The flight from womanhood. In: *Feminine psychology*. New York: Norton, 1967, pp. 54–70.

———(1933). The denial of the vagina. In: *Feminine psychology*. New York: Norton, 1967, pp. 147–162.

Jacobson, E. (1937). Ways of female superego formation and the female castration conflict. *Psychoanal. quart.*, 45:525–538, 1976.

Jones, E. (1927). Early development of female sexuality. In: *Papers on psychoanalysis*. Boston: Beacon Press, 1961.

———(1933). Early female sexuality. In: *Papers on Psychoanalysis*. Boston: Beacon Press, 1961.

Klein, M. (1928). Early states of the Oedipus complex. *Internat. j. psycho-anal.*, 9:167–180.

Kohut, H. (1977). *The restoration of the self.* New York: International Universities Press.

Lamb, M.E. (1977). The development of parental preferences in the first two years of life. *Sex roles*, 3:495–497.

Levenson, R. (1984). Intimacy, autonomy and gender: Developmental differences and their reflection in adult relationships. *J. Amer. psychoanal.*, 12:529–544.

McDougall, J. (1980). *Plea for a measure of abnormality.* New York: International Universities Press.

Mahler, E.L. (1985). "Everybody must be just like me": Observations on female castration anxiety. *Internat. j. psycho-anal.*, 66:331–348.

Mahler, M.S., Pine, F., and Bergman, A. (1975). *The psychological birth of the human infant.* New York: Basic Books.

Mitchell, J. (1974). *Psychoanalysis and feminism.* New York: Pantheon.

Ogden, T. (1987). The transitional oedipal relationship in female development. *Internat. j. psycho-anal.*, 68:485–498.

Person, E.S., & Ovesey, L. (1983). Psychoanalytic theories of gender identity. *J. amer. acad. psychoanal.*, 11:203–226.

Rees, K. (1987). I want to be a daddy. *Psychoanal. quart.*, 56:497–522.

Reich, A. (1940). A contribution to the psychoanalysis of extreme submissiveness in women. *Psychoanal. quart.*, 9:470–480.

Roiphe, H. & Galenson, E. (1981). *Infantile origins of sexual identity.* New York: International Universities Press.

Spieler, S. (1984). Preoedipal girls need fathers. *Psychoanal. rev.*, 71:63–80.

Stoller, R.J. (1968). *Sex and gender.* New York: Aronson.

———(1973). Facts and fancies: An examination of Freud's concept of bisexuality. In: *Women and analysis*, ed. J. Strouse. Boston: Hall, 1985, pp. 343–364.

Torok, M. (1970). The significance of penis envy in women. In: *Female sexuality*, ed.

J. Chasseguet-Smirgel. Ann Arbor: University of Michigan Press.

Tyson, P. (1986). Male gender identity: Early developmental roots. *Psychoanal. rev.*, 73:405–425.

Winnicott, D.W. (1971). The use of an object and relating through identifications. In: *Playing and reality.* Harmondsworth, Middlesex: Penguin, pp. 101–111.

Young-Bruehl, E. (1988). *Anna Freud.* New York: Summit Books.

Part Three

THE DEBATE BROADENS

INTRODUCTION

Eifersucht [jealousy] is a *Leidenschaft* [passion] which *mit Eifer such* [with eagerness seeks] what *Leiden Schafft* [causes pain].
—*joke, attributed to Schleiermacher (SE 8:35)*

While, for the most part, the concept of penis envy has been surrounded in the literature on gender theory with an aura of unease, it has nevertheless dominated the discussion of gender and envy in psychoanalytic thought from Freud's time to the present. Even feminist theorists who focus their attention on women's development in particular generally limit their discussion of the interaction of gender and envy to a critique, endorsement or rejection of penis envy; of 10 recent, well-respected anthologies of writings on women and psychoanalysis, only three had index listings of the word "envy" at all, and two of these were referring to *Envy and Gratitude*. On the other hand, "penis envy" was heavily referenced in each of the volumes, and the average number of pages cited was 25 times greater than that for envy in general and other specific types of envy, such as womb envy or vagina envy, combined. Yet the debates reflected in the first two sections of this volume refer consistently to other forms of and bases for envy which are rooted in the development of psychological gender, each as potentially intricate, complex and controversial as penis envy has historically proven to be.

To approach the question of the relationship between gender and envy from beyond the specific confines of the penis envy debate necessitates an appreciation not only of the range of the psychoanalytic theories of gender development, but of envy as well. Here, the tensions between essentialism and constructivism, monism and pluralism, object-love and identification, are raised all over again, as the reader is forced to face such questions as, "What is envy?" and "What's the difference between envy and jealousy?" and "Is envy an aspect of the unanalyzable bedrock of human nature, or is it, itself, a secondary phenomenon?" and "How, if at all, is envy tethered to the development of gender in general?" The task of approaching these questions is complicated further by the fact that psychoanalytic theories of envy are even less developed than are those of gender; if women were, to Freud, the dark continent of psychoanalysis, envy at this point is an even darker expanse, penetrated only by a very few, albeit quite substantial, inroads.

The first of these, at least in the psychoanalytic literature, was made by Freud himself, as he constructed a theory of the ways in which the child's rivalrous, jealous, or envious feelings resulted in the buildup of internal structures that, in the aggregate, formed his or her character. In Freud's writing, such stories take a myriad of forms; he describes envy and jealousy between siblings, between father and son, between the primal hoard of brothers and their god, between mothers and daughters, fathers and daughters, mothers and sons, and so on, in seemingly endless combination; his letters and autobiographical statements reveal, too, his preoccupation with, and attempts to come to terms with, the envious feelings that arose in his own life. In all these stories, jealousy is taken to be a primary, in some sense unanalyzable, part of infantile life, about which "there is not much to be said from the analytic point of view" (*SE* 18: 223), a foundational sentiment to which all later manifestations can be traced. And indeed, although he does suggest in a few places that this sentiment can be broken down into its components, such as fear of loss, a wound to narcissism, hatred, and omnipotent belief, and at some points implies that jealousy can be distinguished from envy as a later, relational manifestation of it (*SE* 19: 254), he does not attempt to trace its roots down into that pre-oedipal darkness into which, for so much of his life, he was loathe to go.

Klein, however, was not deterred by the vision of that dark portal, and her writing on envy, culminating in *Envy and Gratitude* (1957), has been taken as definitive in psychoanalysis since it, and the controversy that surrounded it from its inception, first appeared (the reader is referred to that essay as essential background reading for an appreciation of the present debate). In that work, Klein describes the foundation for later, gendered forms of envy in a universal envy of the mother's breast that exists from birth, and traces the vicissitudes of this envious feeling as it plays out in the battle between the life and death instincts, and as it contributes to the infant's object relations and orientation to the world. She defines envy, places it within the context of its relationship to gratitude, describes the defenses against it and their effects, pinpoints its role in the development of psychopathology, and discriminates it from the related phenomena of jealousy and rivalry. In her theory, like that presented in the later works of Horney (Keyishian, 1982), envy in its most fundamental form is common to, and indistinguishable in, individuals of both sexes, but she diverges from Horney's view that it is secondary or incidental, and indeed necessarily pathological, when it emerges (Kerr, 1987).

Klein's ideas have provided an apt arena in which debates over what is most fundamental in the human psyche can once again unfold. While her followers, notably Bion, Rosenfeld, and Segal, have expanded upon the fundamental account of envy presented in her 1957 paper, others have taken issue with her idea that envy is a primary building block of character which is constitutionally given, albeit influenced in its outward form by experience. In many respects, the debate about the foundational status of envy has mirrored or coincided with debates about the nature of aggression; while some authors see envy as a primary (Etchegoyen, 1987), irreducible (Berke, 1987), and indeed perhaps unknowable (Schneider, 1988) aspect of human life that is indissolubly linked with aggression, others claim that "Klein's formulations of infantile greed and envy can be applied without presupposition of inherent aggression arising within the child" (Mitchell, 1981). Thus, alternative accounts of the origins of envy have been offered in response to Klein's ideas, the most notable and comprehensive being that of Boris, who traces envy to a frustration in the basic needs for an object which is both similar and different (1994) (an account that seems to offer a context for the self-psychological view of envy as a manifestation of disruption in the twinship transference [Wahba, 1991]). Another important contribution, that of Colman (1991), marks envy as a defense against a premature impingement upon the sphere of omnipotence that surrounds the hermetic field circumscribed in the earliest postnatal period by the infant and its mother.

It is against this backdrop of tension between competing understandings of the natures of envy and of gender per se that the essays included in this section of the book unfold. While most of these were inspired, first and foremost, by an interest in understanding the vicissitudes of gender development, each relies, even if implicitly, upon a particular way of envisioning envy as well, and thus stands to contribute to discussion in both arenas of thought. Of recent efforts to contextualize the penis envy debate within a broader framework, Irene Fast's has been perhaps the most influential and far-reaching. Following Freud's view that the recognition of gender *identity* as perceived by children hinges inextricably upon the recognition of gender *difference*, Fast develops an account of early development as proceeding out of a shared point of origin, although not the phallic one that Freud originally conceptualized. Fast argues that a depiction of this point of origin as male does as little justice to our understanding of boy's development as to the girl's, and she suggests instead that it be reconceptualized as an "undifferentiated and overinclusive earliest matrix" in which children of both sexes lay implicit claim to a broad range of sexual characteristics that, from an adult perspective, might even be seen as contradictory. It is only within the process of discovering limits in general, and limits to their sexuality in particular, as they are forced to come to terms with "losing" characteristics to which they had previously laid claim, that envy arises in both sexes for those relinquished aspects that they imagine to have been retained in others. Thus, in Fast's view, envy in its general and specific forms is an artifact of the struggle with limits, just as a sense of oneself as gendered, in terms of the child's own perception of it, is constructed in the course of development. Although the essay included in this volume can be read apart from the other chapters in her book *Gender Identity*, it does not capture the sweep of her effort to chart the course of gender differentiation and its implications for the development of identity in general, to her more extended discussion of which the reader is thus referred.

The two papers that follow Fast's, by Kittay and by Freud, each focus upon an aspect of envy or jealousy of *women*, as experienced by men in their struggles, in Fast's words, to come to terms with the developmental process of differentiation. In "Mastering Envy," Eva Feder Kittay presents and comments on Bettelheim's book *Symbolic Wounds* (1962), which highlights men's fundamental envy of women's procreative capacities. To be sure, men's envy was well-known to the analytic community prior to Bettelheim's observations; Freud described it in his patients, it was reported on by such psychoanalytic forerunners as Groddeck, Klein, Zilboorg, and Fromm, and Horney took its influence as the basis for phallocentric bias in psychoanalytic theories of women's development. But Bettelheim's work represented the most extended study of the phenomenon to date; he combined observational data gleaned from his work at the Orthogenic School with ethnographic data to argue that "penis envy in girls and castration anxiety in boys have been overemphasized, and a possibly much deeper psychological layer in boys has been relatively neglected...which, for want of a better term, might be called...'vagina envy'" (p. 20). Kittay offers a commentary both on Bettelheim's arguments regarding the prevalence in men of womb envy and their defenses against it, and on his observations about how culture serves to bind and metabolize this envy. Although she finds much of value in his writings on the individual and social ramifications of womb envy, however, she argues that his estimate of the success of the cultures he observes in accommodating it is unrealistically optimistic. Alternatively, she offers suggestions for a more benign cultural resolution of male envy of women. In this regard, Kittay's essay offers an entree into the discussion that unfolds in this book's fifth section concerning the social implications of gender and envy.

While Freud's discussions of envy in men were often overshadowed, at least in later accounts of his ideas, by his attention to the issue of penis envy, he nevertheless devoted a great deal of effort to understanding its role in their psychological lives as well. Despite his assertion that jealousy "plays a far larger part in the mental life of women than of men" (*SE* 19: 254, 22: 125) due to its reinforcement from the current of penis envy, he generally portrayed jealousy and envy in adult life as universal phenomena, isomorphic in the dreams (*SE* 12: 64), transference manifestations (*SE* 16: 442), and general psychological lives of men and women. Although, in the essay by Freud included here, he emphasizes the universality of jealousy in its various forms, he refers substantively only to the cases of male patients, and pays particular attention to jealousy's contribution to homosexuality in men. Inasmuch as both homosexuality and cultural contributions are portrayed as sublimations in males of this earlier rivalrous hatred, the reader might be led to wonder whether jealousy appears more prominent in women precisely because of the opportunities presented by these sublimatory opportunities, more available to men in Freud's time than to women, to metabolize it. Further, the reader is left here to discern whether (perhaps in light of a reading of Freud's 1920 "Psychogenesis of a Case of Homosexuality in a Woman") this mechanism is also important in the development of homosexuality in women, or whether, on the other hand, the role played by jealousy in the development of men's homosexuality might be distinctive to their psychology.

If Freud's essay, discussed above, focuses on the centrality of the envy of men toward other men, Christiane Olivier takes as her object of inquiry the envy she observes between women, attempting to account for its emergence in the course of the girl's development. Although she begins the chapter with a critique of Freud's ideas about penis envy, she quickly moves to an emphasis on envy of the breast as foundational for children of both sexes, suggesting, however, that this common source of envy has very different careers in the psychological lives of men and women. For whereas the boy finds confirmation, in his relationship with his mother, of his existence and adequacy as a sexual being, the girl's capacities to be and to have a sexual object are seemingly endlessly deferred, leaving her to fetishize her body and its accouterments, rather than be a "nothing" in the sense that, according to Irigaray, Freud implies. In Olivier's suggestion that the way out of envy is to focus not on a search for an elusive attractiveness, but in the development of a sense of one's own voice, she perhaps adds further emphasis to Freud's appreciation of cure through sublimation and the creation of culture.

Although both Olivier and Susan Kavaler-Adler locate their inquiries in the domain of the mother-daughter relationship, Kavaler-Adler's focus is not simply on oedipal-level jealousy, as discussed above, but on the deeper dimensions of envy in the pre-oedipal period, as first elucidated by Klein. In general, as noted in the introduction to this volume, gender studies and Kleinian theory alike have suffered from their mutual disregard (although, hopefully, there have been some recent impressive exceptions to this general rule; *viz*, Sánchez-Pardo, 1998). Though Breen (1993, p. 8) proposes that Kleinian theorists may for the most part have lost interest in the topic of gender because of a shift in emphasis in British psychoanalysis from sexuality to separation issues, the relative neglect of Klein's ideas in the field of gender studies nevertheless remains unjustified. Kavaler-Adler's paper constitutes one attempt to rectify this deficit, demonstrating the usefulness of Klein's—and Fairbairn's—ideas not only in understanding the course of women's lives, but in injecting a more visceral, embodied perspective into the study of a topic that is itself inherently grounded in physical, bodily life. In adopting an object relations perspective, Kavaler-Adler begins with the assumption that both envy and essential femininity (as defined, for instance, by vaginal sensations) are primary in women, presenting case and biographical material to illustrate how these elements are interwoven in states of health and illness.

The essays in this section, taken as a whole, highlight the multiplicity of forms taken by envy, and its multipicity of origins, in the psychological lives of both men and women. These essays demonstrate that the differences that give rise to envy may—but need not—be difference of gender. Likewise, however, they also suggest the range of psychosexual meanings that envy can take; from the point of the recognition of difference, loss, deprivation or disillusionment onward, envy shapes experience, including the experience of oneself as gendered. Thus, we might expect that the variety of forms and patterns of envious experience will only increase as the variety of experiences grows across the course of life, and that later manifestations of envy in individuals will build upon the phenomena described in the readings included here. As such, these essays should be read not only for their perspectives on the origins of envy, but as providing the basis for its emergence in its later forms, as detailed in the discussion in Part 4.

REFERENCES

Berke, J. H. (1987). Shame and envy, In D.L. Nathanson (Ed.) *The many faces of shame.* New York: Guilford.

Bettelheim, B. (1962). *Symbolic wounds, puberty rites and the envious male.* New York: Collier.

Boris, H. (1994). *Envy.* Northvale, NJ: Jason Aronson.

Breen, D. (1993). Introduction to D. Breen (Ed.), *The gender conundrum.* New York: Routledge.

Colman, W. (1991). Envy, self-esteem and the fear of separateness. *British journal of psychotherapy, 7* (4), 356–367.

Etchegoyen, R.H., Lopez, B. M., & Rabih, M. (1987). On envy and how to interpret it. *International journal of psychoanalysis, 68* (1), 49–61.

Fast, I. (1984). *Gender identity.* Hillsdale, NJ: Lawrence Erlbaum.

Freud, S. (1905). *Jokes and their relation to the unconscious. SE* Vol. 8.

——— (1911). Psycho-analytic notes on an autobiographical account of a case of paranoia (demential paranoides). *SE* Vol. 12 (pp. 1–84).

——— (1917). *Introductory lectures on psychoanalysis. SE* Vol. 16.

——— (1920). The psychogenesis of a case of homosexuality in a woman. *SE* Vol. 18 (pp. 145–172).

——— (1922). Some neurotic mechanisms in jealousy, paranoia and homosexuality. *SE* Vol. 18 (pp. 221–234).

——— (1925). Some psychical consequences of the anatomical distinction between the sexes. *SE* Vol. 19 (pp. 241–260).

——— (1932/1933) *New introductory lectures on psychoanalysis. SE* Vol 22 (pp. 1–182).

Kerr, N. (1987). 'Wounded womanhood': An analysis of Karen Horney's theory of feminine psychology. *Perspectives in psychiatric care, 24* (3–4), 132–141.

Keyishian, H. (1982). Karen Horney on 'The value of vindictiveness.' *American journal of psychoanalysis, 42* (1), 21–26.

Klein, M. (1957/1975). Envy and gratitude. In *Envy and gratitude & other works, 1946–1963.* New York: Delacorte.

Mitchell, S. (1981). The origin and nature of the "object" in the theories of Klein and Fairbairn. *Contemporary psychoanalysis, 17* (3), 374–398.

Sánchez-Pardo, E. (1998). Melancholia as constitutive of male homosexuality: A Kleinian approach. *Gender and psychoanalysis, 3*(1), 47–79.

Schneider, M. (1988). Primary envy and the creation of the ego-ideal. *International review of psychoanalysis, 15* (3), 319–329.

Wahba, R. (1991). Envy in the transference: A specific self-object disruption. In Arnold Goldberg (Ed.), (pp. 137–154). *The evolution of self psychology.* Hillsdale, NJ: Analytic Press.

9

DEVELOPMENTS IN GENDER IDENTITY: THE ORIGINAL MATRIX (INTRODUCTION TO *GENDER IDENTITY*)

Irene Fast

In psychoanalytic theory the processes of the oedipal period are conceptualized as central in establishing gender identity. During this period the issues to be resolved and the problems in doing so are patterned in part by developments prior to that time, beginning with the original matrix out of which development proceeds.

As this matrix has been conceptualized in psychoanalytic theory, both boys and girls are originally male in functioning anatomical structure. The boy is unequivocally male in embryonic origins and anatomic structure. The girl is anatomically bisexual. The clitoris is embryologically male, the vagina female. Only the clitoris, anatomically a vestigial male organ, is of importance in the girl's early development.

Furthermore, the libidinal orientation in the early years of life has been conceptualized as masculine[1] in both sexes. The boy's development is therefore straightforwardly masculine. The girl's is more complicated. Through the phallic period the girl, in her sexual orientation and experience, is unequivocally masculine. Her genital interest and excitement are clitoral. The clitoris is, in her experience and in anatomical development, a small or vestigial penis. The quality of clitoral excitement, and its aims, are like those of the penis, and thus masculine. She normally has no knowledge of the vagina.

For both boys and girls the first emotional attachment is to the mother. For the boy this provides a heterosexual orientation in his earliest object relations. For the girl this first established relationship is a homosexual one.

The problems to be resolved in the oedipal period are determined in part by the characteristics of this original matrix. The boy has a secure masculine base in anatomy and instinctual orientation, and an orientation toward heterosexuality in his relationship to his mother. The oedipal processes begin for him when he perceives the father as rival for the mother. In order to resolve the oedipal dilemma, he gives up the (incestuous) relationship to the mother because of the threat of castration. He identifies with the father and accepts his values, thus taking a major step in establishing his masculine identity.

---

1 I will follow Stoller (1968) in using the terms male and female when dealing with biological issues, masculine and feminine for matters of psychosocial origin. Some ambiguity occurs where origins are unclear or overlapping but in general the distinction serviceable.

For the girl the problems of the oedipal period are different. The central issue for her is the achievement of a feminine gender identity and heterosexual orientation on a base that is male in its focus on the clitoris, masculine in instinctual orientation, and homosexual in primary object relationship. Oedipal processes begin for her when she becomes aware that her sexual organ is not as large as the boy's or is non-existent. In anger and disappointment she turns away from the mother. She turns to the father and substitutes a wish for a baby from him for the wish for a penis. In this way she takes a major step away from a homosexual orientation toward a heterosexual one. A further significant step in the establishment of her feminine identity remains to be taken after puberty when she transfers her interest from the clitoris with its male anatomy and masculine aims to the vagina with its feminine ones.

In barest outline these processes constitute the major developments in gender identity as Freud conceptualized them[2] and as they continue to be widely accepted in psychoanalytic thinking. As they concern the boy, they have provided a widely accepted formulation, elaborated in a multitude of directions. As they concern the girl, they have seemed less satisfactory. Freud himself offered the formulation in 1925 and reiterated it almost unchanged in 1931, but he continually repeated his dissatisfaction with it. Others, such as Horney (1926), Jacobson (1937), Thompson (1943), and Zilboorg (1944) have offered alternate approaches or modifications, but these have tended to remain unintegrated into the mainstream of psychoanalytic thought.

Recently, stimulated in part by renewed interest in the role of women in western society, but also by interest in more general changes in sexual mores and gender-relevant human characteristics, questions are being raised with renewed vigor about the psychoanalytic theory of gender identity development. New data and insights, experimentally and clinically based, add substance to issues being raised. Three are of particular interest here as immediately relevant to formulations about the original matrix.

The first concerns the biological origins of the clitoris. Basing his thinking on the known biology of his time, Freud conceptualized the clitoris as a vestigial male organ, and its libidinal orientation as masculine. Recent biological data, summarized by Stoller (1975), suggest that this conceptualization is not valid. The clitoris is not a vestigal male organ. It is female in anatomical origin, and the hypothesis that the instinctual aims associated with it are masculine is not supported by available biological data. If both clitoris and vagina are recognized to be female in origin, this anatomic base for the notion of greater bisexuality in women than in men is gone, and to whatever extent the psychological theory depends on this anatomic base, it is called

---

2. On almost every topic Freud expanded his views in various directions, altered them, and offered suggestive ideas which he did not integrate into the main line of his thinking. To assert, without complex qualifiers, that a particular formulation is Freud's, is therefore necessarily to do a disservice to the richness of his thinking. Nevertheless, it has seemed to me that a thorough re-examination of the psychoanalytic theory of gender development requires that its postulates be stated as explicitly as possible. Any reformulation must, of course, take into account the broadest possible range of data and insight, and the degree to which it can do so is a test of its usefulness. This chapter is limited to outlining one aspect of such reformulation and suggesting directions for its elaboration.

into question. The notion that the girl is masculine in gender identity in the first years of life is not necessarily refuted, but it cannot be grounded on accepted data concerning biological origins. Finally, if the clitoris and vagina are both female in origin and integral parts of the female genital organization, the idea that the clitoris alone is functional in childhood without integration with or effect on the vagina is more difficult to accept and requires more support than when clitoris and vagina are seen as of distinctly different and sexually opposite anatomical origins.

A second body of data concerns the little girl's knowledge of her vagina in the early years of development. This issue is not new. Horney suggested as early as 1926 that young girls are aware of their vaginas. Freud, in 1931, and again in 1933, considered the fact that a number of clinicians had made similar observations, but he reasserted his earlier position (Freud, 1925) that the vagina was normally undiscovered by little girls. Jacobson, in 1936, emphasized the importance for optimal development of the girl's knowledge and exploration of her vagina, but this paper was not translated for English-speaking readers until the recent resurgence of interest in this topic. Recently, too, the contributions of Fraiberg (1972), Kestenberg (1968), Barnett (1966), and Torok (1970) address the question, and the notion that the girl has an early awareness of her vagina appears to be finding increasing acceptance in psychoanalytic thought.

Somewhat unexpectedly, the concept that the earliest matrix for gender identity development in boys is unequivocally male and masculine has also been called into question recently. The boy is at birth anatomically male; to whatever extent physiological factors are influential, the direction of his gender identity development is masculine. Stoller (1968) argues, however, that in humans physiological factors have an appreciable but secondary influence on gender identity, and that social factors generally override the physiological ones. Furthermore, he asserts that a major social factor for boys, as for girls, is the early identification with the mother. Thus, Freud emphasized the importance of male anatomy and instinctual orientation in contributing to boys' masculine identity; Stoller sees biological factors as relevant but of secondary importance. Freud focused on the boy's earliest relationship with the mother as heterosexual and contributing to his masculinity; Stoller and, in related work, Greenson (1968), emphasize the identificatory aspect of the boy's relation to the mother and therefore the uncertainty of his earliest sense of masculine identity. Therefore, while Freud considered the early gender development of the boy theoretically uninteresting because all major forces tend to strengthen his masculine orientation, Stoller suggests that contrary forces are normally operative, and that the boy cannot be thought of as unequivocally masculine in identity from the beginning.

These data and hypotheses suggest that neither girls nor boys are best conceptualized as male and masculine from the beginning. The problem, then, is to develop an alternate formulation: if boys and girls are not male and masculine in their earliest experience, what forms might their earliest gender experience take? If a male and masculine base does not underlie oedipal processes and to some extent pattern them, how might that base be conceptualized and what are the implications for understanding oedipal processes? Specifically, if the girl is no longer seen to be wholly male and masculine in orientation from the beginning, the central problem for her cannot be how a feminine identity can be built on a male and masculine base. If the boy is no longer seen to enter the oedipal period unequivocally male in anatomy, masculine in biologically based gender identity, and heterosexual in object relations, the influences on oedipal processes of his early development will need to be considered.

This chapter addresses only the first of these issues: the reconceptualization of the earliest base for the development of gender identity. The hypothesis to be proposed is that at birth boys are biologically male, girls female. Physiological factors probably contribute to sex difference in experience but are in the usual case overridden by social influences. From the time of sex ascription at birth, the caretaking environment treats girls and boys differently. Therefore boys' and girls' gender-related experience differs to some extent from the beginning, influenced by biological factors and differential handling by caretakers. With regard to gender awareness, it is proposed that girls' and boys' early experience is undifferentiated and overinclusive. That is, in the early processes of identification or establishment of self representations, the child has little sense that the characteristics of either femaleness or maleness, femininity or masculinity, are excluded for her or him respectively. Self representations or identifications are in this respect indiscriminate and overinclusive (though due to the caregiving practices of this society probably occur more extensively in relation to the mother than the father). At a later time, probably around the second half of the second year, the child can identify self and others as to maleness or femaleness. However, while such positive identification as girl or boy has been learned, *delimitation* of the characteristics of each has not. This delimitation occurs as part of the processes attendant on the child's recognition of sex difference. It involves renunciation of early gender-indiscriminate self representations and identifications now found to be physically impossible or gender-inappropriate (to grow a baby in one's body, to have a penis, to be physically active, to be tender, to be aggressive, and so forth). It requires attributing sex and gender characteristics, renounced for oneself, to members of the other sex. It includes recognition of the sex- and gender-related limits of the other sex.

This chapter offers evidence that an early period of development occurs in which boys' and girls' self representations or identifications include both male and female, masculine and feminine characteristics, and that there are subsequent processes of sex and gender differentiation and delimitation. Specifically, indications will be offered that early in development both boys and girls do assume that they have characteristics of both sexes. When they become aware of sex differences, probably in the third year of life, they feel a sense of loss or deprivation, a requirement that they renounce self characteristics made their own through early identifications. Angry and painful speculations occur about the reasons for such loss. Even after the child has accepted the fact of his or her own limits, a conviction may persist that it is a personal loss not shared by others. The recognition of the sex- and gender-related limits of the other sex may be incompletely established. Indications of residues of the early undifferentiated period and of the subsequent processes of differentiation will be offered as they occur in the normal development of children, in the arts and ceremonies of normal adulthood, and in cases of emotional disturbance.

The proposed notion of an undifferentiated and overinclusive earliest matrix for gender identity development is in some ways similar to Freud's formulation and in some ways sharply different. Both frameworks posit an early developmental period before sex difference becomes salient and in which children assume that all people are the same. It is in the hypothesized character of that early sameness that the proposed framework differs from the currently accepted one. Freud's view was that boys and girls initially assume all people to be male and masculine. The proposed view is that initially boys and girls may internalize a wide range of characteristics of the people in their environment. No attribute is excluded because it is inappropriate to the child's actual sex and gender. Only retrospectively, when sex differences become salient, will the girl and the boy become aware that attributes included in their developing self structures cannot or must *not* in fact be theirs.

There is some evidence that children do have these overinclusive notions of their sex and gender possibilities. Girls' notions that to be complete is to have a penis are well known. The assumption is often made that such notions constitute a wish to be a boy. There is, however, no explicit suggestion in theory nor evidence in clinical experience that little girls imagine that having a penis would mean *not* having the capacity to bear children.

More salient to the argument are boys' early ideas about their sex and gender possibilities. The accepted view is that boys are male and masculine from the beginning. If, as here proposed, their experience is overinclusive rather than male and masculine, they, too, must have notions that all sexual possibilities are open to them: that, for instance, they too, can have male genitals and also have babies. Evidence is likely to be scanty because this notion has not been part of the theory directing observation. Nevertheless some evidence does exist. It is a familiar clinical observation that in boys, symptoms centering around defecation often represent various aspects of pregnancy fantasies. Erikson's (1950) case of Peter is a well-known example suggesting some directions such ideas may take. That is, some boys at least, conceive of themselves as able to grow children in their bodies.

More direct and explicit evidence comes from Freud's report of Little Hans's conversations with his father (Freud, 1909). In them, despite his father's demurrers Hans, at the age of five, continues to assert that boys can have babies, that his father can, and that he himself will. These notions in no evident way conflict with his sense of himself as a boy with a penis or with his masculine rivalry with his father.

Not only are there indications that girls and boys know unreflectively that all sexual possibilities are open to them, but they attribute this same completeness to others. Freud recognized as early as 1908 that a pervasive fantasy of children is that mothers have penises, and he related the fantasy to the child's notion that everyone is the same. If one posits that in children's ideas everyone is the same, but sexually unlimited rather than male and masculine, one would expect that boys' notions that their mothers have penises would coexist with their knowledge that mothers have babies, and that if everyone is bisexually complete, fathers too have the capacity to bear children. In fact there is evidence that this is so. Clinical experience does not suggest that the notion of the mother having a penis means that the mother becomes boy, or implies that she does not bear children. Little Hans, again, serves us well in his assertions that his father, like his mother, can have babies, an assertion that in no way contravenes his sense of the father's dominating masculinity.

Clearly, this evidence for early notions of undifferentiated sexual completeness in boys and girls is not conclusive. The aim here can only be to indicate the kinds of implications that the proposed hypothesis would have and to show that some evidence for it is available.

The course of events when sex differences become salient will necessarily be different as envisioned in the two frameworks. The processes of differentiation from a prior undifferentiated state of male and masculine experience differ from those based on a prior bisexually overinclusive one. If the original matrix is male and masculine, only the girl need become aware of limits and deal with the consequences: she is in fact not complete as a male. The boy, accurately perceiving his male completeness, need make no such adjustment. However, if the earliest state is overinclusive in both boys and girls, then both must come to terms with limits.

The necessary coming to terms begins when children discover sex differences. Freud suggests that in part biological factors determine this awareness at about age two. Piaget (Flavell, 1963) suggests that the child attains cognitive capacities beginning at about that age that would make the necessary conceptualization possible. The triggering factor for the girl, in Freud's view, is her recognition that she is lacking a penis and that boys have one. With regard to boys, Freud made a suggestion that he did not pursue and that has found no secure place in psychoanalytic theory, but that seems illuminating for the hypotheses being proposed here. In 1908 he conjectured that the event triggering children's sexual interest was their curiosity about where babies come from. In 1925 Freud qualified this statement, saying that this may be the case for boys but it is definitely not so for girls: for girls sex differences become salient with their awareness that they lack the genital organ that boys have. These two notions taken together would suggest that the event precipitating interest in sex difference is the recognition of a limit: for boys the inability to grow babies, for girls the lack of a penis.

In the proposed framework, the notion that interest in sex difference is triggered by the recognition of something unexpectedly unavailable to oneself because of one's sex finds a ready place. Moreover, it seems likely that these triggers (female capacity to bear children, male possession of a penis) become foci or organizers for a larger array of attributes to be accepted for oneself or consigned to the other sex. As boys and girls become aware of sex difference, the gender-indiscriminate identifications or representations comprising their developing self structures must be tested against notions of their own sex and gender. Both girls and boys must begin to deal with necessary renunciations of those characteristics previously included among their self representations which cannot or must not be theirs. For the boy these might include not only biological matters such as the capacity to grow a baby in his body, but gender-related characteristics such as interpersonal interests expressed in doll-play, delight in color, music or art, and free emotional expression. For the girl the focal issue is likely to be that she does not have a penis, but that may become for her the organizer and symbol of such other renunciations as intellectual precocity, physical vigor, freedom of aggressive expression.

The significance of this recognition for the girl has been emphasized in psychoanalytic literature. The importance of the complementary event for boys has not gone unnoticed but has as yet had no comparably intensive investigation. Nevertheless, Freud suggested far-reaching effects of the boy's recognition of the mother's central role in the origin of babies and his concern about a role for males, "This brooding and doubting [about the father's role], however, becomes the prototype of all later intellectual work directed towards the solution of problems and the first failure has a crippling effect on the child's future" (1908, p. 219).

The differentiation processes and phenomena observed to occur in the girl as she makes her peace with the facts of sex difference include feelings that the absence of the penis is a loss, demands for restitution of it, convictions that the mother can make good the loss, painful speculations about the loss as punishment, beliefs (long after she has given up the idea of having a penis herself) that other women are not as ill-equipped as she is, and assumptions that boys suffer no lack. Similar processes in boys and the ways they come to terms with their recognition of limits have not been extensively observed, though some clinical observations noted below offer retrospective data.

If the notion of an undifferentiated and over-inclusive original matrix for gender development and something like the hypothesized differentiation processes occur when sex differences become salient in the course of development, then it should be possible to find residues of such early events in the processes of normal living and, perhaps more vividly, in cases of disturbed development. To the extent that art and mythology express ideas prevalent in a culture, the occurrence of bisexual figures in primitive art may suggest residues of ideas of normal in early childhood. The myth of Hermaphroditus, in whom a man and a woman were united, suggests again that the notion of bisexual completeness is not altogether foreign, and myths in which males bear children, as Zeus bears Athena, suggest a possible prevalence in men of fantasies that they, too, can give birth.

Kubie (1974) and Bettelheim (1954) have drawn attention to wishes in men and in women to have the attributes of the other sex in addition to their own, and have shown relationships between the occurrence of such wishes in cases of disturbance and in the normal cultural experience. Kubie titles his paper "The Drive to Become Both Sexes." He argues that in every person there is such a drive and that "the unconscious drive is *not* to give up the gender to which one was born but to supplement or complement it by developing side by side with it the opposite gender, thereby ending up as both." He first indicates the prevalence of such themes in art and literature. Then, with extensive clinical material he traces effects of such wishes in such varied domains as disturbances in capacities for work, in processes of courtship, in marriage choices, in psychotic disorganization, in particular difficulties in the end-phases of treatment. Bettelheim (1954) focuses on the theme of the duality of the sexes as he was able to observe it in children and as he hypothesizes it to be central in the initiation rites of primitive cultures. He argues that "one sex feels envy in regard to the sexual organs and functions of the other," and that all people wish to have the genitalia of the other sex in addition to their own. He gives examples from his experience with children, of boys' obsessional wishes to possess both male and female genitalia and of corresponding wishes in girls. In his focus on initation rites he suggests that these ceremonies, involving complex ways of taking the roles and functions of one's own and of the opposite sex, are methods of coming to terms with the duality of the sexes, of giving up notions that one can be bisexually complete, and of finally committing oneself to one's appropriate sex role. Neither Kubie nor Bettelheim suggest an original matrix such as the one proposed here, but their findings are clearly congruent with such a hypothesis rather than with one in which boys and girls are male and masculine in their early experience.

Personal observations of relevant clinical material are beginning to accrue, though confidentiality issues prohibit extended case elaboration at this time. They suggest that residues of primitive notions of bisexual wholeness and of the processes of sexual and gender differentiation proposed here may present themselves in clinical work in the complicated ways typical of any aspect of development. For a young man unusually persistent ideas of bisexual wholeness underlay fears of homosexuality and were related to a long-standing sense that he lived both for himself and for a dead sister. In the therapy of a woman they were linked to problems of self-other differentiation. One expression of them was a notion that became conscious in the course of treatment, that in her marriage her husband was not an autonomous individual, but rather served to give her the attributes she required to be complete. To be pregnant as well was the apogee: it implied having the unmistakable insignia of both maleness and femaleness. When the processes of working through these issues were most intense, she suffered transitory but frightening episodes in which she experienced herself as physically merged with him, unable to sense whether a body part was in fact hers or his. Forms that notions of incompleteness consequent to the recognition of limits may take in women are clinically familiar, but have been less extensively explored in men. In one man a sudden acute awareness of his sexual partner's lack of a penis subsumed not only castration fears but also a sense of his own limits: his lack of ability to bear children, a theme that subsequently led to explorations of work difficulties focusing on a sensed inability to be creative or to produce anything worthwhile. In another, one theme in his castration anxiety reflected a repudiated wish: the yearning to recapture the possibility of interpersonal intimacy by giving up the phallic insignia of masculinity that meant an extreme of objectivity and impersonality to him. Persisting notions that others do not suffer the same limits as oneself also occur in both men and women about members of their own and the opposite sex. For one young woman they underlay an intensely critical attitude toward other women's appearance, expressed as: "What's she got that I haven't got?" In a sexually inhibited man they underlay his sense that he had no way to understand women. Women could understand one another because they had the same experience. Other men, too, could understand women. Behind his notion that these men were "experienced" as he was not, lay a profound sense that his sex and gender limits were losses not shared by other men or by women.

These examples, derived from observations of normal development, representations in cultural artifacts and ceremonies, and evidence from clinical work, have been presented in support of a proposed reconceptualization of the original matrix from which gender identity develops. The major difference between this framework and the one Freud proposed is that in Freud's view both boys and girls are originally masculine in their experience, whereas in the one proposed, they are overinclusive in their early experience, not aware of limitations inherent in being of a particular sex. Other differences in conceptualization follow from this one. Freud noted that children have ideas that their mothers have penises. The proposed framework suggests that initially children have ideas of mothers with penises and fathers able to have babies, and that even when they have given up notions of such bisexual completeness in themselves they may still attribute it to others. In Freud's view, when sex difference becomes salient for children only the girl must come to terms with limits: she becomes aware that she has no penis. In the proposed view both boys and girls must become aware of them: the girl must give up the possibility of having a penis and gender-inappropriate self representations; the boy becomes aware that only mothers bear babies and must renounce self aspects previously internalized but now found to be inappropriate to his gender. In Freud's view, because only the girl is lacking, only the girl is envious of the other sex. In the proposed one, the boy's envy finds a place as well. In Freud's view the girl becomes aware that she has no penis in the context of her early masculinity. In the proposed view, both girl and boy become aware they do not have the attributes of the other sex in the context of experience that also includes awareness of their own actual sexual and gender attributes. In the accepted model the female capacity to bear children plays little part. In the proposed framework it is the trigger for the boy's interest in sex difference.

Because the oedipal period has been viewed as central for the establishment of gender identity, these formulations must be seen in terms of their implications for the conceptualization of oedipal processes as well. Detailed elaboration is reserved for a later chapter,[1] but indications can be given here of directions of investigation. For the most part they imply expansion of areas of inquiry rather than denying the importance of those heretofore considered central. A central underlying focus is the place of the mother and of the child's feminine characteristics in the oedipal triangle. In current theory the boy is seen to enter the oedipal period masculine in gender identity and heterosexual in object orientation. His entry into the oedipal period is signaled by rivalry with his father for his mother. Major accomplishments of that period are the establishment of an identification with the father and his values and, under threat of castration, giving up his incestuous relationships to his mother.

In the proposed framework, he is seen to enter the oedipal period not unequivocally masculine but overinclusive in his experience. Entry into the oedipal period requires recognition of sex difference. Therefore it is seen to be signaled by both the boy's rivalry with the father *and* his recognition of the requirement that he relinquish claim to attributes appropriate only to girls and women. His relationship to the mother has been objectively heterosexual since birth, but is hypothesized here to be largely gender-undifferentiated in his experience. Now it becomes masculine in relation to his mother as specifically feminine. One important theme in the boy's relationship to the father is the achievement of a specifically masculine identification. It involves both giving up claim to female/feminine attributes and also sufficiently resolving the attendant envy, sense of loss, and so on, to commit himself to the elaboration of his masculinity. Castration anxiety in this context is seen to derive its power not only from the rivalry-based threat from the father but *also* from the boy's repudiated wishes for the characteristics of the other sex. Masculine protest, the contempt for all things feminine, is seen to be, like its counterpart, women's contempt for all things masculine, a defensive aversion to desired characteristics.

The central problem of the oedipal period for the girl, as Freud saw it, is the construction of a feminine identity on the masculine base with which she enters the oedipal period. Her entry into the oedipal period is triggered by her recognition that she has no penis. In anger and disappointment she turns from her mother to her father and substitutes a wish for a baby for the wish for a penis.

In the proposed framework she is seen to enter the oedipal period with female genitals rather than ones that are partly male and partly unknown. Her gender experience is over-inclusive rather than altogether masculine. The recognition that she has no penis confronts her with limits rather than the loss of the only known genital. It occurs in the context of self representations of her female body and feminine gender characteristics. Her envy of the penis is not bedrock, responsive to actual biological superiority of the male. It is responsive to a forced recognition of limits and is resolved in a change of focus from this lack, to focus on female and feminine characteristics objectively and

---

1. (Ed: of *Gender identity*.)

experientially present. The relationship to the mother is not only one of hatred and disappointment but also one of specifically feminine identification and relationship. The wish for a baby from the father is not only a turning away from the mother, but also an identification with her in her specifically female child-bearing capacity.

REFERENCES

Barnett, M. C. (1966). Vaginal awareness in the infancy and childhood of girls. *J. Am. psychoanal. ass.* 14, 129–141.

Bettelheim, B. (1954). *Symbolic wounds.* Glencoe, IL: Free Press.

Erikson, E. H. (1950). *Childhood and society.* New York: Norton.

Flavell, J. H. (1963). *The developmental psychology of Jean Piaget.* London: Van Nostrand.

Fraiberg, S. (1972). Some characteristics of genital arousal and discharge in latency girls. *Psychoanal. study child,* 27.

Freud, S. (1908). On the sexual theories of children. *SE* 9.

———— (1909). Analysis of a phobia in a five-year-old boy. *SE* 10.

———— (1925). Some physical consequences of the anatomical distinction between the sexes. *SE* 19.

———— (1931). Female sexuality. *SE* 21.

———— (1933). *New introductory lectures on psychoanalysis*: xxx-III. *SE* 22.

Greenson, R. R. (1968). Dis-identifying from the mother: its special importance for the boy. *Int. j. psycho-anal.* 49, 370–374.

Horney, K. (1926). The flight from womanhood. *Int. j. psycho-anal.,* 7, 324–339.

Jacobson, E. (1936). On the development of the girl's wish for a child. *Psychoanal. q.,* 37, (1968), 523–538.

———— (1937). Ways of female superego formation and the female castration conflict. *Psychoanal. q.,* 45, (1976), 525–535.

Kestenberg, J. S. (1968). Outside and inside, male and female. *J. Am. psychoanal. ass.,* 16, 457–520.

Kubie, L. S. (1974). The drive to become both sexes. *Psychoanal. q.,* 43, 349–426.

Stoller, R. J. (1968). *Sex and gender,* Vol. 1. New York: Jason Aronson.

———— (1975). *Sex and gender,* Vol. 2: *The transsexual experiment.* New York: Jason Aronson.

Thompson, C. (1943). "Penis envy" in women. *Psychiatry,* 6, 123–125.

Torok, M. (1970). The significance of penis envy in women. In J. Chasseguet-Smirgel (Ed.), *Female sexuality.* Ann Arbor: Univ. of Michigan Press.

Zilboorg, C. (1944). Masculine and feminine: some biological and cultural aspects. *Psychiatry,* 7, 257–296.

10

MASTERING ENVY: FROM FREUD'S NARCISSISTIC WOUNDS TO BETTELHEIM'S SYMBOLIC WOUNDS TO A VISION OF HEALING

Eva Feder Kittay

We are hardly in need of proof that men stand in awe of the procreative power of women, that they wish to participate in it, and that both emotions are found readily in Western society....My own purpose was to show that some preliterate societies, far from being inferior to us in this respect, made the spontaneous move from the negative experience of fear to the positive experience of mastering it—by trying to make women's power their own.

Symbolic Wounds, (revised ed., 1962, p. 10).

Bruno Bettelheim thought it patently clear that men stand in awe of women's procreative power, and that it required only adequate argument to show that this primitive emotion was better handled in preliterate societies than in our own. In *Symbolic Wounds*, subtitled *Puberty Rites and the Envious Male*, he sets out to show that the pubertal rites surrounding preliterate societies are adaptive behaviors satisfying deep instinctual desires on the part of the pubescent child (male or female): desires to experience the sexuality of the other sex, while advancing the development of their own sexuality as male or female. Bettelheim had taken his cue from the seemingly bizarre behavior of the disturbed adolescents in the Sonia Shankman Orthogenic School of the University of Chicago. These children initiated spontaneous rituals, willingly entered into by the boys, and sometimes initiated by the girls, which involved blood-letting, blood exchange, genital manipulation, and even mutilation, especially on the part of the boys. Freud and his psychoanalytic disciples had already taken note of the envy of some young girls for the male organ. Penis envy had become a central doctrine, one crucial to the Freudian account of female sexuality. The behavior Bettelheim witnessed at the school seemed to indicate that *both* girls and boys envied the genitalia and the sexuality of the other, an envy which came to seek expression at puberty. But for all the obviousness Bettelheim attributes to a parallel envy on the part of men for the sexual organs and capacities of women, a concept of "the envious male" eluded Bettelheim's mentor, the man to whom *Symbolic Wounds* is dedicated. In this book Bettelheim wished not to challenge, but to supplement Freudian theory, to restore the symmetry implicit in Freud's own thesis of our inherent bisexuality, and to reinterpret certain phenomena and behaviors in light of an awareness of men's envy of women.

Freud and Bettelheim shared a cultural heritage. Both were Jewish men who grew up and were educated in the rich milieu of turn-of-the-century Vienna. One was the founder, the other an early pioneer of psychoanalysis. The comparison between Freud and Bettelheim invites the query why Bettelheim could see the importance of men's envy of women, the theme that pervades *Symbolic Wounds*, while Freud never appeared able to assimilate it. Why did Bettelheim see as obvious what Freud so systematically missed? And why, given Bettelheim's prominence in the psychoanalytic community, has the notion of an envy parallel to women's penis envy, an envy we may call "womb envy" for short (meaning by the term not merely the envy of the specific organ but of women's procreative organs, functions, and capacities) not penetrated the heart of psychoanalysis? Despite its merit, *Symbolic Wounds* remains undervalued and too often ignored.

In this article, I will not rehearse the arguments of *Symbolic Wounds*. Nor will I discuss critiques of the book which question the plausibility of Bettelheim's broad brush stroke across cultures and his use of a disturbed population to throw light on so-called "primitive" societies. Bettelheim himself answers some of these doubts in a later edition of the *Symbolic Wounds*:

> Far from "lumping all primitive people together," I am convinced that they share with all of us certain needs and wishes that are basic to mankind. These emotions are so basic that the more varied the societies, the greater the vicissitudes they experience; in some societies they are elaborately repressed, denied, and covered up; in others they are equally elaborately transformed into social customs; or both....These wishes are primitive not as belonging to primitive man (a concept I have no use for) but with the primitive in all men (which interests me greatly). (1962, p.11)

My starting point will be the theme that gives this article its title: while Bettelheim spoke of "symbolic wounds" ritually inflicted by or upon the envious male, Freud spoke of the narcissistic wound suffered by the envious female. Exploring the move from the narcissistic (but only symbolically speaking) "wounds" suffered in early childhood to Bettelheim's flesh wounds ritually inflicted later at the onset of adolescence, the *significance* of which is symbolic, I will put forward some speculative hypotheses concerning two issues: how Bettelheim came to acknowledge male envy and the limitations of his view that may contribute to the persistent neglect of the notion within Freudian psychoanalysis. The substance of my claim will be that, although Bettelheim recognized that male envy is prevalent within our own society and that preliterate societies provided men with a means by which to move from fear to mastery, the adaptive means Bettelheim applauds and the less obvious stratagems employed in modern societies are all less than optimal. The efforts to master envy have themselves perpetrated the domination of women by men. Ultimately we need to build on Bettelheim's insights to find healing salves for envy that aren't at once destructive to women. I will offer one proposal. I invite my readers to join in seeking solutions to the questions raised herein.

FREUD'S BLIND SPOT

Freud gave short shrift to envious inclinations on the part of men. Instead, Freud reinterpreted even the woman's desire for a baby as a compensatory wish for the man's penis.[1] In Freud's case studies, boys or men who expressed desires to give birth were interpreted as expressing anal, autoerotic, or homosexual desires, not envy of women's birthgiving. In the case of the Wolf Man, Freud attributes all indications of the patient's "feminine" stance to expressions of homosexual libido. Freud believed that the Wolf Man's "wish to be born of his father (as he had at first believed was the case), the wish to be sexually satisfied by him, the wish to present him with a child...at the price of his own masculinity, and expressed in the language of anal eroticism" all expressed homosexual desire in "its furthest and most intimate expression" (1918, p. 294). We can well understand that Freud accepted the wish for the Wolf Man to be sexually satisfied by the father as an expression of homosexual desire. But why did the explicitness of the wishes for a child and male birth go without notice, or at least without comment? In the two cases of the paranoid Dr. Schreber and Little Hans, Freud relates the striving to give birth to a child to anal eroticism, citing children's theories of anal childbirth and attempts to produce babies while producing feces. Without denying the power of anal eroticism, one notes, as did Freud (1908, p. 34), that the anal production of children seems a reasonable hypotheses for a male child[2] with childbirth wishes. That such wishes may be reinforced by anal eroticism does not reduce them to desires that take no account of women's capacities for birth-

---

1. [Original journal editor's note.] Cf. Peter Gay, (1988) *Freud, A Man of Our Times.* Gay pursues the more personal, biographical evidence for Freud's life, particularly his self-analysis, that suggests that he did not successfully pursue maternal transference issues, at least not as fully as the paternal transference.

2. It is ambiguous whether the children of whom Freud speaks are to be thought of as including both sexes or are limited to male children. Consider, for example, a passage such as the following (Freud, 1908):

   > The first of these theories begins with a neglect of sex-differentiation, the neglect to which we called special attention at the commencement as being characteristic of children. It consists in attributing to everybody, including women, a penis like the one the boy knows from his own body. (p. 31)

   It can only be the boy child who attributes to everyone a penis, *like his own.* The natural analogue for girls is that they attribute to everyone a vagina, like their own. I have indeed heard anecdotal accounts of girls who thought their daddies had vaginas, and who, upon learning that their father did not possess a vagina remarked, "Poor Daddy." But Freud curiously goes ahead and concludes that girls too suppose that everyone has a penis (like the one the girl knows from her own body?) but that she is a castrate. Such a view is clearly a projection from the male child to the female child that assumes identity without recognizing difference, and in the process setting for Freud himself the beginnings of the great "riddle of femininity."

giving. In the cases of the Wolf Man and Dr. Schreber, Freud interprets all signs of a putative feminine character, such as passivity and the desire to "give birth," as expressions of repressed homosexual libido. In all these cases Freud systematically assigns to all the male desires for female bodily functions,an interpretation presented in autoerotic or homosexual terms, i.e. in terms of the male's relation to a male.

Again, Freud interprets female sexual desires, among which he counts the desire to have a penis, and includes the desire to have a child, as relative to a male sexuality: a woman desires to have a man, be a man, give a baby to a man, give birth to a man. Female desire is for the phallus, but so is male desire. Of course, men have the desired organ. But their possession of the penis is subject to an anxiety that this power may be taken away—the threat of castration looms large.

In his forays into anthropology, Freud proposed to establish phytogenic origins for the fear- and envy-inspiring power not of women's parturition but of men's phallus. A central rite among human males, circumcision is understood by Freud to be imposed by a threatening patriarch to subdue the sexuality of the younger males. In the mythic primal horde, the father threatens his sons with castration if they attempt to co-opt the patriarch's sexual access to the women in the family. This "fear of castration" is a drama that is then reenacted in the psyche of each young boy in his development toward maturity. The agents in this thaumathurgy are all male; women enter only in so far as they are objects of desire, not as they are themselves actors with desirable powers. It is no wonder that femininity remained a riddle for Freud. Female sexuality could be nothing inherent; it was always a lack, a desire for the ever-absent penis. And how can one scientifically study a mere absence?

In another study, I have tried to understand Freud's skewed conception of femininity that is central to his blindness to men's envy of women's procreative powers (Kittay, 1984a). Here I am interested in understanding another psychoanalyst, similarly struck by expressions of men's desire for women's capabilities, who assigns to these a more obvious and, I will argue, more accurate reading.

BETTELHEIM'S INSIGHT

Bettelheim encountered expressions of desire to be a woman or have women's procreative capacities, on the part of the prepubescent and adolescent boys of the Sonia Shankman Orthogenic School. He did not take these to be disguised expressions of homosexual desire, but understood them as the male counterpart of the girl's penis envy. Obvious expressions, at that! He connected these with the rites of passage, the initiation rites, often centering around circumcision, described in anthropological accounts he had read.

The boys that Bettelheim worked with envied the unambiguous signs by which girls became women. "The boys," wrote Bettelheim, "confided to us their envy of girls, who at least *knew* they had grown up sexually when menstruation began. Boys, they felt, could never be so sure" (1962, p. 26). They partook in ceremonies in which they too were made to bleed, and it was these spontaneous rites that Bettelheim found so reminiscent of the pubertal initiation rituals in the ethnographic literature. In *Symbolic Wounds*, Bettelheim quotes two boys, each of whom repeatedly and independently stated that "he felt it was 'a cheat' and 'a gyp' that he did not have a vagina" (1962, p. 30). Bettelheim quotes one of the boys as remarking on another boy's tears: "I know why he's crying—it's because he wants a vagina." Several of the boys wanted to have both genitalia, and "disappointed in this desire and envious of women because, they felt, [they] had superior sex organs, both boys frequently expressed *a wish to tear out or cut out the vaginas* of girls or women" (1962, p. 31, emphasis mine).[1] Others insisted that in the body of women and girls there is only one lower opening, just as in the case of boys, thereby effectively insisting that the rectum and vagina are one. Bettelheim, commenting on a number of boys who seemed to accept their masculinity, writes, "We have often observed a hostility toward female sex characteristics....While these boys do not say they wish for female sex organs, they have many fantasies about cutting off and tearing out breasts and vaginas." For some "extremely disturbed boys" this turns into a "consuming desire" (1962, p. 31). Bettelheim saw a pervasive desire in the boys to be able to bear children and "the feeling of being cheated because it cannot be done." The envy extended to female breasts and lactation:

> A riddle they repeatedly asked was: "What is the strongest thing in the world?" And they never failed to supply the answer: "A brassiere because it holds two huge mountains and a milk factory." Girls never seemed interested in the riddle, but the preadolescent, emotionally disturbed boys were nearly always fascinated. (p. 32)

Of particular interest to Bettelheim was a spontaneous ritual that four of the children, two girls and two boys, had elaborated. The girls had reached menses, and a decision was made that "the boys would cut their index finger every month and mix their blood with that of the menses." Bettelheim goes on to remark on the desire of one of the girls that the boy's blood should come from their genitals, but that this wish "never went beyond intimating that it should come from 'a secret place of their bodies'"—fearful of the possibilities of injury, the staff interceded, and this plan was aborted.

It was the hope for understanding the motivations behind the blood-letting ceremony that led Bettelheim to rethink the initiation rites and circumcision of preliterate societies, especially ones most removed from Western influence, such as the aboriginal culture of Australia. In Australia, New Guinea, and elsewhere the initiation rite involved a symbolic death of the boy, who has been within the maternal domain, and his rebirth as a man, a birth effected by men. Margaret Mead (whose work is cited by Bettelheim in *Symbolic Wounds*), remarked that the structure of the initiation cult "assumes

---

1. As we will see later, this destructiveness is part and parcel of the emotion of envy.

that men become men only by men's ritualizing birth and taking over—as a collective group—the functions that women perform naturally" (Mead, 1949, p. 98). The basic theme of the initiation rites of New Guinea societies, claimed Mead (1949), is that:

> Women, by virtue of their ability to make children, hold the secrets of life....Man has hit upon a method of compensating himself for his basic inferiority....They can get the male children away from the women, brand them as incomplete and themselves turn boys into men. Women, it is true, make human beings, but only men can make men. (p. 103)

Bettelheim saw that circumcision is often practiced and spoken of as a means by which the boy is reborn as a man or by which the penis is reborn as the potent phallus. Far from the castration threat exerted by the male elders, Bettelheim suspected that circumcision arose in answer to the needs of the young male to have some contact with the female experience of sexuality while affirming his own virility. Circumcision is a wound symbolic not of the father's power, but of the son's mastery over his ambivalence with respect to his sexuality. The significance of this ritualized injury is made still more salient in the practice of subincision. In this practice, found primarily among the tribes of central Australia, the penis is incised along the penile urethra, rendering it more vulva-like in appearance. Not only is the wound itself called "vulva," but the blood from the wound is thought to be menstrual from the "menses of the old Wawilak women" (Bettelheim, 1962, p. 105). From his considerations of the behavior of the adolescents in his school and his anthropological researches Bettelheim (1962) thought it necessary to offer hypotheses which ran counter to the received psychoanalytic and anthropological wisdom about circumcision and initiation rites. These he summarized as follows:

1. Initiation rites, including circumcision, should be viewed within the context of fertility rites.
2. Initiation rites of both boys and girls may serve to promote and symbolize full acceptance of the socially prescribed sexual role.
3. One purpose of male initiation rites may be to assert that men, too, can bear children.
4. Through subincision men try to acquire sexual apparatus and functions equivalent to women's.
5. Circumcision may be an effort to prove sexual maturity or may be a mutilation instituted by women, or both.
6. The secrecy surrounding male initiation rites may serve to disguise the fact that the desired goal is not reached.
7. Female circumcision may be partly the result of men's ambivalence about female sex functions and partly a reaction to male circumcision. (p. 45)

FROM THE NARCISSISTIC WOUND TO THE SYMBOLIC WOUND

From these seven postulates, it is clear that Bettelheim understood circumcision and initiation rites as expressions of men's desire to possess women's procreative organs and capacities, of their envy of women, and of their attempts to move from envy to mastery. The title, *Symbolic Wounds*, is certainly an appropriate way to cast a study of such rites, given the bodily mutilations that so often accompany the ceremonies. But the term "symbolic wounds" is ambiguous. It can mean something that is a wound only in symbolic terms, or it can mean an actual flesh wound whose significance lies entirely in its symbolic repercussions. I suggested above that Freud speaks of symbolic wounds in the former sense when he speaks of the imposition of narcissistic wounds in childhood, while Bettelheim's concern is with the symbolic meaning of actual wounds. The "narcissistic wound" is the psychological injury to self-regard which comes about from a loss of love or a failure, made inevitable in childhood by children's limited power and sexual maturity. Not only did Freud take women to suffer from a narcissistic wound, the missing penis—a wound that could be healed only with the birth of a son who possessed the desired penis—but he also saw that all children possess narcissistic scars from the "early efflorescence of infantile sexual life" (1928/1967, p. 42).

A source of such a narcissistic scar is found in the child's attempt "to make a baby himself, carried out with tragic seriousness, [which] fails shamefully" (1928, p. 43). The boy child, though in possession of a penis, suffers a narcissistic wound due in large measure to his inability to create a child from his own body. The young girl too is unable to produce a child, but her wish, unlike her brother's, can be satisfied, even if deferred. While Freud discusses the possibilities of resolving the wound to the girl's self-esteem in literally producing the penis from her body in the form of a male child, Freud has no discussion of what happens to the wounded self-esteem of the boy who wanted to produce babies. Freud seems to have forgotten this source of a narcissistic scar. Instead Freud transformed the narcissistic wound suffered by the boy into a fear of castration rather than a unfulfilled desire to give birth and nurture a child from one's own body.

Bettelheim's title suggests and his subsequent work supports the view that in the initiation rites and through circumcision, the psychological wounds are made flesh, and in being inscribed on the body become attempts to heal the intangible injury to self-esteem. Bettelheim saw the self-imposed mutilations of adolescence as attempts at self-mastery; as attempts to compensate for the sense of loss brought about by the irrefutable facts of human sexual dimorphism. By trying to make their genitalia resemble those of a woman, by making the penis (or some substitute organ such as the finger or the nose) bleed, by enacting scenes of birth, and by giving birth to a "new penis" through circumcision, men seek parity with, if not superiority to, women's evident fertility.

A major aim of Bettelheim's work was to demonstrate the ego-supportive nature of the rites that appear to touch such deep instinctual desires, and to implement the thesis that social institutions, if they are stable and long-lasting, must serve such ego adaptive functions. If initiation rites are to be found throughout the preliterate world, if some form of ritualistic wounding occurs spontaneously among adolescents where there is no such socially sanctioned ceremony, then we must look for the motivations which lie behind and sustain this behavior. For if the institutions are to endure, believed Bettelheim, they must meet the needs of the initiates as well as the elders; they cannot be simply imposed from above and sustained through coercion. For Bettelheim, the question became: What need gets addressed and how is the need satisfied? The need, he maintained, arises from a desire to identify with one who is sexually other; the rites address these needs by allowing for that identification, but also for the control, mastery, or appropriation of the sexual powers of the other. Bettelheim saw the needs of adolescent males and females as entirely symmetrical, though he recognized a significant asymmetry, at least within our own society, of the power between men and women.

For the remainder of this article, I want to argue that Bettelheim's formulation and his turn to ego psychology allowed him to detect the womb envy that had eluded Freud. However, his insistence on the symmetry between the situation of the boy and the girl, and a fixity on the biological determinism of the impulses, yields an analysis that remains inadequate. Bettelheim has moved beyond the picture of female sexuality as being constituted only by a lack (see Irigaray, 1985, and Kittay, 1984a) to a recognition of awe-inspiring possibilities of her sexual physiology; he takes some account of the importance of the pre-oedipal period for both the daughter and the son; and he recognizes the cultural limitations of the image of the threatening father as arising from "the scarcity of appropriate libidinal objects in the modern small family" (1962, p. 39). But, Bettelheim fails to integrate into his picture of the envious male, first, a full recognition of the destructive forces of envy, second, the full importance of the fact of woman's mothering in creating man's envy of woman's procreative power and, finally, the persistent fact of woman's subordination. We will first look at the features to which I think we can attribute Bettelheim's insight and Freud's blindness and then address those factors that Bettelheim too underappreciated even as he recognized the importance of womb envy.

IDENTIFICATION AND MASTERY

I have suggested that in Bettelheim's treatment of castration and other symbolic wounds two central themes emerge: that of identification with an other—one's sexual complement—and that of mastery of, or control over, that otherness. More important still is the particular connection between the two: the depth of understanding achieved through identification allows for the mastery that makes one an agent with control over one's life. According to Bettelheim himself, the importance of identification as a methodology, and of mastery as an aim, became clear to him in his encounter with a child whose disturbed condition manifested itself in the self-infliction of pain.

In an essay, "How I Learned About Psychoanalysis," Bettelheim (1990) recalls his encounter with a child patient, a psychotic boy, in his analyst's parlor in Vienna. The boy, Johnny, had been in therapy with Bettelheim's own psychoanalyst's wife, herself an analyst, for about two years, about the same time that Bettelheim had been seeing his doctor. On this occasion the boy was chewing the spiny leaf of a cactus plant that sat in the parlor, and which the child habitually broke off and put in his mouth, often causing bleeding and, doubtless, causing pain. For two years Bettelheim had witnessed this behavior and he wondered if the therapy was doing the child any good. Against his better judgment, he blurted out: "Johnny, I don't know how long you have been seeing Dr. Sterba, but it must be at least two years...and here you are still chewing these awful leaves" (p. 32). Bettelheim describes the boy growing in stature as he answered, assuming an air of disdain as he faced his interrogator: "What are two years compared with eternity."

This stunning response, from a boy who had never uttered a full sentence, was the basis for a series of reflections which have considerable bearing not only on the issues touching Bettelheim's subsequent work on symbolic wounds, but also on his understanding of the therapeutic situation. Bettelheim realized that his own impetuous comment was the result not of a true concern for the boy's well-being, but of Bettelheim's own doubts about the efficacy of therapy. The concern for the boy was a fake and the child intuited as much. But Johnny also intuited that he had something of importance to communicate to Bettelheim, and which Bettelheim wanted to know, that concerned the slow progress of the therapy. Bettelheim's concern, not for Johnny, but for himself, placed him on a par with the boy—they had both been in therapy for two years and Bettelheim, watching the boy retaining symptoms for that time, reflected on his own lack of progress. It was by virtue of the identification of their concerns that the boy could respond to Bettelheim. Reflecting on the experience, Bettelheim (1990) writes:

> ...In a flash Johnny had taught me how inclined we are to believe that the wellspring of our action is concern for the other rather than self-involvement: and how much we can learn about ourselves from others, provided we accept that what they say or do may reveal things not about them but about us. (p. 33)

Crucial was the understanding, which congealed only after many years of working with psychotics, of the importance that one's "motive in relating to them made in their ability to relate" (1990, p. 35). Bettelheim (1990) writes:

> Only in this one encounter had I treated Johnny as a person who had supe-
> rior knowledge on a matter of greatest significance—was psychoanalysis
> doing much good? At all other times...I had felt superior to him. This time I
> had unconsciously hoped that this crazy child would solve my most press-
> ing problem. And so he proceeded to do exactly that. (p. 35).

There were still more lessons in store. Afterward, Bettelheim realized that
the boy had taken the leaf out of his mouth to speak, something he had never
done before or since, and did not replace it while Bettelheim was still in the
room. It was by virtue of the genuine encounter, the real communication that
took place that the psychotic boy did "not need his symptoms" (1990, p. 35).
Johnny was in control of this communication; it was he who had the superior knowledge, not of what was going on in himself, but on what was going
on in his interlocutor. As for the nature of the symptom itself, it originated
from an early life trauma over which he had no control. Bettelheim (1990)
writes:

> By inflicting on himself a parallel pain, he tried not only to obliterate through
> pain the mental images which tortured him, but to convince himself that now
> he could be in control of a pain over which he had been able to exercise no
> control whatsoever, when it destroyed him as a human being. *Had I under-
> stood this at the time, Johnny would have also taught me all one needs to
> know about the causes and meaning of self-mutilation.* (p. 37, emphasis
> added)

Self-mutilation, as Bettelheim came to see, was an attempt at mastery, at
overcoming a subjection wherein one is rendered impotent. In looking at the
self-inflicted or willingly suffered flesh wounds of the adolescent, both in the
school and in the socially instituted initiation rites with this perspective,
Bettelheim could see these rites as serving a constructive purpose for the
youth, not simply the destructive one Freud envisioned in his theory of circumcision as the imposition of a threat of castration. It is the narcissistic
wound of the "early efflorescence of sexuality" that the adolescent tries to
gain mastery over by the painful rituals of initiation and circumcision. In
boys that narcissistic wound is intimately bound to the failed effort at producing a child from one's own body.

In the same essay, Bettelheim writes that one thing that he had learned from
psychoanalysis was that in order to understand the behavior of another, one
had to see the world from the perspective of the other. Johnny's remark opened
Bettelheim to his own insensitivity to the suffering of the boy. It taught him
"from then on always to believe that whatever the behavior, it would seem the
most natural thing for me to do if I were in the other's situation." But it also
taught him that "when there are strong emotions involved, taking the other's
frame of reference is very difficult" (p. 36). One is far more likely to project
unto the other one's own fears, wishes, and desires, and not notice the differences that mark off oneself from the other. The imaginative leap into the situ-

ation of the other requires that we ask, as Bettelheim did in reflecting on the case of this boy, what would induce me to act in the way this boy did, what would induce me to inflict such physical pain on myself.

Too often the question of identification becomes the question: If I were in the situation of the other how would *I* behave? While this question may allow us to empathize with another, and predict the behavior of another, it can do so only in so far as the interior reality of the other matches one's own. But to ask as Bettelheim did: "What would induce me to act in such and such a manner—no matter how alien the behavior?" is a much deeper and truer identification. It is one that works through the affect of the other, and probably one that is far closer to the sort of identification from which we learn in taking another as a model.

I venture that it is this understanding of identification which permitted Bettelheim his insights into the womb-envying behavior of the adolescent boy. It provided him access to the possible motivation of the initiate. Still more significant, it revealed to him the therapeutic ambitions of engaging in imitative, symbolic activities. These recreate certain conditions present in the situation that first gave rise to the psychological wound. The hope is to exert control, mastery, and agency, where impotence, subjection, and suffering passivity were experienced before. Even with respect to the neurotic, asocial, and delinquent children whom he treated, Bettelheim saw behavior which would appear to be "expressions of the most violent hostility, of 'the id in the raw'" as "actually frantic efforts by the ego to regain rational control over a total personality overwhelmed by irrational instinctual forces" (p. 21).

Bettelheim could then see that an identification with the powerful pre-oedipal mother was crucial to understanding the circumcision undergone by youth and the initiation rites, painful as they may be. This, he saw, was an identification that was called up once again as the young boy witnesses the maturation of the girl into a woman with procreative powers. The early identification with the mother must take different forms within the nuclear family, with its propensity to generate oedipal conflicts, and within societies where men and women live apart and boys remain with the women until they are deemed men. But as the body undergoes the metamorphosis whereby it gets transformed from a child's body to that of a sexually mature male or female, the boy's identification with the mother must bring about some uncertainty, some hesitancy, or ambivalence about the outcome. Will this body turn into a male body or a female body? Is the identification to be with the fertile mother or with the dominant male? How can social institutions encourage the desire in the boy for the latter, when so much of his life has passed in the orbit of the former? Bettelheim projected himself into the situation of the pubescent boy, asking what would have to be true of himself if he were to behave in the same manner. By projecting himself into this situation and identifying with the boy, Bettelheim as analyst and theoretician uncovered a layer of identification which Freud failed to penetrate. That is the identification of the boy with his mother which has as a central feature the desire to give birth and experience the procreative powers of the mother.

Limited by an androcentricism that would not permit the identification of the boy with woman as agent (the only identification countenanced by Freud was the boy's identification with woman as object, the object of male desire), and unable to see and overcome the strong emotions which blocked the theoretician's ability to be able truly to see the world from the frame of reference of the other (the boy child longing for the powers of the mother), Freud held onto the view of women's sexuality as a deficiency longing to be compensated. Bettelheim, seeing the world as the boy might see it, understood the infliction of or submission to the symbolic wound as a way to gain mastery over his (doubtless ambivalent) desire to be transformed into a female— the potent female of his childhood. By identifying with the boy, Bettelheim could access an identification that the boy makes with the mother. In *Symbolic Wounds* (1962) he wrote:

> But the conclusion has been forced on me that just as in the psychoanalytic practice and theory we have learned to go farther back into childhood, beyond the age of the oedipal situation, so too for any adequate explanation of puberty rites we will have to consider much earlier emotional experiences, including the close attachment of the infant, boy or girl, to the mother; the male's ambivalent and positive feelings toward female figures; and the ambivalence of boys and girls originating in pregenital fixations about accepting their prescribed sex roles. (p. 19)

The passage suggests that not only did Bettelheim tag the motivation behind the behavior of adolescents in his school, and the pubescent boys in preliterate societies, as expressing envious desires for woman's procreative parts and functions, but that he traced the motivation of these desires back to the early close attachment of the infant to the mother and the ambivalent feelings toward the early female figure. The ambivalence he cites is related to sex roles as well as sexual organs. In his subsequent discussion, however, Bettelheim loses sight of the importance of these factors and seems to lean heavily on the symmetry of the anatomical differences that mark male and female.

A concomitant of circumcision in many societies is the presentation of the foreskin to the mother (Bettelheim, 1962, pp. 93–95). Bettelheim (see the fourth hypothesis above) speculates that this may be indicative of the role of women in instigating circumcision rites, demanding that men be made to bleed, just as women bleed at menses. But this gesture may also be seen as an exchange on the part of the man. He gives to the woman a portion of his genitalia, in the hope that she will give over some of her fecund powers. The desire to appropriate the woman's power and fecundity, to steal it away and make it man's, Bettelheim saw to be an earmark of the secrecy surrounding the ceremonies and the persistent myth that the rituals were stolen from mythical female ancestors. If the boy can in some way appropriate the power of the woman, steal it away from her or on occasion make a trade for it, then his transformation into a man would be welcomed. Bettelheim's sixth hypothesis at the beginning of *Symbolic Wounds* speculates that the secrecy surrounding initiation rites may be due to the recognition that the rituals do not entirely succeed in their appropriation. Bettelheim saw that the adaptive mechanisms that he praised were limited in their efficacy. Nonetheless his analysis stresses not the shortcomings but the achievements of the rituals. In looking to preliterate cultures for a salve for womb envy, we must attend to the negative consequences for an envy imperfectly resolved. And we must consider if there are not better ways to dissipate envy than to inflict symbolic wounds.

WOMB ENVY IN WESTERN CULTURE

In spite of their limitations, Bettelheim appeared to find the efforts on the part of men in pre-literate societies to be relatively effective strategies in mastering envy, and he found few analogues in Western society. Bettelheim himself does not supply a set of criteria for what is to count as efficacy, but it is fair to presume that he believed that males, both the elders and the young, could satisfy, at least in part, certain parturient yearnings, and act out certain jealousies and fears in a controlled manner—at least as long as the pretense could be maintained. The ritualized behaviors presumably made the transition for the boys into manhood (and, in the case of the couvade,[1] for men into paternity) less fearful or more acceptable. By mastering their envy of women, the men could better fulfill their prescribed gender roles. Bettelheim granted that in most cases the prescribed roles for men involved a position of domination over women. Without being an apologist for male domination, Bettelheim understood male domination as itself serving an adaptive function for women:

> Almost any central institution of society, while it may serve the needs or desires of one sex more than the other, must to some degree satisfy certain needs of the other sex in order to survive permanently. Those satisfactions need not be primary or basics, but may themselves be the consequences of custom. For example, certain passive desires may be activated in women who begin to live in a patriarchical society. But once aroused, they need to be sat-

1. In the couvade, a practice found globally, the man takes to bed after the woman has given birth. He is to rest from the ordeal of childbirth while the women returns to her normal activities almost immediately after birth. Anthropologists have speculated that the couvade is meant to underscore the bond between husband and wife created by the birth of a child or to establish social paternity "by the symbolic assimilation of the father to the mother" (Malinowski as quoted in Bettelheim, 1962, p. 110). To Bettelheim's credit, he sees that such explanations are not adequate. More importantly, argues Bettleheim (1962), "men need [the couvade] to fill the emotional vacuum created by their inability to bear children" (p. 111).

Noting that while the couvade involves a "sympathetic" association, "the man who envies the woman's ability to bear children has no 'sympathy' for her" as she is "even compelled to resume her work irrespective of the toll the childbirth has taken." Nonetheless Bettelheim (1962) assumes that women agree to the couvade: "Women, emotionally satisfied by having given birth and secure in their ability to produce life, can agree to the couvade..." (p. 111). One wants to ask, what becomes of the physical and emotional exhaustion that most women experience after childbirth? Do the women sufficiently identify with their husbands so that their husbands' rest suffices as their own? Or, more reasonably, are there other more coercive factors that motivate women to acquiesce in the couvade? Contra Bettelheim, it should not be assumed that women "agree" to it.

isfied. That such a society frustrates many of women's active desires goes
without saying. Still, it could not have continued to do so had it not also met
some of women's passive wishes. (Bettelheim, 1962, p. 70)

The womb envying strategies he cites are, in his own words, neither "entirely progressive or entirely inhibiting" (Bettelheim, 1962, p. 70). His positive
evaluation of the initiation rites was relative to the sparsity of mechanisms
available to Western men. While Bettelheim recognized the envious desires
in Western man, he may not have fully appreciated the extent to which the
envious male in Western culture also tries to master that envy by trying to
make women's powers his own.

Recent studies of young boys of 3 or 4 (Ross, 1974, 1975) report the children frequently expressing desires to give birth and expressing disbelief or disappointment when they learn that their bodies will not mature into the bosomy
figure of the mother. Perhaps, it is itself a sign of womb-envious behavior that
such expressions on the part of young boys are not often discussed, although
appropriate anecdotes are readily elicited when attention is called to the phenomenon. In another paper (see Kittay, 1984b), I cite other expressions evinced
in our own contemporary society of men's curiosity about, or desires for,
women's birthgiving capacities. Surely we can believe that there is a curiosity
on the part of both sexes with respect to the sexuality of the other. But curiosity is not yet envy. What is enviable must first of all be thought of as a prize
to be sought. Second, it must also be out of reach enough to not be readily
attainable, but not so incommensurate with our powers that we cannot identify with the possessor of what is desired. And third, the desire to possess what
one lacks is marked, more or less pronouncedly, with a negative affect: unhap-
piness or anger or anxiety. Spinoza (1677/1951) defined envy as "hatred, insofar as it induces a man to be pained by another's good fortune and to rejoice
in another's evil fortune" (*Ethics*, Pt III, Proposition 55). One may come to
resent the other who possesses what we wish to have; or one may feel oneself
unworthy of its possession; or one may try to take the desired object away,
even if it means destroying it in the process; or one may try to despoil it, so
that no one can enjoy it if we cannot possess it.

Within the context of societies that live so much closer to the rhythms of
nature and its evident fecundity, there may be little question of the desirability
of procreative powers. Within our own society, the desirability of these powers
is far less evident, especially when women are generally devalued. Bettelheim
points out that, "in any society, envy of the dominant sex is the more easily
observed" (Bettelheim, 1962, p. 56). Still, Bettelheim, I believe correctly, branded a number of behaviors found within our own culture as womb envying.

In an earlier work (Kittay, 1984b), I argue that all sorts of behavior, from the
exclusion of women in intellectual and artistic endeavors to childbirth practices in the modern hospital to the average weight gain of over 20lbs most contemporary American men experience when their wives are pregnant, are
expressions of the envy of men toward women's childbearing. I stress that it is

the third condition, the negative, often destructive, affect that mark these behaviors as envious desires. The imitative behavior of the three year old boy who stuffs a pillow or a puppy under his shirt and upon releasing it announces that he has given birth need not yet be *envious*. It is when he realizes that this power will never be his and that despite woman's devalued status and his own membership in the dominant sex, he still desires to have these powers, that this desire can turn to envy. It is when the boy perceives his incapacity as a wound to his narcissism that the desires and curiosities are transformed to envy, and the behavior it gives rise to has a cutting edge.

Within the psychoanalytic theories of Melanie Klein (1957), envy, more particularly the infant's envy of the mother's breast, is central to the intrapsychic drama that unfolds in each child. Klein developed an intriguing account of breast envy which includes a typology of stratagems deployed by the infant to defend against envy. In her account none of these really succeeds in dissipating the envy. Only the enjoyment of what she calls the "good object" and the gratification that it brings can dissipate envy. In Klein's account breast envy is central to all later forms of envy.

I beg the psychoanalytic reader's indulgence as I make use of Klein's typology and dynamic account of envy without adhering to the theory of breast envy and the intrapsychic nature of the Kleinian account. The Kleinian account is sufficiently rich to permit one to abstract from the account of breast envy to a more general picture of envy, and even of a species of envy which, unlike the breast envy Klein subscribes to, is sensitive to interpersonal relations. I use Klein's discussion as a heuristic that will allow us to interpret certain behaviors as envious ones. Space does not permit me to do more than propose that all the behaviors and phenomena I cite below are womb-envying. (see Kittay, 1984b for more detail).

Here I want to suggest that Western man, no less than preliterate man, seeks ways to defend against envy, to master that envy; but, as Klein suggests vis-à-vis the infant's breast envy, none of the defenses successfully accomplish their aim. Modern men rarely engage in symbolic wounds, but, none the less they look to transform fear and awe into mastery. Modern men lack socially recognized and public rituals specifically designed to effect the transformation. The institutions preliterate man erects to keep the secret that he has not really succeeded in wresting woman's power often are more successful in establishing a mastery over women than a mastery over womb envy. Within modern society the adverse effects of womb envy for both men and women become apparent as we survey the intrusions of womb envy and of the defenses erected against it.

Idealization

One defense against envy is to so idealize the object desired that it appears to be out of the reach of all who may aspire to it. The object desired, in its actual forms, can be disdained. These are taken as mere shadows of the sought for object. In periods of vitalistic romanticism, Mother is idealized as an ever bountiful and awesome Nature. The actual women who are mothers are subordinated to the men for whom the gifts of the idealized Mother are reserved. Male poets can sing of Mother Earth and male adventurers can pursue her. But in these periods actual women are subject to misogyny. Within our own memory, the Romanticism of the 1960's hippie movement glorified "feminine" virtues of love, gentleness, and peace, and hippie men renounced war, wore their hair long, and donned beads and loose-fitting clothes. But hippie women recall with bitterness their exclusion from the central arena of activity, and their confinement to traditional female roles. "Barefoot and pregnant" was the regressive ideal set for hippie women. This is in keeping with idealization of the maternal, for in idealizing women's maternal aspects, the tendency is to reduce women to their reproductive function. In sentimentalizing an ideal mother, each actual mother may be seen as falling short. Mothers and women generally become fit targets for men's anger and disdain, emotions born of an envy whose defense idealizes that which it despairs of possessing.

Devaluation of the Object

The envy of women may be transformed into a devaluation of women's procreativity. This is particularly common in those cultures that are heir to the Greeks and the Judeo-Christian canon. What is valued need no longer be coveted and therefore no longer envied. Mead (1949) points out that women's envy of the male role in Western culture "can come as much from an undervaluation of the role of wife and mother as from an overvaluation of public aspects of achievement which have been reserved for men" (p. 92). The devaluation of the desired object, woman's procreative power, is seen in remarks that characterize the pregnant woman as a "cow," in devaluing birthgiving as a purely animal function, or splitting birth into a spiritual (valued) and a bodily (devalued) aspect where men are responsible for the former, women for the latter. In different forms this strategy can be located in the foundational writings of Plato, Aristotle, and Aquinas.

Devaluation of Self

Alternatively, one can try to defend against envy by devaluing the self, reckoning that one is simply not worthy of what is valued. Contemporary psychiatric literature includes much material on crises men suffer, not uncommonly when their wives or lovers are pregnant, including depressive and suicidal tendencies (see Boehm, 1930, Van der Leeuw, 1958, Knight, 1971, Lacoursiere, 1972), or an extreme aggressivity and hostility which can be used to cover a sense of inferiority (see Van Leeuwen, 1966, Lacoursiere, 1972, Jaffe, 1968). Many of these behaviors may have concomitant causes. Frequently cited is the fear on the part of the man that the new child will displace him in the attention and affections of the woman. But if the man were to think of this conception as a child that he would have a significant role in rearing, who he could love and be loved by, and through whom he could reenact what was desirable in his own childish attachment to nurturer, then the shifting of attention would not be felt as a bitter loss. Both man and woman would lose some spousal attention but be amply compensated by the addition of a child to care for, to love, and be loved by. This consideration hints at the close relation between envy of the child *bearing* capacity itself and the subsequent child-*rearing* role generally assumed by the woman. The conflation, I propose and will argue further below, is what fuels the envy of women's procreativity.

Incorporation/Appropriation

The attempt to appropriate women's powers for oneself is amply exemplified in the initiation rites and the couvade of which Bettelheim speaks. There are reports of men within our own modern societies engaging in behavior imitative of the pregnant woman (see Trethowan & Conlon, 1965, Gottlieb & Wessel, 1982, and Lipkin & Lamb, 1982). More frequently, we find a discourse in which birth serves as a metaphor for activities in which men partake, in which women are excluded, and for which a great respect is reserved. The Pygmalion myth, so often retold in contemporary garb, is the story of a male creator who has the power to give life (biological life in the original myth, social life in the Shavian[1] retelling). A creation modeled on but not limited to procreation, is the prerogative of men within our Western tradition. In Plato's *Symposium,* Diotima expounds on the "mysteries of love" in which love and the desire for immorality are intertwined. Men who are "pregnant in body only, betake themselves to women and beget children." But those men whose souls are pregnant seek other men with whom to create the conceptions of the soul. These are the poets, artists, philosophers, and all who can be thought of as "inventors" (Plato, 1892/1937, p. 209). It is noteworthy that these mysteries of love are put forward by a woman, even though the role of women is devalued. Socrates, like the men of New Guinea, Australia, and the Amazon, learns about the secrets of birth (whether bodily or spiritual) from a woman.

The idea of homosexual love as having a productive outcome has a more corporeal version in the belief among some contemporary young African-American homosexual men that anal intercourse will produce a "blood baby" to which a man gives birth anally. Money and Hosta (1968) have collected personal attestations to such "births."

Male appropriation of creativity is found in the metaphor of artistic and intellectual creation of the male creator requiring the female Muse who inspires him in the production of a "brainchild." (Ong, 1967, p. 252) Poets as diverse as Rilke (Simenauer, 1954) and Browning (Munich, 1987) abound in images of male birth or male appropriations of women's creativity. Joan Landes points to royalist caricatures of the birth of the constitution of 1791. In one such figure:

1. George Bernard Shaw was one of the few preeminent men who openly supported women's emancipation. In his retelling of the Pygmalion myth, the man's role in "creation" is more modest than in the original version. The man's role is to shape the already alive woman, not to breathe life into his creation.

The lawyer Target, deputy of the Third Estate from Paris and member of the committee charged with drafting the new constitution, is seen sitting with his legs spread apart having just delivered a baby (the new constitution). Three males allegorizing the three estates and the female revolutionary Theroigne de Mericourt witness the baby's baptism. (Landes, forthcoming)

Although this is meant as an unflattering portrayal of the Third Estate—where the feminization of the political "birth" is the cudgel used against the revolutionaries—the image is a striking confirmation of the thesis put forward by Carole Pateman (1988) that the story of the social contract tells a modern story of masculine political birth. According to the theory of the social contract—the most influential narratives are told by Hobbes, Locke, and Rousseau—the origin of social life was brought about when men came to see their lives would be much improved if they gave over some of their natural rights to a sovereign power whose entire power would derive from the collective rights individuals have granted it. The story, sometimes told as a mythic tale with historical antecedents, sometimes told as a theoretical construct, is meant to underwrite the extent and limitations of legitimate power of the sovereignty. The sovereign is to retain its power as long as it can protect the individuals who gave over their natural rights to self-protection both from each other and from outside threats. It is to establish a peaceful and well-ordered state in which men could flourish. The constitutional democracies which emerged in the 18th century are implicitly or explicitly founded on such a contractual understanding of a legitimate sovereignty. Pateman cites Hobbes' "Artificial Man," Rousseau's "artificial and collective body," and Locke's "Body Politick" as the creations of reason—a reason from which woman has been excluded. The social contract, argues Pateman, rests on men upholding the terms of the sexual contract by which male sex-right is affirmed and maintained. According to Pateman (1988): "The story is an example of the appropriation by men of the awesome gift that nature has denied them and its transmutation into masculine political creativity" (p. 102).

We can go still further and say that the appropriation of women's birthgiving power, inscribed by initiates in certain preliterate societies on the flesh in the form of symbolic wounds, gets inscribed in the contract that founds the body politic. The French Revolution brought with it the overthrow of the body of the king as the iconic representation of the State. The body of the nation became a "discursive body" (Landes, 1992), a constitutional text or a legal *corpus*. Pateman points out the body politic, to which men give birth, is in the male-gendered image of the civil individual who is constituted by the contract.[1] Bettelheim himself speculates that the larger forms of society may have been created after men "despaired of being able, by magic manipulation of their genitals, to bear children....Society may thus have been founded not on the association of homicidal brothers (postulated by Freud) but on a joint effort of men to master a common problem" (1962, p. 121). The story of the social contract among men may be a prime replacement in Western cultures for those

---

1. See Pateman (1988) for an interpretation of Freud's myth of the primal patricide as an extension of the social contract theory (p. 103).

rituals that Bettelheim admires in preliterate cultures. The exclusion of women within the political domain, the absence of women in the executive, judicial, and legislative branches of our own constitutional government, even after 100 years of woman's suffrage, lends credence to the claim that the social contract is a pact among men. As women demand inclusion in the social contract, the sham of a male birth of a body politic is disclosed, and we must wonder what further defenses will be employed to master envy.

Not only are artistic and political creation figured as appropriations of woman's procreative power, but the scientists too do their share of symbolic thieving. Scientific theories of procreation, from Aristotle to writings at the end of 19th century, refused woman even an equal role in conception. The microscope helped some detect minuscule homunculi in the spermatozoa. Today, of course, scientists know better. But childbirth continues to be a province of powerful men in most maternity wards of modern hospitals. Gynecologists and obstetricians, mostly men, are the heroes of the delivery room where, with the assistance of (mostly female) nurses, the laboring mother is *delivered* of a child. The modern woman, until recently most often anesthetized and generally encouraged to behave in a helpless and regressive fashion (see Lomas, 1966), has been deprived of the triumphant experience of a successful birth. The appropriation of childbirth is not limited to the delivery room. Struggles surrounding reproductive rights and contraceptive controls suggest ways in which men try to dominate the birthgiving process.

Two stratagems for dealing with envy remain—both are still more negative.

Stirring Up Envy in Others

The envious one may attempt to stir up envy in others. One may consider if Freud's theory of penis envy isn't itself such a response. It is interesting to place the theory of woman's defective genitalia, penis envy, and the myth of the vaginal orgasm (where a woman requires the phallus for climax), alongside the Chuga pretense that after initiation the male no longer needs to defecate, since he has had a plug inserted into his anus. (It should be noted that this power is asserted by the Chuga male to be the source of his superiority to women.)

Stifling Feelings of Love and Intensifying Feelings of Hate

The last defense is the most destructive and in the context of contemporary weapons of death, most fearsome. Inverting the values of life and death, birth and destruction, love and hate are exemplified in the macho images from cowboy to football hero, in violent pornography, and militarism. If the birth of a society by male compact is not sufficient to master envy, will the dissolution of the compact by the creation and deployment of powerful weapons capable of destroying all life be the ultimate defense against men's envy of women's power to give life?

According to Georges Bataille (1962), novelist, pornographer, and philosopher, a violent, violating sexuality can supply the participants (most especially the man) with the possibility of each individual losing his discrete boundaries, allowing him to experience himself as a part of a greater whole. I submit that the sense of merger and continuity Bataille seeks is most happily achieved in childbirth and loving sexuality. The deleterious violations glorified by Bataille represent postures of the envious male who cannot merge with another as the pregnant woman does. One defense is to violate the physical integrity of another in acts of violence. If man cannot create life, he can seize for himself the power to end life.

The Destructiveness of Envy and the Elusiveness of its Resolution

Using the Kleinian discussion of defenses against envy as a schema, we have tried to see ways in which men in Western culture, cultures without codified and ritualized defenses against womb envy, have sought to master their fear and envy of the awe-inspiring faculty of women that Bettelheim took to be so evident, but that were for Freud eclipsed by the power of the phallus. The womb-envying strategies of Western man, though more dispersed and less readily identifiable, are, I think, no less efforts at mastery than the infliction of symbolic wounds.

In assimilating some of the above behaviors and institutions to male efforts at mastering their envy, we need consider the theory, suggested in anthropological literature, that only in societies where there is a great deal of father absence, and particularly where men live separately and women have the care of the children, is it necessary to initiate vigorous means by which to dislodge the male child from the maternal sphere. Nonetheless, it is clear that in our own society, and in the traditions which have shaped our society, father absence continues to be the rule, especially in the earliest years of a child's life. As Nancy Chodorow (1978) points out with exquisite simplicity, women mother— only the nature and extent of father absence varies.

If what I have called *womb*-envy is envy only of the biological function of childbearing, then the active engagement of men in childrearing would at best be the ultimate effort to master envy: if I can't bear the child, I can make it my own creation after birth.

If what men desire is to give birth and lactate, then we can predict that a defense against envy that is predicated on the involvement of men in childrearing will, one can foresee, exclude women from child rearing itself. To defend against envy, even to try to master it, is not to dispel it. The envious impulse is to take away or despoil that which is desired. Surely, it would be easier to dislodge the male child from the maternal domain if men were to rear children from infancy. Our own history books record a time when the child was the possession of the father and when all legal and educational decisions were made by the father. But they do not record a time when men did the primary child-care. It is interesting to ask "why?" Was that task *too* onerous? Did women resist too strongly? Or is it perhaps that, in the minds of men, childbearing was so closely allied to child rearing that envy of the physiological is conflated with envy of that close and ambivalent relation the child has to the mother figure? Historically, the question is impossible to answer. But it appears to me that conceptually, the last suggestion has a certain plausibility.

If child rearing is seen as an intrinsic outcome of childbearing and the distinction between bearing and rearing a child is effaced, then woman cannot be replaced in the one case unless she is also displaced in the other. Since men cannot give birth, nor can they lactate, men cannot seize for themselves the biological capacities. If those appear so intimately tied to the role of primary nurturer then the strategies to master envy must resort to imitative substitutes or in efforts to spoil the object. But these efforts only give rise to more destructive forces. The imitative appropriations are a sham that must be protected against revelation, and in the end give rise to a persecutory anxiety—one evinced in the enormous threat women are perceived to pose in many of the preliterate societies of which Bettelheim writes. Some male secret societies are even willing to kill a few young boys in order to deceive the woman into believing that all the boys had been killed by the spirits and that only through the efforts of the men had some been brought back to life. These men destroy highly prized groves of areca palms to demonstrate the viciousness of the male ghosts who kill their sons. Bettelheim (1962, p. 125) comments: "Like the neurotic who will readily destroy important possessions to keep his unrealistic defenses intact, these men destroy the cherished palm trees to impress the women more thoroughly with their power to create life." In some societies, women may even be killed for observing the rites meant only for men. The accounts of womb envy make clear that efforts to spoil the good object only impede its further enjoyment. As Klein so clearly saw: "Greed, envy and persecutory anxiety...inevitably increase one another" (pp. 127–128).

As long as the envious male identifies the biological aspects of woman's difference as the source of his distressing desires, there can be no resolution to womb envy; there can only be defenses which, at best, partially alleviate the envy, often at the expense of women, whose power and aspirations are constrained. At worst, they exacerbate the negative emotions, resulting in behavior destructive to women and men alike. Bettelheim, in stressing the adaptive function of the ceremonies he analyses, paid perhaps not enough attention to the extent to which the defenses failed, and to the negative impact on men and, especially on women of the envious behavior.[1] Adaptive behaviors need not be entirely successful in order to become stabilized, and even when the defenses assure a stable order we need to look for the pernicious fallout from envy.

Within our own society, the failure of men's strategems is reflected in the continuance of male domination: If men have control of women, they have

1. See note 4 on the couvade above.

control of their powers. But even here there is not a total resolution, for a woman may have a baby when the man doesn't want her to, or could refuse to have babies when a man wants her to, or has a child with a man other than himself. The battered pregnant woman stands as a bloody testament to the violence that may stem from escalating envy.

WOMB ENVY AND PENIS ENVY: SYMMETRY OR ASYMMETRY?

Bettelheim treats male's envy as symmetrical to women's envy of the penis. But are they really symmetrical? Women psychoanalysts and feminists, since Karen Horney at least, have granted some validity to the idea of penis envy—there is ample clinical evidence of girls expressing desire and even envy of men's organ—but they have also invited us to consider the extent to which the significance of the penis as a symbol of power and male prerogative is implicated in this envy. If womb-envy is analogous, then it would seem that not the biological function per se, but some social power of women is what is truly envied in womb-envy. But in male-dominated societies why would men desire to be devalued women?

This appears to be a rhetorical question, and as such, I submit, it prevented Freud from developing a concept of womb envy. It continues to block the integration of a concept of womb envy into most contemporary work in psychoanalysis. A psychoanalysis which is heir to Freud's understanding of femininity, and which continues to underestimate the importance and power of the pre-oedipal relation the child has with the mother, is doomed to lose sight of the role of womb envy in a boy's development—no matter how often the phenomenon is discovered and uncovered, and no matter how persuasively it is presented.

Unless one takes account of the effect of the power differential within society, one fails to recognize the fundamental asymmetry in the parallel phenomena. Let us accept that both penis envy and womb envy have biological and social components. If penis envy is taken to be envy of the physiological difference, then womb envy as the female analogue comes to be seen as the envy of women's physiological difference. If penis envy is understood not only to be envy of the biological organ per se, but also of the power and privilege that the organ signifies,[1] then womb envy must also be envy of some power that is not only physiological but social. Only if we look back to the pre-oedipal mother-child relationship (as Bettelheim recognized we must) does the social nature of "womb" envy emerge. In the case of penis envy, the biological organ seems only incidental to the social power it also symbolizes, yet in the case of womb envy the biological capacities seem central to the power of the mother. The child believes that it is *by virtue of giving birth* that the mother has the special power and special tie she has to her offspring.

1. In this context it is interesting to note how often the men of devalued and oppressed groups are feminized (see Gilman, 1985), or, if presented as threatening, are presented as oversexed and as having an exceptionally large penis.

I believe it fair to say that as a physiological organ, deprived of its cultural significance, the penis appears only as a curiosity to a young girl, not as the awesome, enviable object that catapults her into a lifelong inferiority complex. The transformations of the body accompanying childbirth, the fact of a baby forming within the mother's belly and being expelled from there, do in and of themselves seem awesome to girls and boys alike, and potentially a source of envy. Nonetheless, it is the close, early identification of the child with the mother, and with her powers, the child's early ambivalence, the love and attachment together with the sense of dependence and vulnerability, that gives the physiological basis for envy its full force (see Kittay 1984b for the full argument regarding this point). Bettelheim recognized that in a society where one sex dominates, it is easier to recognize the envy of the subordinate group and his aim was to reestablish the symmetry too easily lost sight of by virtue of the gender hierarchy. But an asymmetry remains. For it is one thing to covet that which is possessed by the dominant sex and quite another to envy what marks the subordinate group as different. In male dominated society, it is hardly irrational or self-deprecating for a woman to desire the power of men, and their access to what is valued within society. But although women are devalued with a male-dominated culture, women appear to possess a power that is inherently awesome. They have access to a good that is quite independent of social ordering.

Consider what it must feel like to be a member of a dominant group when your subordinate has something desirable—in this case the man who desires the procreative capacity and the organs and functions that constitute it, that power which in fact defines woman as woman and condemns her to a lower status. That the subordinate possesses such a good makes a mockery of the other's own superior status. Not only is it the case that taking away the desired object is not physiologically possible, but it is inherently *problematic to desire it*. What is desired is at once despised. To possess the desired object would be equivalent to wishing to devalue oneself.[1] This is what makes womb envy far more invidious than penis envy.

When men envy women they experience themselves as anomalous—because the desire itself appears anomalous in a context of male dominance. Codified ways in which men can "steal" women's secret reduce the anomaly, but fail to fully satisfy the desire. Womb envy may or may not be at the origin of male domination. But it is a powerful motor driving male domination.

Nancy Chodorow (1979) has argued that the early mothering of children by women gives rise to differential personality structures of men and women such that nurturing impulses are fostered in females and suppressed in males. The degree of father absence, the exclusivity of the mother-child relation, the

---

1. That is perhaps what is so striking and convincing about transsexual men who feel themselves to be women. One wonders what could be so compelling that the man who has all the privileges of his sex would forfeit them to become a woman? The transsexual answers that he has always felt himself to be a woman trapped in the body of a man, and nothing short of such a response seems to warrant the extreme measures the transsexual man undertakes in hormone therapies and surgery—measures much more frequently taken by transsexual men than transsexual women.

access to adult figures other than the mother—all serve to modulate the degree and the form of the sex-differentiated personalities. But the universal (or near universal) condition of women's mothering, in suppressing relational and nurturant personality traits in men, also serves to perpetuate male dominance.

Insofar as childbearing and childrearing are ineluctably linked, the strong attachments and ambivalence the child experiences toward the early nurturer get displaced onto the already inherently awesome biological fact of women's procreativity. The early identification of the boy child with the mother and the subsequent disappointment of the boy that he cannot replicate the relation that the mother bears to him in his relation to a future child *because* he cannot bear a child result in an *envy*. This envy goes beyond the mere desire of curiosity about the woman's sexual biology. In the context of male domination, the envy takes the particularly bitter flavor I remarked on above.

A HEALING HALVE—A PROPOSAL

If we can follow Klein (1957) in her claim that it is "*enjoyment* and the *gratitude* to which it gives rise that mitigate destructive impulses, envy and greed" (p. 187)—a claim which does not seem particularly tied to the metapsychology she expounded—and if the claim that the child's identification with the mother and her power fuels the envy of the biological difference is correct (see Kittay 1984b), then the participation of men in the process of mothering should go a considerable distance in allaying men's envy, or at least vitiating its more destructive impulses. If the envy itself (not merely the desire or the curiosity evinced) is crucially that of biological difference, then, as I pointed out above, male participation in early child rearing will serve still another defense, accompanied by greed, persecutory anxiety, or depression.

Only a social experiment on a large scale, in which men are actively engaged in early child rearing will tell the difference empirically. As Kyle Pruett's (1987) wonderful book, *The Nurturing Father*, attests, the experiment is being carried out on a small scale today. There are fathers that are primary caretakers of their young children and probably many more who together with their wives share the responsibilities and day-to-day care of young children. Pruett has many fascinating observations about the results on both the fathers and the children. But we have yet to see the full effects of the young boys raised by these men. And we have yet to see the effects on boys whose fathers have substantially shared early child rearing with mothers. Will the assumption of the male role mean the forgoing of nurturant desires for these boys? Will those desires be as tied to woman's procreativity as it is currently for most men? Will they be able to take on the nurturance of their own children with an ease that eluded their fathers? Will they live a life, not necessarily free from an awe of women's procreative powers, but free from a ruinous envy? Will they see their role in the biological creation of the child as giving them the same warrant that the mother's role gives her?

I would urge that these experiments need to be carried out not only in the nuclear family but in other familial and public settings. The two-gendered two-parent family is increasingly not the norm, and the father often has a distinct and distant role. I am proposing that boys and men be exposed to child care at an early age, that men and boys be trained in the care and nurture of others, and that men be involved in nurturant activities inside or outside a home setting. Whether it is their own father or men outside their own home whom the young boy sees in a nurturant role, the possibility of male nurturance becomes available to him.

It will be interesting to see if, under these conditions, the deleterious consequences of womb envy can be curtailed. Most significant would be to see if it will be possible to reverse the systematic subordination of women by intercepting some of the reproductive mechanisms, psychological and social, that sustain it. The possibility of male nurturance may be the soothing salve for the narcissistic wound of womb envy.

Conclusion: Incorporating
Womb Envy

Bettelheim was not the first to discover "the envious male," nor was he the last. (See Kittay, 1984a, and Ross, 1975.) *Symbolic Wounds*, as fascinating and (with some caveats) as persuasive as it is, has done little to bring the concept of womb envy into the central body of psychoanalytic thought nor into contemporary lay culture. If womb envy is to advance beyond the status of marginalia, some theoretical moves are required that push beyond Bettelheim's achievement. What is required for the integration of the concept? A theory of a boy's development that pays sufficient attention to his early attachment and identification with a female figure; a reconceptualization of women's sexuality such that it is not simply perceived as a lack or deficiency; an understanding of the role of male domination in the formation of male and female personality, as these are modulated by cultural and historical differences in family structure and childrearing practices; and a move away from a biological determinism to see the role of culture in shaping what appears so ineluctable and inevitable. Bettelheim understood the importance of identification in human development and the struggle of the ego to replay the source of past hurts so that a way may be found to control the circumstances that gave rise to the injury. His understanding of the role of identification allowed him to understand female sexuality such that there was something enviable. But he overstated the power of the social institutions of circumcision and initiation to control against envy. He did not heed the difficulty of overcoming the destructive quality of envy. And he did not clearly envision the importance of male domination in the formation and consequences of the envy. Although the case for womb envy has frequently been made, it has yet to be heard. Only when we have both a theory adequate to its incorporation and a practice of child rearing that begins to dissipate envy will men face how deep this narcissistic wound cuts and how disastrous have been the symbolic attempts to master the hurt by inflicting still more wounds.

REFERENCES

Bataille, G. (1962). *Death and sexuality*. New York: Ballantine Books.

Bettelheim, B. (1962). *Symbolic wounds, puberty rites and the envious male*. New York: Collier Books.

———(1990). *Freud's Vienna and other essays*. New York: Knopf.

Boehm, F. (1930). The femininity-complex in men. *Int. j. psychoanal.*, 11,444–469.

Chodorow, N. (1978). *The reproduction of motherhood*. Berkeley: University of California Press.

Freud, S. (1908). On the sexual theories of children. In P. Rieff (Ed.), *The sexual enlightenment of children*. New York: Macmillan, 1976. (Ed.: SE 4, 205–226).

———(1928). *Beyond the pleasure principle*. (G. Zilborg, Trans.). New York: Bantam Books, 1967. (Ed: SE 18, 1–64)

———(1918). From the history of an infantile neurosis. In P. Rieff (ed.), *Three case histories*. New York: Macmillan, 1968. (Ed.: SE 17, 1–122).

Gay, Peter (1988). *Freud: A man of our times*. New York: W.W. Norton.

Gilman, S. (1985). *Difference and pathology: Stereotypes of sexuality, race and madness*. Ithaca: Cornell University Press.

Gottlier, S., & Wessell, M. (1982). Gastrointestinal symptoms among expectant fathers. *Connecticut med.*, 46:715–718.

Irigaray, L. (1985). *Speculum of the other woman* (G. C. Gill Trans.). Ithaca: Cornell University Press.

Jaffe, D. S. (1968). The masculine envy of woman's procreative function. *J. Amer. psychoanal. assoc.*, 16, 521–548.

Kittay, E. (1984a). Rereading Freud on 'femininity' or why not womb envy? *Women's stud. intern. For.*, 7, 385–391.

———(1984b). Womb envy: An explanatory concept. In J. Trebilcot (ed.), *Mothering: Essays in feminist theory*. Lanham, MD: Littlefield and Adams.

Klein, M. (1957/1975). Envy and gratitude. *Envy and gratitude and other works: 1946-1963*. New York: Delacorte.

Knight, J. A. (1971). Unusual case: False pregnancy in a male. *Medical aspects of human sexuality*, March, 58–67.

Lacoursiere, R. B. (1972). Fatherhood and mental illness: A review and new material. *Psychiatr. q.*, 46, 109–123.

Landes, J. (1992). Representing the body politic: The paradox of gender in graphic politics of the french revolution. In S. Melzer & L. Rabine (Eds.), *Rebel daughters: Women and the french revolution*. Oxford: Oxford University Press.

Lipkin, M., & Lamb, G. (1982). The couvade syndrome: An epidemiologic study. *Annals of internal medicine*, 96, 509–511.

Lomas, P. (1966). Ritualistic elements in the management of childbirth. *Brit. j. med. psychol.*, 39: 207–213.

Mead, M. (1949). *Male and female*. New York: William Morrow.

Money, J., & Hosta, G. (1968). Negro folklore of male pregnancy. *J. sex res.*, 4, 34–50.

Munich, A. A. (1987). Robert Browning's poetics of appropriation. *Browning institute studies: An annual of victorian literary and cultural history,* 15, 69–78.

Ong, W,. (1967). *The presence of the word.* New Haven and London: Yale University Press.

Pateman, C. (1988). *The sexual contract. Stanford,* CA: Stanford University Press.

Plato. Symposium. *The dialogues of Plato* (1892/1937). B. Jowett (Ed. & Trans.). New York: Random House.

Pruett, K. D. (1987). *The nurturing father.* New York: Warner Books.

Ross, J. M. (1974). *The children's children: A psychoanalytic study of generativity and nurturance in boys.* Ph.D. Dissertation, New York University.

———— (1975). Paternal identity: A critical review of the literature on nurturance in boys and men. *J. Amer. psychoanal. assoc.,* 23, 783–818.

Simenauer, E. (1954). "Pregnancy envy" in Rainer Maria Rilke. *Amer. imago,* 11: 235–248.

Spinoza, B. (1677/1951). *The ethics.* R. H. M. Elwes (trans.). New York: Dover Publications.

Trethowan, W., & Conlan, M. (1965). The couvade syndrome. *Brit. j. psychiatry,* 111, 57–65.

Van der Leeuw, P. J. (1958). The pre-oedipal phase of the male. *Psychoanal. study child,* 13, 352–374.

Van Leeuwen, K. (1966). Pregnancy envy in the male. *Inter. j. psychoanal.,* 47, 319–324.

IN THE BEGINNING WAS FREUD (AND OTHER EXCERPTS FROM *JOCASTA'S CHILDREN*)

Christiane Olivier

In the face of such uncertainty it is most unfortunate that Freud insisted on proceeding so far in constructing a psychology of women.
—Kate Millett, *Sexual Politics* (London, 1971), 178

Why is Freud so virulently attacked by women? Why Freud rather than some other man? We are well aware that he is not the only sexist, the only phallocrat, the only enemy of femininity. We are indeed; but he alone built up 'his' truth into an objective-seeming science, 'his' sexuality into a universal sexuality.

In psychoanalysis we find a conception of woman that has been dreamed up by a man; a woman such as many men might wish her to be, but one perhaps unrelated to what 'woman' really is.

From Freud onward there occurs a distortion of feminine sexuality which women now are challenging as totally unrelated to them.

What has to be remembered is that, if there hasn't yet been a woman to remember the story of her early girlhood, there was, at the outset of psychoanalysis, one solitary man who recalled his early boyhood with his mother...Let us not forget that Freud had been adored by his mother, who was young, pretty, desirable, married to a much older man, and with a son who gave her satisfactions which must have greatly puzzled young Sigmund himself. From this life with his mother, this little boy, when he became a man, drew conclusions concerning masculine development which have never yet been successfully challenged. It would appear that the analysis he gave was pertinent indeed. But when it comes to women, it is a different story.

The clear pattern of development in the boy seems to have drawn him into a sizable trap, for in the earliest phase of his work he strove to establish the girl's development as *symmetrical* with the boy's. This led him into some strange flights of argument concerning little girls, since he wanted to establish symmetry round a fundamental asymmetry (that of the sexes), and since for him male supremacy seemed unquestionable (which may raise a smile nowadays). He had no end of difficulty in working out a theory—given detailed exposition as early as 1905 in the *Three Essays on Sexuality*—which seems to us now to be packed with improbable notions, of which the two most obvious are: penis envy, and the renunciation of the clitoris.

PENIS ENVY, OR ENVY FOR THE PARTS ONE HASN'T GOT

One of the earliest claims we come across in the *Three Essays* on the subject of infantile sexuality seems wholly unexceptionable: 'It is self-evident to a male child that a genital like his own is to be attributed to everyone he knows'.[1] But it opens straightaway on to a question: what do little girls believe? These girls who also know no genital apparatus other than their own, are they capable of imagining a different one? Now Freud, determined to confer primacy on the male sex, answers the question, with no discernible logic: 'The assumption that all human beings have the same (male) form of genital is the first of the many remarkable and momentous sexual theories of children.'[2]

And in case we hadn't understood he adds, later on: 'We might lay it down that the sexuality of little girls is of a wholly masculine character.'[3]

Or again: 'It would even be possible to maintain that libido is invariably and necessarily of a masculine nature, whether it occurs in men or in women.'[4]

Here, in this primacy of the male, is a rather striking convergence between the earliest analytic theory and the dominant ideology. And, more curiously still, it is a theory to which Freud will remain attached all his life. Penis envy, set off by the girl's suffering from not having a male sexual organ, is a datum which regularly recurs throughout Freud's writings on infantile sexuality in girls. Whether it is in the *Three Essays* or the later papers, the form of words is practically always the same:

> Little girls do not resort to denial of this kind when they see that boys' genitals are formed differently from their own. They are ready to recognize them immediately and are overcome by envy for the penis.[5]

> They notice the penis of a brother or playmate, strikingly visible and of large proportions, at once recognize it as the superior counterpart of their own small and inconspicuous organ, and from that time forward fall a victim to envy for the penis.[6]

And from this envy, Freud will go on to draw conclusions that are congruent with his views on women in general. What a shame that his premises should be so dubious:

1. Sigmund Freud, *S.E.* 7, 195.
2. ibid.
3. ibid., 219.
4. ibid.
5. ibid., 195.
6. Freud, *S.E.* 19, 252.

> The physical consequences of envy for the penis, in so far as it does not become absorbed in the reaction-formation of the masculinity complex, are various and far-reaching. After a woman has become aware of the wound to her narcissism, she develops, like a scar, a sense of inferiority....Even after penis-envy has abandoned its true object, it continues to exist: by an easy displacement it persists in the character-trait of jealousy.[1]

Freud must have been confident indeed of possessing the only worthwhile sex (or needed desperately to persuade himself that he did) for him to set up envy and jealousy of the boy's genital as the mainsprings of psychological development in girls. For, as a little reflection shows, it is by no means certain that every little girl is in a position even to see the 'large penis' of brother or cousin. For if the penis is large, it must be the case that the boy is at least adolescent; and would he, at that age, agree to display it?

Add to this unlikeliest of scenarios that a girl would have to be oddly blind, or have a strange imagination, to see anything in the boy's sex that remotely resembled hers. It's hard to see how the girl's 'slit' and the boy's external 'appendage' could ever be equated.

The whole thing is a figment of the imagination of a man absolutely set on establishing a comparative relation between the sexes, instead of establishing that the evidence pointed to a radical difference between them.

We have to wait until a different research reaches us; by a woman this time, and with a very different message. In 1974 Luce Irigaray finally decided to abjure this Freudian dogma that bore so little resemblance to reality, even if it meant that her Freudian colleagues would not understand.

No doubt she was breaking up the pattern of received ideas, transmitted all the way along psychoanalytic doctrine; no doubt she was rather too brutally upsetting the calm certainty established by Freud as to the supremacy of the male gender.

Luce Irigaray challenges the claim that femininity is founded exclusively on envy and jealousy of the male sexual organ. She works patiently through the whole history of this famous 'primary,' evaluative gaze directed at one sex by the other. She takes a dim view of the fact that this recognition of difference leads on to a devalorizing of the feminine.

> Why does the term 'envy' occur to Freud? Why does Freud choose it? Envy, jealousy, greed are all correlated to lack, default, absence. All these terms describe female sexuality as merely the *other side* or even the *wrong side* of a male sexualism...'Penis envy'...means nothing less than that the little girl, the woman, must despise *her own* pleasure in order to procure a...remedy for man's castration anxiety.[2]

In short, women, according to Luce Irigaray, are seen as losing or having lost something so that men can be spared seeing themselves as losing, as unprovided with. For it is very much the case that man is not 'all', any more than woman is; with nothing to show but vestigial breasts and missing

1. ibid., 253–4.
2. Luce Irigaray, *Speculum of the Other Woman* (*Speculum de l'autre femme*), trans. Gillian C. Gill (New York, 1985).

womb. And this woman analyst goes on to say, with a logic that is now unmistakably feminine:

> The *desire to have it* would confirm man in the assurance that he has it....If it were not so, why not *also* analyse the 'envy' for the vagina? or the uterus? or the vulva? Etc. The 'desire' felt by each pole of sexual difference 'to have something like it too'? the resentment at being faulty, lacking, with respect to a heterogene, to an other? the 'disadvantage' mother nature puts you to by providing only *one* sex organ?[1]

And so envy, it is argued, is not after all specifically feminine but common to both sexes, and bears on the sexual attributes of the 'other.' This is amply confirmed by children's play, where each child will try to see what the other one has. And it looks as if each one, as a result, feels distinctly aggrieved at discovering that he or she is missing something that the other one has. Hence those games of pretend, where the placing of cushion or ball varies with the sex of the child.

All through his disquisitions on penis envy, we find, don't we, Freud mentioning 'his own' envy of the breast, femininity, maternity—all those things that men have dreamed of having since time began, and which, since literature began, the poets have sung? There is no end to the celebration in literature of our curved neck and bosom, our breasts, our tiny waist: in short all the things which men don't have and envy us for having. The locus of male envy is indeed the bosom, continually hymned, extolled, bedecked with all the qualities of loving-kindness, fullness, and softness attributed to mothers.

But does the man's 'breast envy' allow us to infer the existence of 'penis envy' in the woman? What is all this new psychoanalytic stuff that suddenly comes along and sets itself up against so many hundreds of years of poetry, of literature in general? And can anyone show me that other poetry, by women, which sings the charms of men? When are we to see the new feminine poetry or literature that takes as its subject the male body and the penis, in all their alternating strength and fragility?

For there are no two ways about it: the male organ, which Freud taught us was the object of such envy by women, hardly ever appears in the graphic arts or in literature unless the artist is a man—Greek statuary, Etruscan pottery; the paintings of Picasso, Chagall, Dali; the novels of D. H. Lawrence, Henry Miller, and so on.

But on the distaff side: a blank; silence; the word unheard. This precious, eminently coveted object has failed to attract the pen or the brush of any woman (with the very recent exception of Benoîte Groult, and her description of it is anything but flattering).

No, it is the men who have something to envy. They are the envious ones, the jealous ones, but, by an astonishing reversal of the facts, we find ourselves saddled with their shortcomings and inadequacies. As Annie Leclerc so rightly points out: 'We had a sex that was so rich in events, adventures, experience that men might have paled with envy at the mere mention of it—

1. ibid., 51–2.

and what happens? They have actually managed to turn us, with all our wealth, into the envious ones.'[1]

The same writer goes on unhesitatingly to relocate envy, inviting us to share in the endlessly renewed joys of the female body. And it may well be that this penis envy that has been attributed to women is merely the obverse, the reverse of men's breast envy.

Breast, which we all of us came to know at the very beginning, in our mother's arms. Breast, which, later, we all lost, and have always dreamed of finding again. Loss that only women are capable of making good, both because it is there on their own bodies and because they see that men have something that can be given to them, in the same way that long ago their mother 'gave' it. For what men see as virile aggression, women receive as generous breast (penis = breast). 'When we make love, I am full of you, enchanted by you, by the song of you wandering near, the murmur of you wandering far; but not taken, not ravished: *there*, more than ever there, and full, more than ever full.'[2]

This is how women express themselves when finally they take the liberty of talking about their sexuality without reference to what men may make of it. Not ravished or possessed or raped, but enchanted, filled, marvellously fed: that is how women feel during lovemaking. Of course they need the man's penis, but they don't envy it or wish to keep it. Not at all: what they want is for the other to give it to them. What they want is to make it welcome, to take it in, sometimes to keep the fruit of it.

No, in this area, the 'underequipped' one is the man, for he has no means of making good the primary loss, except by looking at and touching as many breasts as he can (cf. men's magazines and the photos in them). Men are, quite simply, avid for breasts, and this unquenchable longing of theirs they have managed to plant on us, deceiving both themselves and us at the same time.

In the end, behind the apparent contrast between the gentleness in the writing of men poets and the aggressiveness of feminist writers lies one and the same fantasy, one and the same envy: envy of the maternal breast, forever lost, forever sought by men as by women. But to take this as an axiom is to challenge the entire phallocratic theory of sex. Annie Leclerc again:

> They invented sexuality in its entirety in the absence of any sound from our side. If we invent our own, they'll have to rethink the whole of theirs. Men don't like women; not yet. They go after them, they desire them, they subdue them, but they don't like them. But women hate women.[3]

Now this opens up a whole new field for psychoanalysis: it is necessary not only to rethink feminine sexuality, but to explain the hatred women have for 'other women'; to explain, not jealousy and envy of the penis but aggressive desires directed at the mother, first of the women that the little girl meets along her way.

* * *

1. Annie Leclerc, *Parole de Femme* (Paris, 1975).
2. ibid.
3. ibid.

THE DEVELOPMENT OF THE BOY

We start with him since it was his development that Freud called 'more logical' and easier to interpret than the girl's.

And what in fact do we see? An extremely simple infantile situation: from
the moment of birth the boy finds himself exposed to the opposite sex, since
his love-object is his mother, and therefore already in an elementary oedipal
position, since the famous 'incestuous' object is right there by the cradle. For
the male child there will be no problem about setting up the oedipal relation
or getting into it since he is in it from the outset as a result of his birth—at
the hands of a woman. Rather, it might be said, he falls into it head first, and
the really hard thing for him is coming out again, getting out of this 'fatal'
conjunction of the sexes while managing to keep his integrity.

For it is in her son that the mother has her only chance of seeing herself
in male form. This child that has come out of her belongs to the other sex,
and so the woman gets the chance of believing in that ancient dream that all
humans have: bisexuality, so often represented in Greek statuary in the guise
of the androgyne.

Just watch how proudly she carries this son who has come along to complete her in a way that no-one else can. Just look at the utter satisfiedness
painted on the faces of all those 'virgins with child.' Surely all those Italian
Madonnas are giving praise to the woman-and-mother who achieves happiness and wholeness without involving herself with the father, here banished
to a myth. God the Father—a religion of men, laid down by men who recognize nothing in women but the womb that bore them. An Oedipal religion, if
ever there was one, since the father is pushed out to make more room for the
mother—just as he is in our own day.

Motherhood: for the man, paradise lost, haunting him so much that he
wants to be master of it, be the one who decides on it. If he can't carry the
child, let him at least be able to compel 'the other' to do the carrying. The
woman 'gets' pregnant, in the phrase everyone knows. As if with brutal sud-
denness she had contracted something by accident, something unexpected
that would lay her low. Men whom we have seen angrily buzzing round the
problem of motherhood and abortion in a display of extraordinary violence;
men who will build up the mother in order the better to put down the
woman, who, it appears, has no right even to the 'desire' for a child—that is
something that can be settled on her behalf. No question of her being in command. What have we not had to suffer, all because of the farrago of myths
and envious feelings that the man always carries along with him on the subject of our reproductive organs!

It's a lucky woman that has a son! Is that perhaps why Lacan vengefully
reminds her that 'woman is not everything'? Let her not imagine that she
might occupy that position that causes so much envy in the man, who sees
himself condemned to the solitary experience of single-sexedness.

No, no, don't worry: this mother is not 'everything'—even if she is strongly tempted to think that she is—for this little boy is neither her nor hers and if, briefly, she may have thought that she had the other sex in her possession, her son as he grows will not fail to take away her illusions. The longer the mother believes in her oneness with her son, the more violent and perdurable will be the opposition he puts up.

And if the first months of dependence and of mother-child symbiosis seem to hold fewer problems for boys than for girls, it is a different story as far as the next period is concerned, the period of anal opposition and self-assertion. For then the difficulties will fall on the boy who, in this phase, will have to defend himself against the maternal fantasy of completeness so as to win his independence: an independence which his mother is less than wholehearted about wanting.

The woman has unconscious difficulties about giving up the only male she has ever been able to keep by her; she whose father let her down and whose husband is more often away than at home.

There is a further difficulty (not described by Freud) which the little boy has to overcome, for he has to make his escape from the oedipal stage *against* his mother, who does not want him to go away and leave her. This is the start of the longest but least obvious of wars against female desire; the place where the boy joins battle in the oedipal war of the sexes. Against his own mother.

When his mother says to him: 'You'll be grown up soon enough,' is she not giving expression to her desire? Is this not a way of holding on to him? Have I not known mothers who urged their sons to pull out their first facial hairs, that token of the onset of male adulthood?

Is it not on account of this desire of the mother's that the boy stays 'little' so much longer than the girl of the same age? Do we not learn from tests that there is a considerable gap in maturity between the sexes up to puberty and even beyond?

Here surely we are seeing the outward sign of the difficulty in growing up that is experienced by the boy pinioned in the maternal love-trap. Is it not the boy who wets the bed, who soils himself, who, in a word, refuses to grow up? The bad time that the male child goes through here leaves its mark on him forever, in the form of a deep fear of female domination.

It looks as if the famous 'trap' so often alluded to by men must be the trap of a symbiosis with the mother that is seen as 'imprisoning.' Symbiosis, psychosis? At all events, a 'prison' that sets off panic in the man at the thought of any symbiosis with any other woman. Never again to be caught up in the same place, in the same desire as the woman: this is the main driving force of the man's misogyny. Holding the woman away from him, keeping her confined to areas designed for her alone (family, schooling, home) is the primary objective of the masculine campaign.

Setting up at all points a barrier, whether physical or social, between him and her, standing out against her desire in any and every way, keeping his distance by any and every means will be the man's greatest obsession. Even his sexual behavior will be affected: he will be that much more sparing of the gestures and words that might recall something of his symbiotic loving-ness with the mother.

So: no painless escape from the oedipal stage; it will never be irreversibly achieved, and it will leave the man forever suspicious of women. Sometimes, no escape at all, which will bring mother and child to the psychotherapist's door. At this stage in the life of the human being we see three times more boys than girls (their turn will come later). That fact alone is proof of the order of difficulty that this battle with the mother faces the boy with. Where there is neurosis, it will be because the battle has made the boy into:

Either a child who has been so keen to resist the mother that he has forgot-ten to exist for his own sake: a child dead to all desire. Such a one will be spoken of as featureless; he will speak neither at home nor at school, for the shut-down is total. In order to find out how to get rid of 'her' and her per-manent desire, he has had to jettison all desire.

Or a child who has turned aggressive: first with his mother, and later, by extension, with all and sundry; defying the teacher, picking fights with the boys, being mean to the girls. Wherever he is, battle is never very far away; wherever he goes, his arrival rings the alarm bell, for he is set on proving that he is the tough one. Tougher than 'her', and then tougher than anyone. What he really wants is to get the better of his mother and her control. Unstable sometimes, his increasing fidgetiness is a sign of his urge to get away from her at every moment.

And what about the father? What is he doing all this time? Where is he? Can he not see, does he not know, from having gone through it all himself, what is happening? Of course he knows. Of course he remembers. But he does not dare pull his son free of female power: the only power his wife can enjoy undisturbed, since all other forms of power fall to him. The son has little hope of being able to count on his father to get him out of the bad time he is hav-ing with his mother, for the father deliberately keeps out of this conflict. More often than not, the first the boy will know of homosexuality will be in adoles-cence, with other boys of his age who are just emerging from the dangerous labyrinth. And in that context homosexuality in males acts as defense against mothers, women, girls. Homosexuality in boys is above all a way of defending themselves against the opposite sex. We shall see later that homosexuality in girls is wholly unrelated to this way of being.

Here then, in summary form, are the general nature and effects of the prob-lem of the male Oedipus complex; the story of the man's coming into being, as fruit of the fateful congress of the sexes, at the hands of a woman. For the man, what is born here is the tenderest of all loves, followed by the most long-drawn-out of wars. From this the man emerges showing signs of distrust, silence, misogyny; in a word, all the things women reproach men with.

It costs the man no small effort to get to the point where he can shake free of the woman he has loved best (no mother will contradict me if I say that boys are far more loving than girls) and who has loved him best. And all this is the result of cross-sex dealings within the family, where only the mother has the child-rearing role, only the mother has to live close up against her son.

In the old days there would have been grandfathers and great-grandfathers, uncles, cousins—any number of male images to break up this dangerous one-to-one. Nowadays the all-powerful mother lives with her son, who satisfies all the longings she had long ago, makes up for the father who was never there and the husband who has gone away. The little boy *is* there, so he must pay for them. After all, a woman has to get a man wherever she finds him: too bad if it's in the cradle!

After the terrible struggle with this all-powerful mother, how could men possibly avoid opting for wariness in anything to do with women and their power, that power which must be held in check? How could they possibly not spend their time setting limits to our world, shutting us away with our duties and responsibilities? How could a man's love for a woman be anything but ambivalent?

Is there a man, is there a son anywhere who can say that he really has got rid of his mother? Oh, he'll have left her, all right, but how far did he get? At what age? Left her for whom? Is there a mother anywhere who could say that she has given up her son, even when she's 80? He is still 'the one,' even where no word is said, even if respect for others requires that nothing be said, even if there really are brave men and mothers above reproach.

The bond that is woven in the darkness of infancy between mother and son binds them forever. When a woman marries, she can only ever marry another woman's son. Hence the clashes that go on between mothers-in-law and daughters-in-law over the same man, until such time as the younger one has a son of her own. Until she abandons the battle for the past in favour of the battle for the future with her son; this for want of the chance to hold on to the adult male, who is unavailable because invariably, mysteriously, tied up with his mother; because he is still ambivalent as between his past and his future.

Which is how the story carries on from one generation to the next: a son, secretly bound to his mother, takes a wife so that he can really get going, so that he can reproduce; but keeps his distance from her and allows her no rights beyond love–bed or child–bed. A woman without a husband, without a male equal, will foot the bill for the war in which she finds herself involved for no other reason than that she has taken over from the mother; a woman who will find in her son the only male that is really close to her. The circle has been closed, the loop looped: because the woman has been kept at a distance by her husband, she will invest in her son and prepare in him the ground of 'distance' for the other woman, the one who is yet to come. Misogyny is a crop sown by one woman and reaped by another.

THE DEVELOPMENT OF THE GIRL

Now let us take a look at what is happening on the other side: while the boy is desperately struggling to break free of his mother's fondness for him, what

is the girl going through–this little girl whom the same mother is conspicu-
ously not binding to herself with hoops of steel, since in the mother daughter relationship there is no sexual desire?

One question may be put straightaway: might the girl not be better off,
since she avoids the 'fateful' combination of the sexes? Alas, not at all. But
the risks are not the same, and neither are the results: if the boy finds it hard
to get rid of a love-object which is 'too adequate,' the terrible thing for the
girl is failing to find any adequate object along her way, and so having to
stay outside oedipal relations until well into her life. The boy may start out
from fusion/complementarity; the girl's early experience is of the body/mind
split: she will be loved as a child but not desired as a girl's body. She is not
a satisfactory object for her mother in sexual terms; only for her father could
she be one.

Only the father could give his daughter an easy (because fully sexed) position, since he sees the female sex as complementary to his own and therefore indispensable to sexual pleasure (something that the mother only rarely
feels about her daughter's sex, for, outside exceptional cases, the mother does
not desire her own sex as object of pleasure, but rather the sex that is complementary to her own, that is, the man's).

The girl, as a non-oedipal object for her mother, will feel that she is unsatisfactory, incapable of satisfying. This is the first of the consequences of her
mother's non-desire: the girl–and later the woman–is never satisfied with
what she has or what she is. She is always yearning for a body other than
her own: she would like a different face, different breasts, different legs.
Every woman, by her own account, has something about her body which
does not look right.

For the first thing that did not look right was indeed something about the
body, since it was about her sex not triggering desire in her mother. The little girl, in her mother's eyes, will be sweet, lovable, graceful, good–anything
but sexually alive, tinged with desire. The color of desire will not be found
in the little girl that has been handled by a woman.

And yet, even at that time, her sex is a fact, and the vulvo–clitoral area is
hypersensitive to the mother's touch when she cleans the child; but that sex
is not an object of desire for the mother who, in line with the culture, does
not see this part of herself as 'typically female', rather reserving that distinction for her vagina, which the man has pronounced 'fit for orgasm.' It is the
mother, then, who first bars the way to her daughter's clitoral orgasm and
institutes silence on the subject of that orgasm.

The 'thou art a clitoral child' is replaced by the 'thou shalt be a vaginal woman
who will come to climax with a man–later on'. A present tense which is forbidden for the sake of a future which must be waited for: that, alas, is how it will
be for a great many women, still caught up in the wait for the orgasm of the
adult woman who, like the little girl, knows that there is a climax lying ahead
but is never aware of one at the time. So the girl is denied in her own sexuality
and told to wait for her future sexuality as a woman; she must keep to herself

what she is (a clitoral child) and believe in what she is not (a vaginal woman).

Grasping the dialectic that is being imposed on her, guessing that only the woman is regarded as a sexual being, she plays at being a woman: she borrows the tricks of her trade: the lipstick, the high heels, the handbag. The little girl gets herself up as a woman, just as later on the woman will disguise herself to look like another woman, different from the one she is.

That is the origin of the permanent 'displacement' of the woman with respect to her own body: there's never any harm, in her view, in the odd bit of cheating if it means being accepted as a woman. Her real sex is not enough; she is always having to make more of it. And what do women's magazines go on about, if not the 'really natural woman,' the 'womanly woman,' the 'woman that *is* a woman,' and so on? As if there always had to be something added to the woman's own sex, as if the woman were not woman by nature, as if her sex were not the signifier of her femininity. Surely all this is—once more, once again—the story of the little girl who has to show herself as sexed differently from how she actually is? And was it not right back in childhood that the woman first started to tell lies about her actual sex? There are no genuine little girls; there are only make-believe little women.

Everyone knows that to get yourself recognized as a girl, it is not enough just to be one: you have to be continually adding on proofs of femininity which, often, have nothing to do with sex.

> The boy is desired for his own sake....The girl is desired—if and when she is so according to a scale of values....
>
> –girls are more loving...,
>
> –they are more grateful...,
>
> –they are sweet and charming...,
>
> –they help about the house....[1]

All in all, the girl is pronounced 'girl' for a thousand reasons which never have anything to do with her actual sex; she is given conditional recognition as 'girl,' while the boy is recognized as boy entirely because of his sex. The girl always has to bring forward proofs of her femininity. Following on from that, how could women not be haunted by the need to put the signs of that femininity on public display? What a life it is for the woman who thinks she has to go on proving all her life long that she really is a woman! A woman—something even she is never wholly certain of being, since her social identity seems never to have stemmed from the sex of her body.

A painful dialogue in which *identification* (being like) matters more than *identity* (being oneself), in which *make-believe* replaces *genuine*. Identity

---

1. Elena Gianini Belotti, *Du Côté des petites filles* (Paris, 1976).

blocked by lack of desire from the other sex, identification imperiled by the difficulty she has in seeing her own body as being like her mother's: these are the twin hazards that lie along the girl's road.

The little girl's trouble is that her body is not like anyone's. She possesses neither a sex like her father's nor the distinguishing features of her mother (who has breasts, comes in at the waist and out at the hips, has pubic hair). The little girl sees herself as naked, flat, and with a slit—something like the sexless dolls on sale in shops.

She does have something which really is 'like,' but it is something she can't see, something hidden away inside her slit. And noone ever tells her about this clitoris, the only sexual point of comparison with her mother.

For anyone who really wants to see some lightening of the darkness that surrounds women's sexuality, the clitoris—so much built up by feminists, so much played down by male chauvinists—may well be one of the earliest links that must not be bypassed in the developmental chain. For when the girl is not told about this part of her sexuality, what happens is that she is denied mention of what she has, and told instead, in general terms, about her as yet non-functioning genital endowment. She is told about what she does not have (periods, reproductive processes) and her mother does have.

And because of all this, the mother cannot be a locus of identification for the girl. Homosexual feelings between them are ruled out: only in adolescence will the girl discover that there are bodies like hers—hence the importance of friendship between girls in that period, setting up the femininity which could not be set up with the mother.

On the other hand, faced with this mother who is unlike her, who is better endowed than she is, the girl does discover envy and jealously which do not— as Freud thought—stem from the relationship with the male body, but from the overwhelming comparison with that of the woman-and-mother.

It is not uncommon to see a little girl touching first her mother's breasts and then her own chest and saying 'Katie no boobs.' Long before the man's penis, is it not rather, in view of the mother's predominant presence, the sexual attributes of the mother that are felt as missing from the child's body? Creating in the boy the irreversible lack and enduring fantasy of the comforts of the maternal breast, and, in the girl, the endless comparing with and jealousy of any other breast (any other body) better shaped than her own?

In any case, if that is where women are stuck, and if jealousy has taken the place of homosexuality, it is because the mother, first and foremost of the women to be encountered, was unable to bring herself to recognize or name that part of her daughter's body which in fact is like part of hers. Out of shame? Out of fear? No woman ever talks to her daughter about the clitoris.

And so, in despair at having no sex (the clitoris unrecognized), and no sexual object (the father absent), the little girl will go on, not, as Freud thought, to repress her sexuality, but to displace a sexuality which, as such, is impossible.

If there is nothing sexual in her sex, there will be enough and to spare everywhere else. The girl sexualizes everything: her body, which has to be feminine, her acts, which have to be in line with those of her kind, her language, which becomes seductive. The woman will sexualize whatever can be seen by the other. Since her sex got no recognition when she was a little girl, the woman will contrive to get it for the other, unsexed parts of her body. With the result that sometimes she will take her whole body as a sexual signal and then will be afraid to display it; like the woman who said to me one day: 'When I have to get up and speak, and everyone can see me, I get confused about what I want to say, my mind goes blank. I'm overcome with shame, all I can think of is my body, and then I just don't know where to put myself.'

The woman learns in childhood to use her external features to signify her internal sex. The little girl spends her time giving external proofs of her femininity, which the adults round her keep a closely guarded secret, and, following on from that, she will stop being able to tell what is sexual about her and what is not.

It will be said of her that she becomes hysterical because she appeals continually to the gaze of the other to guarantee her sexual identity. What difference is there between her and the man, other than that the man is given this desiring gaze from the outset, by his mother? The absence of any paternal gaze in earliest childhood seems to register in the girl as sexual anxiety, as an identificatory doubt that has forever to be allayed, forever made good by the gaze of another in adulthood.

* * *

THE SPIDER'S WEB

* * *

As Freud says, mothers would be amazed if anyone told them that when they look at their children, their gaze has in it not only love but desire for the opposite sex, and therefore desire for their sons; and that no male child can take that on without feeling afraid. This, as we have seen,[1] is a fear which does not appear straightaway, since the primary symbiosis seems to work to the little boy's advantage, and even strengthens his narcissism. This fear only appears at the anal age, when the child has to take the strain of learning to be clean and of discovering the difference between the sexes.

The source of evidence for the difference between the sexes is the mother (she who is closest to the child), both for the girl, who witnesses her superiority, and for the boy, who sees her with 'something missing' where the sex organs are. If witnessing the mother's superiority sets off envy in the girl, the sight of his mother's inferiority sets off *fear* in the boy, for, as Freud says, every child believes that everyone else is made in the same image, and if his

---

1. At the risk of seeming repetitious, I go on here to restate a number of points developed earlier. I do so, not from any want of confidence in the reader, but so that I can group these points together, in order to bring out more clearly the way in which male psychology is built up.

mother 'hasn't got one,' it can only mean that she hasn't got one *any more*, that she's lost it, etc. This 'something missing' in the mother's body is immediately regarded as a loss, as some kind of disappearance, as a possible castration. Here we have it, then, this dreadful affliction that hangs menacingly over the rest of the boy's life: he fears castration. He is afraid that any human with 'something missing' (and therefore all women, including his own mother) will attack him, who 'has one'.

The mother, then, is a twofold danger: she 'hasn't got one,' and she unconsciously wants the man's—even if the man is her own son. This the little boy experiences as *threat*: in Freud's terms, fear of castration. The whole of Freudian history is there: castration anxiety will take hold in man and drive him to defend himself, first against 'the woman,' then against women. Mere male fantasy, this claim that women feel 'penis envy.' This envy is a figment of the man's imagination, hunted and haunted by the idea that she is going to take it from him: that she may actually castrate him.

If psychoanalysis had been written by a woman, no doubt there would never have been any mention of castration. Castration is a little boy's notion; envy is a little girl's.

You will have noticed that when they get to adult years, in practice the woman tries to acquire the greatest possible sexual distinctiveness, while the man tries to preserve his, as far as he can, by commanding respect as a male. Envy belongs on the woman's side of the line. There is no end to women's envies, women's dreams: it seems as if they are always waiting for something else, something different. Defences belong on the male side. Men keep accumulating powers that will consolidate their supremacy. In the end, the woman's strong desire to take, to have (a highly generalized desire, by no means only—perhaps indeed hardly at all—directed at the man's sex: is it not true that every little girl dreams of being a queen, that is, of having everything?) triggers in the man the fear of being possessed, robbed, trapped, as he so often puts it.

* * *

12

SOME NEUROTIC MECHANISMS IN JEALOUSY, PARANOIA, AND HOMOSEXUALITY

Sigmund Freud

A

Jealousy is one of those affective states, like grief, that may be described as normal. If anyone appears to be without it, the inference is justified that it has undergone severe repression and consequently plays all the greater part in his unconscious mental life. The instances of abnormally intense jealousy met with in analytic work reveal themselves as constructed of three layers. The three layers or grades of jealousy may be described as (1) *competitive* or normal, (2) *projected*, and (3) *delusional* jealousy.

There is not much to be said from the analytic point of view about normal jealousy. It is easy to see that essentially it is compounded of grief, the pain caused by the thought of losing the loved object, and of the narcissistic wound, in so far as this is distinguishable from the other wound; further, of feelings of enmity against the successful rival, and of a greater or lesser amount of self-criticism which tries to hold the subject's own ego accountable for his loss. Although we may call it normal, this jealousy is by no means completely rational, that is, derived from the actual situation, proportionate to the real circumstances and under the complete control of the conscious ego; for it is rooted deep in the unconscious, it is a continuation of the earliest stirrings of the child's affective life, and it originates in the oedipus or brother-and-sister complex of the first sexual period. Moreover, it is noteworthy that in some people it is experienced bisexually. That is to say, a man will not only feel pain about the woman he loves and hatred of the man who is his rival, but also grief about the man, whom he loves unconsciously, and hatred of the woman as his rival; and this latter set of feelings will add to the intensity of his jealousy. I even know of a man who suffered exceedingly during his attacks of jealousy and who, according to his own account, went through unendurable torments by consciously imagining himself in the position of the faithless woman. The sensation of helplessness which then came over him and the images he used to describe his condition—exposed to the vulture's beak like Prometheus, or thrown bound into a nest of serpents—were referred by him to impressions received during several homosexual acts of aggression to which he had been subjected as a boy.

The jealousy of the second layer, *projected* jealousy, is derived in both men and women either from their own actual unfaithfulness in real life or from impulses towards it which have succumbed to repression. It is a matter of everyday experience that fidelity, especially that degree of it required in marriage, is only maintained in the face of continual temptations. Anyone who denies these temptations in himself will nevertheless feel their pressure so strongly that he will be glad enough to make use of an unconscious mechanism to alleviate his situation. He can obtain this alleviation—and, indeed, acquittal by his conscience—if he projects his own impulses to faithlessness on to the partner to whom he owes faith. This strong motive can then make use of the perceptual material which betrays unconscious impulses of the same kind in the partner, and the subject can justify himself with the reflection that the other is probably not much better than he is himself.[1]

Social conventions have wisely taken this universal state of things into account, by granting a certain amount of latitude to the married woman's craving to attract and the married man's thirst to make conquests, in the expectation that this inevitable tendency to unfaithfulness will thus find a safety-valve and be rendered innocuous. Convention has laid down that neither partner is to hold the other accountable for these little excursions in the direction of unfaithfulness, and they usually result in the desire that has been awakened by the new object finding satisfaction in some kind of return to faithfulness to the original object. A jealous person, however, does not recognize this convention of tolerance; he does not believe in any such thing as a halt or a turning-back once the path has been trodden, not that a flirtation may be a safeguard against actual infidelity. In the treatment of a jealous person like this, one must refrain from disputing with him the material on which he bases his suspicions; one can only aim at bringing him to regard the matter in a different light.

The jealousy that arises from such a projection has, it is true, an almost delusional character; it is, however, amenable to the analytic work of exposing the unconscious phantasies of the subject's own infidelity. The position is worse as regards jealousy belonging to the third layer, the true *delusional* type. It too has its origin in repressed impulses toward unfaithfulness; but the object in these cases is of the same sex as the subject. Delusional jealousy is what is left of a homosexuality that has run its course, and it rightly takes its position among the classical forms of paranoia. As an attempt at defence against an

---

1 Cf. Desdemona's song [*Othello* IV, 3]:
    I called my love false love; but what said he then?
    If I court moe women, you'll couch with moe men.

unduly strong homosexual impulse it may, in a man, be described in the formula: 'I do not love him, *she* loves him!'[1] In a delusional case one will be prepared to find jealousy belonging to all three layers, never to the third alone.

B

Paranoia.—Cases of paranoia are for well-known reasons not usually amenable to analytic investigation. I have recently been able, nevertheless, by an intensive study of two paranoics, to discover something new to me.

The first case was that of a youngish man with a fully developed paranoia of jealousy, the object of which was his impeccably faithful wife. A stormy period in which the delusion had possessed him uninterruptedly already lay behind him. When I saw him he was only subject to clearly separated attacks, which lasted for several days and which, curiously enough, regularly appeared on the day after he had had sexual intercourse with his wife, which was, incidentally, satisfying to both of them. The inference is justified that after every satiation of the heterosexual libido the homosexual component, likewise stimulated by the act, forced an outlet for itself in the attack of jealousy.

These attacks drew their material from his observation of minute indications, by which his wife's quite unconscious coquetry, unnoticeable to any one else, had betrayed itself to him. She had unintentionally touched the man sitting next her with her hand; she had turned too much towards him, or she had smiled more pleasantly than when alone with her husband. He was extraordinarily observant of all these manifestations of her unconscious, and always knew how to interpret them correctly, so that he really was always in the right about it, and could furthermore call in analysis to justify his jealousy. His abnormality really reduced itself to this, that he watched his wife's unconscious mind much more closely and then regarded it as far more important than anyone else would have thought of doing.

We are reminded that sufferers from persecutory paranoia act in just the same way. They, too, cannot regard anything in other people as indifferent, and they, too, take up minute indications with which these other, unknown, people present them, and use them in their delusions of reference. The meaning of their delusion of reference is that they expect from all strangers something like love. But these people show them nothing of the kind; they laugh to themselves, flourish their sticks, even spit on the ground as they go by—and one really does not do such things while a person in whom one takes a friendly interest is near. One does them only when one feels quite indifferent to the passer-by, when one can treat him like air; and, considering, too, the fundamental kinship of the concepts of 'stranger' and 'enemy,' the paranoic is not so far wrong in regarding this indifference as hate, in contrast to his claim for love.

1 See the Schreber analysis (1911c) [Part III]. (Ed: *SE* 12: 1–84).

We begin to see that we describe the behaviour of both jealous and persecutory paranoics very inadequately by saying that they project outwards on to others what they do not wish to recognize in themselves. Certainly they do this; but they do not project it into the blue, so to speak, where there is nothing of the sort already. They let themselves be guided by their knowledge of the unconscious, and displace to the unconscious minds of others the attention which they have withdrawn from their own. Our jealous husband perceived his wife's unfaithfulness instead of his own; by becoming conscious of hers and magnifying it enormously he succeeded in keeping his own unconscious. If we accept his example as typical, we may infer that the enmity which the persecuted paranoic sees in others is the reflection of his own hostile impulses against them. Since we know that with the paranoic it is precisely the most loved person of his own sex that becomes his persecutor, the question arises where this reversal of affect takes its origin; the answer is not far to seek—the ever-present ambivalence of feeling provides its source and the non-fulfilment of his claim for love strengthens it. This ambivalence thus serves the same purpose for the persecuted paranoic as jealousy served for my patient—that of a defence against homosexuality.

The dreams of my jealous patient presented me with a great surprise. They were not simultaneous with the outbreaks of the attacks, it is true, but they occurred within the period which was under the dominance of the delusion; yet they were completely free from delusion and they revealed the underlying homosexual impulses with no more than the usual degree of disguise. Since I had had little experience of the dreams of paranoics, it seemed plausible at the time to suppose that it was true in general that paranoia does not penetrate into dreams.

This patient's homosexual position was easily surveyed. He had made no friendships and developed no social interests; one had the impression that only the delusion had carried forward the development of his relations with men, as if it had taken over some of the arrears that had been neglected. The fact that his father was of no great importance in the family, combined with a humiliating homosexual trauma in early boyhood, had forced his homosexuality into repression and barred the way to its sublimation. The whole of his youth was governed by a strong attachment to his mother. Of all her many sons he was her declared favourite, and he developed marked jealousy of the normal type in regard to her. When later he made his choice of a wife—mainly prompted by an impulse to enrich his mother—his longing for a virgin mother expressed itself in obsessive doubts about his fiancée's virginity. The first years of his marriage were free from jealousy. Then he became unfaithful to his wife and entered upon an intimate relationship with another woman that lasted for a considerable time. Frightened by a certain suspicion, he at length made an end of this love affair, and not until then did jealousy of the second, projected type break out, by means of which he was able to assuage his self-reproaches about his own unfaithfulness. It was soon complicated by an accession of homosexual impulses, of which his father-in-law was the object, and became a fully formed jealous paranoia.

My second case would probably not have been classified as persecutory paranoia, apart from analysis; but I had to recognize the young man as a candidate for a terminal illness of that kind. In his attitude to his father there existed an ambivalence which in its range was quite extraordinary. On the one hand, he was the most pronounced rebel imaginable, and had developed manifestly in every direction in opposition to his father's wishes and ideals; on the other hand, at a deeper level he was still the most submissive of sons, who after his father's death denied himself all enjoyment of women out of a tender sense of guilt. His actual relations with men were clearly dominated by suspiciousness; his keen intellect easily rationalized this attitude; and he knew how to bring it about that both friends and acquaintances deceived and exploited him. The new thing I learned from studying him was that classical persecutory ideas may be present without finding belief or acceptance. They flashed up occasionally during the analysis, but he regarded them as unimportant and invariably scoffed at them. This may occur in many cases of paranoia; it may be that the delusions which we regard as new formations when the disease breaks out have already long been in existence.

It seems to me that we have here an important discovery—namely, that the qualitative factor, the presence of certain neurotic formations, has less practical significance than the quantitative factor, the degree of attention or, more correctly, the amount of cathexis that these structures are able to attract to themselves. Our consideration of the first case, the jealous paranoia, led to a similar estimate of the importance of the quantitative factor, by showing that there also the abnormality essentially consisted in the hypercathexis of the interpretations of someone else's unconscious. We have long known of an analogous fact in the analysis of hysteria. The pathogenic phantasies, derivatives of repressed instinctual impulses, are for a long time tolerated alongside the normal life of the mind, and have no pathogenic effect until by a revolution in the libidinal economy they receive a hypercathexis; not till then does the conflict which leads to the formation of symptoms break out. Thus as our knowledge grows we are increasingly impelled to bring the *economic* point of view into the foreground. I should also like to throw out the question whether this quantitative factor that I am now dwelling on does not suffice to cover the phenomena which Bleuler [1916] and others have lately proposed to name 'switching'. One need only assume that an increase in resistance in the course taken by the psychical current in one direction results in a hypercathexis of another path and thus causes the flow to be switched into that path.[1]

1. [The idea underlying this goes back to the picture of the psychical apparatus which Freud had already drawn in his 'Project' of 1895 (Freud 1950a).] (Ed: *SE* 1: 281–393).

My two cases of paranoia showed an instructive contrast in the behaviour of their dreams. Whereas those of the first case were free from delusion, as has already been said, the other patient produced great numbers of persecutory dreams, which may be regarded as forerunners of or substitutes for the delusional ideas. The pursuer, whom he only managed to escape with great fear, was usually a powerful bull or some other male symbol which even in the dream itself he sometimes recognized as representing his father. One day he produced a very characteristic paranoic transference-dream. He saw me shaving in front of him, and from the scent he realized that I was using the same soap as his father had used. I was doing this in order to oblige him to make a father-transference on to me. The choice of this incident for his dream quite unmistakably betrays the patient's depreciatory attitude to his paranoic phantasies and his disbelief in them; for his own eyes could tell him every day that I was never in a position to make use of shaving-soap and that therefore there was in this respect nothing to which a father-transference could attach itself.

A comparison of the dreams of the two patients shows, however, that the question whether or not paranoia (or any other psychoneurosis) can penetrate into dreams is based on a false conception of dreams. Dreams are distinguished from waking thought by the fact that they can include material (belonging to the region of the repressed) which must not emerge in waking thought. Apart from this, dreams are merely a *form of thinking*, a transformation of preconscious material of thought by the dream-work and its conditions. Our terminology of the neuroses is not applicable to repressed material; this cannot be called hysterical, nor obsessional, nor paranoic. As against this, the other part of the material which is subjected to the process of dream-formation—the preconscious thoughts—may be normal or may bear the character of any neurosis; they may be the products of any of the pathogenic processes in which the essence of a neurosis lies. There seems to be no reason why any such pathological idea should not be transformed into a dream. A dream may therefore quite simply represent a hysterical phantasy, an obsessional idea, or a delusion—that is, may reveal one or other of these upon interpretation. Observation of the two paranoics shows that the dreams of the one were quite normal while he was subject to his delusion, and that those of the other were paranoic in content while he was treating his delusional ideas with contempt. In both cases, therefore, the dream took up the material that was at the time forced into the background in waking life. This too, however, need not necessarily be an invariable rule.

C

Homosexuality.—Recognition of the organic factor in homosexuality does not relieve us of the obligation of studying the psychical processes connected with its origin. The typical process,[1] already established in innumerable cases,

---

1. [Described by Freud in Chapter III of his study on Leonardo (1910c).] (Ed: *SE* 11: 59–138).

is that a few years after the termination of puberty a young man, who until this time has been strongly fixated to his mother, changes his attitude; he identifies himself with his mother, and looks about for love-objects in whom he can re-discover himself, and whom he might then love as his mother loved him. The characteristic mark of this process is that for several years one of the necessary conditions for his love is usually that the male object shall be of the same age as he himself was when the change took place. We have come to know of various factors contributing to this result, probably in different degrees. First there is the fixation on the mother, which makes it difficult to pass on to another woman. Identification with the mother is an outcome of this attachment, and at the same time in a certain sense it enables the son to keep true to her, his first object. Then there is the inclination towards a narcissistic object-choice, which in general lies readier to hand and is easier to put into effect than a move towards the other sex. Behind this latter factor there lies concealed another of quite exceptional strength, or perhaps it coincides with it: the high value set upon the male organ and the inability to tolerate its absence in a love-object. Depreciation of women, and aversion to them, even horror of them, are generally derived from the early discovery that women have no penis. We subsequently discovered, as another powerful motive urging towards homosexual object-choice, regard for the father or fear of him; for the renunciation of women means that all rivalry with him (or with all men who may take his place) is avoided. The two last motives—the clinging to the condition of a penis in the object, as well as the retiring in favour of the father—may be ascribed to the castration complex. Attachment to the mother, narcissism, fear of castration—these are the factors (which incidentally have nothing specific about them) that we have hitherto found in the psychical aetiology of homosexuality; and with these must be reckoned the effect of seduction, which is responsible for a premature fixation of the libido, as well as the influence of the organic factor which favours the passive role in love.

We have, however, never regarded this analysis of the origin of homosexuality as complete. I can now point to a new mechanism leading to homosexual object-choice, although I cannot say how large a part it plays in the formation of the extreme, manifest and exclusive type of homosexuality. Observation has directed my attention to several cases in which during early childhood impulses of jealousy, derived from the mother-complex and of very great intensity, arose [in a boy] against rivals, usually older brothers. This jealousy led to an exceedingly hostile and aggressive attitude towards these brothers which might sometimes reach the pitch of actual death-wishes, but which could not maintain themselves in the face of the subject's further development. Under the influences of upbringing—and certainly not uninfluenced also by their own continuing powerlessness—these impulses yielded to repression and underwent a transformation, so that the rivals of the earlier period became the first homosexual love-objects. Such an outcome of the attachment to the mother shows various interesting relations with other processes known to us. First of all it is a complete contrast to the development of persecutory paranoia, in which the person who has before been loved becomes the hated persecutor, whereas here the hated rivals are transformed into love-objects. It represents, too, an exaggeration of the process which, according to my view, leads to the birth of social instincts in the individual.[1] In both processes there is first the presence of jealous and hostile impulses which cannot achieve satisfaction; and both the affectionate and the social feelings of identification arise as reactive formations against the repressed aggressive impulses.

This new mechanism of homosexual object-choice—its origin in rivalry which has been overcome and in aggressive impulses which have become repressed—is sometimes combined with the typical conditions already familiar to us. In the history of homosexuals one often hears that the change in them took place after the mother had praised another boy and set him up as a model. The tendency to a narcissistic object-choice was thus stimulated, and after a short phase of keen jealousy the rival became a love-object. As a rule, however, the new mechanism is distinguished by the change taking place at a much earlier period, and the identification with the mother receding into the background. Moreover, in the cases I have observed, it led only to homosexual attitudes which did not exclude heterosexuality and did not involve a *horror feminae*.

It is well known that a good number of homosexuals are characterized by a special development of their social instinctual impulses and by their devotion to the interests of the community. It would be tempting, as a theoretical explanation of this, to say that the behaviour towards men in general of a man who sees in other men potential love-objects must be different from that of a man who looks upon other men in the first instance as rivals in regard to women. The only objection to this is that jealousy and rivalry play their part in homosexual love as well, and that the community of men also includes these potential rivals. Apart from this speculative explanation, however, the fact that homosexual object-choice not infrequently proceeds from an early overcoming of rivalry with men cannot be without a bearing on the connection between homosexuality and social feeling.

In the light of psycho-analysis we are accustomed to regard social feeling as a sublimation of homosexual attitudes towards objects. In the homosexuals with marked social interests, it would seem that the detachment of social feeling from object-choice has not been fully carried through.

---

1. Cf. my *Group Psychology and the Analysis of the Ego* (1921c). (Ed: *SE* 18: 65–144).

13

VAGINAL CORE OR VAMPIRE MOUTH: THE VISCERAL LEVEL OF ENVY IN WOMEN: AN EXPLORATION OF THE PROTOSYMBOLIC POLITICS OF OBJECT RELATIONS

Susan Kavaler-Adler

Melanie Klein's understanding of envy as distinct from oedipal-level jealousy, and of primal oral envy as distinct from a later level of penis or womb envy, was a revolutionizing contribution to psychoanalytic theory. Although Klein did not write about the developmental deficits that contribute to the dissociation or repression of primal envy, which I believe are highly significant, she did write about the instinctual base with which the developmental issues interact. Furthermore, in her essay "Envy and Gratitude" (1957), she writes of envy at the level of psychic fantasy as a vivid, visceral, and body-level phenomenon. Klein did not run from the body as many modern-day theorists have done. And in articulating psychic fantasy in the body, she brought to life a protosymbolic level of pre-oedipal experience that had been neglected in psychoanalytic literature, which until then was focused on the oedipal level of experience. Klein's contribution regarding primal envy, which has influenced theorists such as Wilfred Bion, Otto Kernberg, James Grotstein, and Betty Josephs, has allowed the infant mother relationship to be understood in all its encapsulated forms within the adult psyche. To the degree that her work has been neglected by current psychoanalytic theorists of all persuasions, and by gender studies theorists in particular, the subjective voice of the unconscious has been neglected. To that degree psychoanalysis has lost its "body" and become a disembodied postmodernist abstraction, a self psychological idealization, or an ego psychological function (Kavaler-Adler, 1995).

My own passion for Melanie Klein relates to my particular interests in the mourning process and what I have called "developmental mourning" in my two books, *The Compulsion to Create* (Routledge, 1993) and *The Creative Mystique: From Red Shoes Frenzy to Love and Creativity* (Routledge, 1996). My theoretical writing has followed Klein's original writing on mourning in

"Mourning and Manic-Depressive States" (1940) in which she asserts that mourning is a critical clinical and developmental process. My writing also has followed Klein's focus on body-level manifestations of psychic need as expressed by Klein in her seminal paper "Envy and Gratitude." In writing about gender and envy, I now come upon another opportunity to speak of the visceral level of experience I have studied in both my research on female writers and artists and in my own analysands in object relations psychotherapy and psychoanalysis.

In this chapter I will look at the contrast between two cases. The first is a well-known female poet, Sylvia Plath, who shows pathological arrest at a level of psychic starvation manifesting as envy and splitting off of the central body core, or vaginal core. The second is an analysand in my practice, Ms. Z, who is successful in resolving such split-off body manifestations of envy and psychic starvation through a therapeutic mourning process in an object relations treatment context.

Sylvia Plath evidences a pathological mourning state in which psychic starvation resulting from inadequate object internalization and integration leads to an addiction to a persecutory object, which in its masculinized primal object form I call a "demon lover god muse," and which she calls her "Lord of the Mirrors." Such a psychic addiction can be related to Ronald Fairbairn's (1952) pathological clinging to an inadequate real primal object, which he calls a "bad object," an "internal saboteur," or an "exciting and rejecting object." The psychic addiction also relates to Melanie Klein's paranoid-schizoid position, in which the negative aspect of the psychic fantasy primary object is experienced as hostile and persecutory. Envy is an essential part of such an addictive position, in which the insatiable hunger for a split idealized and demonic object substitutes for contact with a good object, that is, an object that could be internalized to provide psychic structure at a core self level.

In my exploration of Plath's predicament, I will link the concept of an object tie split off from the central self to the bodily based expression of insatiable oral hunger. This split-off object tie eludes contact and connection with an other through the psychic channel of the woman's vaginal core. This results in a demon lover addiction with vampirelike body imagery at the level of oral craving, prior to any differentiated subjective self desiring object connection. The sealed-off, starved self, akin to Fairbairn's internal closed self and object system, is associated with dependency on an "empty core" mother in early phases of development (see Seinfeld, 1990). It is exacerbated by the lack of a whole object father who could relate and be penetrated by his daughter's psychic experience, and further by the early death of that father during the latency stage. Both Plath and Ms. Z have had a latency-age experience of the father's death. Early object loss intensifies all the earlier levels of psychic deprivation with both mother and father. Such early loss therefore intensifies the dynamic of envy that can sometimes manifest as a vampire-mouth insatiability, with all its self-sabotaging modes of spoiling in relation to sustained object connection.

Both the mother of symbiosis and of separation-individuation play a role in enhancing or modifying envy. The dynamics of envy can range from toxic destruction of all dependent object ties to a more moderate form of conscious hunger and ambition. For the female child, the mother's primal role as both symbiotic object and agent of separation is not only formative of an autonomous and yet related self, but also determines the capacity to move on to oedipal-level desires to connect with the father as a differentiated other, one who is also the subject of erotic desire. When there is a failure of mothering in the early stages of critical self-formation, the erotic longings for the father are not differentiated, and the father himself is not differentiated. The father comes to play the role of an extension or mirror of the mother. When the mother is an empty core mother, who lacks a separate and subjectively alive affect-self of her own, the father becomes a father-mother extension of mother. He is destined to be experienced as seductive and abandoning (like Fairbairn's "exciting and rejecting object"), because his presence can never provide the fulfillment of object connection and object relations internalization that was missed during the critical pre-oedipal eras of symbiosis and separation-individuation (Mahler, 1975). When the father is lacking in object-related capacities in his own right, manifesting as narcissistic, borderline, or schizoid modes of character pathology, the experience of him as a bad object exacerbates object starvation and the envious manifestations of psychic insatiability. This can be eroticized, so that he is seen as a demon lover figure by a daughter who splits off her own erotic impulses. The death of such a father, who despite his failings still stands as an "other" in reality, separate from the primal mother, only further exacerbates the depth of psychic and sexual arousal in the daughter, as well as the degree of frustration in the further effects of psychic deprivation.

Sylvia Plath's poetry illustrates this insatiable object craving quite vividly. In many poems Plath speaks of a vampire image as synonymous both with herself and with the demon lover (father-mother) part-object that she hungers for as a compensation for the emptiness within the self. The early object loss in relation to a mother who can't facilitate an adequate separation process is felt through the later object loss of the father's death, and its personified form becomes that of a masculine demon—as in Emily Dickinson's "metallic god who drills his welcome in" (Kavaler-Adler, 1993), who turns into the image of death. The negative phallic god, like Edith Sitwell's yearned-for father in an "atomic bomb mushroom cloud," (Kavaler-Adler, 1993) can produce only death, not babies. For he rapes, murders, abandons. He eludes the contact, connection, tenderness, relatedness, and emotional touch that can promote positive psychic internalizations.

THE DEMON LOVER

The lust for the demon lover god father is an insatiable hunger for an omnipotent other which, in women, denies not only body limits, but vaginal limits. The insatiable craving comes from a profound sense of an internal void, a void often felt painfully at the visceral level, although the real void is in a lack of inter-nalization of a responsive, differentiated other. As long as the illusion lasts that the god-muse will somehow cork and enclose the vast black void, and that tran-scendence will take place, the woman with a pre-oedipal arrest in psychic devel-opment focuses all her yearnings on the god muse that she wishes to merge with. Thus, Emily Brontë yearns for transcendence through creative ecstacy as she expresses her wish for merger with the power of language and poetry that he, her god-muse, represents to her, crying, "My outward sense is gone/My inner essence feels." She anticipates the yearned-for merger with a masculin-ized god figure. However, the original psychic trauma of her childhood—the loss of her mother to cancer during the critical separation-individuation phase—is destined to repeat itself in her encounter with her masculinized muse. As we read in the poem "The Demon Lover" (Gerin, 1971), Emily Brontë's one brief moment of creative ecstacy and anticipated transcendence turns to possession by the god as he manifests his demon side. She loses her voice as a poet as she submits to his possessive form of power, and the last stanza of the poem ends in the image of a graveyard. To be possessed by the demon lover is to end up in the arms of death, as seen in the poetry of both Brontë and of Emily Dickinson, both of whom moved away from the world and into seclusion in their father's homes, committing psychic incest with their fathers in poetry and rejecting real men in the interpersonal world.

Emily Dickinson's demon lover, the god who "Deals one Imperial Thunderbolt that scalps your naked soul," leads her to the land of death in the form of a gentleman caller. This is after she has refused to marry a man she truly loved, Judge Otis T. Lord. She declares that "No" is the most excit-ing word in the human language and "Renunciation is a Piercing Virtue" (Kavaler-Adler, 1993, p. 207, Sewall, 1974, p. 656), as she refuses his mar-riage proposal. Dickinson, like Brontë, moves away from life and into a secluded world in her father's home, where she survives states of extreme depersonalization through writing her internal experience down as poetry that openly expresses the pain of the void. But as she ages and her state of seclusion intensifies, her creativity dries up, and the god-muse turns into a demon lover leading her to the land of death.

SYLVIA PLATH'S UNRESOLVED ENVY IN RELATION TO A DEMON LOVER

In the case of Sylvia Plath, we see a 20th century woman addicted to a demon lover, and the hunger of the insatiable self emerges even more clear-ly in her poetry, resulting in suicide rather than seclusion. In Plath, her hunger, and therefore her envy, is more apparent than the anoretic refusal of interpersonal relations in the world. Her murderous wishes accompany her passion for her demon lover.

Plath's psychic hunger can be felt as an oral hunger that is vampirelike at a vaginal level, as oral cravings for a primal mother-object merge with oedipal longings in an aborted self-structure. The void within from early separation-individuation trauma at the pre-oedipal level combines with split-off erotic intensities derived from oedipal longings. Potential oedipal desires manifest as split-off intensities due to the dissociation in the core self structure. Through the dissociation of her own instinctual longings, combined with projective identification, Plath creates her god daddy/demon lover. Then she projects her child view of her lost and dead father onto him. She creates him and spoils him. Her devaluation combines with her lust, and we see the dynamics of destructive envy at work, along with psychic starvation in a visceral form in the woman's vaginal core:

Daddy, I have had to kill you.
You died before I had time—
Marble-heavy, a bag full of God,
Ghastly statue with one grey toe
Big as a Frisco seal.
***

Not god but a swastika
So black no sky could squeak through.
Every woman adores a Fascist,
The boot in the face, the brute
Brute heart of a brute like you.
***

I was ten when they buried you.
At twenty I tried to die
And get back, back, back to you.
I thought even the bones would do.

But they pulled me out of the sack,
And they stuck me together with glue.
And then I knew what to do.
I made a model of you,
A man in black with a Meinkampf look

And a love of the rack and the screw.
And I said I do, I do.
So daddy, I'm finally through.
The black telephone's off at the root,
The voices just can't worm through.

If I've killed one man, I've killed two—
(Plath, 1961, pp. 49–51)

Envy is an attempt to gain what the other has in a perverse act of destroying it, as if murdering the tantalizing power of the other will empower the self. Klein (1957) shows such murderous wishes in her own analysands as she as analyst is perceived as the god power, the muse with magic and tantalizing power. In the case of Plath, a poet with father loss, the muse is seen through the symbolized personality of the father. Ultimately merger with the muse-father does just the opposite of empowering the daughter-poet, as Emily Brontë finds when she loses her voice at the moment of merger with her masculine muse god. In a state of envy the power is either all in the other or all in the self. There is no interactive mutuality of power nor of identity. In merging with the masculine muse the female poet loses her identity as symbolized by the loss of voice.

In Plath's "Daddy" poem, the visceral experience comes increasingly to life. Plath suggests that the demon lover is created through the psychic resonance in a sealed-off female self. "The love of the rack and the screw" suggests the vaginal cravings within such a sealed-off female self and the insatiable aspect is heard through cries of retaliatory rage. The delusional omnipotence of the grandiose self is projected into the idealized and masculinized primal object, seen in its phallic form, and in its displacement to the image of the "toe," big as a frisco seal. It is in the delusion of omnipotence that destructive envy is seen, but the envy is also in the body's hunger for penetration by an omnipotent god. There is the suggestion of a delusion that the vagina has no limits. The instinctual vaginal cravings that have been numbed in the body of a woman with a sealed-off self are converted into psychic fantasies of rape that can express split-off erotic desire, a kind of diffuse eroticism of an undifferentiated pre-oedipal form. The demon lover is all eroticism, with no tenderness and no touch, the essence of a personified image of destructive envy. He is split-off impulse without relationship. He is the sealed-off self's narcissistic image and counterpart. In Melanie Klein's language he is a part-object endowed with the instinctual cravings of the primary unconscious. In Ronald Fairbairn's view, he would be seen as a bad object. Fairbairn would emphasize his origins in the female's early real experiences with the primal mother, a mother whose inadequacies create a bad object in the child's psyche as the primal object is incorporated, but not digested in the internal world.

When there is an addiction to the demon lover part-object, we see the demon lover complex, which is an expression of the traumatic frustration resulting when the female is deprived of a mother's tenderness and separate subjective self (Stern, 1985). In his book *The Empty Core*, Jeffrey Seinfeld (1990) writes of the real deprivation that results in schizoid pathology. Psychic deprivation marks the entire state of mind in such personalities, and when I apply Seinfeld's term "empty core" to the female with such deprivation, which is often manifested interpersonally in dynamics of dissociated envy, I speak of the vaginal core as an insatiable mouth, possessing a vampire quality in its incessant craving. In its less extreme form, it is felt as a biting mouth, as in the words of one of my patients (Lois in *The Creative Mystique*), who spoke of the fantastic urge to bite her sister's nose off.

In Seinfeld's terms, the demon lover can be swallowed by the empty core self as a natural expression of the object-hungry self when the parents' and child's subjective experiences are dissonant, lacking connection. Without connection there is always envy. However, in the pathological case of the demon lover complex, as seen in Sylvia Plath, the demon lover part-object becomes a prime replacement for whole self- and other-relationships because of severe gaps in real self and other connections during early development.

In *My Life Has Stood a Loaded Gun* (1990), Paula Bennet, the feminist literary critic, writes of Sylvia Plath's mother, Aurelia Plath, that she had never been supported in her own strivings toward self-expression and authentic autonomy (pp. 163–164). Bennet writes: "Beyond the sympathy that comes from a recognition of likeness, true empathy requires a respect for difference as well, and that learning sometimes not to give, not to help out, and not to be kind, is also necessary not just for growth, but for survival" (p. 163). Indeed, "Parental giving unchecked by a recognition of boundaries is in its own way a form of abuse. Without a father present to model otherness or to balance Aurelia Plath's excess of devotion, Sylvia Plath was lost" (p. 163).

What Aurelia Plath bequeathed her daughter had very little to do with conscious choice. In some ways, she was an outrageously attuned mother, extremely devoted to the children that filled her life when her own strivings toward self-expression were blocked by marriage and circumstance, and later by the death of her husband. Yet, her need to deny her own resentment, rage, pain, and loss kept her hidden behind a false self, and Sylvia Plath sensed these hidden pressures in her mother through an aura of "disquieting Muses" (Plath, 1968, pp. 58–60). Needing to avoid this rage and pain, Aurelia Plath failed to hear the real concerns of her daughter (Bennet, pp. 107, 110) or to allow her to fail, because she remained sealed off from true emotional contact with both herself and her daughter in the hollow shell of the "empty core." This was Sylvia Plath's heritage. What Aurelia Plath lacked was a separate self, a responsive inner core of her own that could respond to her daughter. Authentic tenderness and nurturance of a separate self and soul cannot come from an empty core mother. Instead, the normal projective-identification between mother and child becomes grossly pathological. The child craves the mother's reflection of her, as well as her authentic responsiveness to her child as a separate other, an other who can be touched and touch from an alive emotional core. The child of the empty core mother, of the internally dead schizoid parent, easily becomes ensnared in the trap of being an identity confined to the outlines of the mother's mirrored image, because there is no nurturance through intersubjective responsiveness to counter this phenomenon. I believe that it was in these terms that Sylvia Plath became locked in her mother's mirroring view of her, and then in her father's. Her oedipal strivings, her own erotic lust, and the natural yearnings for her father's tenderness all thrust her toward her father's profound influence.

Sylvia Plath's father, Professor Otto Plath, was as schizoid as his wife. His grandiose view of himself sought reflection in his daughter. His entertainment with 5-year-old Sylvia consisted of having her perform for him and his friends, and reciting polysyllabic Latin terms (Butscher, 1976). When he became ill with diabetes that he refused to attend to, and ended up bedridden with progressive gangrene, his daughter was let in to perform for him each evening (Stevenson, 1989). She engaged him as a mirror in a contrived setup that hardly allowed for the dynamic of a spontaneous self even if the father had such a dynamic within him. Sylvia became addicted to her performance before the detached paternal giant's mirror. Later, when she speaks to her father in her poetry, he becomes a part-object, whom she calls "Lord of the Mirrors" (Kavaler, 1985, 1986; Kavaler-Adler, 1993). He is also "herr professor," her "colossus," her judge, her demon. He is idealized and demonic at once. In Fairbairn's (1952) terms, her father's detached and yet adoring personality constructed the mold for Sylvia's sealed-off internal world demon. Yet, her elaboration went beyond her father's real personality and resonated with the instinctually endowed unconscious "phantasies" depicted by Melanie Klein (1940, 1957). Within a primary unconscious, a basic grammar of the mind, similar to Chomsky's language grammar (see Ogden, 1986), the psyche can carve out a god-demon mold that is turned into a myth. For Plath, any man on whom she depended emotionally could be seen only as a manifestation of that idealized and demonic myth.

Therefore, when Plath declares her retaliatory rage and kills off her father, she kills not one man, but two. Her husband is the "vampire" in the poem "Daddy," "The vampire who said he was you, And drank my blood for a year, Seven years, if you want to know" (Plath, 1961, p. 51). Plath refers to her husband of seven years, the poet Ted Hughes, upon whom she focused her primal envy, which turned into a jealousy of all other women her husband spoke to (Stevenson, 1989). The vampire image of the husband, the mirrored reflection of the demonic mirroring father, "Lord of the Mirrors," is the projected image of the vampire self, the starved self sealed away in infancy, prior to adequate separation and whole object internalization. The husband takes on the image of the sealed-off self's hungry, devouring mouth in the poem "Other" (Newman, 1971, p. 50), in which he comes in late "licking his lips," rapaciously inserting himself between "myself and myself." Here is the vampire-infant self reflected in the paternal male. Plath's own children take on the air and attitude of the insatiable vampire self as well. The poet writes of the baby god in "I Want I Want" who "Open-mouthed...Immense, bald, though baby-headed, Cried out for the mother's dug" as "The dry volcanoes crouched and spit. Sand abraded the milkless lip. Cried then for the father's blood" (Plath, 1968, p. 39). Plath had no adequate therapist to enter her sealed-off self's domain. She had only electric shock and a therapist's platitudes advising her that she could hate her mother (Plath, 1972; Stevenson, 1989).

Sealed off, Plath's vampire hunger is the entrapping snare of her narcissistic lust for perpetual mirroring. What might appear as overt envy in a paranoid personality appears as insatiable craving for mirroring in the narcissist. No Stolorowian "functional definition of narcissism" (Stolorow & Lachmann, 1980) can adequately address the insatiable passion in this lust for the mirror, and the body level on which this lust enacts hunger and rage. No such functional definition can capture the instinctual vaginal cravings that accompany the psychic structure impoverishment in the female narcissist, with her schizoid empty core, and with the paranoid vulnerability that stems from an intolerance of mourning and grief, and the corresponding terror of facing the inner despair that threatens the moment one is touched by another. A functional definition of narcissism, defined in terms of a need for a positive self-image and positive self-feeling, cannot capture the delusion of the no-limit vagina, nor the craving for the demon lover who instills terror and awe, but who promises body sensation to a numbed-out vagina whose cravings are split off and projected outward into the demon lover image. For the schizoid narcissist, as for all those in the state of mind called Klein's paranoid-schizoid position, the schizoid barrier seals off more profoundly than the repressive barrier of the depressive position neurotic (see Ogden, 1986). The schizoid barrier deadens, and the raging hunger of the sealed-off craving—the starving mind split off from its body—is projected outward into the demon lover whose lust leads to seduction, and then to abandonment into death. In the myth of the demon lover the female must leave her home. She must leave her mother so as to be destroyed by the seductive and rejecting father. She becomes psychically possessed by the paternal male who abandons her. Envy of the male's power marks her impotent state of dependence on the indifferent and possessive power of the demon lover.

I propose that Plath, in this state of envy, is the perfect victim of the demon lover that potentially lives within all our unconscious minds. Perfect, since she is encased in implacability, as she is parented by an implacable mother and by an implacable and seductive father. Plath's mother mirrored her rather than relating to her, and I speculate that the mirroring itself was not embodied, as her mother was divided from her body. In *The Bell Jar* (1972), Plath writes of her sealed-off self-imprisonment in terms of attempts to relate to an unreachable mother. The mother she depicts does not respond back (Orgel, 1981).

In the end, Plath psychically marries her demon lover and turns herself into a witch. The essence of the witch's power is the will to act out a primal envy. She throws her husband out (Stevenson, 1989), and dances around a fire, a fantasied funeral pyre, in which she has deposited her husband's manuscripts, letters, and fingernails (Bennet, 1990). She sings incantations. The neighbors see her. As a narcissist, she lusts for the exposure, for the mirroring, for the intensity craved to feel that she exists at all with a numbed-out vaginal core. In her poetry, she marries the male demon of "Daddy": "the man in Black with the Meinkamph look and the love of the rack and the screw" (1961 p. 51). Then she returns to mother, but the mother she returns to is the moon, the dark shadow side of woman. The mother moon's light beguiles, but is merely the shadow form of a father sun. Inside she is dark! The moon's darkness is symptomatic of the undeveloped female self. In "Edge," a poem Plath wrote shortly before her suicide, she claims the moon as mother, and her mother is a mother who is denied the depressive position healing power of love-endowed grief.

Without the healing power of grief and sadness, Plath's sealed-off vaginal core, with its insatiable hunger and envy, and with its swallowed demon lover, is the subjective view of the vagina dentate. The sealed-off vaginal core cannot tolerate sensation from an external male. When sealed off, the woman's fears of vaginal- and thus of self-containment remain split off and unconscious, and she is left with the delusion of having no limits.

THE CASE OF MS. Z

When we first see the paranoid-schizoid patient in psychotherapy, we must help her tolerate the arousal by containing it in our bodies, holding it until an interpersonal dialectic can be used to contain it. As Jeffrey Seinfeld articulates (1990), it is our combination of holding through our presence, confrontation, and empathy that allows the patient to begin to contain overwhelming desire that has numbed out the self. In the case of Ms. Z, I will relate her journey from a paranoid-schizoid psychic state, in which she enacts the hunger of an empty biting mouth—constantly attacking me to resist internalizing me—into the state of a woman with an aroused vagina, who must experience that the vagina, unlike the delusional vampire mouth, has limits. In this latter state, Ms. Z will be seen to have psychic conflict that is experienced on the bodily level as a fear of vaginal sensation containment. This bodily level, within the overriding psychophysical experience, resonates with the object-related psychic dynamics of conflict between her need for me and her persistent fear of internalizing me. I'm needed both as a potentially good internal object and as an external love object.

In the beginning, Ms. Z called me "the battering ram." She relinquished this term after she changed from acting out the dynamics of a starved self as biting mouth, and began to express her desire for me in terms of having an aroused vagina. Although the battering ram was projected onto me in the transference, in her dreams she herself appeared in the form of the battering ram. She appeared as a metallic breast-mother, who forced her breast into a helpless infant. The infant coughed, choked, and spit up. The infant in her dreams could not take in her breast.

In the transference dyad, Ms. Z portrayed me as the intrusive persecutory breast, and her as the helpless infant. Her aggression was disowned, yet displayed, in the way she spoke to me, with biting sarcasm, spoiling or devaluing comments, and a tendency to cut me off and switch topics abruptly to deflect my touch, impact, or penetration. She further displayed her aggression through the way she evaded listening to me, so that my attempts to get through to her banged up against her wall of resistance. Such a wall can be seen to be reflective of an internal schizoid barrier, a barrier between mind and body. The barrier deflects emotional contact and interpersonal touch. In this hostile aggressive manner, Ms. Z could actually provoke, through the projective identification of the internal metallic breast mother, the intrusiveness of the battering ram. She could also induce an infant's helplessness, as she rendered me impotent with her evasiveness and her warding-off attacks. The dyad of mother infant in the dream, and in the transference and countertransference, can be seen as an enactment of a sealed-off internal world scene in the endopsychic model of Fairbairn. It is the scene of an early intrusive mother, disconnected from her body, that Ms. Z may in fact have experienced as an infant. It is the scene of the exciting and rejecting primary mother object, who allures with her breast and then makes it impossible for the infant to take her in. If this mother were to be masculinized and combined with the paternal image, as the bad object mother is by Sylvia Plath, she could easily be seen as a demon lover figure. She would become the huge and overpowering omnipotent phallus, which persecutes with rape, and yet tempts to arouse long-numbed-out vaginal sensations in the woman's core. In Ms. Z, such numbed-out vaginal sensations had been regressively converted into the dynamics of an empty biting mouth, an empty-core vaginal mouth, full of sarcastic comments, raging with hunger and with the retaliatory biting of bitterness and blame.

The therapist-as-battering-ram would be interpreted as a psychic fantasy part-object mother, a persecutory breast mother, a bad breast. In Klein's view (1957), the dominance of the bad persecutory object in Ms. Z's psyche would be viewed as a sign of Ms. Z's degree of envy toward the mother, or the part-object good mother, the breast. Ms. Z.'s biting sarcasm can be seen in terms of envy, as she attacks me if I sound happy, or if she has revealed her need for me, of which she has felt profoundly ashamed. A vicious cycle of self-starvation intensifies the envy and its biting attacks. The object is seen as having too much good inside of it, as an alien other who cannot share. If the therapist is happy, then she is seen by the patient as having robbed her of her potential to be happy. The mental splitting of self and object into a polarized dichotomy, so that if one is the "have" the other is the "have not" may have an instinctual basis, as Klein suggests in "Envy and Gratitude." But real infant and child deprivation prevents the tendency to split in this manner from being modified. Instead of internalizing the goodness of the object, the person in an envious state devalues and spoils the goodness in the object within her own mind; therefore there is nothing nutritious to be had from the other. Not only concrete food or nurturance is rejected, but all its potential symbolic representatives. Therefore, the food of psychic nurturance is itself rejected, wherein an adequate experience with the external other could be potentially internalized in a symbolic form to build psychic structure. As the capacity to build psychic structure is obviated in this way, the inner need for the other touches a perpetual and exaggerated extreme of emotional and psychic starvation.

I confronted Ms. Z's hostile aggression and empathized with her fear of emotional contact and the powerful craving for touching me that lay behind it. In order to speak to Ms. Z about this, I needed to help her understand the shame she felt in relation to needing me. My interpretations pointed out to Ms. Z. how she deprived herself of the very thing she was starving for. Once I survived the rage she expressed in the transference, I could speak to her about how she heard my confrontations of her aggression as accusations that she was all bad. Through such empathic interpretations, Ms. Z was able to hear what I was actually saying. I could then tell her that she was walling me out with her biting hostility and with her attempts to twist my words into a counterattack. I pointed out repeatedly her switching away from a moment of potential contact, potential psychic feeding, and on a psychophysical vaginal level, from potential penetration. As Ms. Z yielded, I could offer her an empathic reflection of her shame about letting me in, about letting me be important, about needing me. I could touch her with my voice, and her cold rage might turn into a flicker of sadness that expressed her underlying need. Moments of sadness began to expand into working periods in which I could be with Ms. Z, rather than being treated as under her or over her in a projected internal battle for control.

Ms. Z began to acknowledge the loneliness spoken through her sad depressive affect. She began to warm up, to become more human and somewhat more feminine. Gradually I could appeal to her to let me in to help her with her acknowledged loneliness, the loneliness that she began to connect with her outer life. Reaching her sadness, her empty core changed from a raging vampire mouth into a core of lonely longings. She began to mourn. The mournful affects became the avenue to contact renewed between us, expressed and then warded off. However, increasingly, now, Ms. Z uses the defenses of the depressive position, particularly the manic defenses of contempt and control, which demonstrate that the fear of depressive affect has been becoming more prominent in her developmental mourning process than the fear of persecution by a retaliatory other.

As Ms. Z grows into the depressive position, she listens to me more and more. She sustains more emotional contact. She tells me fantasies she has concerning me, focusing increasingly on sexual fantasies about me that she feels while with me, experiencing a state of arousal. Her empty biting mouth has been transforming into an aroused vagina. Her hunger for me is now primarily vaginal. Her psychic core and her vaginal core are less and less sealed off, and she expresses a feminine form of craving, mirrored by her view of me as a feminine being. Now, in the negative transference, I am a critical mother, not just a part-object battering ram (or bad breast).

Mourning has been the avenue to all this psychic change. Through the mourning process, Ms. Z has become an "interpreting subject" (Ogden, 1986) who is capable of taking in the symbolic meaning of interpretations, rather than hearing them as assaults, because she is increasingly able to experience that she is interpreting her own experience and shaping the meaning of her perceptions, rather than just reacting as though she is a victim. Ms. Z is beginning to tolerate a view of her own destructiveness toward me. In this way, she can have the good part of me. She can now reflect on how having the good in me depends on her capacity to feel the sadness of grief concerning the antagonism she has attempted to set up.

Ms. Z's grieving has appeared with each moment of psychic and emotional touch between us. As she lets in my voice, my body behind it, she allows penetration and begins contemplation. Her self-reflective capacities develop as the grief affect of sadness emerges repeatedly. This progressive developmental process occurs along with moments of connection and with repetitions of her forgetting me and attacking me. The emergence of sadness is at first painful, but the pain is modified with contact. The new opening of psychic space through contact between us allows for the pain in sadness to transform into a love sadness. I, as the object, then become alive, and so too can Ms. Z's self come alive as she consciously feels the love and also receives it. Now Ms. Z is able to tolerate some conscious guilt, as opposed to the former unconscious guilt in the form of paranoia. Winnicott (1965) speaks of "held guilt," which comes about as an object-related concern develops. Ms. Z begins to hesitate prior to envious attacks. She begins to give warnings, and to sometimes modify the tone and attitude with which she expresses her envy and defensive contempt.

Yet, as Ms. Z's body comes alive and seeks connection, this has its own threats for Ms. Z. In one session, Ms. Z sees me crossing my legs. She is afraid she cannot contain her reaction. Such a fear is a sign that Ms. Z is now in her body much more than in the past. She is now aware of limits. The vagina, unlike the vampire mouth, has limits. Fearing the vaginal sensations that arise just prior to each session now, Ms. Z says she must wear pants despite how masculine she thinks she looks. The pants provide the barrier, when the paranoid-schizoid barricade is down. To wear a skirt is to risk more free-flowing vaginal sensations, she thinks. She goes shopping but cannot bring herself to buy a skirt. Meanwhile, at work she begins to wear a skirt and a scarf, tentatively testing out her fledgling femininity. She receives complements from her coworkers. Yet, in my office, still seated in pants, she tells me the following:

> I am imagining you undressed. I see your breasts. I see you touch them, then move your hand to your cunt—you're feeling yourself—you're touching your clitoris—I see your finger going in and out of your cunt. Now I remember a porno ad in a men's magazine, men's cocks. On the way up in the elevator of your building today there was a man who was flirting with me. It hasn't happened for a long time. If I didn't have to get out of the elevator he might have asked me out.

I reflect Ms. Z's words back to her. She's sitting on the couch, not lying. We look at each other as she tells me her thoughts, and I reflect them back to her, emotionally holding her by containing her in an aroused fantasy state, psychically containing her now that she can experience the vulnerability of not being able to contain. Subsequently, she begins to sustain a connection to the vaginal core as a container, rather than splitting her inner experience off into the defensive aggression of the vampire biting mouth.

Each step toward psychic containment and internalization brings a backlash reaction. Ms Z uses a manic defense, expressing contempt, as a manifestation of both envy and underlying guilt about sexual pleasure, as she tries to stay on top of it all. I interpret to her: "How can you have me, and feel pleasure in your body, if your mother didn't have this pleasure?" She agrees that she has to pull back to deprive herself. She repeats the deprivation to hold on to the object—but also has guilt about having what she believes her mother didn't have. She holds onto her mother by holding on to the bad object.

Yet she has to realize her guilt toward her mother. I tell her she creates battles to avoid her inner conflict: the guilt over having pleasure, the pleasure she thinks her mother never had. She is beginning to digest such an interpretation now, because she can grieve her guilt, and realize that her attacks on me are a sign of her guilt, as well as a fear of love, need, and vulnerability. In grieving, she yields to my presence as a good object that can be internalized. I come to exist as a true other. In existing, I threaten her with pleasure, particularly with the pleasure of loving, and with love's sexual tones of arousal and crescendo.

Ms. Z is leaving her self-depriving closed system, her imprisoned system of split-off thought, in which her body is held hostage. She is changing her belief that she is entitled only to a little bit: a little love, a little sex, a little femininity. However, to have more is scary, for it is exciting! To have more incites envy, her internal mother's envy, other women's envy! The starved real mother, Plath's mother, who is internalized early on, is certainly an envious mother, but when exaggerated by an inner fantasy mother, the threat is even greater. Ms. Z's self-deprivation will continue as long as fears of an internal envious mother remain unconscious. But in the depressive position, the fear is less, and the guilt is more. The depressive position fear is of the depressive pain that comes in recognizing the loss of good feeling when the mother's body is depleted by one's own envy. If Ms. Z can have only a little bit, it is because she is emptying me out, me as her transferential mother, with envious and spoiling attacks. It is painful for Ms. Z to face that it is she, herself, who is the self-perpetuating agent of her own psychic and emotional deprivation. Her own hate kills off the loved others in her internal world, empties them out with swallowing modes of envy, or attacks them with biting spite.

Our own self-sabotage is difficult for us all to face. However, without facing that pain we end up repeating the vicious cycle of self-sabotage again and again. In Fairbairn's terms, we hold on to the bad object, and seal ourselves off from any vision of the whole and more loving objects in the external world. For Klein, when we kill off what the mother has because of envy, and in the unconscious this is experienced very much on the body level as the devouring of flesh, the scooping out of her breasts, the stealing of the other woman's vaginal sexuality, then we are depleting and depriving ourselves. In the primary unconscious that Melanie Klein addresses, the mother and the self always have a fluid boundary (1940). What is in one's own body can easily be seen as having been extracted—stolen from the mother, leaving her empty, just as one's own vaginal core is experienced as having been depleted by mother's hunger to feed and fill her own body. If we deplete our internal mother, we feel depleted.

Ms. Z's depressive pain is her route to healing, but only as such pain allows the opening for her therapist to be with her. If she can acknowledge her need for me with tolerated shame, my presence can be internalized. With me sustained inside of her, she can risk the recognition of guilt toward her mother. Then guilt can be tolerated and guilt can transform to concern, to a sustained caring. Fairbairn's antilibidinal ego—the real bad parent that has been internalized into hard core self-structure—now softens and yields. The metallic object, whether seen in Emily Dickinson's poetry as a metallic god "who drills his welcome in," or in Ms. Z's dreams as a "metal pole" mother, yields and softens. The yielding is in the body as it is in the soul. It is in the walls of the vagina.

With sustained mourning, there is sustained self and other connection, and sustained love. There is the contact for Ms. Z to tell me that she has fantasies about my life. There is an atmosphere of sufficient trust for Ms. Z to tell me about her body. Winnicott's (1971) transitional space is created, and the patient can then reflect, and digest interpretations. She begins to experience a responsiveness that can be transitional to sustained love in all relationships. She becomes an agent, rather than remaining a snipping guerrilla fighter. She develops an observing ego that can allow her to look at her feelings and thoughts as feelings and thoughts, rather than as persecutors motivated by the object's retaliatory wrath and envy. She can experience internal conflict, and her resistance to experiencing it can now be interpreted.

Resistance interpretations now yield quick response and new awareness. For example, when Ms. Z comes in with her old routine of looking compulsively for something to blame on me immediately following any generosity on my part or an experience of more intimacy between us, I can now interpret her guilt about her resistance to gratitude and about her fear of giving to me. She can now tolerate feeling the grief of regret or the grief of recognition concerning her own resistance to object love and to the development of involvement with another. She can now experience her own coldness, and with my empathic view that she doesn't have to set her coldness in "stone" as her mother did, she begins to melt.

In between this session and the next, Ms. Z feels intense loving passion, revealed in a dream of two women turning and passionately kissing two men. Her associations suggest that these men represent me in the transference, as I am now being experienced as a man in other dreams, and in sessions in which she fears and wishes for penetration at a vaginal level. Ms. Z can now accept the interpretations about her suppressed passion. Then we both recognize the familiar backlash impulse to attack me. Ms. Z can now acknowledge the impulse to attack, without acting out the attack full force as before. I can tell her now that her experience of her coldness has allowed her to turn warm, but her warmth brings new fear of love leading to me penetrating her. She needs to take me in and internalize me, but for this to happen, for love, and my inner presence to warm her, she has to let me penetrate her. Her coldness is now an attempt to ward off phallic penetration as she experiences me as a man, a step beyond the ever-repeating resistance view of me as the metal mother.

Ms. Z can now tolerate ambivalent feelings toward me. She can love and hate me in her need for me, seeing her hateful backlash reactions as responses to her need for me. Ms. Z herself can speak of her backlash reaction. She is barely beginning to conceptualize her alternations of object connection with me and her backlash of attack and withdrawal as internal conflicts about being in a primary position of vulnerability to need. Much alternating work on the self's shame and the object-oriented envy has been needed. Also, much work has been needed on the painful guilt that only now can be tolerated. It is our therapeutic object relationship (Grunes, 1984) that allows the guilt to be contained so that it can be tolerated. Ms. Z's guilt can be tolerated as it can begin to be grieved.

These are Klein's depressive position achievements. But they are also the gains that come when Fairbairn's sealed-off internal world opens to external object connection, and when the transitional mourning of Klein brings sustained connection and an opening of Winnicott's transitional, psychic, and analytic space. The bad part-object of the internal world becomes transformed to a good whole other person, an external object, whose badness becomes tolerable faults and lacks that can be understood as a result of the other's, the parents', own pain. The faults become tolerable as they are symbolized through mourning. In this way the parental object, just like its body sensations, can be contained. When the object can be contained, ongoing relationships can be sustained, and the vomiting up of the object in splitting and projecting modes of self-fragmenting defense can be greatly modified. As a "good-enough" object (Winnicott, 1971) is internalized and sustained, the self develops a solid core. The empty core becomes a transient feeling rather than a psychic state. With this solid feeling comes warm and loving affect, so that empathy for the internal parent emerges, expanding the view of a whole object. For a woman, the vaginal core at her center comes alive.

When I pointed out to Ms. Z that she was protecting her mother against her anger by attacking herself at one point, which was different than her former characterological mode of split-off blaming, she came in the next day crying. She was feeling the pain of her love for her mother. She said, "If I want to protect my mother I must love her," painfully admitting her wish to love. Her ultimate bad object is turning good, since now it can be loved. In conjunction with such a shift in her maternal object her dead father can now be idealized less, and fondness for her brother can be felt, where formerly there was only contempt or idealization.

At one point in her treatment, Ms. Z dreamed of a satiated infant, of a fulfilling feed. She reluctantly admits this to me some time after I interpret her guilt about having the pleasure of sexual arousal in her body, a pleasure that she believes her mother never had. But then, possibly in a retreat from her growing connection with me and with her inner self and her body's vaginal core connection, she develops a neurotic symptom. She does not return to a more primitive level of envious attack on me as the external object, but rather expresses her conflict though a somatic symptom of bleeding gums. She must go to the dentist for problems with her bite. What was formerly enacted with me, with her playing the part of the empty biting mouth, is now being experienced in protosymbolic form in her body, with a precurser to verbal symbolism in the symbolism of the body. I believe she regressed back to the biting mouth because of her fears of containing her vaginal arousal with me, and as a way of protecting me from the envious attack from that mouth. Her impulse to attack is turned against herself and she creates pain for herself, her bleeding gums, impairing the area of the teeth that symbolize the impulse to regress into a biting attack on me. Ms. Z is not regressing all the way back to the former paranoid-schizoid mind, and its defensive mode in which she is compelled to get rid of awareness of the internal biting mouth by depositing it in me, the battering ram. Instead, now Ms. Z can block out awareness with repression. She achieves hysterical body symbolism, as she begins to achieve neurotic conflict with the depressive position coming through mourning.

As the depressive position developmental achievements are reached, the empty core transforms. The vampire mouth becomes a biting infant mouth, and then an aroused vagina. Ms. Z expresses excitement to see me on the night before Thanksgiving—telling that her mother always spoke about having a big date on that occasion. Following this, she retreats and visualizes hearts carved in the design of a wicker screen in my office as negative and spoiled. Her guilt toward her internal mother about having me brings a backlash reaction. Her shame about needing me causes the backlash as well. This is all part of a dynamically alive hunger in her empty core turned vagina. She has a dream of foreplay, in her words: "touching a man's cock—not 'going all the way'." These are the words of her teen years. She pulls back with me: "It's hot in this room," she says. I ask her, "Is it hot inside of you?" The empty core is now a vaginal core of conflict. She can now feel depression as she retreats. She can now feel that she is actively constricting herself, suppressing her arousal into a state of repression. She realizes that her loneliness comes from killing off the tenderness and love that goes with the erotic sensations. Awareness of this allows her to go forward. Ms. Z's awareness of herself as the agent of aggression is a sign that her internal good and bad objects have combined and created a whole object, a whole self, and a whole therapist. Thus, the demon lover as lust devoid of tenderness is converted. In the case of Ms. Z, the battering ram becomes a desired man with a sensual penis.

REFERENCES

Bennet, P. (1990). *My life a loaded gun...Dickinson, Plath, Rich, and female creativity.* Urbana: University of Illinois Press.

Butscher, E. (1976). *Sylvia Plath: Method and madness.* New York: Simon and Schuster.

Fairbairn, R. D. (1952). *Psychoanalytic studies of the personality.* London: Routledge.

Flockouer. I.N., (1996). *Holding and psychanalysis.* Hillsdale, NJ: Analytic Press.

Gerin, W. (1971). *Emily Brontë.* New York: Oxford University Press.

Grunes, M. (1984). The therapeutic object relationship. *Psychoanalytic review,* 71 (1), 123–143.

Kavaler, S. (1985). Mirror mirror on the wall.... *Journal of comprehensive psychotherapy,* 5, 1–38.

——— (1986). Lord of the mirrors and the demon lover. *American journal of psychoanalysis,* 46 (4), 336–344.

Kavaler-Adler, S. (1993). *The compulsion to create: A psychoanalytic study of women artists.* New York: Routledge.

——— (1996a). *The creative mystique: From red shoes frenzy to love and creativity.* New York: Routledge.

——— (1996b). The instinctual self. *American journal of psychoanalysis,* 55 (1), 73–81.

Klein, M. (1957/1975a). Envy and gratitude. In *Envy and gratitude & other works, 1946-1963,* New York: Delacorte.

——— (1957/1975b). Mourning and its relation to manic-depressive states. In *Love, guilt and reparation and other works, 1921-1945.* (pp. 344–369). London: Hogarth.

Mahler, M., S. F. Pine, and A. Bergman (1975). *The psychological birth of the human infant.* Northvale, NJ: Jason Aronson.

Newman, C. (Ed.), (1971). *The art of Sylvia Plath.* Bloomington: Indiana University Press.

Ogden, T. H. (1986). *Matrix of the mind.* Northvale, NJ: Jason Aronson.

Orgel, S. (1981). Fusion with the victim: A study of Sylvia Plath. In J. T. Coltrera. (Ed.), *Lives, events and other players.* Northvale, NJ: Jason Aronson.

Plath, S. (1961). *Ariel.* New York: Harper & Row.

——— (1968). *The colossus.* New York: Vintage.

——— (1972). *The bell jar.* New York: Bantum.

——— (1982). *The journals of Sylvia Plath.* New York: Dial.

Seinfeld, J, (1991). *The empty core.* Northvale, NJ, Jason Aronson.

Sewall, R, (1974). *The life of Emily Dickinson.* New York: Farrar, Straus & Geroux.

Stern, D. (1985). *The interpersonal world of the human infant.* Northvale, NJ: Jason Aronson.

Stevenson, Anne, (1989). *Bitter fame.* Baston: Houghton Mifflin.

Stolorow, R. and Lachmann, F., (1980). *Psychoanalysis of developmental assests.* Madison, CT: International Universities Press.

Winnicott, D. W. (1965). The development of the capacity for concern. In *The maturational processes and the facilitating environment.* Madison, CT: International Universities Press.

——— (1971). *Playing and reality.* Middlesex, England: Penguin.

Part Four

GENDER AND ENVY
THROUGH THE LIFE-SPAN

INTRODUCTION

It's a really extraordinary thing to live with sexual desire past the age of its being accommodated.

—Diana Trilling

Since its inception, psychoanalysis has had an anxious if often fruitful relationship with the studies of adolescence, adulthood, and aging. Freud himself was skeptical regarding the usefulness of psychoanalytic practice for individuals of too great an age, feeling that "old people [that is, people 'near or above the 50s'] are no longer educable" (*SE* 7: 264). Both the nature of psychoanalytic theory itself, the foremost concern of which was to illuminate the first principles from which later life was to unfold, and Freud's therapeutic practice, which seemed to be, in regard to his treatment of older patients, something of a disaster (*SE* 6: 122–125, 177), led him to view the emergent properties of advanced adulthood as inherently less interesting than those of the early years. Further, Klein's view that good adjustment in old age depended upon the positive outcome of childhood struggles (1957, p. 203–204), as enhanced by the later capacity to vicariously identify with the pleasures of youth (1957, p. 259), left little room for an appreciation of the aging process in itself (although later theorists have found Klein's theories useful in their studies of life-span psychology (Feak, 1992; Woodward, 1988). Yet despite misinterpretations to the contrary, psychoanalysis is in its very nature a theory of development, an antireductionistic world view in the context of which, in accordance with the principle of *Nachträglichkeit*, meaning can only but be emergent. Following Erickson's groundbreaking publication of *Childhood and Society* in 1950, which extended the view of development as consisting of a series of distinct challenges and transformations into adulthood and beyond, theorists began to exploit the potential of a psychodynamic viewpoint in a systematic way to illuminate the entire breadth of the life-span.

Though Erikson's book provoked a discrete movement within American psychoanalysis devoted to the study of longitudinal continuity and change, an appreciation of life-span issues was already alive in psychoanalytic studies of women, no doubt in part because of the prominence of motherhood as a central concern of both women and men. Although Helene Deutsch's writing has fallen out of favor of late—feminists generally see her as something of a Freud *manqué* in view of her rigid if unwitting biologism, her allegiance to an account of women as passive and masochistic, and her tendency toward prescription over description—she can nevertheless be credited with developing the first psychoanalytic life-span study of women's lives in her books on girlhood (1944), adolescence (1967), and motherhood (1945). These studies, augmented by Theresa Benedek's writings of the 1930s to the 1970s on women's psychological configurings of such physiological events as menstruation, motherhood, and menopause (1973), had a momentum of their own which was enhanced, rather than created, by the life-span focus brought to psychoanalysis by Erikson's followers and elaborators.

Recent psychoanalytically-influenced life-span studies are divided in their emphasis on the creation of general theories of life development and on the development of insights into particular life stages, although a number of efforts have been made to combine the two strains through the creation of anthologies of specific studies from which theories can be created. Among general psychoanalytic studies of life-span development, many are written from a self psychology perspective (Galatzer-Levy & Cohler, 1993; Honess & Yardley, 1987)—not surprising given Kohut's emphasis on the need for self-object ties throughout life—and others stress particular aspects of the progression of life-course experience (Lerner & Erlich, 1992). Further, life-span studies have been given new vitality of late in the writings of practitioners concerned to understand the distinctive experiences of gay men and lesbians in all phases of life. While these studies draw upon classic models of development in general (Cornett & Hudson, 1987; D'Augelli, 1994), they also highlight new perspectives and issues that point to the possibilities for modification of those models (Dominici & Lesser, 1995; Glassgold & Iasenza, 1995; Isay, 1996; O'Connor & Ryan, 1993). Writings on specific life-course issues have focused on adolescence (Blos, 1975; Anthony, 1988; Ladame, 1991; Shapiro & Esman, 1992; Eigner, 1996); on adulthood issues such as work, parenting, and midlife adjustment (Grey, 1989; Michels, 1993; Pines 1978); and on old age (Hildebrand, 1987; Jacobowitz & Newton, 1990; Pollock 1994). In general, psychoanalytically informed discussions of specific periods of life have taken as their focus the opportunities granted by later-life challenges for individuals to rework unresolved issues from childhood (Benedek, 1973; Blos, 1979). Of edited psychoanalytically-oriented works on life-span issues, the series compiled by Pollock & Greenspan (1989-1993) is perhaps the most currently visible.

Many of the most recent writings either limit their focus to the experiences of one gender or explicitly acknowledge gender as a determining factor. Most commonly, these studies combine psychoanalytic and other perspectives (Gergen 1997; Levinson, 1979, 1996), though broad studies of gender in life-span development can also be found within the mainstream psychoanalytic literature (Bernay & Cantor, 1986; Colorusso, 1995; Henwood & Coughlan, 1993). As might be expected, the gender-specific literature on parenthood is far more developed in regard to women than to men (Guttieres-Green, 1992; Langer &

Hollander, 1992; Pines, 1988; Vengetti & Jason, 1996), though recently father-hood has begun to receive attention in the mainstream psychoanalytic litera-ture (Fogel et. al., 1986/1996; Shapiro et. al, 1995). In general, psychoanalytic studies of gender and old age continue, for the most part, to be "restricted, neg-ative and scarce" (Gergen, 1990).

It perhaps goes without saying that there have been virtually no systemat-ic attempts to chart the transformations of envy in the years following laten-cy. Thus the essays in this section are breaking new ground; taken together, they constitute an outline for future inquiry. In his essay "Reflections on Envy, With Special Attention to the College Years," Robert May writes about a spe-cific, culturally embedded rite of passage defined by the four-year span of the college experience, raising the question as to whether envy is operative in this time of life in distinctive ways, whether it is gendered, and, if so, how we might best understand its emergence in developmental context. May finds the writing of Klein particularly useful in this context, highlighting its capacity to illuminate the sources of the particular within-gender rivalries that he finds most prominent in people of that age. Peter Shabad, in his paper on parental possessiveness, inverts Klein's perspective, moving the focus of observation away from the child's envy of the parent to concentrate on the parent's envy of the child. He suggests that while both mothers and fathers tend to share in the "rivalry for a new beginning" that emerges between them and their chil-dren, in other respects, envy takes distinctive forms in the psyches of men and women in the context of child rearing. As Shabad attempts to alert both the-orists and practitioners to the often silent role of envy in the sexual abuse of daughters by fathers, David Gutmann, in his essay "Male Envy Across the Life Span," focuses on the ascendancy of men's envy of women that comes later on, in the context of a "postparental transformation." At that time, he argues, as men and women are reversing their respective associations with power and dependency, men at last make good on a promissory note regarding their envy of women written earlier in life, when womb envy was overshadowed by a preoccupation with same-sex rivalries and identifications. As the only life-span study of gender and envy to date, Gutmann's paper lays the groundwork for the development of more extensive theorizing regarding the career of envy in both men's and women's lives.

The challenges faced by those who attempt to develop psychoanalytical-ly-informed theories regarding the interaction of gender and envy across the life-span mirror the difficulties that present themselves to theorists of life-span development more generally. Among the most central of these is the task of discerning the role of origins in determining, influencing, or providing the ground for the experiences of later life. The life-span researcher must thus articulate not only a particular view of the genesis of gender and envy as psy-chological phenomena, but an account of how the points of origin it describes unfold, perhaps backward and forward, within their psychological, physical, familial, social, and cultural surrounds. The obstacles to such a task abound; a tendency toward reductionism, a pessimism regarding the subject of aging, an appreciation of the increasing complexity of life over time. Yet a life-span perspective stands to transform even our understandings of the origins of psychological life by providing an enriched context for the development of retrospective meaning. The papers in this section constitute a step toward that end, and an impetus to take this effort further.

REFERENCES

Anthony, E. J. (1988). The creative therapeutic encounter at adolescence. In *Adolescent psychiatry: Developmental and clinical studies, Vol. 15*. Chicago: University of Chicago Press.

Benedek, T. (1973). *Psychoanalytic investigations*. New York: Quadrangle.

Bernay, T. & Cantor, D. (1986). *The psychology of today's woman: New psychoanalytic visions*. Cambridge, MA: Harvard University Press.

Blos, P. (1979). The second individuation process of adolescence. In *The adolescent passage*. New York: International Universities Press.

Colarusso, C. (1995). Traversing young adulthood: The male journey from 20 to 40. *Psychoanalytic Inquiry*, 15 (1) 75–91.

Cornett, C. W., & Hudson, R. A. (1987). Middle adulthood and the theories of Erikson, Gould and Vaillant: Where does the gay man fit? *Journal of Gerontological Social Work* 10 (3–4), 61–73.

D'Augelli, A. R. (1994). Lesbian and gay male development: Steps toward an analysis of lesbians' and gay men's lives. In B. Greene & G.M. Herek (Eds.), *Lesbian and gay psychology: theory, research and clinical applications*. (pp. 118–132). Thousand Oaks, CA: Sage Publications.

Deutsch, H. (1944). *The psychology of women. Vol 1: Girlhood*. New York: Grune & Stratton.

——— (1945). *The Psychology of Women. Vol 2: Motherhood*. New York: Grune & Stratton.

——— (1967). *Selected problems of adolescence*. New York: International Universities Press.

Domenici, T., & Lesser, R. C. (Eds.) (1995). *Disorienting sexuality*. New York: Routledge.

Eigner, A. (1996). The status of psychic reality in adolescence. *International Journal of Psycho-Analysis*, 77 (6) 1169–1180.

Erikson, E. (1950). *Childhood and society*. New York: W. W. Norton.

Feak, M. (1992). Kleinian contributions to a life-span psychology: Preliminary considerations, with some interpretations from folk tales and literature. *Melanie Klein & Object Relations*, 10 (1), 46–61.

Fogel, G. I., Laine, F. M., & Liebert, R.S. (Eds.), (1986/1996). *The psychology of men: Psychoanalytic perspectives*. New Haven, CT: Yale University Press.

Freud, S. (1901). *The psychopathology of everyday life. SE*, Vol. 6.

——— (1905). On psychotherapy. *SE*, Vol. 7 (pp. 255–268).

Galatzer-Levy, R., & Cohler, B. (1993). *The essential other: A developmental psychology of the self*. New York: Basic Books.

Gergen, M. (1990). Finished at 40: Women's development within the patriarchy. *Psychology of Women Quarterly*, 14 (4), 471–493.

Gergen, M., & Davis, S. (1997). *Toward a new psychology of gender*. New York: Routledge.

Glassgold, J. M., & Iasenza, S. (Eds.) (1995). *Lesbians and psychoanalysis: Revolutions in theory and practice.* New York: Free Press.

Grey, A. (1989). The analytic career: Identity change through adult work role. *Contemporary Psychoanalysis,* 25(4), 641–662.

Guttieres-Green, L. (1992). The child and/or the picture: Motherhood and creativity: Their vicissitudes. *International journal of psycho-analysis,* 73(3), 505–516.

Henwood, K., & Coughlan, G. (1993). The construction of "closeness" in mother-daughter relationships across the lifespan. In *Discourse and lifespan identity, Vol 4.* Newbury Park, CA: Sage.

Hildebrand, P. (1987). Psychoanalysis and aging. *Annual of Psychoanalysis,* 15,113–125.

Honess, T., & Yardley, K. (Eds.) (1987). *Self and identity: Perspectives across the lifespan.* New York: Routledge.

Isay, R. (1996). *Becoming gay.* New York: Pantheon.

Jacobowitz, J., & Newton, N. (1990). Time, context, and character: A life-span view of psychopathology during the second half of life. In R. A. Nemiroff & C. A. Colarusso (Eds.), *New dimensions in adult development* (pp. 306–332). New York: Basic Books.

Klein, M. (1957/1975). Envy and gratitude. In *Envy and gratitude and other works, 1946–1963.* New York: Delacorte.

———— (1959/1975). Our adult world and its roots in infancy. In *Envy and gratitude and other works,* 1946–1963. New York: Delacorte.

Ladame, F. (1991). Adolescence and the repetition compulsion. *International Journal of Psycho-Analysis, 72* (2), 253–273.

Langer, M., & Hollander, N. C. (1992). *Motherhood and sexuality.* New York: Guilford.

Lerner, H. D., & Erlich, J. (1992). Psychodynamic models. In V. B. Van Hasselt & M. Hersen (Eds.), *Handbook of social development: A lifespan perspective* (pp. 51–79). New York: Plenum Press.

Levinson, D. (1979). *Seasons of a man's life.* New York: Ballantine.

———— (1996). *Seasons of a woman's life.* New York: Basic Books.

Michels, R. (1993). Adulthood. In G. Pollock & S. I. Greenspan (Eds.), *The course of life, Vol. 5,* Madison, CT: International Universities Press.

O'Connor, N., & Ryan, J. (1993). *Wild desires & mistaken identities: Lesbianism and psychoanalysis.* New York: Columbia University Press.

Pines, D. (1978). On becoming a parent. *Journal of Child Psychotherapy. 4* (4), 19–31.

———— (1988). Adolescent pregnancy and motherhood: A psychoanalytical perspective. *Psychoanalytic Inquiry,* 8 (2), 234–251.

Pollock, G. (1994). *How psychiatrists look at aging, Vol. 2.* Madison, CT: International Universities Press.

Pollock, G., & Greenspan, S. I. (Eds.) (1989–1993). *The course of life, Vols. 1–6.* Madison, CT: International Universities Press.

Shapiro, J. L., Diamond, M. J., & Greenberg, M. (Eds.). (1995). *Becoming a father: Contemporary social, developmental and clinical perspectives.* New York: Springer Publishing.

Shapiro, T., & Esman, A. (1992). Psychoanalysis and child and adolescent psychiatry. *Journal of the American academy of child & adolescent psychiatry,* 31 (1), 6–13.

Vegetti Finzi, S. & Jason, K. (1996). *Mothering: Toward a new psychoanalytic construction.* New York: Guilford.

14

REFLECTIONS ON ENVY, WITH SPECIAL ATTENTION TO THE COLLEGE YEARS

Robert May

Envy: a feeling of discontented or resentful longing aroused by another's better fortune.

—(*The Concise Oxford Dictionary*, Ninth Edition, Clarendon Press, Oxford 1995)

Envy has a curiously shrunken existence in classical psychoanalysis. Both the index to Freud's writings (Richards, 1974) and Laplanche and Pontalis's (1973) dictionary of psychoanalytic terms list envy only under "penis envy." From a current perspective this seems one of the odd things about Freud's theory, as if the only "better fortune" that mattered were literally gendered and genital. Meanwhile, our personal and clinical experience suggests that envy is all around us, and in us. As a young boy watching my parents playfully running together along the beach, I threw sand at them and angrily told them to stop being so foolish. They had seemed very happy together. It was a pleasant, even a rare, occasion. Why would I want to interrupt, to shatter, that scene? The classical theory would talk about oedipal jealousy. True enough, but I think too limited a view.[1]

There is a psychoanalytic theory that gives envy its proper due: the work of Melanie Klein (see especially Klein, 1957. All subsequent page references are to this work). The genealogy of American psychoanalysis had to do with Anna Freud and what came to be called "ego psychology," and the American tradition was slow to credit Klein's work. Both Otto Kernberg (1975) and Thomas Ogden (1989) have been useful importers of Klein into mainstream American psychoanalysis. There are still difficulties in reading Klein. The structure of her writing is associative and organic rather than logical and systematic. The exclusive focus on the events of early infancy and the seeming total acceptance of historical positivism make hers a difficult approach to embrace these days. Freud's writing had such productive complexity and ambivalence that his

---

1. In what follows, it will become clear that I do not subscribe to the traditional division of jealousy from envy, whereby jealousy involves three people and envy two, jealousy a desire to have and envy the desire to be. This distinction parallels that between object choice and identification in classical psychoanalysis, and overemphasizing that distinction is one of the ways in which classical psychoanalysis became unfortunately polarized around gender. An object relations theory sees things differently. I will side with both the *Oxford Dictionary* and with Melanie Klein in seeing jealousy as a particular type of envy.

archaeological metaphors, those suggesting a "real" history actually recovered in analysis, are tolerable because they are constantly being usefully undermined and complicated (see May, 1990; Morris, 1993). Klein often seems to take the archaeological metaphor literally. The postmodern consciousness is bound to have difficulty with Klein's seeming assumption that complex psychological events are not only observable in an infant a few months old but also literally recapitulated in the transference. But Klein's epistemology has more to do with the time in which she was writing than with any basic flaw of the theory. The Kleinian focus on fantasy, with its phantasmagoric breasts with teeth and infants wanting to scoop out the penises and babies inside mother's body, can best be used as a rich vein of metaphor. Her basic concepts, about splitting, projective identification, and the paranoid/schizoid and depressive positions, have shown considerable clinical richness (Ogden, 1982, 1989).

Klein sees envy as a fundamental, pervasive, and painful human experience. In her view envy operates from the beginning of life. It has a constitutional basis, while also being significantly influenced by the vicissitudes of experience. She defines envy as "the angry feeling that another person possesses and enjoys something desirable—the envious impulse being to take it away or to spoil it" (p. 181). Kleinian theory is based on a primal splitting. Klein took seriously the duality of life and death instincts that Freud had begun to develop. She believed that early psychic life, which forms the template for later experience, revolves around the "innate conflict between love and hate" (p. 180). The infant's inevitable discomfort and hunger are projected outward and result in the creation of "bad objects." Thus, the bad is split off to ease the threat of pain or even annihilation. Counterposed to that process is the idealization of a "good breast," representing not just food but also freedom from painful destructive impulses and persecutory anxiety. Envy enters early on: "Envy contributes to the infant's difficulties in building up his good object, for he feels that the gratification of which he was deprived has been kept for itself by the breast that frustrated him" (p. 180). The basic developmental task is the repeated toleration of envy and then regaining (re-creating) the good object. If things go well enough this repeated process allows the creation of a "whole" (neither totally good nor totally bad) object and the achievement of what the Kleinians refer to as the depressive position. Klein mentions a number of typical defenses against envy: idealization, flight from the mother, devaluation of the object, devaluation of the self, greedy possessiveness, the stirring up of envy in others, and the chronic stifling of love in favor of hate (leading to indifference and withdrawal). What one hopes for if defenses do not dominate is the modest goal stated repeatedly in Klein's writings: the mitigation of hatred by love.

Gender plays a very different role in Kleinian theory than in the classical Freudian view. The central relationship is the one to the mother, and the sacred organ is the breast, in contrast to Freud's narrative of penises and oedipal fathers. More importantly, Kleinian theory does not posit separate developmental lines for the two sexes. Klein avoids polarizing the genders partly because she sets the basic drama early enough in life so that gender can hardly be a significant factor. Klein thus differs from Freud in not distinguishing between the sexes in the area of envy. By emphasizing the human "desire to take away the attributes of the other sex" (p. 201), she anticipates the work of Bettelheim (1954) and Fast (1984) on the basic narcissistic injury of the recognition of gender differences.

Melanie Klein developed the first "object relations" theory in the proper sense of the term. As opposed to Freud's theory of contentless energy, Klein believed that there was no impulse without an object. In her view mental life from the very beginning is constituted of images and representations. That is to say, the internal object world *is* psychic life. The psyche is a realm of (part) self and (part) object pairs. Freud's theory of sexual development was centered on a duality: identification on the one hand, and object choice on the other. Although Freud believed in psychic bisexuality, it is the shadow, a minor chord in his theory. The plot line of oedipal theory leads each sex to desire one parent and identify with the other. The object relations emphasis on pairs of self and object representations stresses the links between elements and leads us to a view of gender that has more to do with dialectic than with duality (see May, 1986). The world that Klein sets up begins to erase the distinction between wanting to be and wanting to have. Lust, admiration, and identification are the braided channels of one river. And so Klein sees jealousy as a type of envy rather than as something distinct.

WHAT IS ENVIED?

Any general theory of envy has to start with the question of what is envied. Freud's basic assumptions in this regard fitted a world seen through male eyes (see Schafer, 1992, on the gender-based limitations of Freud's theory). Freud saw the little girl's envy of the penis as inevitable: "She makes her judgment and her decision in a flash. She has seen it and knows she is without it and wants to have it" (1925, p. 252). The maleness of this vision is hilariously evident as Freud describes "the penis of a brother or playmate, strikingly visible and of large proportions." When he goes on to describe the girl's "small and inconspicuous organ" he is doing precisely what he describes the young boy doing: disavowing the girl's genitals by minimizing them. Thus Freud's theory folds back on itself, enacting male castration anxiety as it purports to describe the girl's thoughts. The fearful male conviction that there is, in the female, only an absence leads the boy to look away and to try to reassure himself of his own superior size.

Melanie Klein's vision of the first occasion of envy is quite different. "My work has taught me that the first object to be envied is the feeding breast, for the infant feels that it possesses everything that he desires and that it has an unlimited flow of milk, and love which the breast keeps for its own gratification" (p. 183). As a paradigm for envy this certainly has the advantage of being nongendered (even the breast is an "it"). To use this as a model does not necessitate a historically literal or reductionist view that would transpose all envy to the infantile feeding situation. The paradigm may show us basic structural qualities of envy, while the content of envy will vary widely both developmentally and situationally.

Following this paradigm, envy has three primary elements: desire (the self as needy), confrontation with otherness, and imagining the other's state of pleasure. The basic drama is of a self (representation) in some painful state of want, and an object (representation) that is recognized as different and then imagined to posses whatever it is that would make the self happy or satisfied. What is envied is a state which the self desires and the other is imagined to have: the full and gratified breast, the happy parents, the confidently powerful or beautiful person. The essential envious thought is "I want to feel the way I think he/she feels." Envy is a fantasy, a projection that includes both idealization and hate. When it is accompanied by persistent attempts to control the other, then we are entitled to see the envy as part of a process of projective identification (see Ogden, 1982). We can also see that the envious idealization is necessarily linked to a view of oneself as lacking, deficient, even shameful. The good has been evacuated into the envied object, where, as idealization shades into envy, it is spoiled by hate. There also is in envy a characteristic failure of empathy as a consequence of the splitting involved. Envy thinks in terms of all good and all bad rather than of a whole person with whom one might feel empathy.

The particular content of envy varies with one's life stage and situation. Gender is certainly one of the areas likely to be an important site of envy. Sex and age (size) are universal categories that children recognize early on. The confrontation with otherness and difference, often in the context of desire, is a primary characteristic of gender and sexuality. The work of Bettelheim (1954), Fast (1984), and Mayer (1985) elaborates the childhood confrontation with gender difference and the resulting struggle with narcissistic injury.

THE COLLEGE YEARS

I have been asked to comment in particular on envy in the college years, because my primary work for the last 25 years has been as director of a college counseling and mental health service. There are cultural, developmental, and situational reasons that make envy important in the college years. On the cultural level, students coming to college are media children. They have grown up surrounded by television and magazine images. In these images it is increasingly difficult to tell the advertising from the text. Envy is the motor that drives our economy. Those maniacally smiling and improbably beautiful images presented to us are meant to stir in us the envious aspiration to be as happy as they are pretending to be, through buying whatever seems to make them happy/beautiful/successful. The illusory message is that anyone can be like those people simply through the liberal use of a credit card. College students have been more or less marinated in this media culture and are thus already past masters at "scoping" the world to rate who is looking good and who is doing well.

Developmentally the late adolescent/young adult still makes primary use of idealization and splitting as ways of organizing the world. Heroes and villains populate the landscape. Both in their inclination for combat with the older generation and in their capacity for rapid and intense crushes, college students display their dual capacity for hopeful idealization and bitter disappointment. This tendency toward splitting also underlies the unfortunate potential for failures of empathy, even cruelty, in groups of this age. And there is a developmentally necessary narcissism that serves to protect a still unstable, or at least not yet defined, representation of self. It is crucial for the college student to have fantasies, to have dreams of the future; in fact many important things, such as work, sex, and a continuing love relationship, are often primarily experienced in imagination. Without the fantasy of immortality and unlimited possibility the late adolescent and young adult would lack the courage for the required risks and adventures.

The particular context in which I work is a rich environment for the observation—not to say experience—of envy. Amherst College is a highly selective and intensely competitive institution. On a good day that amounts to high standards, and on a bad day to arrogance. The students who come to this college have all been very good at something, and most of them are used to being at the top of their class. Put 1,600 such people together, and the mutual inspection and evaluation will be intense. It is an environment where being "the best" is considered not only desirable but possible. People try to look good, to look cool, to seem smart and self-assured. Although the majority of students come from public high schools, within the first week every student seems to be convinced that every other student comes from a fancy private school! To every student other students seem so assured, both academically and socially. Such an environment presents endless opportunities for both idealization and envy.

My experience of watching the workings of envy in a college group tends to support Klein over Freud in the sense that envy does not seem to be a primarily or extensively gendered experience. At least on the level one sees it in relatively brief psychotherapy, envy is more likely to be focused within one's own gender, along lines of potential identification. Or one envies another's talents or advantages regardless of gender. However, there are some patterns in which envy is structured by gender. The man envies the woman's seeming possession of desire, which he experiences as the power to stir him up, and he wants to force a response. Men speak of feeling needy compared to women because the woman seems less in the grip of desire. Women are envied and resented for seeming not to have as strong sexual needs, for being able to remain cool and above it all, even during sex. The man is trying to "get" something and to evoke a response.

The woman may envy the qualities of activity and doing to that she thinks men have more access to, so she projects her own forbidden activity into the other and then takes pleasure in controlling him. Some women speak of the powerful pleasure of being able to single out a man at a party and draw him over, and being able to do so at will with different men. For other women that process remains more covert. The activity is put into the man in such a way that she reacts with alarm or outrage and experiences most of her competence in then saying no. Given the failure of empathy which typifies envy, and the high level of anxiety and wordlessness which is associated with sex for many college students, these gender-typed envy patterns can mesh malevolently, resulting in at best a painful experience and at worst an episode experienced as sexual harassment or assault.

Sometimes with college students one sees the theme that is central in the struggle with envy in midlife: the confrontation with one's own limitations and incapacities. But characteristically in the college years the adaptive grandiosity and prevalence of idealized fantasy serves to protect a fragile self from those painful blows. But there are some students, most clearly and sadly those facing serious physical illness, extraordinary economic pain, or particularly cruel family circumstances, for whom the work is to accept limits. Certainly the college years are not immune from the painful realization that the world is not fair: Intelligence, beauty, and financial good fortune are not fairly distributed.

The central therapeutic work in the area of envy is to clarify the self and object representations involved in the envious fantasies. As one elaborates, in the context of each individual's unique story, the hoped-for ideal and the past and present sense of inferiority or shame, while honoring the feelings of love and hate embedded in these images, it becomes more possible to arrive at a view that mixes good and bad and tempers envy with gratitude.

Let me end by returning to the child on the beach. How does such envy become bearable? Partly through seeing that the blissful happiness I felt so excluded from was in good part my own idealization. And empathy allows me to be thankful that my parents did have moments of mutual enjoyment and pleasure, given all the pain and struggle of other times. Those moments of happiness and pleasure are a heritage deserving of gratitude. If I hate something about those parents, it is more likely to be the anxiety or self-involvement which went along with their conflict and pain. It was more *that* which threatened to leave me on the outside. To be angry at their happiness only destroys the good resources that were there for me to share. If I couldn't literally be part of that happy twosome at that moment, at least I could imagine finding it for myself.

REFERENCES

Bettelheim, B. (1954). *Symbolic wounds: Puberty rites and the envious male.* Glencoe, IL: Free Press.

Fast, I. (1984). *Gender identity: A differentiation model.* Hillsdale, NJ: Erlbaum.

Freud, S. (1925). Some psychical consequences of the anatomical distinction between the sexes. *SE,* Vol. 19.

Kernberg, O. (1975). *Borderline conditions and pathological narcissism.* New York: Jason Aronson.

Klein, M. (1957). In R. Money-Kyrle (Ed.), *Envy and gratitude: the writings of Melanie Klein,* (Vol. 3, pp. 176–235). London: Hogarth.

Laplanche, J., & Pontalis, J.-B. (1973). *The language of psychoanalysis.* London:

Hogarth.

May, R. (1986). Concerning a psychoanalytic view of maleness. *The psychoanalytic review*, 73(4), 175–193.

———— (1990). The idea of history in psychoanalysis: Freud and the "Wolf-Man." *Psychoanalytic psychology*. 7(2), 163–183.

Mayer, E. L. (1985). "Everybody must be just like me": Observations on female castration anxiety. *International journal of psychoanalysis*. 66, 331–347.

Morris, H. (1993). Narrative representation, narrative enactment, and the psychoanalytic construction of history, *International journal of psychoanalysis*. 74, 33–54.

Ogden, T. (1982). *Projective identification and psychotherapeutic technique*. Northvale, NJ: Jason Aronson.

———— (1989). *The primitive edge of experience*. Northvale, NJ: Jason Aronson.

Richards, A. (1974). *Index to the standard edition of the complete psychological works of Sigmund Freud*. London: Hogarth.

Schafer, R. (1992). Problems in Freud's psychology of women. In *Retelling a life* (pp. 59–81). New York: Basic Books.

15

THE EVIL EYE OF ENVY: PARENTAL POSSESSIVENESS AND THE RIVALRY FOR A NEW BEGINNING

Peter Shabad

Wilt thou set thine eyes upon that which is not? For riches certainly make themselves wings; they fly away as an eagle toward heaven.

—T. H. Huxley

DAVID AND THE EVIL EYE

The tremendous literal power of the evil eye was highlighted for me during a 3-year-long psychotherapy with a 5-year-old child whom I will refer to as David. David's sense of emptiness became apparent in our first session together as he immediately began to dig a deep hole in the sandbox of our clinic playroom. When I asked him what he was doing, he replied that he was digging a hole to China in order to get some food. To help build our relationship, I made it a habit for us to go at the beginning of each session to the hospital cafeteria, where typically he would buy a bag of Doritos corn chips.

During these visits to the cafeteria, he would require that I not watch while he inserted the coin into the vending machine. Afterward, whenever I glanced casually at his newly acquired possession, he became very angry and hid the bag out of my view. On our way back from the cafeteria, we usually stopped at a wishing fountain where he would silently make a wish to himself. Again, David became irritated if I did not avert my eyes from him while he was making his wish as if the malevolent potency of my "evil eye" could reach inside of him omnipotently and steal his private pleasures.

David's exquisite sensitivity to the fragile boundary between the presence and absence of valued objects emerged as a major theme in his play. A continuing thread tying our sessions together was David's recurring attempt to master his acute sense of helplessness through a magical process of reversal and undoing. Session after session, David spontaneously created an ongoing script in which I was to express an anticipatory fear of undergoing all sorts of tortures and torments—most of which revolved around the experience of being abandoned. At these times, he appeared to derive a special delight in seeing me "cry" plaintively at being left all alone.

Initially, I complied with my assigned role of sufferer. More and more, however, I began to play with the script that David had laid out for me. Occasionally, he would become upset and annoyed at my not following his instructions. At other times, however, he would adjust to my improvisations and play along with me. With this newly shared spontaneity—and my modeling of self-protectiveness—David began to gain a new confidence and flexibility in recognizing the free agency of others without undue anxiety. David's sense of emptiness stemmed from his difficulty in internalizing and retaining "good" things for himself. At the age of 6, he was already begrudging himself the pleasures of life. Because of his problem in establishing emotional object constancy or what Adler and Buie (1979) have called "recall evocative memory," David had little sense of his personal past or feeling of an individual identity. Without the stabilizing anchor of an internal center of gravity, David felt a tremendous sense of vulnerability and exposure to the arbitrary whim of forces beyond his control. Much of David's anxiety derived from his sense that his fate depended helplessly on the purposes of others and their envious designs upon his cherished possessions.

Four months before the psychotherapy ended, David and I began to reclaim some of our therapeutic heritage. David, fascinated with the discovery of the lost *Honeymooners* episodes at that time, began spontaneously to discuss our own "lost" episodes—our past sessions. We took turns reminiscing and re-creating bygone sessions in which we were, of course, the celebrity stars. As the stars, we answered questions from the imaginary studio audience on the Donahue show about the different episodes of our shared history—all the while giving credit generously to each other for the success of a particular episode in true show-biz style. In this way, piece by piece, we reconstructed our therapeutic roots together which, in time, helped generate and establish for David an internalized memory of our relationship.

"YOUR EYES ARE BIGGER THAN YOUR STOMACH"

David struggled with the loss or abandonment of treasured objects, good introjects, memories, and images to a sadistic, envious evil eye set on depriving him. The metaphor of the evil eye and David's anxiety concerning its malevolence reveals a vivid, meaningful underlayer of primary process thinking and imagery.

A rich and substantive literature in mythology and anthropology lends credence to David's experience. In the myths of the Medusa, Orpheus, and Narcissus, a stare, a glance, or even a brief glimpse has a petrifying effect upon its victim. In many primitive cultures people avoid being photographed for fear of being robbed of their souls. In clinical work, paranoid patients may ask defensively, "Why are you staring at me like that?" Virtually all languages, ancient and modern, contain a word or expression for the evil eye or its equivalent (Ellworthy, 1895/1970).

What is the envious evil eye after? Whenever as a child I would complain of being extremely hungry and my mother would respond by saying "Your eyes are bigger than your stomach," she was pointing out the obvious fact that I would always aspire to eat more than I could ever hope to consume. This saying alludes also to a deeper, tragic aspect of the human condition: The fulfillment of our desires and ambitions always will be frustrated by the limitations of living within one mortal body. For the eye does not seek so much what it possesses already, but what it does not have. The eye seeks to transcend the limitations of stomach and body; it aspires to more. It is the expressive vehicle of desire, greed, and ambition.

Dundes (1981) states, "Man is born with only so much life force and therefore ever anxious to replenish it" (p. 267). This is especially true of an unrealized life. When something does not go well, we all would wish for another opportunity to correct it. The future is potentially an inexhaustible wellspring of renewal by which the past can be undone and perfected.

Yet while time may be thought of as an ever-flowing river, a human lifespan eventually runs down. A human order of a shifting cycle of generations, conforming to the dictates of mortality, marks off the ascending and descending transitions of our biological clocks. As the entreaties of aging beckon and the illusion of an indefinitely extending future erodes, reverberating pangs of regret threaten to consume the person in despair.

The missed "dead" opportunities of an idealized past can be revived, however, if they are imagined as "living" opportunities that have been stolen and are being realized in the now-idealized lives of others. This sense of having been robbed of the life to which one feels entitled justifies the envious person's coveting of the futures of others. The greed for an eternal flow of life, having encountered the roadblock of death, finds an alternate route to salvage the past through envy.

In his cross-cultural study of the evil eye, Dundes (1981) notes that if a baby returns to the breast after having been weaned, it is said to cause the baby to have the evil eye. Perhaps we could say that those persons who possess the envious evil eye have an overweening desire to turn the unidirectional course of human time, as delimited by a cycle of generations, on its head and grab more than their allotted share.

The envious evil eye is characteristic of those who have had a turn at one or another time of life, but who crave more. Like the mythological vampire who feeds off the blood of the living to sustain itself, envy fights the constant dying of the light by capturing and drinking from budding life that is in the process of becoming. In his classic survey on the evil eye, Ellworthy (1895/1970) notes that its main effects are on "everything that is vital yet incomplete in the process of becoming; everything that is beautiful and precious yet easily harmed."

In the following, I will discuss the different ways that parents look at their children's fresh start in life with a covetous eye. First, I will examine how parents generally seek to neutralize envy by identifying with and participating vicariously in their children's burgeoning lives. As children develop increasing autonomy from parental encroachment, the desire of parents to possess and grab back may become more manifest. Mothers, in particular, may exhibit a "separation envy" and cast an evil eye to freeze the developing child in his or her tracks. Fathers, on the other hand, may display a "womb envy" by bringing their daughters prematurely, either sexually or emotionally, into their narcissistic spheres.

PARENTAL IDENTIFICATION AS A NEUTRALIZATION OF ENVY

Parents repeat the hated behavior of their own parents in interactions with their children all too frequently. Why would a parent call his children stupid repeatedly, knowing how it felt when it was done to him? Why would a father consistently break promises to his child, if he could not tolerate it when his own father did that to him? Perhaps we can discern a subtle revenge and envy in these parents' perpetuating of the wrongs done unto them.

Many adults who have devoted their early years to the labor of worrying and caring for their parents' emotional lives have the sense of having grown up too quickly. The resentful afterimages of being cheated out of their rightful childhood can burn ragefully bright many years later. For at the very same time that such persons were evicted prematurely from their innocence, they began to harbor unconscious yearnings to retrieve that of which they feel robbed and to which they now feel entitled. These adults externalize their regret for their own lost innocence into an envy of children who they imagine are living it out.

When such individuals become parents, the advent of a new generation may stimulate powerful ambivalences. There is now a new field on which to reclaim a life that never had been lived out—a life of hopes, dreams, and possibilities. One constructive way that parents can improve on their own childhoods is through identification.

Identification neutralizes envy by enabling the parent to take sufficient "possession" of the child's growth so that the parent feels that he or she is participating in the child's life as well. Through empathic identification with their children, parents can construct an illusion of their own new beginning.

Conversely, children, by allowing their parents to take identificatory participation in their developmental accomplishments, can placate the parental appetite for a new beginning. By offering "food sacrifices" to the deceased ancestors of the parent's bygone "dead" childhood, children can ward off parental envy of their budding lives. In this regard, parenthood, and perhaps motherhood more intensely, becomes a natural therapeutic means by which parents can heal the wounds of their childhood by partaking in the better life that they are generating for their children.

Although such parents may believe it is too late for them to "go home again," it is not too late for their children. Their children, possessing the precious innocence that they themselves lost years earlier, now become the idealized links to a past from which the parents feel alien. A hope for a rejuvenating new beginning is transmitted from their own future to that of their children; their sons and daughters come to represent the "best" parts of themselves.

To the extent that it is difficult to mobilize aggression toward those whom we idealize, some parents may find it difficult to set the containing limits needed for the provision of a safe holding environment for their children. Thus, some parents, instead of saying "no" to their children's misbehavior, may say something like, "Well, that's just the way 5-year-olds are." For such parents their children's expressiveness has a precious naturalness that should remain untouched by any barriers of sullying restrictions.

The problem of putting children in positions of authority over their own lives in this way can be illustrated through the metaphor of questions and answers. Perhaps a generation or two ago, when children asked questions of their parents they would receive answers, guidance, directions, even rules to live by. Although child rearing was less encouraging of individual self-expression and more autocratic, parental decisiveness formed a containing umbrella that enabled children to feel less alone in the world. The advantage was, as it is in any dictatorship, that parental answers, be they right or wrong, provided a circumscribed environment that allowed children to remain children and not worry about their own welfare.

In today's world, not unlike the psychotherapeutic situation in which a patient's question is responded to with a question, a child may not receive a firm answer to his or her question, but rather a return question that puts the burden of decision back on him. Although in some instances the democratic offering of choice to one's children can have salutary effects, at other times the return posing of questions to children offers only a semblance of freedom. For it is a freedom that cannot be meaningfully actualized without the "holding environment" provided by some "answers."

When a parent responds to a question with a question, what looks like encouragement of freedom of expression may be an unconscious pressure on the child to be the authority figure who will care for the parent. As both parent and child search for answers from a larger containing authority, we see the common unconscious roots of envy and admiration in the rivalry for a new beginning.

PARENTS AND CHILDREN: THE RIVALRY FOR A NEW BEGINNING

The rivalry for the possession of a new beginning is based on what Foster calls the "image of the limited good." Whether it be a life-giving manna, regenerative youth, or food, there is only so much life to go around. Thus, Boris (1994) suggests that envy has roots in the rivalry of natural selection. If one lives, then the other dies.

This sort of rivalry for a limited good forms the basis for an antagonistic zero-sum principle of social interaction in which if one person succeeds, the other must go down to defeat. When one person is happy, then the other must be unhappy, and if one is unhappy it must mean that the other is doing well. If one belongs to the communal procession of life, participating busily in its becoming, then the other must be on the outside, looking in, passive, and watchful with the envious evil eye. In this regard, rivalrous envy, especially of young women, is a fundamental motive animating the malevolence of witches.

In the renowned film version of *The Wizard of Oz*, the Wicked Witch of the West covetously eyes (green with envy) Dorothy's ruby-red slippers which will eventually return Dorothy to her home. Here the Wicked Witch—locked coldly out of her own inner space (water eventually melts this witch-like block of ice)—seeks to possess the red slippers as magical vehicles by which she can be delivered to the home and childhood from which she feels exiled. In *Snow White and the Seven Dwarfs*, the evil stepmother/witch begrudges her stepdaughter her beauty.

Some parents are tempted to bitterly begrudge the passing on of a better life to children, who are viewed unconsciously as rivals for a "new beginning." These parents might say to their children something like, "If I had to walk two miles to school, why can't you?" When queried about this statement, such a parent might respond, without imaginative access to a vision of his own ideal childhood, by saying, "That's what my parents did with me." In thus replicating and passing on the misfortunes of their own upbringing, such parents hope unconsciously to displace their children from an opportunity for an idealized new beginning and grab it for themselves.

SEPARATION ENVY: MATERNAL POSSESSIVENESS AND CASTING THE EVIL EYE

Parental admiration and idealization of children thus is a reaction formation to parental envy, its flip side. As long as parents can bind the invigorating freshness of their children's innocence to and for themselves via identification, they will not have a great urgency to grab or spoil it enviously. Through their identification with the new beginning of their child, parents can cultivate the illusion of reliving their own childhood in a better way. In this parental identification with the child, there is an illusion of continuity in which, to a greater or lesser degree, the distinction between past and present is obliterated.

When a child grows further away from the parent, however, the parent's illusion of identification/continuity with his or her own childhood is ruptured, as the generational difference between parent and child now is exposed. The promise of renewal evaporates as the dream of identity between past and present gives way to the reality of time and history. Here, we can speak of a separation envy of the developing child who is involved so centrally in the process of becoming.

For such parents who are consumed with envy, it is not a simple matter to accommodate themselves generously to the unpredictable fits and starts of a child's developmental needs. Instead, the parent, desperately grasping at the straws of eternal youth, may rear a covetous head of envy and attempt to grab, hold back, and take possession of the child's growth. Mothers, in particular, have the profoundly intimate experience of carrying their children within their bodies for nine months. This is a tie so intimate, in fact, that nature has seen to it that the baby's birth does not rupture the bond but merely punctuates it with the mutually binding give-and-take of suckling and being suckled. This intensity of attachment gives way only grudgingly to ever-greater spaces of separateness.

For certain narcissistically fragile women who feel worn down from giving of themselves unilaterally all their lives, the fullness of pregnancy may bring with it a wonderful sense of compensatory renewal. Giving birth then may come to signify that, yet again, they are being deprived of a supremely significant possession. As the child almost literally empties the mother of life-sustaining milk, uses her up and then leaves her, the mother may feel her primary access to a "new beginning" is being removed once again.

If we do not define the concept of castration too narrowly or biologically, we can say that castration refers to the annihilating, denuding loss of a person's particular source of procreative power. For mothers, castration then refers to the separation and growing independence of the child from her creative influence.

Although from Klein's (1957/1975) viewpoint it is the infant who, full of greed, envies the mother her breast, it is also plausible to say that the mother envies the infant its opportunity to nurse from her breast—especially if she feels forgotten and unappreciated. Of course, as Klein herself noted, a mother's real withholding actions may stimulate the infant's greed and envy.

When a mother withholds provision for the infant's growth and increasing separateness, she simultaneously is expressing an urge to grab back, to regain what she feels is hers, and thereby make herself a bearer of new life again. In this light, it is interesting to note that in Latin the root meaning of evil eye derives from *fascinatio*, to fasten one's eye on another or to bind one substance to another. To the extent that the newborn's physical separateness and individual life are narcissistic insults to the mother's momentary glory of being the creative source of a new beginning, the primary manifestation of the envious evil eye is to begrudge the child its independent life by regaining possession of it. Just as primitive mythology has it that ancestral spirits rise up to devour children, so the "ancestral spirits" of the mother—the ghosts of her own missed childhood—are tempted to reincorporate via the envious evil eye the budding life of her own child.

These ideas lend a necessary human dimension and motive force by which to understand Rheingold's (1967) concept of unconscious maternal destructiveness. For Rheingold, maternal destructiveness reflects the mother's unconscious urge to reincorporate the life to which she gave birth. Roheim (1955) also states that to possess the evil eye means to have oral aggression or a desire to eat the child. A baby's impulse to put a brightly colored object in its mouth exemplifies the close primary connection between visual stimulation and oral incorporation, or as the French have the expression, "to devour with your eyes." Muensterberger (1969) also notes, "The belief in devouring demons is a projective manifestation of ideas which are clearly pre-oedipal and are very often connected with food sacrifices to deceased ancestors" (p. 209).

When a mother fastens her eyes adoringly on her child these fantasies of maternal incorporation become manifest in phrases such as "You are the apple of my eye," or "You are so sweet I could eat you up." And for those maternal appetites that cannot tolerate any delay of gratification, it is interesting to note that the closest equivalent for the evil eye in the Philippines is "bati" or "hot mouth" (Flores-Meiser, 1976).

THE WOLF IN SHEEP'S CLOTHING: THE DANGERS OF MATERNAL ADMIRATION

It is not an accident that doting words, compliments, and praise, especially of young children, are viewed as particularly threatening to the well-being of the child. Behind the cloak of praise and admiration, the envious desire to possess lurks hidden. Farber (1966) observes insightfully:

> Whereas true admiration keeps its distance, respecting the discrepancy between the admirer and the admired one, envy's assault upon its object with a barrage of compliments serves not only its need to assert itself in the costume of admiration, but also the lust of the envier to possess the very quality that initially incited his envy. (p. 122)

Because the parent's covetousness of the child's new beginning may be disguised by doting involvement, the fear of the envious evil eye may more accurately reflect a diffuse anxiety concerning a hidden fear instead of a more focused fear of a tangible danger. The persecutory anxiety of paranoia has more to do with the enemy that is shrouded in darkness than the threat that is apparent.

These persecutory anxieties can be accentuated by a mother's angelic, overprotective solicitousness, which the child may perceive unconsciously to be a mask for her hidden destructiveness. Because there is little opportunity to work through these anxieties by directing overt aggression and consequent acts of reparation toward a seemingly saintlike mother, the child is hard-pressed to resolve his or her ambivalence toward this fantasied "wolf in sheep's clothing."

The child instead splits the image of the mother into the "good," angelic, doting mother who is visible and the hidden mother who is imagined to be voraciously possessive and witchlike. In the fairy tale *Hansel and Gretel*, the witch tempts and entraps the two children with the "sweetness" of her home in order to make them prisoners for her next meal.

Where antagonism rules, a person may be inclined to present the other with a spiteful gift of misfortune. Such spiteful gifts, for example, may take the form of witches casting spells on the blooming of young life. A primary meaning of casting the evil eye on children thus has to do with the act of bewitching.

In *Sleeping Beauty*, the evil fairy, uninvited to the baptism of the newborn princess, arrives at the celebration to cast a spell that will cut short the princess's future. In some versions of *Hansel and Gretel*, the witch's house is made up of children who have been frozen in place. It is only after the witch dies that her spell is broken and the children come to life again.

When the envious evil eye targets a developing child, it petrifies the movement of the child on the spot. Similarly, when a mother is threatened with the growing independence of her children and exposure to her own mortal vulnerability, she may bind the child to herself by halting the child's process of separating in its tracks. By usurping the desires of the child and absorbing his life-sustaining passion, a mother can transform a freely willing child into a captured object of the mother's territorial domain.

The envious evil eye thus becomes a metaphor by which the mother's narcissism is directed toward the child. The depersonalizing effects of the narcissistic usage of children, of transforming the independent person of child into a mother's possessed self-object, is a modern-day version of suffering under a spell cast by a witch's envy.

The fresh blood of raw innocence offers a tempting target of exposure and vulnerability to the evil eye of envy. Wherever some cherished form of new life is created and is in the process of becoming revealed, whether it be a child about to be born or a newly conceived idea about to be spoken, that revelation of passionate life must be concealed from danger. In order to retain a physical and psychological sense of integrity, the child must learn to ward off the possessive gaze of the mother.

We might say, "With such gifts, who needs enemies?" No wonder compliments are trusted so rarely, and so few people handle them with grace. A suspiciousness of the motives of the giver of compliments runs very deep. We seem to look upon praise and admiration suspiciously because we suspect that the envious evil eye with its "lean and hungry look" and unquenchable desire to possess lurks underneath. Thus, defensive strategies to protect against too much kindness, such as jinx and concealment, are evident in belief systems throughout the world.

By revealing a hopeful thought or fervent wish, or by exposing one's happiness, one has jinxed or ruined the possibility of good fortune. Birthday children are urged to keep their wishes private lest they not come true if they are revealed. If one does err in pronouncing one's good luck out loud, then it is imperative to "knock on wood" to undo the mistake of revelation.

In Romania a newborn is referred to as "ugly thing" to shield it from the evil eye. In the traditions of the Masai tribe, when a child is born, they declare openly that the child is bad, but to themselves they say the child is good. For to avoid praise, as is said in the nation of Mali, is to avoid the evil eye. In our own language, we say "break a leg" when we wish someone well. Perhaps even the gruffness with which many adults, often of peasant stock, speak to children reflects the defensive need to disguise their affections from the evil eye.

PLACATING MATERNAL ENVY WITH THE MASK OF COMPLIANCE

A primary form of defense that has been used against the evil eye is the mask. The word *mask* is a corruption of the older Greek meaning of amulet, the purpose of which was to attract and absorb the malevolent influence of the evil eye. Various charms and brightly colored stones have been employed as magical amulets in this way. In a similar sense, because a person with charm can attract and hold the gaze of the evil eye, he is able to serve as a protective buffer for the exposed and vulnerable.

It is interesting to note here that *mask* also derives from the Latin *Masculus* or "virile male" (Thass-Thienemann, 1973). In ancient Rome, there were Societies of Masks or Male Secret Societies whose function was to terrify women. Perhaps it is only the charming male who is attractive enough to divert a mother's evil eye from her vulnerable daughter, hence his appeal. In many fairy tales it is the kiss of Prince Charming that finally can break the spell cast by the stepmother or witch on her stepdaughter. Similarly, fathers may have a primary function of protectively diverting the mother's enviously possessive gaze away from her separating and individuating child.

The exposed and vulnerable child, however, cannot depend totally on the parent for protection. The child must find a way to fend for himself and safekeep his endangered dignity, for the very same parent who is shielding the child may also be claiming him as his own possession.

Napier (1986) points out that masks, worn during various transitional rites and rituals, have the purpose of concealing and overseeing the authentic passion of developmental changes and transformations as they occur. Masks are designed to preserve life-in-process from annihilation at all costs. In nature, too, camouflage, like that of the chameleon, frequently serves as a protective shield against predators.

This use of a mask or "double face" to preserve a core self is reminiscent of Winnicott's (1960/1965) distinction between the False Self and True Self. The child constructs a False Self to protect the True Self from the exploitations of the outside world. In this sense we might view the False Self as a mask of compliance designed to placate the voracious, narcissistically exploitative appetite of the parent's evil eye.

The strange, contorted faces of the mask thus may be viewed as a means of compliantly reproducing the imaginal representations of that which is most feared so as to co-opt its power. In wearing the mask of the enemy and merging with the source of one's fear, the power of the parent's antagonistic evil eye can be neutralized by imitative or "sympathetic" magic. The imitative reproducing involved in the compulsion to repeat a dreaded experience, for example, may be viewed as a vehicle by which the child can inoculate himself with the representation of threat so as not to be overwhelmed by its actuality.

By reproducing imitative replicas of the way things were, a child placates the possessive envy of parental ancestors. In so doing, he assuages also his own sense of separation guilt by giving away a semblance of himself before his whole self is taken over. In this sense the replication and maintenance of ritual and tradition is a means of lending a representation of oneself to possessively envious ancestors before going on with life again.

Sometimes, however, the child goes too far in offering pacifying gifts to the evil eye. In wearing the mask of complicity with the envious mother, the child sometimes gives himself away to such a degree that he can no longer retrieve himself. When he not only takes on but also takes in or inoculates himself with the countenance of the enemy too deeply, the masks of narcissistic defense become entangled confusedly with the narcissistic attacks they were designed to diffuse. The enemy now lies within. Through an identification with the "aggressor" of the mother's envy, the child inhibits and renounces the very same passions that the evil eye would begrudge.

Far from being "fair weather" friends, the relations between parent and child become governed by the "misery loves company" maxim of "rainy day" friendships. As in a large enmeshed family, the mutual possessiveness of "one for all and all for one" guarantees that the interests of parent and child will be tied together through the lowest common denominator of shared commiseration. By equalizing the fortunes of all, this sort of leveling is a means of placating the parent's evil eye with the reassurance that no one has anything worth envying. Kierkegaard (1846/1962) elaborates:

> In a passionless and strongly reflective age envy is the negative unifying principle which establishes itself in the process of leveling and while a passionate age spurs on, lifts and casts down, raises and lowers, a reflective passionless age does the opposite, it strangles and inhibits and levels. (p. 51)

The child's efforts at self-preservation, manifested in the donning of a compliant False Self mask, come at the sacrificial cost of the expressive and revelatory quality of the child's life. Insulated behind the self-inhibiting masks of character defense, the child gains a compromised security without a revitalizing passion.

Segal (1979) has used the term self-envy to describe this tendency to spoil, inhibit, and paralyze one's own progressive creative capacities. Self-envy is characteristic especially of adults who secretly idealize those unassimilated aspects of childhood innocence that have been left behind and continue not to be realized. Such individuals often find, to their envious chagrin, these missed, idealized aspects of themselves in the lives of others, often children, as if they were enjoying their innocence illicitly. With their placating masks of character defense in tow, envied children have thus become self-envying adults who begrudge others what they do not allow themselves.

INCEST: THE CROSS-GENERATIONAL TRANSFERENCE OF DESIRE AND ENVY

It is for good reason that the developing child shields himself from the parent's evil eye. For within the cauldron of possessive desire and envy lie the messy entanglements of physical and emotional incest. Nowhere is it more obvious how the parent binds the child to himself than through the narcissism of incest. In subtle and sometimes not-so-subtle ways, the parent plays out his heart's desire for a new beginning by grabbing at the child's innocence.

In soliciting her father's protection from her mother's evil eye, a daughter ironically may fall prey to the father's narcissistic sphere of influence, and to his "womb envy." Men in particular who have felt that their mothers withheld their life-giving sustenance are prone to act out their womb envy with their daughters. Such fathers may seek to bind their daughters very closely to themselves and, in some cases, molest them physically.

Sexual abuse may be viewed as the culminating action of envious and rivalrous impulses. The abuser, trapped in the fantasied limited goods universe of antagonistic envy, imagines he can regain the stolen innocence that he spoils for the child. His lack of success in this endeavor drives him compulsively to repeat the same actions again and again.

When children are idealized, admired, and envied, and elevated unconsciously to positions of higher authority, the transfer of passions is apt to cross generational boundaries. In family after family, whether in broken homes or intact families with faulty marriages, children are used as hidden consorts for opposite-sex parents and as loyal duplicates of same-sex parents.

At the very same time that a husband and wife are grounding themselves in a life of security with each other, the husband's transference of possessive passion may leapfrog generations from his mother to his daughter and for his wife from her father to her son. The pervasiveness of oedipal victories through cross-generational favoritism is a primary means by which children are evicted prematurely from their innocence into an impinged-upon world of knowledge and responsibility for the significant adults in their lives.

Mothers, who seek to retain some sense of their girlhood, may elevate their sons into the position of the protective father who was not there when the mother needed him most as a little girl. Far too quickly, her son then becomes the father to the man in himself. This pattern of de facto oedipal victories is especially evident in a culture of broken homes in which fathers leave their sons to fill the void for the mothers.

This same son, attempting effortfully to meet his mother's needs, but feeling overwhelmed and inadequate to the task of satisfying a full-bodied adult woman, becomes the man seeking to regain a little boy's confidence. He may take his tender-aged daughter from her relatively compliant mother and bring her prematurely into his paternal sphere to shore up his fragile sense of narcissism and authority. In so doing, he attempts to undo his sense of inadequacy in being unable to meet his mother's erotic needs by creating the same passions with his daughter. Now he has the grown-up body and a regained sense of being a powerful little boy.

Even if the boundaries of her bodily integrity are not crossed, this little girl, flattered by the narcissistic charms and attentions received from her daddy, may become drawn via emotional incest into his sphere of influence. Perhaps beginning with puberty and later as a grown woman, she, feeling alienated from her mother, may turn on her early loving experiences with her father and renounce her girlhood complicity in them. She longs, instead, to return to the slow rhythms and idealized restfulness of a mother-daughter relationship, free of the possessive influences of male intrusion.

From the daughter's standpoint, the father as outsider has introduced alien reality into her life with her mother before she was ready. If only her father had not been so overzealous in his involvement, she fantasizes, she would have received what she needed from her more reticent mother. In the daughter's mind, the voluntariness of the graduated separation-individuation process was unnecessarily and unfairly preempted by her father's involuntary "kidnapping" of her away from her rightful place next to her mother. Perhaps sexual abuse has caught the public imagination because, in addition to its real exploitative features, it has become a metaphor for this sort of premature "phallic" intrusion by the father into the "womb" of the shared mother-daughter relationship.

The incestuous desire of parents to take possession of their children's developmental souls dovetails closely with the admiration/envy that are central to the fear of the evil eye. The aim of the evil eye to freeze the ongoing development of the child in its tracks is enacted in incest when the child is rendered a sexually or emotionally possessed prisoner of the parent's narcissism. Like narcissism, incest is antidevelopmental in that it is a means of holding on to the familiar and foreclosing the novel.

Although a parent may warn of the dangers of the outside world, as he is doing so, he is also claiming the child as his own. Thus, inoculating a child against the evil eye by means of spitting, baptizing, or circumcising can also be a way that the parent puts a territorial stamp on the child. In this way, members of enmeshed families use the mistrust of strangers as a pretext to huddle together indefinitely. In the meantime, the development of the children in such families, which necessarily must traverse the unfamiliar outside world, is brought to a halt. Time, however, eventually will wind down anyway.

REFERENCES

Adler, G., & Buie, D. (1979). Aloneness and borderline psychology: The possible relevance of child development issues. *International journal of psycho-analysis, 60,* 83–95.

Boris, H. (1994). *Envy.* New York: Jason Aronson.

Dundes, A. (1981). Wet and dry, the evil eye: An essay in Indo-European and Semitic worldview. In (Ed.). *The evil eye: A casebook.* Madison: University of Wisconsin Press.

Ellworthy, F. (1895/1970). *The evil eye.* New York: Collier.

Farber, L. (1966). *The ways of the will.* New York: Basic Books.

Flores-Meiser, E. (1976). The hot mouth and evil eye. In C. Maloney (Ed.), *The evil eye.* New York: Columbia University Press.

Kierkegaard, S. (1846/1962). *The present age.* New York: Harper.

Klein, M. (1957/1975). *Envy and gratitude.* New York: Delacorte.

Muensterberger, W. (1969). Psyche and environment: Socio-cultural variations in separation and individuation. *The psychoanalytic quarterly, 38,* 191–216.

Napier, A. (1986). *Masks, transformation and paradox.* Berkeley: University of California Press.

Rheingold, J. (1967). *The mother, anxiety and death.* Boston: Little, Brown.

Roheim, G. (1955). *Magic and schizophrenia.* Bloomington: Indiana University Press.

Segal, H. (1979). *Klein.* London: Fontana Modern Masters.

Thass-Thienemann, T. (1973). *The interpretation of language, Vol. 2.* New York: Jason Aronson.

Winnicott, D. W. (1960/1965). Ego distortion in terms of True and False Self. In *The maturational processes and the facilitating environment* (pp. 140–152). New York: International Universities Press.

16

MALE ENVY ACROSS THE LIFE-SPAN

David Gutmann

The lust for the possessions and prerogatives of the other that we know as "envy" or "avarice" is a potent theme across history, across societies, across families, and across the human life-span. Envy is a major dynamic of social relations, particularly in preliterate, agrarian societies. The witchcraft beliefs that are common in such societies are typically based on the idea that the witch—or the one who procures the witch's services—is driven by envy of the victims' possessions. Within families, it is a truism that siblings are routinely, even necessarily, envious, begrudging the rations of love and attention that the parents mete out to their "rivals." The degree of envy and its targets also vary within individuals, according to the seasons of the life cycle. Thus far, psychodynamic investigators have confined their studies to women generally, and to children of both sexes. Thus, in classic Freudian theory, penis envy is regarded as a feature of the female psyche, organizing the relations to self and others across the life-span; and children, as we have already noted, are presumably in the strong grip of sibling envy during their years of maximum dependency.

But there is a strange asymmetry in the study of envy. While we concentrate on envy in women and children, its manifestations in men, and in elders of both sexes, go ignored. This paper represents a beginning attempt to restore the missing symmetry. In it, I will put forward some observations concerning the phrasings of male envy across the seasons of the masculine life cycle, particularly in the later years. I will flesh out these ideas with clinical and ethnographic vignettes, as well as descriptions of the work produced by male painters and graphic artists in their adulthood and old age.

When we think of men generically and genetically—that is as members of the human species, rather than as members of a particular community or tribe—we can observe that the life cycle of the human male has four major divisions. He starts life, in the psychological, as well as the physical sense, as the child of his mother, and if things go as they should, he soon graduates to the status of "father's son." From there, he ascends to his own paternity as the father of sons and daughters. And finally, at the end of life, he relapses back to the psychological status that predominated at the beginning of life—he becomes once again a "mother's son."

The first three periods, during which we observe the man's evolution from being parented to being a parent, have been closely studied by developmental and psychodynamic psychologists. In this brief paper, we will look at the neglected fourth season, comprising the "return to the mother," and the associated shifts in the politics of male envy. By way of preparation, we will begin with the first stanza, with the little boy who has been weaned in the physical sense, but who remains bonded to the mother in the psychological sense.

Envy (male as well as female) is probably at its highest pitch during these earliest years. The boy is needy for both physical and emotional nutriment during this time, and both seem to have their major source in the mother. While the weanling's love goes to his mother, envy is directed at the other siblings, of either sex, particularly those who appear to have the best places at the feeding trough. To the degree that the father receives evident donations of the mother's love, he too is envied—first, as a kind of larger sibling, the one who shares the mother's bed. Later, as the rivalry takes a more specifically oedipal form, the father will be resented, on narcissistic grounds, as a successful rival, and envied for the powers that gained him the victory. The stage of oedipal envy phases out when the boy, realizing that he cannot co-opt the father's powers by defeating him in open competition, decides to "join" him through identification and emulation. Accepting that he cannot steal the father's powers, the son accepts the principle of delay, becomes the father's apprentice, and begins, through protracted learning, to inherit the father's coveted powers. He enters the latency period.

In sum, the son's dangerous oedipal dilemma is solved through a shift in allegiances: The son gives up the dangerous, envy-ridden status of "mother's son" and achieves a partial separation from her in the new, less dangerous and "politically" advantageous status of "father's son."

The boy's "rebirth" as father's son—or as son of the collective fathers—is celebrated in many cultures via rites of passage that range from penile subincision by cowrie shells as among the Papuan natives to the Bar Mitzvah ceremony of religious Jews. But whether the trial takes a physically demanding or intellectually challenging form, an ordeal is always involved, a test of manhood that is laid on by the communal fathers, who observe the candidate closely for signs of weakness. Whiting and Child (1953) found that the severity of the ordeal varied, across cultures, with the length of the breast-feeding period. The ritual is clearly a passage away from the mother, and since late weaning implies a strong maternal bond, a stringent ordeal is required to break it. Thus, if the boy is too visibly frightened and tearful, then he has not passed the crucial test: He has cried for his mother, he still belongs to her world, and he has not been reborn as father's son and junior colleague into the company of men. But if the lad endures with some grace and fortitude, then he has begun to make it as a man: He is one of the "twice born," reborn as a son of the collective fathers and as an age-grade brother of the initiates who have endured the trial with him.

Bruno Bettelheim (1954) has documented the ways in which the ritual serves also to cool the boy's residual envy of women and their strange powers. As he points out, the rites of passage involving subincision of the penis, as well as other forms of scarification, inflict symbolic wounds that leave the boy with vaginal representations engraved in his flesh. In effect, the son surrenders his rivalrous envy with the powerful mother, the residues of his sojourn as the "mother's son," via identification: In the rituals, he grafts the symbols of her powers into his skin. Thus endowed, he can let go of the real mother "out there" and go on, now as a father's son, to eventually become a man and a father in his own right. His envy of female power has been put on hold; during the time of young manhood and adulthood, his envy as well as his regard will be centered on his male peers—particularly those who surpass him in the manly pursuits, those who earn praise and advancement from the fathers. When he was a mother's son, he envied the siblings, male and female, with whom he had to share her attention and love; now, as a father's son, he envies mainly the male peers against whom he strives for the "old man's" tokens of honor and recognition. Young boys are envious of love; mature men—even when they become fathers of sons—are more prone to envy the prestige and honor held by other men.

The major psychological transitions of a man's life are keyed to his procreative and parental status. Thus, men separate decisively from their mothers, bond to their fathers, and attempt the first tests of manhood at about the time when their bodies make the transition from the prepubertal to the pubertal condition. At that point in their bodies's history, when their physiology moves toward procreation, their psyche prepares for manhood and parenthood. They give up sexual bimodality, concede feminine qualities to the mate, and establish an unambiguous masculinity. But the male capacity for procreation in the physical sense outlives the male commitment to paternity and to male autonomy from maternal persons. The male investment in the ways of the fathers, in the paternal orientation, and the suppression of feminine qualities, begins with the onset of procreativity and phases out as the "emergency" period of active parenthood comes to a close. As children mature, as the sense of parental emergency ebbs, men recover the feminine aspects of self as well as the maternal identifications that had been put on hold, lived out vicariously through the wife during the period of active paternity. In effect, the male engagement in unalloyed masculinity lasts about as long as the female window of fertility; as that window closes, men take over or reclaim the feminine qualities that the women relinquish. In any event, in this postparental transformation, men return to the status of "mother's son" that they abandoned during the preparental years, as they prepared for paternity. Following this restoration of the *status quo ante*, maternal persons, both real and fantasied, again loom large in the mental life of the older man.

Across cultures older men become preoccupied with women as powerful rather than seductive: They discover in women the aggressive strength that is diminishing in themselves. When men are younger, they envy males of superior prowess, prestige, and sexual potencies. In later life, women acquire, in the eyes of older men, the same strengths that these elders once *envied* in their male peers and superiors.

The older man's envy of the powerful woman is rarely acknowledged openly; it can only be inferred from their covert fantasies and artistic productions. For the remainder of this paper, I will concentrate on the latter: the drawings and paintings produced by accomplished artists across the span of their creative years, from adulthood to old age. While artists may differ from the nonartistic majority in that they coin their inner life into created works, these interior contents—their preoccupations, their appetites, their excitements—will be like those of "generic" men in the same life stage. The artist's creative act does bring into being a work unlike anything that has existed before, but the work grows out of the same soil and is shaped by the same concerns that prompt the actions of ordinary men. The investigation begins with a study of two *New Yorker* cartoonists, George Price and William Steig, both of them chosen because they have had long and productive lives, because their superior draftsmanship merits the designation "artist," and because the approximate location of each drawing in the timeline of the artist's *oeuvre* is easily determined from the *New Yorker* issue in which it appears.

As men age, they revive images of the woman as mother: the "good mother," the man's haven in a sea of troubles; and the "bad mother," who dominates or disappoints the man while mocking his impotent anger. The body of work by William Steig traces, over time, the thinning out of aggression-laden, male-oriented themes, in favor of later-life depictions of the "good mother."

Steig was born in 1907, and his early cartoons, drawn for the *New Yorker* when he was in his 30s, give a picture both of his times and of his own concerns as a younger man. We find a group of early cartoons that feature little guys who are trying to make it in the world of Real Men. In a locker room crowded with large, muscular males, a spindly little fellow tries to get their attention by loudly singing a World War I song, "Mademoiselle from Armentieres." Another cartoon series, titled "Small Fry," amusedly but sympathetically portrays spunky kids who test their courage and mimic adult male behaviors. A later series, from World War II, titled "Dreams of Glory," depicts, again with a kind of wry sympathy, the grandiose dreams of small boys intent on impressing their big brothers and their fathers. Thus, a jubilant little cowboy, brandishing man-sized six-guns, is shown breaking into Hitler's headquarters to capture him single-handedly.

If Steig the younger has envy, it is directed toward men of superior size, courage, and exploit, those who could achieve or have achieved the "dream of glory."

However, upon entering his middle years, Steig seems to disparage the masculine ideal rather than envy it. He produces a series of drawings that ridicule armed, warlike men as posturing though dangerous fools. In the same early midlife period, a large number of drawings depict angry men, out of place in a world they never made; men resolutely turned against women; men and women struggling together in a tight, entrapping net; and men and women as discordant, opposing parts of the same larger body.

In his young manhood, Steig clearly envies the big guys, and gently

ridicules his own wish for acceptance by them. But in his middle years he perhaps manages his envy by ridiculing "real men" and the standards that define
them as such. But even as he rejects the aggressive versions of masculinity, in
his middle years Steig is at the same time troubled by an emerging feminine
aspect, represented by a man and a woman at odds within the same body, that
he seems to recognize, uncomfortably, as a part of himself. Having put aside
the idea of aggressive masculinity, Steig discovers—like his age mates around
the planet, and with a thrill of horror—a hidden quality of softness and femininity at the very core of self. Represented in Steig's drawings of this period
are the conflicts over emerging androgyny that are generic to midlife men.

However, as Steig enters the sunset years, his crisis of androgyny appears
to end. In his 60s and early 70s, Steig produced drawings that show a profound
change in content and execution. His line, which was once definite, boundary-
defining, and boundary-cutting, is now open, rounded, and impressionistic. This
shift in his later artistic style, toward a softer and more sensual line, is in
keeping with the drastic changes in pictorial content of the same period.
Now, instead of depicting imposing male athletes and soldiers, the majority
of Steig's later drawings are filled with imposing women: bounteous, queenly
women, or Venuses attended by diminished men. Whereas in his early years
no more than 10 percent of Steig's drawings depict easy relations between
men and women, in his elderhood at least 35 percent of the sample portray
comfortable and even loving male-female relations, usually with the man
paying court to a woman who may or may not respond. Now the man is the
needy one, and the woman has the power to satisfy him, or to rebuff him.
The radiantly sensual and buxom women that Steig so lovingly draws are
clearly the ideal and envied figures of Steig's later years. The aging Steig, like
the generic men that we have studied, divests himself of aggression, or uses
it to obliterate the masculine rather than the feminine principle. As a young
man he tried to please and to be accepted by the envied fathers and big
brothers; older now, he tries to please the adored (and clearly envied) mothers,
rather than the fathers.

By contrast, George Price—a contemporary of Steig's at the *New Yorker*—
shows us the "bad mother." Like Steig, when Price was in his 30s and 40s, 60
percent of his cartoons had to do with the world of men: males in competition
or in collaboration, mainly in outdoor public spaces, with women either absent
or relatively insignificant. A typical early cartoon shows a group of straining
runners at the moment of breaking the finish-line tape while a man in the
background clocks them with an hourglass. In another cartoon from the same
period, two men holding strike signs picket, in wheelchairs, a surgical supply
store, while the angry owner looks on. Despite their manifest differences, both
cartoons do have in common a struggle among men, observed by men, in outdoor public spaces that are empty of women.

But when Price reaches his early 50s, striking shifts take place. The majority
of his cartoons no longer depict the world of men, and women are portrayed as
being dominant in male-female encounters. In the depiction of space, Price

also shifts away from the outdoor, public world of men, and toward the domestic interior, the preserve of women: Two-thirds of the later drawings depict household rather than outdoor scenes.

A typical cartoon from Price's middle years shows three generations of men—a son, a father, and a grandfather—frantically pedaling their bicycles around the living room table, while the woman of the house, joined by a female friend, looks on dubiously. She remarks: "It's not enough I let them have a six-day race. Now they want I should put up money for sprints!" From this same middle period, another cartoon shows an elderly man in cowboy costume sitting on a spavined horse, shading his eyes as though gazing out over vast Western ranges. But in actuality, his horse stands within a small, junk-filled, fenced-in backyard. Again there is a disgusted-looking woman who complains to a female visitor, "You'd think it was a ten-thousand acre estate he's looking over!"

These are transitional cartoons. In both cases, men act in ways—competitive (bike riding) or ascendant (horseback riding)—that belong to the male arena but not to the domestic zone (where they come under the disparaging view of the resident woman). In the earlier cartoons, women, if they appeared at all, tended to admire and (by implication) envy the men. But now, in the later drawings, women have gained their own enviable power: They disparage men who are ridiculous rather than heroic.

Later, in Price's seventh and eighth decades, the reversals of sex roles and milieux of action are almost complete. The world of men is now a relatively neglected arena. Four out of every five cartoons are concerned with male-female relations, and the female is dominant in at least half of these. Regarding the milieux of action, these become exclusively domestic: one room, without doors or windows to an outdoor world, and this interior space crammed with the presence of a hostile older wife. In a cartoon from Price's eighth decade, the mild husband and the burly wife are drawn with matching T-shirts: hers reads "Fight" while his reads "Flight." In Price's senescent fantasy, it is the man who quits the field and the woman who goes into combat.

Between them, Steig and Price show us the two images into which aging men, universally, have split the empowered maternal image: Steig shows us the woman as a kind of "Horn of Plenty," the wellhead of good power, while Price shows us the dangerous "witch," she who concentrates bad power and who becomes, in place of men, the enemy of the weakened male. In the eyes of these older artists, women have taken the enviable powers—whether to do good or to do harm—into themselves.

These age shifts, by gender, in the assignment of ascendant qualities is not limited to cartoonists, or to a special historic cohort of artists. In our time, long-lived fine artists show the same age-progression as Price and Steig: from being centered on competitive and productive "masculine" concerns to being centered on women's works and on the fate of men in the interior, domestic world of women. Consider, for example, the lifework of Edward Hopper (1882-1967), a contemporary master of some importance who painted continuously—again, without any loss of his powers—from his youth until his death in the ninth decade. True to form, as a young man Hopper painted the world of men: impersonal action by large, powerful machines (locomotives, tugboats, etc.). However, in his middle years, Hopper becomes interested—though at first from the outside—in domestic structures, in houses. At first he paints houses as an architect might; they are structures that inhabit a larger exterior space. Somewhat later, though still as an outsider looking in, Hopper becomes intrigued by the domestic interior rather than by the exterior architecture. Now he looks in through the windows from the outside, to discover and paint a warm, enclosed world populated by women. And in his last painterly years, Hopper (like George Price) has completed his journey from the vital outside to the more quiescent, "womanly" interior. In his last paintings, Hopper is inside looking out. His ego now lives in an enclosed space, one typically furnished at its very center with a compelling (and often nude) woman. As was the case with Steig, the women of Hopper's final years are idealized and powerful. Again, we assume that envy follows idealization.

This age transition of the artist is not limited to a particular artistic style; and it is not limited to a particular era. Consider the lifework of Jean-Auguste Dominique Ingres (1780–1867), a French master of the early 19th-century classicist period. Predictably, we find that the young Ingres painted land battles, sea battles, and the deeds of mythic heroes—and the heroes are always male. If women appear in his youthful works, it is only as victims of male-inspired warfare and as the occasions for manly heroism: Helpless (and sometimes topless) they can only adore while the gallant knight rescues them from the dragon. Women admire men; by implication, what women admire they also envy.

But time brings about a reversal of gender priorities. As Ingres ages, his males become weakened and inwardly troubled. Though they may have public stature, they do not seem to have an inner fortitude to match it. Women are depicted as the power behind the throne—the true sponsors of male accomplishment. Finally, true to form, in the seventh and eighth decades of his life Ingres paints, almost exclusively, the virtues and worlds of women: nursing Madonnas and the magnificent Odalisque canvases—the signature paintings of his entire career—which limn the sealed, inner world of the harem. And these naked women of Ingres's harems might have been imagined by Steig: They are masses of lovingly painted, opulent female flesh. Again, as a young painter, Ingres calls up the outdoor, action-filled vistas of the male perimeter; but in his later years, he re-creates the domain that is familiar to little boys who have not yet left their mothers: the enclosed, hothouse climate of the woman-filled domestic interior. Toward the end of life love and its dark partner, envy, return to their beginnings.

REFERENCES

Bettelheim, B. (1954). *Symbolic wounds: Puberty rituals and the envious male,* Glencoe IL: The Free Press

Gutmann, D. (1994). *Reclaimed powers: Men and women in later life,* Evanston IL: Northwestern University Press

Whiting, J.W. & Child, I. (1953). *Child training and personality: A cross-cultural study.* New Haven: Yale University Press

Part Five

GENDER AND ENVY IN SOCIAL AND CULTURAL LIFE

INTRODUCTION

The psychological origin of inequality, as Rousseau brilliantly sketched it in the Second Discourse, comes when "solitary" man begins to assemble and finds that the strongest, the handsomest, the best dancer and the best singer get an undue share of the goods. Envy begins to show its face.... If consumption represents the psychological competition for status, then one can say that bourgeois society is the institutionalization of envy.
—Daniel Bell (1976/1996)

Shakespeare would love this. This is all Shakespeare. This is about love and hate and cheating and distrust and kindness and disgust and avarice and jealousy and envy.
—Senator Alan Simpson at the hearings on the confirmation of Clarence Thomas, as quoted in Garber (1993)

Although psychoanalysis prescribed a method of treatment, to describe it simply as a clinical theory is not only to impoverish it, but to distort its original intent. For psychoanalysis was simultaneously a literary theory from its outset, that is, from the time that Freud first wrote to Fliess in 1897 about his thoughts on reading *Oedipus* and *Hamlet*, and, equally intrinsically, a full-fledged social theory from the time of his earliest consideration of repression, sublimation, and the microcosmic relational universe of the family romance. If some writers stress the primacy of clinical techniques, insights, and data over the literary or "academic" aspects of the psychoanalytic project (Trosman, 1996), Freud himself referred readers in search of psychoanalytic insights as often to the world of the poets as to the world of the couch, and currently much of the vitality of psychoanalysis, particularly as it pertains to gender, can be viewed as derived from its use within the realms of literary, cultural, and social studies. If the goal of this book is to gesture toward a preliminary framework for the development of self-conscious, psychoanalytically-informed insights into the nature of the interaction between gender and envy, then we might as well have started as have ended here.

Though psychoanalysis was a social theory from its inception, however, it was never comfortably so. Indeed, intrapsychic and sociocultural concerns have often been viewed as at odds; such was the objection to Horney's work, that it "sociologized psychoanalysis" (Sayers, 1991, p. 127) by focusing on the external determinants of neurosis. Protests against Horney's ideas, however, arose perhaps most forcefully from that group of psychoanalysts, following Otto Fenichel, whose own social agenda had attempted to bridge the intrapsychic-sociological divide by offering a rigorous integration of sociopolitical ideas with such central psychoanalytic concepts as the unconscious and infantile sexuality (Jacoby, 1983, p. 106). This debate regarding the relationship and relative balance between intrapsychic and sociocultural factors in character formation and identity formation has been reiterated over the past 20 years within the arena of psychoanalytic gender theory. Though psychoanalysis has been welcomed in some circles (Mitchell, 1974) as providing a basis for understanding the universality of patriarchy and thus for feminist critique, and though many of the most important current writers on psychoanalysis and gender theory (including Choderow, Benjamin, and Chasseguet-Smirgel) have approached the topic from a background in political or social theory, other writers have emphasized the dangers inherent in allowing sociological and psychoanalytic explanations to become too carelessly intermingled. If, for some authors, psychoanalysis provides insight into how the structure of social life manifests itself in individuals, and how it might be modified for women's (and men's) psychological good, others see its greatest contribution as its power to illuminate the unavoidable "failures of identification" that result in the divergence of individuals from their socially-determined roles (Rose, 1986, p. 354), and thus to provide a haven for understanding the ways in which the unique and delicate internal environment resists and transforms what would otherwise be deterministic social pressures.

In assessing the extent to which this contribution can be preserved, and the ways in which it can most widely made use of, however, the need to evaluate psychoanalysis's potential as a resource for the illumination of sociocultural life is not so much done away with as refined. In this context, the question is not *whether* psychoanalytic theorists need to pay attention to that aspect of the "complemental series" (Freud, 1917, *SE* 14, p. 347) that constitutes the sociocultural environment, but *how*. This debate in itself has been a recent generative locus of a range of theoretical responses. Some generally more traditional theorists tend to focus on the ways in which cultural products and social visions can be understood by reference to the individual psychologies of those responsible for them. Others, in essence following in the footsteps of Fenichel and the radical Freudians, question whether psychoanalytic insights might be brought to bear on policy and thus serve to dictate social change. Kittay, in her exposition and critique of Bettelheim's work above, pointed out the crucial function played by sociocultural practices in structuring and metabolizing (men's) envy, as well as the disastrous consequences attendant on their failure to do so. In addition, such authors as Benjamin (1988), Choderow (1978, 1989) and Olivier (1989) stress that their psychodynamically informed observations have implications for the restructuring of family and society; likewise, the recently founded

Journal for the Psychoanalysis of Culture & Society and its parent organization, the Association for the Psychoanalysis of Culture & Society, aim to "use psychoanalysis to formulate social and cultural practices that can alter the psychological roots of socially destructive attitudes and behavior" (Bracher, 1996, p. 1). The practical motivation for such an endeavor is to redress specific socially problematic phenomena, in the hope that doing so will simultaneously enliven psychoanalytic discourse; Young-Bruehl's book *The Anatomy of Prejudices* (1996) demonstrates how useful, indeed essential, a psychoanalytic perspective can be in supplementing a purely sociological one for understanding racism in its various forms. Adams's work *The Multicultural Imagination* (1996) likewise stresses both the vacuum of attention within psychoanalysis to issues of race, and its potential both to illuminate and be illuminated by this field of inquiry. Yet the theoretical motivation of still other recent endeavors is, in some cases, even more radical: to pave the way for the development of a psychoanalysis of culture itself, in the context of which cultural cure might be accomplished.

Perhaps more radical still, from the perspective of current clinical theory, is Teresa Brennan's suggestion that the view of individuals as discrete, contained beings is, at base, an illusion, an artifact of our times, and one that psychoanalysis can help to account for. Her goal, rather, is to attempt to arrive at an understanding of the social psychosis, born three centuries ago, of which this illusion is merely one symptom. If Daniel Bell, in *The Cultural Contradictions of Capitalism* (1976/1996, p. 22), decried the almost total neglect of the idea of envy by sociological and economic theorists attempting to account for capitalism's spread, Brennan points the way toward appreciating envy's central place in creating the structure of life at all levels. She does so by reinterpreting Klein's insights into the child's destructive wishes toward the mother's breast as formative in the creation of a foundational fantasy that fixes and defines objectification, and therefore exploitation, as a social actuality. Brennan's project is extraordinarily rich and far-reaching, and it is impossible to capture its sweep in an excerpt of a length appropriate for this book. Thus, the selection that follows should be thought of as only an introduction to her broader project of elucidating what Lacan calls the "ego's era." Here she outlines the elements of the fantasy that grounds our collective malaise, of which a disabling view of femininity and an institutionalized impulsive voracity are but two troubling aspects.

If Brennan's work testifies to a current emphasis upon a reworking of earlier approaches to the psychoanalytic appreciation of social life, psychoanalytic studies of culture, and of the specific arts and other practices that comprise it, have likewise undergone a transformation. In some respects, this transformation has led psychoanalytic cultural criticism full circle; whereas from the outset Freud looked to literature as a wellspring of insight into the further reaches of psychological life, and thus saw it as the source of theory as well as the object of its analyses, later generations of literary scholars focused most often upon the latter point of view, offering demonstrations of the power of analytic theory to explain the motives of characters, authors, and creative mechanisms, often in a reductive manner. When, in his essay "The Idea of a Psychoanalytic Literary Criticism" (1987), Peter Brooks, following Shoshana Felman (1977) and others, questioned the hegemony of theory over text, arguing for a circular pattern of influence between the two domains, he spoke for a whole range of psychoanalytic scholars and critics who were charting the reverberations between psychoanalysis and their respective disciplines, literature among them.

In many ways, the emerging field—or rather, "blurred genre" (Geertz, 1983)—of cultural studies was the beneficiary of this move to view the encounter between theory and its subject as mutually determinative, though in other respects, it had also been born of a similar movement within the field of anthropology. Likewise, although the integration of gender theory into literary criticism required a protracted effort marked by a series of turning points, an awareness of gender issues was integral to the emergence of cultural studies in its current form. Perhaps because cultural studies was raised from birth with an awareness of the vicissitudes of gender and of theory, it has generally provided a comfortable and nurturing context in which to chart the play of gender and envy across the modalities of our cultural surround. In Marjorie Garber's essay "Fetish Envy," she demonstrates the mutual nourishment of examples from literature, theater, pop music videos, and the psychoanalysis of Freud and Lacan, toward the creation of an appreciation of envy (of the phallus, of the fetish, of the fantasy of gender) as "foundational to theater itself" (p. 306), and (complementing Rene Girard [1991]) of the theater as the essence of envy. In that context, she highlights penis envy as but one instance, and not the first, of the workings of the economies of loss and desire, as fueled by the omnipresence of fetish envy. Thus, she extends Brennan's argument regarding the participation of envy, in its gendered manifestations, in the creation of the foundations not only of social, but of cultural life.

Implicit in the arguments of both Brennan and Garber is an appreciation of the power of envy itself as a motivating force in and beyond the psyche of the individual. In his essay "Castration Envy," Clayton Koelb enriches our appreciation and understanding of this power through a reading of Nietzsche's account of the feminine. In light of Jacques Derrida's discussion in *Spurs* (1979), Koelb highlights the way in which disgust in response to the body of woman and its lack, as portrayed in Nietzsche's writing, serves to veil the "irresistible might" stemming from the power of woman's castration in the eyes of men. In the trope of the woman/saint as his unfulfillable ideal, the artist's most fundamental anxiety is not derived from his vulnerability to being brought to a similar state, but from his appreciation of the far more potent force which is created in that vacuum. Koelb's reading is interesting not simply as a point of philosophical scholarship, however; rather, it throws into relief hidden aspects of Freud's own discourse that might function all the more powerfully there because of Freud's quite deliberate cleavage of Nietzsche's ideas from his own. For Koelb's argument points the way toward a recognition of another side of the story of penis envy and castration anxiety that Freud puts forward in his essays on female development, one toward which Freud gestures elsewhere—for instance, in his 1922 essay "Medusa's Head" (*SE*, p. 273), in which woman's castration is the source of the strength of Athena, the virgin warrior goddess. Koelb's interpretation, thus, sends us back to the beginning of this book, to reread Freud's original ideas in light of the philosopher's insights. For indeed, it is only through the circular process of leaving and returning to the ideas about gender and envy to which we currently have access, and thus appreciating the power and importence of these ideas in new ways, that new insights into the forms of their mutual determination might, over time, emerge.

REFERENCES

Adams, M. V. (1996). *The multicultural imagination: "Race," color and the unconscious.* New York: Routledge.

Bell, D. (1976/1996). *The cultural contradictions of capitalism.* New York: Basic Books.

Benjamin, J. (1988). *The bonds of love.* New York: Pantheon.

Bracher, M. (1996). Editor's introduction. *Journal for the psychoanalysis of culture & society,* 1(1), 1–14.

Brooks, P. (1987). The idea of a psychoanalytic literary criticism. *Critical inquiry,* 13(2), 334–348.

Chodorow, N. (1978). *The reproduction of mothering.* Los Angeles: University of California Press.

——— (1989). *Feminism and psychoanalytic theory.* New Haven, CT: Yale University Press.

Derrida, J. (1979). *Spurs/Nietzsche's styles.* Chicago: University of Chicago Press.

Felman, S. (1977). *Literature and psychoanalysis.* Baltimore, MD: Johns Hopkins.

Freud, S. (1917). *Introductory lectures on psycho-analysis. SE,* Vol. 16.

——— (1922). Medusa's head. *SE,* Vol. 18, pp. 273–275.

Garber, M. (1993). Character assassination: Shakespeare, Anita Hill and JFK. In M. Garber, J. Matlock, & R. L. Walkowitz (Eds.), *Media spectacles,* New York: Routledge. p. 23–39

Geertz, C. (1983). *Local knowledge.* New York: Basic Books.

Girard, R. (1991). *A theater of envy: William Shakespeare.* New York: Oxford University Press.

Jacoby, R. (1983). *The repression of psychoanalysis: Otto Fenichel and the political Freudians.* New York: Basic Books.

Mitchell, J. (1974). *Psychoanalysis and feminism.* New York: Random House.

Olivier, C. (1989). *Jocasta's children.* New York: Routledge.

Rose, J. (1986). *Sexuality and the field of vision.* London: Verso.

Sayers, J. (1991). *Mothers of psychoanalysis.* New York: W. W. Norton.

Trosman, H. (1996). *Contemporary psychoanalysis and masterworks of art and film.* New York: NYU Press.

Young-Bruehl, E. (1996). *The anatomy of prejudices.* Cambridge, MA: Harvard University Press.

17

THE FOUNDATIONAL
FANTASY[1]

Teresa Brennan

Of what then does the foundational fantasy consist? The difficulty with describing it is that it is perceived necessarily from a present standpoint, although I am assuming that it is a kind of mindset or psychical fantasy which is reinforced historically and acted out technologically. In the present, I have suggested, the subjective psyche is shaped and thoroughly overdetermined by the technological acting out of this fantasy, as the totalizing trend eliminates difference. If I am right, we are reaching a point where the fantasy can have no clear locus in either the psyche or the social order, so we need to focus on a point midway between both.

Such a point is provided by the commodity (in the narrow sense of a "consumer good"), a thing that is socially produced for exchange and psychically desired. A second reason for focusing on the commodity is that we know ourselves best by what we do. Or what we make. In this world, we make commodities. To the extent that commodities are shaped by our desires, they indicate what those desires are. There are of course problems with beginning with the commodity, which I come to in a moment. But a psychoanalysis of the desires encapsulated in commodities will eventually yield the rudiments of the fantasy that founds us. As time must be central in this fantasy, let us start with the desire for instant gratification, described by Freud and realized in a proliferation of commodities.

The vending machine that provides instantly upon the insertion of a coin, the fast-food establishment that promises no delay, the bank card that advertises itself as the one that does away with the need to stand in a queue, all promise the abolition of *waiting time.* Yet a little reflection shows that commodities cater to more than a desire for instant gratification. They are also marked by an attitude of appealing availability: the "I'm here for you" message signified by the trolley at the airport that asks you to "rent me," or the advertisement that once asked you to "fly me." These appealing items are akin to those that promise service, such as the credit card that delivers the

1. (Ed: In this excerpt from *History after Lacan*, Brennan describes the "foundational fantasy" that undergirds the collective psychosis characteristic of the present "ego's era" that started in the 17th century. At that time, Lacan suggested, the ego (as a social phenomenon) began "its progress to the center from the wings" of our collective life, "seeking to make over all that exists in its own image" [Brennan, 1993, p. 3].)

object of desire to your door. "Pick up the phone; we come to you." More than the abolition of waiting time is offered here; one will also be *waited upon*. And if the promise of service appeals to a desire for domination and control, it has to be noted that the illusion of control is also provided by vending machines and their ilk. The consumer makes it happen; or rather, the consumer is catered to via the fantasy of making it happen with minimal effort, even none at all. In this connection, the car is an exemplary commodity. It provides mobility without much activity to a passive director. At the same time it pollutes the surrounding environment.

In proposing that the desires encapsulated in commodities embody a foundational fantasy, I am proposing that we treat the commodity as an expression of it. But immediately, this proposition raises three problems. The first is that the desires encapsulated in commodities do not tally exactly with any existing account of a psychical fantasy. The second problem of course is demonstrating that the fantasy expressed in commodities is in fact foundational. This problem is exacerbated by a third, which figured in the last chapter, particularly in that Lacan neglects the technological dimension when it relates to the economics of profit. This is the problem of why it is that a fundamental psychical fantasy is expressed in a form which is on the socio-historical increase. For commodities, whether in the form of consumer goods or in the form of the technologies that underlie their production, are evidently increasing.

We are not entirely in a void when it comes to considering these problems. As noted at the outset, while there is no extant account which tallies precisely with the psychical fantasy I am assuming commodities encapsulate, a synthetic reading of certain psychoanalytic theories will provide one. In addition, that synthetic reading coheres because it makes central the psychical fantasies Klein describes about the mother's body. This focus on Klein also reveals just what objectification, and with it the subject-object distinction, entails. The focus is appropriate in another way, given that it is a feminist reading of Klein, as well as Lacan, that raised the question of the relation between fundamental or even transhistorical psychical fantasies and socio-historical circumstances.[1] But Freud comes first.

Persistently, consumer goods appeal through visual media. This, together with the desire for the instant gratification these commodities encapsulate, directs us to Freud's pleasure principle. Freud's pleasure principle, more strictly his principle of *Unlust* or unpleasure as he first defined it, is about an hallucinatory visual world where instant gratification is paramount. It is also about how psychical reality as distinct from "material reality" comes into being.[2] When the longed-for object (initially the breast or mother) is not present it is hallucinated in its absence. This hallucination founds psychical reality; the breast is present in the imagination, but not present in the material here and now. The act of hallucination provides instant gratification, but the satisfaction it affords is only short term. For the breast is longed for because the

1. This idea is elaborated in Brennan (1988) and (1989). While the word transhistorical is used in the psychoanalytic, feminist writing the point is simply that a psychical fantasy *can* exist independently of and across a variety of historical circumstances, not that it must always do so.
2. The distinction between psychical and material reality is Freud's. It has been criticized by Laplanche and Pontalis (1968).

infant is hungry, and the hallucination cannot appease the unpleasure of the need for food. In other words, unpleasure is due to the tension of need. Any need (to eat, urinate, defecate, ejaculate) increases quantitatively, and pleasure is felt when the need is relieved. An hallucinated breast does not of itself relieve the need. Indeed it ultimately leads to more unpleasure, in that it generates motor excitations it cannot dispel; the expected satisfaction that accompanies the hallucination gears the body up, but the energy amassed through this excitement cannot be relieved, any more than the original need itself.[1]

It should be clear that Freud's (un)pleasure principle is an economic or quantitative principle: it is about the quantitative build-up of tension or need. In Freud's own terms, it is a matter of psychical economy, loosely based in Fechner's psycho-physics.[2] The economic or quantitative physical aspects of Freud's theory of the pleasure principle are frequently criticized. Its descriptive aspects are more generally accepted; few commentators have problems with the notion of instant gratification, or with that of visual hallucination. Yet, as I said in the Introduction, it is the fact that Freud had a reference point in physics, even if it was the wrong reference point, that will be of most use in the long run.

Moreover, if one reconsiders the desires implicit in commodities, will be plain that while the pleasure principle accords with the desire for instant gratification that they express, and with their visual presentation in various media, it does not account for the other desires revealed in their design, namely: the desire to be waited upon; the desire to believe one is the source of agency who makes it happen; the desire to dominate and control the other who is active in providing, but whose activity is controlled by a relatively passive director, and the aggressive desire towards the other, if we take pollution as evidence of aggression.

The last-named desire returns us to Klein. In her theory, the infant desires to spoil and poison the breast (and the mother) with its excrement. In discussing the infant's desires in Klein's theory, I should repeat the brief caveat on the notion that "the infant" is the sole culprit when it comes to pinpointing the origin of the aggressive desires under discussion. "The infant" is always that origin for Klein, although we will see later that the question of culpability is more complicated, as is the idea that the target of all this aggression is simply "the mother." But for the time being, I shall continue to write in terms of monstrous infants and mauled mothers. As well as desiring to poison, the infant also desires to devour and fragment the mother's body. "Cutting up" the mother's body is a recurrent theme in Klein's analyses of small children. She ties this cutting impulse to the drive for knowledge: the urge to get inside, grasp and in this sense understand what is hidden and in the process destroy it.[3]

For Klein, the desires to poison, devour, dismember, and to know through

1. See in particular the well-known seventh chapter of *The Interpretation of Dreams* (Freud 1900). (Ed: *SE* 5: 509–622).
2. For the most thorough discussion of Freud's relation to Fechner, see H. F. Ellenberger (1970). As with most of my references to Freud, this is discussed in more detail in Brennan (1992).
3. For representative illustrations of these and many of the following Kleinian ideas from different periods of Klein's work, see Melanie Klein, "Early stages of the Oedipus conflict," (1928) and "Envy and gratitude" (1957).

dismembering are prompted by two interrelated forces. The first is the strength of the death drive working within. The second the envy of the creativeness embodied in the mother and mother's breast. While the death drive and envy motivate these fantasmatic attacks on the breast, they also lead to a fear of retaliation. The fear is that the aggressed breast will respond in kind; this fear results in what Klein terms the paranoid-schizoid position. It is paranoid because the infant projects its own aggressive desires onto the other, and the retaliation it fears (being cut up, poisoned, devoured) mirrors its own desires. It is schizoid because this paranoid projection involves a splitting both of the ego and of the other. For to deal with its dependence on the breast as the source of life, and its simultaneous fantasy that the breast is out to get it, the infant splits: there is a 'good' breast, and a 'bad' one. Yet because the badness the infant fears originates within itself, the splitting of the other presupposes and perpetuates a splitting of the ego. The ego, by depositing its own aggressive desires in the other, impoverishes itself by the splitting, and the repression or 'denial' that this entails.

The ego can only recover its full potential by reclaiming that which has been cast out. This reclamation, when it occurs, can lead to depression: the recognition that the erstwhile projected badness lies within. It may also lead to reparation: the attempt to repair the damage done in fantasy;[1] this reparation is manifest in creativeness or, I think, creative labour, both means to integrating a psyche felt to be in pieces. Lacan too thinks the infant feels itself to be in pieces, due to its premature (relative to other mammals) birth, and consequent lack of muscular co-ordination. The mirror-stage, in part, is founded on the appeal of an erect posture; the infant idealizes not only its whole image, but an image in which it is standing up (1949, p. 7).[2] But while these accounts have a certain phenomenological similarity, Klein injects an ethics into the realization of wholeness, and a pathway to it other than that of erection.

Leaving that hopeful note aside: It is important to add that the extent of the splitting, and of the poisoning, devouring, dismembering fantasies that accompany splitting, is mediated by anxiety. For Klein, anxiety derives from the death drive working within. In the last analysis, she posits that the strength of the death drive, and envy, are innate. Moreover, Klein's account of the splitting process presupposes a psychical fantasy which has no direct correspondence with reality (the breast is not really cut up, etc.). It is a psychical fantasy, and clearly not a consequence of the infant's actual social environment or social events. It is also important to note that the splitting of the good and bad breast is remarkably similar to the splitting of women into two types, mother and whore, which suggests that the Oedipal, symbolic split embodies an earlier one. The psychical fantasy of woman, for all it is meant to be a bulwark against the ego's era, only comes into being at a "certain historical moment." Klein's account of the splitting into good and bad has more

1. The most representative if difficult account of the views summarized in this paragraph is "Notes on some schizoid mechanisms" (Klein 1946).
2. Standing up is actually a recurrent preoccupation of Lacan's, and he finds a similar interest in it in Heidegger's use of the term *Dasein*. "The idea of standing erect, of life, of evolving is what comes of an etymological analysis of [the verb 'to be'] completed by a grammatical one" (1955-6b, p. 339).

claims to generality, as we shall see, and will help explain why the expression of this split in the fantasy of woman contributes to the ego's era.

Thus far, we have a theory that accounts for the desire to poison or, in commodity terms, the desire to pollute. We also have some elements of a theory that accounts for the desire to dominate and control (insofar as the desire to get inside, cut up, devour and so on involve control and domination). It remains to tie this theory to the instant hallucinatory gratification embodied in the pleasure principle, and the desire to be waited upon from a passive though authoritative position. Here Klein's analysis of envy provides an indirect clue.

> Though superficially [envy] may manifest itself as a coveting of the prestige, wealth and power which others have attained, its actual aim is creativeness. The capacity to give and preserve life is felt as the greatest gift, and therefore creativeness becomes the deepest cause for envy. The spoiling of creativity implied in envy is illustrated in Milton's *Paradise Lost*, where Satan, envious of God, decides to become the usurper of Heaven. Fallen, he and his other fallen angels build Hell as a rival to Heaven, and becomes the destructive force which attempts to destroy what God creates. This theological idea seems to come down from St. Augustine, who describes Life as a creative force opposed to Envy, a destructive force.
>
> (Klein 1957, pp. 201–202).

This passage is interesting because it points out, although it does so obliquely, that envy superficially focuses on attributes or possessions, rather than the creative force which may (or may not) result in them. The quotation from Klein also points out that envy will attempt to rival that which it envies, and that it will do so by constructing an alternative. More generally, Klein's analysis of envy in the essay from which the above quotation comes shows that while envious motivations are readily recognizable in destructiveness or calumny, they are less recognizable, although present, in denial. This is the form of denial which simply ignores or forgets that which is displeasing to the ego. It is present in the denial of the labour involved in creativity. I add that we recognize it where creativity is seen as accidental, or where it is attributed to a lucky circumstance or an unearned possession.

Let us add to these observations a notion that is best elaborated by Freud. This is that the infant, or small child, imagines the reversal of the actual state of affairs, and imagines that the mother is a dependent infant (Freud 1931, p. 236). In reversing the passive experiences of childhood into active ones in his play with a cotton-reel, Freud's grandson not only masters the mother's absence and introduces himself to deathly repetition (Freud 1920); nor does he only, if simultaneously, enter the world of language through the mother's absence that forces him to call. He also makes the mother into a fantasized small child which he controls, a child which is also an inanimate *thing*.

If the notion of the reversal of the original state of affairs is made central, rather than the incidental aside it is for Freud, it has the advantage that it reconciles otherwise diverse findings. When realities are seen in terms of their opposites, the fact of nurturance and the means to grow becomes a threat to narcissism; it establishes the reality of dependence. From this perspective, the envy of the mother's breast is the resentment of that dependence, and the reason why nurturance, or love, or protection, or assistance, are interpreted as assertions of superiority and power. "Only saints are sufficiently detached from the deepest of the common passions to avoid the aggressive reactions to charity" (Lacan 1948, p. 13). There is a related, if less relevant, offshoot of the reversal of the original state of affairs into its opposite, an offshoot which we might usefully term "imitating the original," in which rivalry with the original is clearly apparent. The child imitates the mother; the commodity, harking back to this chapter's point of departure, is often an imitation of the original.[1] Writing this, I went to the corner store for orange juice, and found only artificial orange drink in an orange shaped container, with green leaves. (It is not a good store.) I also took in late night television, worst amongst it *The Stepford Wives*, which is all about constructing a reliable and completely controllable imitation of the original wife and mother, and *Star Trek II*, where "Project Genesis" shows us humans reinventing the entire process of creation.

The idea that we live in a culture of simulacra is developed by Baudrillard (1981 and 1986), whose study of *America* (1986) shows how much of its culture is a copy of a copy, and sometimes of yet another copy. In Baudrillard's world of hyper-real, more real than real copies, the disappearance of the distinction between the original and the imitation is due to the inability to locate an origin or referent for meaning.[2] Yet in the *Zeitgeist* what is lost, in fact explicitly rejected is any notion of an original; an original is a notion of a foundation, hence suspect. I am challenging this suspicion by focusing on the mother's body, an origin before the foundation, of which more in a moment.

But keeping to the main thread: the tendency to look at realities in terms of their opposites is manifest at another level, which will explain the desire to be waited upon. Originally, the infant is perforce passive, and dependent on the mother's activity for survival. Yet it would be consistent with a fantasmatic reversal of the original state of affairs if the infant were to correlate its actual dependent reality with the fantasy of control through imagining that the mother's activity takes place at its behest. The infant does not wait upon the mother; the mother waits upon it. It is precisely this fantasy that is catered to by the commodities with which we began. But a little of reality lingers on, in the association between passivity and luxury, which recognizes that it is not the passive controller, or "the infant," who labors. At the same time, the labour activity involved in fulfilling the wish is denied in so far as its intelligence is denied. In fantasy, the mental direction and design of what labor effects is appropriated,

1. The imitation of the original is an often implicit and sometimes explicit theme in discussions of women and technology, particularly reproductive technology. For a general representative collection on this theme, see Stanworth (1987). For a discussion which bears more closely on the issues discussed here, see Haraway (1985).

2. Baudrillard also identifies the loss of the sense of history in America as a fact, not a theoretical lapse.

only the manual activity is left out. Thus the mental whim and control is the infant's. The work goes elsewhere.

The split occasioned by this fantasy prefigures a deeper dualism between mind and body, in which direction or agency is seen as mental and mindful, while activity, paradoxically, is viewed as something that lacks intelligence. By an ineluctable logic, the activity of women as mothers is presented as passive. In fantasy, it lacks a will of its own; it is directed. And because direction is too readily confused with a will of one's own, this denial can readily be extended to living nature overall. In this connection, it is worth noting that the oft-repeated association of women and nature can be explained not by what women and nature have in common, but by the similar fantasmatic denial imposed upon both of them. In the case of women, it is one's will that is denied. In the case of living nature, its own inherent direction is disregarded. The denial of will also holds for people of color, in terms of "a belief structure rooted in a concept of black (or brown or red) antiwill, the antithetical embodiment of pure will. We live in a society where the closest equivalent of nobility is the display of unremittingly controlled wilfulness. To be perceived as unremittingly without will is to be imbued with an almost lethal trait" (Williams 1991, p. 219).

That creativeness is not viewed as intelligent or directed activity is consistent with envy's predilection to focus on creativity as the possession of certain attributes, rather than as a force in itself. Creativeness is seen less as what one does, than what one has. Or, to say a similar thing differently, the dialectics of envy conduct themselves at the level of images. It is appropriate that the word envy is derived from the Latin verb *videre*: the derivation signals the tie between the concept of envy and visualization.[1] What matters is the appearance of the thing, rather than the process of which it is part.

To say that what is envied is the mother's possession of the breast is to work already within the terms of envy, which are those of possessions, things, appearances, discrete entities, separable and separate from an ongoing process. Which brings us to the crux of the matter. While a fantasy of controlling the breast cannot survive at the level of feeling (pain or pleasure), it can survive at the literally imaginary level of hallucination. In fact, the controlling fantasy can be perpetuated through hallucinations, and this ability to perpetuate it must contribute to the addiction to the pleasure in hallucination, despite its unpleasure at other levels. In other words, by this account, the fantasy of controlling the breast and the act of hallucination are one and the same, which means that the amazing visual power of hallucination is tied to a desire for omnipotence from the outset.[2]

Of course feelings of omnipotence, for Freud, are infantile in origin, and tied

1. Conceptual ties such as this are fascinating pointers to the notion that Benjamin's 'prelapserian state', in which the expressive value of a word was tied to the signifier, may have something to it. Cf. the discussion of Freud's 'common source' below.
2. A qualification. While omnipotence is tied to the act of hallucination, most non-Western cultures do not regard an hallucination as deceptive necessarily. What is likely in this culture to be dubbed hallucinatory could as well be styled a vision, or spirit-possession. It is only in the psychoanalytic vision that hallucination is tied in its origin to infancy. I have followed this vision, but its cultural specificity, and the phenomenology it presupposes, is questioned in the book's conclusion.

to narcissism. But while there has been some discussion of how it is that narcissism can only come into being through fantasy or hallucination, the other
side of this issue, which is how it is that hallucination is by nature an omnipotent or narcissistic act, has not been discussed.[1] It is one thing to concentrate
on how it is that the subject's sense of itself as a separate being is inextricably
linked to narcissism; that is to say, that it is only by the narcissistic act of fan-
tasizing about its own body or circumference that it establishes its separate
self. It is another to think about how the narcissism involved is also, and simultaneously, an omnipotent fantasy about controlling the other. For to establish
itself as separate, the subject has to have something to be separate from. This
much is foreshadowed by Lacan's *object petit a.*

But by this account, the thing the subject is separate from is the breast or
mother it imagines as available to it, subject to it, and towards whom it feels
the aggressive desires that lead in turn to paranoia. Moreover, in the omnipotent act of hallucinating a breast it controls, the nascent subject separates
and gives priority to its own visual capacity for imagination over its other
senses. It is this visual capacity that allows one to imagine that things are
other than as they are; it is this capacity that enables one to focus on the distinctiveness of entities other than oneself, rather than the senses or feelings
that connect one with those others; it is this capacity that enables the subject to believe in (and even achieve) a situation where mental design and
direction can be divorced from bodily action.

By this account, hallucination should be the mechanism by which Lacan's
split subject, which is the human condition for him, comes into being. But at
the same time, the tie between hallucination and envy means that the very
act of hallucination can never be neutral. In St. Augustine's imagery, if the
fallen angel of light (Lucifer: *lux* = light, *ferre* = bring) fell because of envy
there is no reason for supposing that he lost his power of light altogether;
rather, in the act of hallucination, light becomes actively distorted and re-
directed as an imaginary and necessarily envious vision. Lacan, like Klein,[2]
also refers to Augustine, who, of course, is writing long before the ego's era
began. In this quotation, Lacan is discussing the individual ego as such, and
the death drive.

> The signs of the lasting damage this negative libido causes can be read in the
> face of a small child torn by the pangs of jealousy, where St. Augustine recog-
> nized original evil. "Myself have seen and known even a baby envious; it could
> not speak, yet it turned pale and looked bitterly on its foster brother."...
>
> (Lacan 1953a, p. 16)[3]

It is after quoting Augustine that Lacan moves swiftly on to Hegel's master-

1. Although Borch-Jacobsen comes close when he pinpoints the core of megalomania in many of
   the dreams Freud analysed (Borch-Jacobsen 1989). Borch-Jacobsen's analysis of why narcissism
   is necessary, in fact the key, to the constitution of the subject is the outstanding discussion of
   this theme. Also important are Laplanche and Pontalis (1968) and Laplanche (1970).
2. In addition to those aspects of Lacan's indebtedness to Klein discussed above, it is worth
   adding that he also writes of art and its relation to aggression against the mother's body, citing Klein. See Lacan (1959–60, p. 126).
3. Lacan does not give a reference for the quotation from St Augustine. It comes from the

slave dialectic, and the attempted destruction of the other consciousness, or other within, that the dialectic foretells. While Lacan makes it plain that that dialectic is the key to the "most formidable social hell" (1949, p. 7) of the ego's paranoid era, the nature of the destructive objectification involved in the master-slave dialectic needed elucidation, and requires still more.

By this argument, the desires to poison, fragment and destroy the mother's body constitute the process of objectification, a process which has a physical reality. We have seen that turning the other into an object also means fragmenting it (in order partly to know it) or poisoning or in other ways attacking it, as well as making it a controllable thing. A very similar point is made by Kristeva, who, in an argument which echoes that of Mary Douglas, makes "abjection" the foundation of objectification. Abjection is the feeling that one has revolting (including excremental) substances within; objectification comes from the need to exclude these substances by depositing them in the other, which brings the other, as object, into being.[1]

Some of the resonances between Klein's theory of the infant and Lacan's theory of the ego's era should now be evident. I will assume that the links between their arguments on the role of anxiety in 'objectification' can be taken for granted. Also, Klein's account ties the objectifying desires to the drive for knowledge. While she does not stress visualization in this connection herself, the fact that Foucault ties objectifying power/knowledge to visual mechanisms of control fits the theses I am elaborating.

The objectification of knowledge, for Lacan, is paranoid precisely because it is knowledge based on a need for control. It is knowledge tied to a "positivist" worldview in which what is seen, or what can be tested or proved to exist, especially on the basis that it can be seen, is privileged. The objectification of knowledge helps construct a world in which only objects (or discrete entities?) are recognized, and they can only be recognized by subjects. In turn these subjects are affected, if not driven, by the objects they construct,[2] objects whose energetic process of construction will be discussed below, in an account that builds on Lacan's assumption that the subject-object distinction is tied to sexual fantasy, and his ethologically based belief that the impact of an image was both social and physical, and critical in the nature of the objectification that founds the ego.

Confessions. The context is an argument that sin is present in infancy. When considering various possibilities, St Augustine asks whether as infant he sinned by endeavouring to harm 'as much as possible' those larger beings, including his parents, who were not subject to him, 'whenever they did not punctually obey [his] will'. ('*Non ad nutum voluntatis obtemperantibus feriendo nocere niti quantum potest....*') One sentence later comes the observation that Lacan also quotes: '*vidi ego et expertus sum zelantem parvulum: nondum loquebatur et intuebatur pallidus amaro aspectu conlactaneum suum.*' S. Aureli Augustini (c. 400, p. 8). For my purposes, it is the failure to *punctually* obey, in connection with envy, that is interesting.

1. Kristeva (1980, pp. 17–32); Douglas (1966). Douglas's cross-cultural enquiry lends further weight to the notion that what we are dealing with here is a foundational fantasy with a very wide application in some of its aspects.

2. Although at one point Lacan indicates that objectification means turning the other into a controllable thing, he does not pursue this point. Lacan is more concerned with the objectification of knowledge as such; in this concern, he is again at one with Heidegger, although Heidegger centralizes the objectification of nature as 'standing reserve', and the technocratic drive for mastery over nature, in a way that Lacan does not. Cf. Heidegger (1938).

Thus far it seems we have an account of a psychical fantasy which tallies with the desires encapsulated in commodities. It is this psychical fantasy I am positing as a foundational psychical fantasy. That is to say, I am positing that the desire for instant gratification, the preference for visual and "object"-oriented thinking this entails, the desire to be waited upon, the envious desire to imitate the original, the desire to control the mother, and to devour, poison and dismember her, and to obtain knowledge by this process, constitute a foundational psychical fantasy.

It is a fantasy which accords certain attributes to the subject, and dispossesses the other of them as and by the process that makes the other into an object, a surrounds (as Heidegger might say), an absent background against which it is present. It is a fantasy that relies on a divorce between mental design and bodily action to sustain its omnipotent denial. In this fantasy, the subject must also deny its history, in so far as that history reveals its dependence on a maternal origin. There is no "before" before this very present subject. We have also seen how the subject denies time, how it must do this to sustain its fantasy, by imagining that there is no delay between what it desires and its presence.

REFERENCES

Baudrillard, J. (1981). *Simulacres et simulation.* Paris: Galilee.

———(1986). *America* (Trans. C. Turner). London & New York: Verso.

Borch-Jacobsen, M. (1989). *Lacan: The absolute master* (Trans. Douglas Brick), Stanford: Stanford University Press.

Brennan. (1988). Controversial discussions and feminist debate, in N. Segal and E. Timms (Eds.) *Freud in exile: Psychoanalysis and its vicissitudes.* New Haven and London: Yale University Press, p. 254–274.

———(1989). Introduction to *Between feminism and psychoanalysis* (Ed. T. Brennan). London and New York: Routledge, p. 1–23.

———(1992). *The interpretation of the flesh: Freud and femininity.* London: Routledge.

———(1993). *History after Lacan.* New York: Routledge.

Douglas, M. (1966). *Purity and danger: an analysis of concepts of pollution and taboo.* New York: Praeger.

Ellenberger, H. F. (1970). *The discovery of the uncounscious: The history and evolution of dynamic psychiatry.* London: Allen Lee.

Freud, S. (1900). *The interpretation of dreams. SE* Vol. 4 & 5.

———(1920). *Beyond the pleasure principle. SE* Vol. 18.

———(1931). Female sexuality. *SE* 21, 221–43.

Haraway, D. J. (1985). A manifesto for cyborgs: Science, technology, and socialist feminism in the 1980s, in L.J. Nicholson (Ed.) (1990) *Feminism/postmodernism.* New York and London: Routledge, p. 190–223.

Klein, M. (1928). Early stages of the Oedipal complex, *International journal of psycho-analysis* 11, 167–80.

———(1946/1975). Notes on some schizoid mechanisms. *Envy and gratitude and other works, 1946–1963* (Collected writings, vol. 3). London: Hogarth Press and the

Institute of Psycho-Analysis, p. 1–25.

———(1957/1975). Envy and gratitude. *Envy and gratitude and the other works, 1946–1963* (Collected writings, vol. 3) London: Hogarth Press and the Institute of Psycho-Analysis, p. 176–235.

Kristeva, J. (1980). *Powers of horror: An essay on abjection* (Trans. Leon S. Roudiez). New York: Columbia University Press.

Lacan, J. (1948/1977). Aggressivity in Psychoanalysis. *Ecrits: A selection* (Trans. Alan Sheridan) London: Tavistock, 8–29.

———(1949/1977). The mirror stage. *Ecrits: A selection* (Trans. Alan Sheridan). London: Tavistock, 1–7.

———(1953). Some reflections on the ego. *International journal of psycho-analysis*, 34: 11–17.

———(1955–56/1966). *Le seminaire livre II: Les psychoses.* Paris: Seuil.

———(1959-60/1986). *Le seminaire livre VII: L'ethique de la psychanalyse.* Paris: Seuil.

Laplanche, J. and Pontalis J.-B (1968). Fantasy and the origins of sexuality. *International journal of psycho-analysis* 49, reprinted in V. Burgin, J. Donald and C. Kaplan, *Formations of fantasy.* London and New York: Methuen, p. 5–34.

Laplanche, J. (1970). *Vie et mort en psychanalyse.* Paris: Flammarion (trans. J. Mehlman). *Life and death in psychoanalysis.* Baltimore: Johns Hopkins University Press, 1976.

Stanworth, M. (Ed.) (1987). *Reproductive technologies: Gender, motherhood and medicine.* Cambridge: Polity Press.

Williams, P. (1991). *The alchemy of race and rights.* Cambridge: Harvard University Press.

18

FETISH ENVY

Marjorie Garber

Whose underwear is under there? Fruit of the Loom. 'Cause it fits.
—Advertising jingle for Fruit of the Loom underwear

A fetish is a story masquerading as an object.
—Robert J. Stoller, M.D., *Observing the Erotic Imagination*

Few women are ready to go to a party dressed in a skimpy white toga that reveals of pair of shorts embellished with a large drawing of a phallus.
—Gladys Perint Palmer, "Fashion Famine Plagues London"

A fetish gave my patient the power to ignore a man and deny his penis. Her bitter resentment against men for her lack of a penis and for her great need of them, stemming from oedipal sexual disappointment, was expressed in an attachment to fetishes. This was especially notable when she lavished attention on her denim jacket and turned away from the analyst.
—David A. Raphling, M.D., "Fetishism in a Woman"

In recent years, feminist literary criticism and film theory have been preoccupied with issues like female fetishism and male subjectivity—issues linked by a common desire for equality, or reciprocity. If he has it, we should have it. Or, if we have it, he ought to have to have it too.

"Female subjectivity" is itself, I think, a recuperative strategy; its apparent counterpart, "male subjectivity," is a fantasy construct designed to obscure the fact that the male equivalent of "female subjectivity" is not "male subjectivity" but, alas, "subjectivity,"' just as the male equivalent of "female transvestism" in most psychoanalytic and popular discourse is not "male transvestism" but "transvestism" *tout court*. Men who are surgically transformed into women are transsexuals; women who are surgically transformed into men are "female-to-male transsexuals." (Unfortunately, in most of the literature, neither are described simply as "women" or "men.")

At the end of her provocative essay on female fetishism, Naomi Schor raises this point directly, confessing to "a persistent doubt that nags at [her] as [she] attempt[s] to think through the notion of female fetishism. What if the appropriation of fetishism...were in fact only the latest and most subtle form of 'penis envy'?"[1]

---

1. Naomi Schor, "Female Fetishism: The Case of George Sand," in *The Female Body in Western Culture*, ed. Susan Rubin Suleiman (Cambridge: Harvard University Press, 1986), p. 371.

What I am going to suggest here, using examples from Shakespeare's plays, modern theatrical productions, psychoanalysis, evolutionary biology, and pop music videos, is that this question, though highly pertinent, is wrongly posed, because it is, finally, tautologous. Penis envy *is* phallus envy; phallus envy *is* fetish envy. It is not clear that it is possible to go "beyond ideology" here; the ideology of the fetish is the ideology of phallocentrism, the ideology of heterosexuality.

"If the penis were the phallus," writes Eugénie Lemoine-Luccioni, "men would have no need of feathers or ties or medals."[1] The penis is an organ; the phallus is a structure. What does it mean to say that envy for the one is envy for the other? Here we might remind ourselves of what Freud has to say directly about "penis envy": that it marks the castration complex of the young girl; that she wishes to be able to exhibit the penis she does not have (as, for example, by urinating while standing up); that a "successful" maturation toward adulthood will convert this female wish for the penis into a wish for a baby; and that the "ultimate outcome of the infantile wish for a penis...in women in whom the determinants of a neurosis in later life are absent [is that] it changes into the wish for a *man*, and thus puts up with the man as an appendage to the penis."[2]

Why is fixation on the phallus not called a fetish when it is attached to a man? The concept of "normal" sexuality, that is to say, of heterosexuality, is founded on the naturalizing of the fetish. And this in turn is dependent upon an economics of display intrinsic both to fetishism and to theatrical representation.

In general, according to Freud, men have perversions, women have neuroses. Perversions have to do with having something and neuroses with lacking something. Thus, when Freud articulated for psychoanalysis both the idea of "penis envy" and the psychoanalytic concept of the fetish as "a substitute for the woman's (the mother's) penis that the little boy once believed in and...does not want to give up," he privileged the "man's penis" as the "normal prototype of fetishes."[3] The "woman's real small penis, the clitoris," was, he claimed in the same essay, "the normal prototype of inferior organs," where "organ-inferiority" became the basis of all neuroses. Men had the penis; men had the fetish.

Lacan, in moving from penis to phallus, from the level of anatomy or "nature" to that of the unconscious and of representation, addressed the question of fetishism in relation to the phallus as the mark of desire. Thus, commenting on "the absence in women of fetishism," Lacan notes (after Freud) that the "imaginary motive for most male perversions is the desire to preserve the phallus which involved the subject in the mother." Since fetishism represents "the virtually manifest case of this desire," he concludes that "this desire," the desire to preserve the maternal phallus, "has a different fate in the perversions which she [i.e., woman] presents."[4] Again follow-

1. Eugénie Lemoine-Luccioni, *La Robe* (Paris: Seuil, 1983), p. 34.
2. "On Transformations of Instinct as Exemplified in Anal Erotism," trans E. Glover in *The Standard Edition of the Complete Psychological Works of Sigmund Freud*, ed. James Strachey, (London: The Hogarth Press and the Institute for Psycho-Analysis, 1955) 17: 129.
3. Sigmund Freud, "Fetishism," *SE* 21: 157.
4. Jacques Lacan, "Guiding Remarks for a Congress on Feminine Sexuality," in *Feminine Sexuality: Jacques Lacan and the école freudienne*, ed Juliet Mitchell and Jacqueline Rose, trans. Jacqueline Rose (New York: W. W. Norton, 1982), p. 96.

ing Freud and Ernest Jones, Lacan locates both this desire and this perversion in "the homosexual woman," who exemplifies the patterns of "courtly love" in that she "excels in relation to what is lacking to her." So it is the lesbian, and not the straight woman, who follows the path of something analogous to fetishism. Lacan notes "the naturalness with which such women appeal to their quality of being men, as opposed to the delirious style of the transsexual male," and takes this as a sign of the path leading from feminine sexuality to desire. It is the trajectory of desire which is at issue here—the position of "the homosexual woman" as not the object but the subject of desire.

Thus Lacan can claim, in a complex but suggestive passage, that "feminine sexuality appears as the effort of a *jouissance* wrapped in its own contiguity (for which all circumcision might represent the symbolic rupture) to be *realized in the envy* of desire, which castration releases in the male by giving him its signifier in the phallus."[1] "*The envy* of desire." In the woman who lacks the penis but "has" the phallus (that is, who "has" it by becoming aware of its lack), it is phallus envy, the desire for desire, that motors and motivates her actions. "Having" the phallus, having the fetish, becomes therefore a matter of one's position in the symbolic register and in the economy of desire. "Men" have the phallus; "men" have the fetish. What is at stake is the ownership of desire.

What I will be arguing is that fetishism is a kind of theater of display—and, indeed, that theater represents an enactment of the fetishistic scenario. Thus Freud's "penis," the anatomical object, though understood through Lacan's "phallus," the structuring mark of desire, becomes reliteralized as a stage prop, a detachable object. No one has the phallus.

In contrast to other animals, sexual visibility in humans is marked in the male rather than the female. In most mammals, readiness for sex (and for reproduction) is displayed by estrus, a regularly recurrent period of ovulation and excitement—what is also called "being in heat." The human animal substitutes erection for estrus, the overt, signalized sexual readiness of *man* for the overt, signalized sexual readiness of woman. It is no accident, I think, that the invention by humans of recreational sex (sex not for reproductive purposes but for fun) is coextensive with this shift from female to male display. Since the theory of fetishism employs a developmental narrative which implies loss, here is another version: phallocentrism is *loss* of estrus. So that the loss or lack that is described in the Freudian fetishistic economy as castration is itself a substitution for another loss or lack. Phallic fetishism—which is to say, fetishism—is already a substitution and a displacement. And Freud's attempt to make the fetish part of the *female* body is both denial and displacement.

As Naomi Schor notes "it is an article of faith with Freud and Freudians that *fetishism is the male perversion par excellence.* The traditional psychoanalytic literature on the subject states over and over again that there are no female fetishists; female fetishism is; in the rhetoric of psychoanalysis, an oxymoron."[2] For the same reason, there have traditionally been in the psy-

1. Lacan, "Guiding Remarks," p. 97.
2. Schor, "Female Fetishism," p. 365.

choanalytic literature no female transvestites, although the fantasies collected by Nancy Friday in *My Secret Garden* (for example, a woman admiring
herself in the mirror wearing jockey shorts with a Tampax protruding from
them), self-help manuals for female-to-male passing transvestites (for example, how to pin rolled-up socks to the inside crotch of your underwear to
enable you to pass in the men's room ["dress socks, that is...be realistic"],
recent medical acknowledgements (for examples, that items like "blue denim
Levis," "engineer boots," or a false moustache have in fact produced orgasmic sensations in women),[1] and a wealth of historical research from the
medieval and early modern periods have turned up innumerable cases of
women who were, or are, fetishizing cross-dressers.

Freud describes the fetishist as someone who both believes in the "reality" of castration and refuses to believe it. "*Je sais bien,...mais quand
meme...*" says the little boy in Mannoni's example; "I know, but still...."[2] As
Sarah Kofman argues, "since there can be no fetishism without a compromise
between castration and its denial and because the fetishist split—this is what
distinguishes it from psychosis—always preserves the two positions, the fetish
can in no sense be a simple *Ersatz* of the penis; if there were really a *decision* in favor of one of the two positions, there would no longer be any need
to construct a fetish."[3] And Derrida, reading Freud, observes that it may be
possible "to reconstruct from Freud's generalization a 'concept' of fetish that
can no longer be contained within the traditional opposition *Ersatz/non
Ersatz*, or even within opposition at all."[4] An example of an "undecidable"
fetish is in fact given by Freud, in his description of a garment that rendered
the wearer's gender unknowable:

> The case of a man whose fetish was an athletic support-belt which could
> also be worn as bathing drawers. This piece of clothing covered up the gen-
> itals entirely and concealed the distinction between them. Analysis showed
> that it signified that women were castrated and that they were not castrat-
> ed; and it also allowed of the hypothesis that men were castrated, for all of
> these possibilities could equally well be concealed under the belt.[5]

Whose underwear is under there?

This is where the transvestite comes in, not as a mask, or masquerade, or
male *or* female, but as a theoretical intervention. For the transvestite is the
equivalent of Lacan's third term, not "having" or "being" the phallus, but
"seeming" or "appearing": "the intervention of a 'to seem' that replaces the
'to have,' in order to protect it on the one side, and mask its lack in the
other."[6]

1. Robert J. Stoller, *Observing the Erotic Imagination* (New Haven: Yale University Press, 1985),
   pp. 135 36.
2. Octave Mannoni, "'Je sais bien...mais quand meme' la croyance," *Les Temps Modernes* 212
   (1964).
3. Sarah Kofman, *The Enigma of Woman*, trans. Catherine Porter (Ithaca: Cornell University Press,
   1985), p. 87.
4. Jacques Derrida, *Glas* (Paris: Editions Galilee, 1974), pp. 232ff.
5. Freud, "Fetishism," pp. 156 157.
6. Jacques Lacan, "The Signification of the Phallus," in *Ecrits: A Selection*, trans. Alan Sheridan
   (New York: W. W. Norton, 1977), p. 289.

That the fetishistic patient is sometimes *in fact* a transvestite renders more complex but also more plausible the argument that the transvestite on stage or in culture is himself/herself a fetishization. The fetish is a metonymic structure, but it is also a metaphor, a figure *for* the undecidability of castration, which is to say, a figure of nostalgia for an originary "wholeness—in the mother, in the child. Thus the fetish, like the transvestite—or the transvestite, like the fetish—is a sign at once of lack and its covering over, as in the case of Freud's patient's athletic support-belt—a garment very similar to devices worn, as it happens, by some present-day female-to-male transvestites.

The history of the fetish in representation (and this is not just, as the anthropological nature of the term implies, in non-Western cultures) indicates that the fetish *is* the phallus; the phallus *is* the fetish. Let us look at some examples. I will be concentrating here, at least initially, on the plays of Shakespeare, in part because Shakespeare has virtually come to define theatrical representation in Western culture, and also because there has been so much recent attention to cross-dressing in his plays, though it has tended to focus on social and political rather than theoretical issues.

Shakespeare's plays are famously full of moments in which characters express castration anxiety—or threaten castration. Iago to Brabantio: "Look to your house, your daughter, and your bags" (*Oth.* 1.1.80); Solario, mocking Shylock's loss, ventriloquizing his imagined voice: "two stones, two rich and precious stones, /Stol'n by my daughter! Justice! find the girl,/She hath the stones upon her, and the ducats" (*MV* 2.8.20–22)—*Jessica* as phallic woman; Malvolio, caught in his erotic daydream, a masturbatory fantasy: "having come from a day-bed, where I have left Olivia sleeping....perchance wind up my watch, or play with my—some rich jewel" (*TN* 2.5.48–60); Viola, in a *double entendre* clearly aimed by the playwright at the audience: "A little thing would make me tell them how much I lack of a man" (*TN* 3.4.302–303).

To best make an argument about fetishism in the plays, though, I select an obvious example from Renaissance theatrical representation: that of the codpiece, itself, bizarrely, a sign of gender undecidability, since it is the quintessential gender mark of "seeming," and thus interposed between "having" and "being" the phallus: the space occupied, as I have argued, by the transvestite. The codpiece is the thinking man's (or woman's) bauble, the ultimate detachable part.

It may seem curious to choose the codpiece to demonstrate something about "*female* fetishism," but in fact it is perfectly logical to do so. For the codpiece, like Freud's undecidable underpants, is a sign of what might—or might not—be "under there." A woman with a codpiece—what in *The Roaring Girl* is called with fear and titillation a "codpiece daughter"—is the figure of the phallic woman, the ultimate fantasy of male transvestite scenarios (if the psychoanalysts are to be believed). At the same time, the woman with the codpiece is the onstage simulacrum of the female transvestite, a crossover figure who, whether or not she exists in psychoanalytic theory, has a substantial claim to existence in history and in representation.

More importantly—and less intuitively—the codpiece confounds the question of gender, since it can signify yes or no, full or empty, lack or lack of lack. It is the stage equivalent of Freud's equivocal underpants. The codpiece is therefore a theatrical figure for castration—which is to say, a theatrical figure for transvestism itself. We might call it a foundation garment.

One thing that sticks out about the codpiece in all of Shakespeare's direct references to it is its explicitly (and precariously) artifactual nature. For example, when Julia and her waiting-woman Lucetta in *The Two Gentlemen of Verona* discuss Julia's transvestic disguise (in terms that anticipate a similar conversation between Portia and Nerissa), the *pièce de résistance* of her male costume is clearly the codpiece:

> *Lucetta.* What fashion, madam, shall I make your breeches?
> *Julia.* That fits as well as, "Tell me, good my lord,
>   What compass will you wear your farthingale?"
>   Why, ev'n what fashion thou best likes, Lucetta.
> *Lucetta.* You must needs have them with a codpiece, madam.
> *Julia.* Out, out, Lucetta, that will be ill-favor'd.
> *Lucetta.* A round hose, madam, now's not worth a pin,
>   Unless you have a codpiece to stick pins on. (*TGV* 2.7.49–56)

Like Portia's comment that she and Nerissa, once cross-dressed, will appear "accomplished/With that we lack" (*Merch.* 3.4.61–62), this exchange draws attention to what is absent, to what seems. Since the original "actresses" in their parts were boys, they in fact "have" what they seem to "lack"—or do they? That the codpiece is to be ornamented by sticking pins in it is not entirely comforting—and in the case of Julia, the whole codpiece itself will be an ornament, pinned on, rather like the socks in the jockstrap of the passing female-to-male transvestite. We are dealing with a detachable part.

But Julia is, of course, a woman in disguise. (Although "she" is also a boy in disguise as a woman in disguise.) Surely there are "real men" in the plays, with real contents in their codpieces? It's not so clear.

In *Much Ado About Nothing*, the scoundrel Borachio refers to "the shaven Hercules in the smirch'd worm-eaten tapestry, where his codpiece seems as massy as his club" (3.3.136–137). The *Riverside* editors, like others, suggest that this "shaven Hercules" is a representation of the hero as subjugated by the Eastern Queen Omphale, dressed as a woman and put to work spinning among her maids.[1] An earlier reference to Hercules in the same play (2.1.253) cites this incident. But A. R. Humphries in the *Arden* edition finds an allusion to the cross-dressed Hercules unlikely (although he has no satisfactory alternative to suggest) because "Borachio's Hercules is in man's dress with a club."[2]

The "man's dress" to which Humphries refers, however, is a hypothetical, metonymic expansion of the codpiece, the only item of clothing specifically

1. G. Blakemore Evans, et al., *The Riverside Shakespeare* (Boston: Houghton Mifflin, 1974). p. 349.
2. A. R. Humphries, *Much Ado About Nothing*, in The *Arden Shakespeare* (London: Methuen, 1981), p. 161.

mentioned. The whole malappropriate discussion comes in the context of a description of "fashion," of a "deformed thief" who "giddily...turns about all the hot bloods between fourteen and five-and-thirty" (3.3.121–129), so that we might expect some connection between male erotic energy and this item of self-advertising sartorial style that "puts the goods in the shopwindow," as used to be said of low-cut blouses for women. Indeed, both editors characterize the "codpiece" in determinedly nonanatomical terms, as if it were itself a totally whimsical deformation of fashion with no reference to the body: "the bag-like flap at the front of men's breeches" (*Riverside*); the "projecting forepiece of men's breeches" (*Arden*). Whose underwear is under there?

So the "codpiece" of *Two Gentlemen* is pinned to the pants of a cross-dressed woman, and the "codpiece" of *Much Ado* marks the representation of a hero who may well be wearing the classical version of drag. In neither case does there seem to be a phallus in the case–or rather, what is represented is the transvestite fantasy, the phallic woman. The anxiety of male aritfactuality seems already much in evidence. And things are not made more reassuring by the "codpiece" references in *The Winter's Tale, Love's Labor's Lost,* and *King Lear.*

In *The Winter's Tale,* Autolycus boasts that it is easy to "geld a codpiece of a purse" (*WT* 4.4.610–11). In *Love's Labor's Lost,* Berowne, decrying the power of Cupid, calls him "king of codpieces," using "codpieces" as the metonymic equivalent for "men," and the Fool in *Lear* does the same: "The codpiece that will house/Before the head has any" (*Lr.* 3.2.27–28). In both cases the part is detached by metonymy. And the Fool, of course, also refers to *himself* as a codpiece ("Marry, here's grace and a codpiece–that's a wise man and a fool" [3.1.184–85]), alluding to the common wisdom that fools had extra-large genital equipment to compensate, so to speak, for their lack of brainpower–the celebrated "fool's bauble."

In a recent one-man show in San Francisco called "Feast of Fools," actor-mime Geoff Hoyle presented, in a series of vignettes, the history of the fool in Western culture. In sequence after sequence the Fool was defined by his comic interactions with a detachable phallus, from the medieval "bauble" to Pantalone's money bag to modern sight gags involving a third leg or a large, red, preternaturally sensitive nose.

The New York-based Mabou Mines troupe has been performing an experimental version of *King Lear* in which *all* the roles are cross-dressed ("a kind of homage to Charles Ludlam," says the director). As a result, many of the Fool's lines play like phallic jokes, especially his advice to Lear, "delivered," wrote one reviewer, "with a reference to his own anatomy–'have more than thou showest.'"[1]

And what about men dressed as women?

The Dame of English Panto had, we might say, an early incarnation in the figure of the cross-dressed Falstaff in *The Merry Wives of Windsor.* As it happens, the cultural production of *The Merry Wives* is linked to a famous "historical" incident of cross-dressing, the founding of the Order of the Garter, when King Edward III supposedly picked up a garter dropped by the count-

1. Jim Beckerman, "A Cheer for Standing Lear on its Ear," *The News Tribune* (Woodbridge, New Jersey), January 10, 1988, p. C-11.

ess of Salisbury at a dance and rebuked his critics with the words that became the Order's motto, "*Honi soit qui mal y pense*." Editors following Leslie Hotson have suggested that the play was written for the Garter Feast of 1597, and several scenes take place at the Garter Inn; an extended passage in Act 5 describes the festivities that attend the installation of a Knight (5.5.57–74). Recent criticism of *Merry Wives* has stressed the historical and cultural links among the Order of the Garter, Queen Elizabeth, and courtly forms,[1] but in emphasizing a female ruler's association with a male order, critics have occluded—or repressed—the fantasy of the founding scenario, which imagines a transvestism of the opposite (gender) kind, the king wearing the countess's garter. (Whose underwear is under there?)

The overdetermined presence of male-to-female cross-dressing in the play—from Falstaff to the boys costumed as (and substituted for) Anne Page in the comic denouement—is related, I would suggest, on the one hand, to this "foundational" subtext, and on the other, to the omnipresent pun on "page" as a surname, a male-to-female disguise, and a code word for a male homosexual love object.

Yet Falstaff is not often discussed in the context of Shakespearean cross-dressing; he represents no ideal figure, either for women *or* for men, dressed as he is like an old woman, carried onto the stage in a basket, his motive seduction, his cause both ludicrous and offensive. He thus satisfies neither the feminist "role-model" progress narrative of the early 1970s nor the recuperative image of the Shakespearean "sensitive man." If the Falstaff of the history plays is often seen these days as a pre-oedipal figure, a pre-oedipal mother, even, the Falstaff of *Merry Wives*—always carefully kept separate from the history Falstaff—is seen as something of an embarrassment, not a glamorous drag queen like Antony in Cleopatra's tires and mantle, but rather the quintessence of what is known in transvestite circles as "cod drag."

"Cod"—as in *codpiece*. Eric Partridge's *Dictionary of Slang and Unconventional English*[2] defines *cod* as "the scrotum," or in the plural, "the testicles." Since 1690 (that is, after Shakespeare), "cod" has also meant "a fool." In its verbal form, "to cod" is "to chaff, hoax, humbug; to play the fool." Adjectivally, it connotes "burlesque; especially *cod acting*, as in acting a Victorian melodrama as through it were a post-1918 farce of burlesque." Since 1965, Partridge adds, "it has been used colloquially for 'pretence, or mock'—e.g., *cod German, cod Russian*." So *cod* means both scrotum or testicles, and hoax, fool, pretence, or mock.[3] The anxiety of male artifactuality is here summed up, as it were, in a nutshell.

---

1. See, for example, Peter Erickson, "The Order of the Garter, the Cult of Elizabeth, and Class-Gender Tension in *The Merry Wives of Windsor*," in *Shakespeare Reproduced*, ed. Jean E. Howard and Miriam F. O'Connor (New York: Methuen, 1987), pp. 116–140.
2. *Eric Partridge's Dictionary of Slang and Unconventional English*, ed. Paul Beale, 8th ed. (London: Routledge & Kegan Paul, 1984).
3. Indeed, we might even consider "cod" as in "codfish." It is no accident, I think, that one of the most overt and outrageous Dame figures of the twentieth-century stage, Captain Hook of Barrie's *Peter Pan*, is taunted by Peter in a famous scene in which Peter calls him a "codfish." Hook is of course the living embodiment of castration and consequent phallic display, his right hand having been severed by Peter in an earlier encounter. See my chapter "Fear of Flying, or, Why Peter Pan is a Woman," in *Vested Interests: Cross-Dressing and Cultural Anxiety* (New York: Routledge, 1991).

What is particularly important to note here is that, traditionally, transvestism on the Western stage and in clubs and drag acts has turned on the artifactuality of *women's* bodies—balloon breasts, fluffy wigs, makeup. Is it possible that this overt acknowledgment of artifice—often a source of consternation to women and to feminists—masks another (I hesitate to say, a deeper) concern—about the artifactuality and the detachability of maleness? What if it should turn out that female fetishism is invisible, or untheorizable, because it coincides with what has been established as *natural* or *normal* for women to fetishism the phallus *on men*? In other words, to deny female fetishism is to establish as natural the female desire that the male body contain the phallus. Heterosexuality here—as so often—equals nature. Female fetishism is the *norm* of human sexuality. That is why it is invisible.

We might note that when the English stage ceases, after the Restoration, to be a transvestite theater—when actresses appear on the public stage in roles previously reserved for men—their appearance coincides with the redesign of the playhouse to include the Italian innovation of the front curtain. The curtain is a veil that marks off the "not real" from the "real." The work done by transvestism in putting the phallus under erasure is now done by a different kind of theatrical punctuation. The one substitutes for the other—the curtain for the transvestite troupe, both marking theatrical difference. The phallus does its work only when veiled: veiled by a difference which makes it difficult to know whether there is difference or not (since "having" and "lacking" can both be kinds of "seeming"); veiled by the curtain that says, "this (and only this?) is theater." Or, to put it another way, the substitution of female actresses for boy actors is not a naturalizing move that returns theater to its desired condition of mimesis, replacing the false boy with the real woman. It is, instead, a double substitution—a rerecongnition of artifice—something tacitly acknowledged by Restoration critics when they praised the women for playing female roles almost as well as the boy actresses did, just as later critics would praise nineteenth-century actresses playing Hamlet, Othello, or Iago for their fidelity in representation—*not* for being dogs walking on their hind legs. "Mrs. Waller's Iago, last night, was truly great," "worthy of being ranked with the best Iago we have ever seen," "the best 'Iago' which has been produced on our stage since the days of the elder Booth."[1]

And here it will be useful to look, briefly, and in conclusion, at yet another contemporary instance, which could be compared to Emma Waller's celebrated moustachioed Iago, or to the cross-dressing of Viola in the style of her "lost" brother Sebastian—an impersonation which turns on Viola's (supposed) "lack." My example is drawn not from a Shakespearean production but from the cross-dressing and fetishization which has become so noticeable a part of the performance of contemporary rock and pop music—specifically, the triangulated relationship of Michael Jackson, Diana Ross, and Madonna.

1. *Opinions of the Press of Emma Waller*...[c. 1876], Harvard University Library. (Newspapers cited are: the Chicago *Herald*, New Orleans *Picayune*, St. Louis *Herald*, Boston *Transcript*, Cincinnati *Commercial*, Cincinnati *Index*, Buffalo *Post*, Buffalo *Express*, Memphis *Bulletin*, and the Memphis *Avalanche*.) Cited in Frank W. Wadsworth, "Hamlet and Iago: Nineteenth Century Breeches Parts," *Shakespeare Quarterly* 17 (1966): 137.

That Michael Jackson has literally remade himself as a figure for transvestism itself seems to me evident not only from his three nose jobs (which have made him more and more resemble Diana Ross) but also from other signatory gestures of "castration," like his glittery clothes, his long lustrous hair, and the fact that his singing and speaking voices have become higher rather than lower over the years—a phenomenon that has led some to speculate that he has altered himself in some fundamental way in search of a voice "that can sing both high and low." As for Madonna, in some of her most recent theatrical self-representations she has made herself into a figure of and for Michael Jackson. Here I have in mind, in particular, a music video called "Express Yourself" and the moment she chose to perform from that video at a recent Music Video Awards Show.[1]

Appearing in a men's double-breasted suit (the mammary description of this garment almost surely a kind of unexpressed pun), as she does periodically throughout the longer version of "Express Yourself," she danced before the audience in a style deliberately imitative of Michael Jackson, mimicking many of his moves, and wearing the signature items of his look, white socks and shiny black men's shoes. Flanked by two female backup singers in pin stripes, she assertively claimed all possible gender space, at one point stripping off her jacket to reveal a lacy teddy beneath, so that she became a kind of sartorial centaur. But the moment that scandalized critics was a moment of sheer quotation from Michael Jackson, when Madonna danced toward the audience and squeezed her crotch. Now, Michael Jackson does this all the time, and no one ever complains—quite the contrary. But Madonna, squeezing what she hadn't got (or *had* she?) emblematized the Lacanian triad of having, being, and seeming. Squeezing the crotch of her pants became for her, onstage, the moment of the claim to *empowered transvestism*, to seem rather than merely to have or to be—*not* (and this distinction is important) just a claim to empowered womanhood. In this moment, and by the very fact that she chose the cross-dressed costume from her longer video to present at the opening of the awards show, Madonna became transvestism itself, the more so since she was so deliberately troping off Michael Jackson.

"Good *madonna*, give me leave to prove you a fool" (*TN* 1.5.57). The speaker is Feste the clown, who surely knows if anyone does about the fool's bauble which is the codpiece. Madonna is a famous female star who is impersonating a famous male star who is impersonating a woman. She is, that is to say, a transvestite impersonating a transvestite.

Why is it shocking when she grabs her crotch, repeating as she does so a gesture familiar to anyone who has watched a two-year-old male child reassuring himself of his intactness? Not because it is unseemly for a woman to do this—although it may be, to some people—but because what she is saying in doing so is: I'm not intact, he's not intact; I *am* intact, this is what intact is.

Theater elicits, produces, and panders to *fetish envy* in both its male and its female spectators. Female fetishism, fetish envy, is indeed possible in a theatrical space where the symbolic nature of the maternal phallus makes it

---

1. I am grateful to Nancy Vickers for calling both the video and the awards show to my attention.

the only phallus that is real. Thus the transvestite in Shakespeare—both the boy actor and the cross-dressed woman—becomes not an accident of historical contingency but the necessary intervention that makes fetishism not only possible but foundational to theater itself.

19

CASTRATION ENVY:
NIETZSCHE AND THE FIGURE OF
WOMAN

Clayton Koelb

It would be difficult nowadays to approach the topic of woman as metaphor in Nietzsche without crossing through the formidable terrain of Derrida's *Spurs*. My particular formulation of the topic in fact situates its discourse squarely within the territory explored by that essay, though perhaps paradoxically; for Derrida announces specifically that the phrase "figure of woman" (*figure de la femme*) does *not* belong in his discussion. He speaks of the "question" and not the "figure" of woman "precisely because we shall bear witness here to her *abduction,* because the question of the figure is at once opened and closed by what is called woman."[1] I wish to pursue the question of the figure, not by any means to refute Derrida's claim, but on the contrary to explore (in perhaps a somewhat different vein) its ramifications.

One of those ramifications is Derrida's demonstration of a powerful connection in Nietzsche's thinking between the notions of "woman" and "castration." The connection both affirms and puts in abeyance the questionable figure of the woman as a man-without-a-penis and focuses attention on the issue of weakness, the ethos of power-in-powerlessness that Nietzsche finds in Christianity. Derrida shows how Nietzsche's characterization of the early Christian church is explicitly linked on the one hand to the realm of the feminine (Nietzsche calls it *weiblich*) and on the other to an ethos of extirpation and denial he refers to as *Kastratismus* in a passage Derrida quotes from *Twilight of the Idols*.[2] From his reading of this and other Nietzschean discourses on women, Derrida claims to have found a "principle [*règle*], which might be resumed in a finite number of typical and matrical [*matricielle*] propositions" (*Spurs*, pp. 94/95). He offers three of them. We need not cite the first two; we need only note that "woman, up to this point then, is twice castration: once as truth and once as nontruth" (*Spurs*, pp. 96/97). In Derrida's third formulation of the Nietzschean principle of woman, he finds something different: "In the instance of the third proposition, however, beyond the double negation of the first two, woman is recognized and affirmed as an affirmative power, a dissimulatress, an artist, a dionysiac. And

1. Jacques Derrida, *Spurs: Nietzsche's Styles / Eperons: Les Styles de Nietzsche*, trans. Barbara Harlow (Chicago: Univ. of Chicago Press, 1979), pp. 40/41.
2. "The church resists passion with extirpation in every sense: its practice, its 'cure' is *Kastratismus*" (KSA 6:83; cf. TI p. 487).

no longer is it man who affirms her. She affirms herself, in and of herself, in man. Castration, in the sense I just spoke of, does not take place" (*Spurs*, pp. 96/97[1]).

Derrida is very careful here: he does not say that castration in every sense does not take place, but only that it does not take place "*au sens que je disais tout à l'heure.*" His careful language is entirely obligatory in this instance because there is good evidence that even this third, more positive proposition about woman carries with it strong associations with castration in some sense. Here is a poem from "Joke, Cunning, and Revenge"—the collection of verses that opens *The Gay Science*—that will serve as a case in point:

Lost His Head
She now has spirit—how did it happen that she found it?
A man recently lost his reason over her,
His head was rich before this pastime:
His head went to the devil—no, no! to the woman!
(KSA[2] 3:364; cf. GS[3] p. 63)

The woman with intellect and spirit (*Geist*), the "affirmative" woman of Derrida's third proposition, appears in this little drama as the beneficiary a man's dismemberment. He is intellectually castrated by his love for her, whereas she miraculously gains the potency he has lost. The castration anxiety is displaced in the poem's imagery from the penis to the head, but the nature of that anxiety—the fear of a loss of male power associated with bodily dismemberment—reveals its fundamental sexual nature. Nietzsche suggests here that love brings about a reversal of gender roles that essentially moves the phallic power from man to woman.

One might argue, however, that the poem offers an example not so much of castration as of anticastration: the woman's intellectual/spiritual power seems to be the result of her acquisition of a male body part, not its loss. The male seems indeed to be castrated, but he is also no longer spirited. There is an association of castration with spiritual power here, but it is an association of opposition. Is there any evidence to suggest that Nietzsche believes the association could be more complex and more intimate?

Derrida himself cites some of the best evidence of such a complex relationship when he quotes another passage from *Twilight of the Idols* that follows almost directly the one mentioned above: "The same means in the fight against a craving—castration, extirpation—is instinctively chosen by those who are too weak-willed, too degenerate, to be able to impose moderation on themselves....Just look at the whole history of the priests and philosophers, including the artists" (KSA, 6:83; TI,[4] pp. 487–88*; quoted in *Spurs*, pp. 92/93). We

1. [An asterisk following a reference indicates that a published translation has been used, but altered].
2. [KSA = *Sämtliche werke: Kritische studienausgabe in 15 einzelbänden*, ed. Giorgio Colli and Mazzino Montinari (Munich/Berkin: dtv/de Gruyter, 1988).]
3. [GS = *The gay science*, trans. Walter Kaufmann (New York: Vintage, 1974).]
4. [TI = *Twilight of the idols, or: How one philosophizes with a hammer*, in *The Portable Nietzsche*, trans. Walter Kaufmann (New York: Penguin, 1976).]

must not overlook the fact that Nietzsche seems to count among the weak-willed and degenerate adherents of *Kastratismus* not only priests, as we would expect, but also artists and philosophers. These are the very groups with which Nietzsche regularly associates himself (carefully constructing his own persona as both artist and philosopher) and with which Derrida understands him to associate the notion of woman in his third and more affirmative "proposition." We may not, then, understand Nietzsche to be setting up a simple opposition such as, say, "potent artist vs. castrated priest" any more than we may suppose that "woman" is excluded from the company of philosophers. Woman, priest, and philosopher/artist all have something in common. Oddly enough one of these common traits is complicity in an ethos of castration.

An association of woman with the castration syndrome of self-effacement is clearly present even when Nietzsche seems to be stressing the positive, powerful fecundity which women share with artists: "Pregnancy has made women kinder, more patient, more timid, more pleased to submit; and just so does spiritual pregnancy produce the character of the contemplative type, which is closely related to the feminine character: it consists of male mothers" (KSA, 3:430; GS, §72 p. 129). Here are some familiar notions in a somewhat different context. Patience, timidity, and submission are traits Nietzsche regularly associates with the feminine, but more often with the "negative" feminine; that is, they belong to the ethos of castration. Here, though, he brings them in contact with the "contemplative type," a concept perhaps in need of further specification. Nietzsche speaks of the contemplative type often, and in the broad category of contemplatives we find not only priests and hermits but also the artist/philosophers among which he numbers himself. Another passage makes the explicit connection: "We who think and feel at the same time are those who really continually *fashion* something that had not been there before: the whole eternally growing world of valuations, colors, accents, perspectives, scales, affirmations, and negations....Only we have created the world *that concerns man!*—But precisely this knowledge we lack,...we fail to recognize our best power and underestimate ourselves, the contemplatives, just a little" (KSA, 3:540; GS, §301, pp. 241-42). The "we" who create the world are the contemplatives who appear otherwise as male mothers; that is, they appear in the figure of woman. They are immensely powerful, but their power is not phallic potency. On the contrary, it appears to depend critically on the absence of the phallus. It depends on a constellation of elements that include all of the negatives linked elsewhere with *Kastratismus*: self-effacement, the affectation of weakness, and the paradoxical power which weakness exerts.

The woman/artist of Derrida's third proposition, then, does not by any means escape the rhetoric of castration. Derrida is surely right, though, in wanting to make a distinction between those instances in Nietzsche's discourse where "woman" appears to be equivalent to "castration" and this one, where castration is present but is not part of any such direct equation. A careful scrutiny of the argument in the passage from *Twilight of the Idols* under discussion makes clear that priests, philosophers, and artists (and also, by implication, the figure of woman that stands for and explains them) are not linked to castration by a logic of equivalence or of similarity; they are linked by a logic of desire. Their weakness and degeneracy are not a matter of their having practiced castration upon themselves or others but rather part of a psychic constellation that includes a kind of wish for castration. If we examine "the whole history" of the priests, philosophers, and artists, Nietzsche tells us, we will discover in them not the impotent themselves, not genuine ascetics, but instead "those who might really have needed to be ascetics" (KSA, 6:83; TI, p. 488*). The priests, artists, and philosophers in question here are "impossible ascetics" who advocate and perhaps even long for an "extirpation" they are incapable of achieving.[1] The denial of a "craving" (*Begierde*) involves a craving of another sort, a craving for the extirpation of cravings. Nietzsche's language even acknowledges this strange double edge of desire when he says that those who are too weak-willed to impose moderation on themselves choose castration "in the fight with a craving." Nietzsche's original German (*wird instinktiv im Kampfe mit einer Begierde von Denen gewählt*) allows an instant of uncertainty as to whether the phrase *mit einer Begierde* modifies the noun *Kampf* or the verb *gewählt,* an uncertainty therefore as to whether the "craving" in question is something the weak-willed oppose or possess. When one considers the rest of Nietzsche's argument, it is clear that both alternatives are affirmed. The choice of the preposition *mit* allows and even encourages the suspicion that desire remains a powerful force even as it is being denied. The uncertainty may be easily resolved on the syntactic level, but on the conceptual level it remains in force, strengthened at last by the admission that these weak-willed folk are not full-fledged eunuchs but only those who "might really have needed to be ascetics."

Nietzsche does speak elsewhere of a certain religious figure—an ideal figure, to be sure—as actually achieving the castration that these others only dream of. "The saint with whom God is well pleased," he declares, "is the ideal eunuch [*Castrat*]" (KSA 6:85; TI p. 490*). But the concept of "saint" is not coextensive with that of "priest." The saint embodies what the priest may wish to be but falls short of achieving. He is precisely the "ideal *Castrat*" whose castration is understood paradigmatically as an object of emulation, and not as a metaphor of achieved reality. His castration represents the standard toward which others, the others referred to as "impossible ascetics," aspire. Granted Nietzsche's irony, granted even his evident contempt for "saints" such as this, the use of the term *ideal* is both instructive and appropriate.

It is even consistent with Nietzsche's own view of himself. At times he sees himself as participating in just such a longing for self-abnegation and extirpation. Consider these closing lines from the poem "On the Poverty of the Richest," a piece he thought highly enough of to use twice. It serves as the conclusion of both the *Dionysus Dithyrambs* and *Nietzsche contra Wagner* and expresses an unmistakable longing for a (probably impossible) self-effacement:

---

1. "Just look at the whole history of the priests and philosophers, including the artists: the most poisonous things against the senses have been said not by the impotent, nor by ascetics, but by the impossible ascetics, by those who might really have needed to be ascetics" (KSA 6:83; TI p. 488*). See also *Spurs*, pp. 92/93.

You must become *poorer*,
wise Unwiseman,
if you want to be loved.
People love only those who suffer,
they give only to those who starve:
first give yourself away, O Zarathustra!
—I am your truth.
(KSA 6:410 and 6:445)[1]

Zarathustra's "truth" sets him the goal of a radical self-abnegation. He must extirpate his "excess" (*Überfluss*), his wealth (*Reichthum*), the source of both his pride and his pain, in order to attain the power to attract love. Nietzsche dramatizes himself (in the persona of Zarathustra) as one of those "impossible ascetics" often found among the contemplatives, one of "those who might really have needed to be ascetics." He presents the divestiture of spiritual "wealth" not as (or not only as) a loss but as a goal toward which Zarathustra should strive.

Here as elsewhere he characterizes this "ideal" condition to which contemplative types look with longing, this extirpation of the phallus, as at once an almost impossible transcendent goal and the most frightening, the lowest condition imaginable. He also, of course, understands it as the mysteriously permanent condition of woman. Woman is the alternative version of the saintly ideal, the other paradigm of Christian morality, who shares with the saint the whole constellation of (often contradictory) values gathered under the term *Kastratismus*.

Nietzsche's complex rhetoric thus places two related but somewhat different versions of "woman" on *both* sides of the relationship of desire: since she is in one guise a kind of artist, she is the desiring subject; but because she may also appear in another form as the embodiment of impotence, as the already-castrated body, she is also the object of desire. In this second guise she is the object of something one might call, if the reader will forgive the impertinence, "castration envy."

I ask for the reader's indulgence here on three counts: first because I insist on the implausible notion that something so self-evidently undesirable as castration could be an object of desire; second because I propose that Friedrich Nietzsche (of all people!) was an advocate of this notion; and third because I am playing fast and loose with Freudian terminology. The first count I will deal with shortly. On the second count I offer in defense the evidence already presented. I believe it substantiates the claim that Nietzsche's texts urge us to think of "desire" and "castration" as compatible concepts. These texts link elements explicitly identified as part of the syndrome of *Kastratismus* with a rhetoric of an "ideal" self-effacement that is part of the writer's own system of values. On the third count I can only plead guilty and throw myself on the mercy of the court. I am indeed playing fast and loose with Freud's notion of

---

1. [Kaufmann omits this poem from his translation of *Nietzsche contra Wagner*, original ed.]

"penis envy." But I venture to suggest that "castration envy" is not, when all is said and done, much more outrageous an idea than the one it plays upon. If "castration envy" seems a paradoxical and ridiculous notion, especially perhaps to many men, "penis envy" has seemed no less so, especially perhaps to many women. If we are willing to entertain the one, then, we had better not dismiss the other. And since the issue of penis envy has become an open and indeed vexed question in the light of its reexamination by feminist criticism, we might welcome rather than reject the possibility that it could have a hitherto unsuspected opposite.

Now let me address the question of the ostensible implausibility of the very idea of "castration envy." In the first place, we must recognize that the notion of "castration" as it appears in Nietzsche is rather different from the concept worked out by Freud. Nietzsche's "castration" is not so much a psychological as a philosophical metaphor, and it figures in a discourse that aims to account for cultural, not individual, behavior. Freud uses castration anxiety and penis envy primarily as part of an attempt to explain the psychohistory of particular persons, while Nietzsche looks to explain the genesis of ethical and epistemological categories. One might say that Nietzsche's "castration" is more purely a metaphor than Freud's, for Nietzsche is rarely if ever concerned with actual sexuality or actual body parts. He uses sexuality in general and the penis in particular as figures, principally for generative power in the intellectual realm, but also in other ways.

That having been granted, however, it remains to show also how and why this evidently negative notion could be turned into a positive value and to demonstrate that "castration envy" forms a coherent part of Nietzsche's thinking.

It is necessary to return first to the figure of woman, a figure both castrated and castrating, who appears regularly as the trope through which Nietzsche approaches the most enduring and perhaps most fundamental questions in philosophy. We can start with one of the most traditional and recognizable of these tropes, in which nature appears as a (usually nurturing) woman. Nietzsche proposes a variation on this old chestnut of a figure when he describes the Greek view of her in *The Birth of Tragedy*: "In these Greek festivals, nature seems to reveal a sentimental trait; it is as if she were heaving a sigh at her dismemberment into individuals" (KSA 1:33; BT[1] §2, p. 40). Nature is thus a dismembered woman, but mysteriously still whole, still complete, and still powerful. Her completeness *as body* is stressed in another passage from the same work: "The essence of nature is now to be expressed symbolically; we need a new world of symbols; and the entire symbolism of the body is called into play, not the mere symbolism of the lips, face, and speech but the whole pantomime of dancing, forcing every member into rhythmic movement" (KSA 1:33–34; BT, §2, p. 40).

As Nietzsche reconstructs the Greek figuration of nature, then, it appears as a female body that is on the one hand subject to dismemberment but on

1. [BT = *The birth of tragedy, or: hellenism and pessimism. New edition with an attempt at self-criticism*, in *The birth of tragedy and the Caseo of Wagner*, trans. Walter Kaufmann (New York: Vintage, 1967).]

the other enormously powerful. One of the principal arguments of *The Birth of Tragedy* hinges upon the power of that body and its effects on the Greek mind: "That overwhelming dismay in the face of the titanic powers of nature...was again and again overcome by the Greeks with the aid of the Olympian *middle world* of art; or at any rate it was veiled and withdrawn from sight" (KSA, 1:36; BT §3, p. 42).

This last formulation is particularly interesting in that it links the rhetoric of one female body, *natura*, with another, the veiled *veritas*. Both are stock figures, but by bringing them together Nietzsche moves them in a new direction. We recognize the trope of "veiled truth" not only from its frequent appearance elsewhere in Nietzsche's writings (about which more below) but also from its extensive use by theologians and rhetoricians from the Middle Ages onward. Augustine used it to describe the way in which truth is clothed in figurative language in the Bible, and Boccaccio reformulated it in his defense of secular poetry: "*Fabula* is a way of speaking under [the cloak of] a figure/fiction so as to serve as a pattern or point something out; and if its surface [lit. "husk"] is penetrated, the intention of the author shows forth. And so if something sensible is ascertained under the veil of fiction, it cannot be superfluous and useless to compose fictions."[1] In all of these versions, part of the argument is that an unmediated vision of the bare truth, *nuda veritas*, is neither safe nor proper for mere mortals. There is an implication, sometimes stated and sometimes only implied, that looking at the naked truth would be just as difficult and dangerous as looking directly at the sun and just as improper as gazing at actual naked women. The veil that covers the body of the truth is thus a matter of moral decency as well as epistemological necessity. Boccaccio says that the goal of literary invention is "to cover the truth with a marvelous *and seemly* veil."[2] When Nietzsche uses the trope, he calls upon this tradition with all its implications. One of the most often-cited passages in *The Gay Science* suggests that he did so quite consciously: "'Is it true that God is present everywhere?' a little girl asked her mother; 'I think that's indecent'—a hint for philosophers! One should have more respect for the bashfulness with which nature has hidden behind riddles and iridescent uncertainties. Perhaps truth is a woman who has reasons for not letting us see her reasons? Perhaps her name is—to speak Greek—*Baubo*?" (KSA 3:352; GS-P §4, p. 38). The naked truth is not attainable because the woman who is truth (and nature) chooses to keep it concealed. It is not desirable because what she conceals is something we would not wish to see. The clear implication is that *veritas/natura* is hiding something downright repulsive.

That there is something unpleasant, even repellent, about the female body is surely one of Nietzsche's more offensive notions, but (in this version at any

1. Giovanni Boccaccio, *Genealogie deorum gentilium libri*, ed. Vincenzo Romano, 2 vols. (Bari: Gius, Laterza & Figli, 1951), 2:706. This is my translation of the following: "Fabula est exemplaris seu demonstrativa sub figmento locutio, cuius amoto cortice, patet intentio fabulantis. Et sic, si sub velamento fabuloso sapidum comperiatur aliquid, non erit supervacaneum fabulas edidisse."

2. "Velamento fabuloso atque decenti veritatem contegere" (*Genealogie*, 2:699; translation and italics are mine).

rate) it may tell us at least as much about the writer's view of nature as it does about his misogyny. It is important to realize that Nietzsche's negative attitude toward the body of woman is linked to his sense of woman's closeness to nature. "Woman is more closely related to nature than man," he wrote on one occasion, and on another: "When we love a woman, we easily conceive a hatred for nature on account of all the repulsive natural functions to which every woman is subject. We prefer not to think of all this....We artists! We ignore what is natural" (KSA 3:422-23; GS §59, pp. 122-23). It is probably not possible to decide here whether woman is repulsive because she is nature or nature is repulsive because she is female. All we can say for certain is that Nietzsche's rhetoric binds together the notions of woman, truth, nature, and revulsion into a single idea.

One cannot avoid the conclusion that for Nietzsche the scandal of the female body is not only or even primarily the "natural functions" of menstruation, lactation, and so forth, but the absence of a visible organ. What Mother Nature needs so urgently to hide from view is not so much what she has as what she lacks. Nietzsche suspects a void at the center of the body of nature. He does not name that void "castration" in his early writings; he names it instead with other figures: Moira, the vulture devouring Prometheus, the curse of the house of Atreus, the wisdom of Silenus; but it is the same dismembered body with a gap in the middle.[1] It is the abyss from which the Greeks sheltered themselves by creating their own veil, the golden world of the Olympian gods. For the most part, though, we do not have to weave veils for ourselves; nature herself withholds from us the sight of her castrated body by offering only mediated visions of the scandal at her center.

There is anxiety—indeed stark terror—that comes with the recognition of the abyss, but it is not exactly castration anxiety. The revulsion that comes from a recognition of nature's appalling dismemberment does not arise from a fear that something similar could happen to us. A sufferer of castration anxiety fears the loss of power that accompanies the loss of the penis. But in Nietzsche's figuration of nature, the castrated body is not the locus of a loss of power; quite the contrary, the feminine body of nature is the most potent force imaginable—and not merely in spite of but to a large extent because of the void at its center. The anxiety Nietzsche depicts in the Greek facing the uncovered body of Mother Nature is not the fear that he might become like her; it is rather a fear that comes from the knowledge that he can never have a power anything like hers. He is in awe of the overwhelming negativity that defines her, a negativity which she ordinarily graciously hides from view.

The potency of the penis is negligible in comparison to the irresistible might figured by its absence. Castration is the trope that stands for the ultimate power, an object as much of envy as of fear. All the positive values of life, all of life's powerful magic, indeed even life itself, are subsumed under the figure of the veiled female body: "I mean to say that the world is over-full of beautiful things but nevertheless poor, very poor when it comes to beautiful moments and unveilings of these things. But perhaps this is the

---

1. See section 3 of The Birth of Tragedy (KSA 1:34 38; BT 3, pp. 41 44).

most powerful magic of life: it is covered by a veil interwoven with gold, a veil of beautiful possibilities, sparkling with promise, resistance, bashfulness, mockery, pity, and seduction. Yes, life is a woman" (KSA 3:569; GS §339, pp. 271–72). Consider also figuration of life as a seductive woman (Helen) in the following: "We hear nothing but the accents of an exuberant, triumphant life in which all things, whether good or evil, are deified. And so the spectator may stand quite bewildered before this fantastic excess of life, asking himself by virtue of what magic potion these high-spirited men could have found life so enjoyable that, wherever they turned, their eyes beheld the smile of Helen, the ideal picture of their own existence, 'floating in sweet sensuality'" (KSA 1:35; BT §3, p. 41).

One might imagine that such a powerful figure—woman-as-nature, woman-as-truth, woman-as-life, not to mention woman-as-artist and woman-as-philosopher—could evade the ethos of castration. But she does not, because power resides in the place of castration. The artist and the philosopher, the lovers of nature and truth and life, recognize this, and so castration haunts their dreams. They dream such disquieting dreams, Nietzsche suggests, even more often and more vividly than do the priests. But they are dreams indeed, not nightmares. The "impossible ascetics," the artists and philosophers, do not fear the extirpation of the sensual any more than the priest does: they long for it. If woman is an artist, then she too longs for the castration which—as a figure—she represents.

The philosopher, the woman, and the poet are of imagination all compact, though as imagined bodies they are radically different. The figure of woman stands for the fulfillment of an imagined impossibility. No one can truly know her (sexually or intellectually), since to know her would undo knowledge.[1] She is the locus of absolute power. Because her power is an infinite void, an irremediable absence, she is appalling; but because her power is enormous, all those who possess a will to power must envy the void that is its source.

1. Derrida speaks of a similar effect of what he calls the "question" of woman: "The question of woman suspends the decidable opposition of true and non-true" (*Spurs*, pp. 106/107). Nietzsche's usual term for woman, *Weib*, even suspends the opposition between male and female, as it possesses neither masculine nor feminine (grammatical) gender. Because *Weib* is both grammatically neuter and sexually female, the word can be the antecedent of either feminine or neuter pronouns, a possibility which Nietzsche's rhetoric occasionally exploits.

PERMISSIONS

The editor thanks the publishers and agents for permission to reprint the following:

"Some psychological consequences of the anatomical distinction between the sexes" and "Certain neurotic mechanisms in jealousy, homosexuality and paranoia," by Sigmund Freud: Reprinted by permission of BasicBooks, a division of HarperCollins Publishers, Inc., from *The standard edition of the complete psychological works of Sigmund Freud*, translated and edited by James Strachey. In addition, the above works: Sigmund Freud © Copyrights, The Institute of Psycho-Analysis and The Hogarth Press for permission to quote from *The Standard Edition of the Complete Psychological Works of Sigmund Freud*, translated and Edited by James Strachey.

The flight from womanhood by Karen Horney: From *Feminine psychology*, by Karen Horney. Copyright © 1967 by W. W. Norton & Company, Inc. Reprinted by permission of W.W. Norton & Company, Inc.

Early stages of the Oedipus complex by Melanie Klein: reprinted with the permission of The Hogarth Press and The Free Press, a Division of Simon & Schuster from *Love, guilt and reparation and other works*, 1921–1945 by Melanie Klein. Copyright © 1975 by The Melanie Klein Trust.

"Another cause—castration" and "Penis envy," by Luce Irigaray: Reprinted from Luce Irigaray: *Speculum of the Other Woman*. Translated by Gillian C. Gill. Copyright © 1985 by Cornell University. Used by permission of the publisher, Cornell University Press.

"The significance of penis envy in women," by Maria Torok, and "Feminine Guilt and the Oedipus Complex," by Janine Chasseguet-Smirgel, from *Female sexuality*, ed. Janine Chasseguet-Smirgel © 1970 by The University of Michigan Press.

INDEX